Asian Business and Management

ASIAN BUSINESS AND MANAGEMENT

THEORY, PRACTICE AND PERSPECTIVES

SECOND EDITION

EDITED BY

HARUKIYO HASEGAWA AND CARLOS NORONHA

First edition 2009
Second edition 2014

Published by
PALGRAVE MACMILLAN

Palgrave Macmillan in the UK is an imprint of Macmillan Publishers Limited,
registered in England, company number 785998, of Houndmills, Basingstoke,
Hampshire RG21 6XS.

Palgrave Macmillan in the US is a division of St Martin's Press LLC,
175 Fifth Avenue, New York, NY 10010.

Palgrave Macmillan is the global academic imprint of the above companies
and has companies and representatives throughout the world.

Palgrave® and Macmillan® are registered trademarks in the United States,
the United Kingdom, Europe and other countries.

ISBN 978–0–230–36738–8

This book is printed on paper suitable for recycling and made from fully
managed and sustained forest sources. Logging, pulping and manufacturing
processes are expected to conform to the environmental regulations of the
country of origin.

A catalogue record for this book is available from the British Library.

A catalog record for this book is available from the Library of Congress.

Typeset by MPS Limited, Chennai, India.

Printed in China.

Contents

PART I ASIAN BUSINESS SYSTEMS MAJOR ISSUES

PART II VARIETIES OF BUSINESS SYSTEMS IN ASIA

List of Tables and Figures

Figures

Tables

Notes on the Contributors

Mai The Cuong holds a BA and a PhD in international economics from the National Economics University, Vietnam and an MBA focusing on marketing from the International University of Japan and is currently a Lecturer in the School of Trade and International Economics at the National Economics University. He has taught international business, international procurement and marketing. He has designed and facilitated marketing and sales programs for enterprises in Vietnam. His papers have been published in several books and journals. He networks with businesses, policymakers and researchers from Vietnam, Thailand, Malaysia and Japan. He also works as an independent consultant in evaluating official development assistance (ODA) projects.

Philippe Debroux is a Belgian citizen resident in Japan since the 1970s. He has a PhD in applied economics from the Free University of Brussels and holds a MBA degree from INSEAD, France. He is Professor of International Management and International Human Resource Management at Soka University in Japan. At the same time he teaches at National Economics University (Vietnam); Rennes University (France) and at Sophia, Rikkyo and Chuo University (Japan). His research focuses on the development of CSR, human resource management, innovation and entrepreneurship (especially female entrepreneurship) in Japan and other East and Southeast Asian countries.

Tony Garrett is in Korea University Business School, Seoul. Prior to his arrival in Korea, he was a Senior Lecturer in Marketing at the University of Otago, Dunedin, New Zealand. His PhD (University of Otago) examined national culture and group dynamics in new product development, focusing on New Zealand and Singapore. His main research focuses on innovation, branding and national factors affecting the adoption of new products. He has published a number of chapters and articles, including articles in *Industrial Marketing Management, European Journal of Marketing, Journal of Business Research, International Journal of Services Management, Services Management Journal, Journal of Business Research* and *Journal of Product Innovation Management*. Prior to his academic career he had business experience in the development of international brands in the New Zealand market.

Axèle Giroud is President, Euro-Asia Management Studies Association. She is currently working for the Investment Issues Section in the Division on Investment and Enterprise at UNCTAD (United Nations Conference on Trade and Development). She is on leave of absence from her position as Reader of International Business at the Manchester Business School, University of Manchester. She obtained her PhD from the Bradford School of Management, United Kingdom. Her main research interests are multinational corporations, Asian business, international strategy, knowledge and technology transfer, and inter-firm linkages. She has published numerous articles in journals such as *Asian Business & Management, Journal of World Business, International Business Review, Management International Review* and *World Development*.

Vipin Gupta (PhD, Wharton School) is Professor and Co-director of the Global Management Center at the California State University San Bernardino. He has been a Japan

Foundation fellow, and a recipient of the Society for Industrial Organizational Psychologists' 'Scott M. Myers Award for Applied Research–2005'. His research focuses on culture, sustainable and comparative strategy and management, organizational and technological transformations, emerging markets, entrepreneurial and women's leadership, and family business models. He has authored or edited 16 books, including the GLOBE book on culture and leadership in 62 societies, 11 on family business models in different cultures and a strategy textbook.

Harukiyo Hasegawa is Honorary Fellow of the White Rose East Asia Centre at the University of Sheffield. He was Professor of Global Management and Human Resource Management at Doshisha Business School in Kyoto, Japan until 2013. He served as chairman of the Euro-Asia Management Studies Association from 2008 to 2011. He has authored, co-edited and contributed to numerous publications, among them: *Steel Industry in Japan: A Comparison with Britain* (Routledge, 1996); *Japanese Business and Management: Restructuring for Low Growth and Globalization* (Routledge, 1998); *The Political Economy of Japanese Globalization* (Routledge, 2001); *Japanese Responses to Globalization* (Palgrave Macmillan, 2006); *New Horizons in Asian Management: Emerging Issues and Critical Perspectives* (Palgrave Macmillan, 2007); and *Asian Business and Management* (Palgrave Macmillan, 2009). He is the founding editor of *Asian Business & Management* (SSCI, Palgrave Macmillan) and was Series Editor for the Palgrave Macmillan Asian Business Series (2004–2013).

Martin Hemmert earned his PhD from the University of Cologne in Germany and is now Professor of International Business at Korea University Business School in Seoul. His current research interests include the international comparative analysis of innovation alliances, innovation systems and management systems. He has published several books including *Technology and Innovation in Japan* (Routledge, 1998) and *Tiger Management: Korean Companies on World Markets* (Routledge, 2012), and numerous articles in journals such as *Industrial and Corporate Change, Research Policy, Management International Review, Journal of Product Innovation Management, Journal of World Business* and *Journal of Engineering and Technology Management.*

Pornkasem Kantamara earned her doctoral degree in General Administrative Leadership from Vanderbilt University, the United States. Currently, she is a lecturer at the College of Management, Mahidol University, Bangkok, Thailand. Her research interests include change management, leadership, educational reform and cross-cultural management. Currently, Pornkasem is an author on a team writing a book on the implementation of the Sufficiency Economy philosophy and how it affects various sectors, such as the agricultural sector, SMEs, large organizations – public and private alike.

Mari Kondo is Professor and Program Dean of Global MBA at Doshisha Business School in Kyoto, Japan. She obtained her MBA and MA (development economics) from Stanford University and her PhD from Kyoto University, Center for Southeast Asian Studies, by conducting an in-depth study of management in the Philippines. She was a faculty member of the Asian Institute of Management in the Philippines for more than 15 years, after a stint at the World Bank in Washington, DC working on projects for East Europe, Asia and Africa. Prior to Doshisha, she was a professor at the Ritsumeikan Asia Pacific University in Japan. Her Philippine related publications include 'Twilling bata-bata into meritocracy' in *Philippine Studies* (2008), 'The Philippines' in the *Oxford Handbook of Asian Business Systems* (Oxford University Press, 2013). She teaches in the areas of strategic management, Asian business and business and society.

Leonard Lynn is Professor Emeritus of Management Policy at Case Western Reserve University, where he was chair of the Department of Marketing and Policy Studies for 10 years. He received BA and MA degrees in Asian studies from the University of Oregon, and MA and PhD degrees in sociology from the University of Michigan. Lynn is now working with colleagues around the world on studies of the globalization of technology development. Lynn has published three books, as well as articles in *Science*, *IEEE Transactions on Engineering Management*, *Research Policy*, *Asian Business & Management*, *Organization Studies*, *Change* and *Issues in Science and Technology*. He has received the 'Excellence in Research Award' from the International Association for the Management of Technology, and is a past president of the Association for Japanese Business Studies.

Nguyen Thi Tuyet Mai is currently Associate Professor at the National Economics University, Vietnam. She holds a PhD in marketing from the National University of Singapore, an MBA from Boise State University, United States and a BA from the National Economics University, Vietnam. Dr Mai's research interests include international marketing, consumer behaviours in transitional economies, knowledge-based management and entrepreneurship. Her research has been published in international journals such as *Asian Business & Management*, *Journal of International Marketing*, *Journal of Business Venturing*, *Journal of Marketing Theory and Practice*, *Journal of Asia-Pacific Business* and *Journal of Macromarketing*.

Carlos Noronha holds a PhD from the University of Sheffield and is Associate Professor of Accounting in the Faculty of Business Administration, University of Macau, China. He serves as a Senior Editor for *Asian Business & Management* (Palgrave Macmillan). His major current area of research is in corporate social responsibility disclosure of Asian, particularly Chinese, enterprises. His research has been published in various journals such as *Asian Business & Management*, *Advances in International Accounting*, *Managerial Auditing Journal*, *Corporate Social Responsibility and Environmental Management* and *Social Responsibility Journal*. He is the author and editor of *The Theory of Culture-Specific Total Quality Management* (Palgrave, 2002) and *Asian Business and Management: Theory, Practice and Perspectives* (with Harukiyo Hasegawa, Palgrave Macmillan, 2009), respectively. He is also a Visiting Professor of Global Accounting and Visiting Scholar at the Doshisha Business School, Doshisha University, Japan. He is a Fellow of CPA Australia and the Association of International Accountants in the United Kingdom.

Gordon Redding teaches at INSEAD and is also Secretary-General of the HEAD Foundation, a think-tank in Singapore devoted to the theory linking social capital and societal development. He was at the University of Hong Kong for 24 years, as founding director of its business school. Active in the study of comparative capitalism he has taught extensively in the region and globally. The author of 12 books, including *The Spirit of Chinese Capitalism* (DeGruyter, 1990), he has recently co-edited the *Oxford Handbook of Asian Business Systems* (Oxford University Press, 2013) and *The Hidden Form of Capital* (with Peter Berger, Anthem, 2010).

Andrew Staples is the Director of the Economist Corporate Network in Japan and adjunct Associate Professor of International Business at Doshisha Business School. His areas of expertise include Japan's political economy, the globalization of Japanese companies and the foreign firms in Japan. His publications include *Responses to Regionalism in East Asia: Japanese Production Networks in the Automotive Sector* published as part of the Palgrave Macmillan Asian Business Series and chapters in edited volumes and textbooks. Andrew has an MSc in East Asian business and a PhD in international political economy from the University of Sheffield and was a research scholar at Hitotsubashi University in Tokyo. Before joining the Economist Group he previously held positions at universities in Japan and the United Kingdom.

Robert Taylor was formerly Director of Chinese Studies and Reader in Modern Chinese Studies at the University of Sheffield. He is the author of a number of books and academic articles relating to China's management systems and Chinese foreign policy, including *Greater China and Japan* (Routledge, 1996) He also edited the volume *International Business in China: Understanding the Global Economic Crisis* (Routledge, 2012) His special interests encompass labour policy and foreign direct investment in China, as well as business networks in Asia. He has published extensively in academic journals, including the *Asia Pacific Business Review* and *Asian Business & Management*.

Rosalie L. Tung (PhD, University of British Columbia) holds the Ming and Stella Wong Chaired Professorship at Simon Fraser University (Canada). She was formerly a Wisconsin Distinguished Professor, Business Administration, with the University of Wisconsin System. She is an elected Fellow of the Royal Society of Canada, the Academy of Management, the Academy of International Business, the British Academy of Management, and the International Academy for Intercultural Research. She served as the 2003–2004 President of the Academy of Management, the leading association of 19,000 professors of management from around the world. She is the author or editor of 11 books and many articles.

Michael A. Witt is Professor of Asian Business and Comparative Management at INSEAD and an Associate in Research at Harvard's Reischauer Institute. He is lead editor of the *Oxford Handbook of Asian Business Systems* (Oxford University Press, 2013) and General Editor of *Asian Business & Management*. Michael's prior works include *Changing Japanese Capitalism* (Cambridge University Press, 2006), *The Future of Chinese Capitalism* (with Gordon Redding, Oxford University Press, 2007) and *Asian Business and Management* (Sage, 2012). Michael has published in leading journals, including *Socio-Economic Review*, *Journal of International Business Studies*, *Asia Pacific Journal of Management* and *Asian Business & Management*. He holds a PhD and MA from Harvard University and an AB from Stanford University.

Preface

Asia represents an immensely complex and evolving matrix of capitalist variations, including China, Vietnam and India, currently in transit towards a market economy. Without a solid theoretical framework it can be challenging to obtain a sound grasp of business and management in Asia. Hence, this textbook offers a perspective – that of Gordon Redding's business systems theory – from which to consider the on-going realities of business and management in Asia. This theoretical framework offers a comparative institutional and systemic perspective that provides a coherent and holistic understanding of Asian business, with all its situational implications for business policy formulation.

This second edition takes note of feedback received on the first edition and also constructive input regarding this follow-up; it has been revised, improved and updated extensively, while maintaining the key two-part structure. The main revision involved bringing the chapters more into line with our adopted theoretical approach. We have contributions from leading scholars from a variety of backgrounds in terms of nationality, geographical location and institution. Although we hope the textbook holds a general sense of unity under the umbrella of business systems theory, each chapter can stand alone, reflecting the author's viewpoint, interest and individuality, enhancing the sense of Asia's complexity and diversity.

This volume is suitable for third- and fourth-year undergraduates and MBA/MA students, as well as managers and executives seeking a more realistic understanding of business and management in Asia as an evolving adaptive system, including further important issues such as globalization, regionalism, corporate social responsibility and ethics, and sustainability. We believe our primer on such issues will address concerns that are becoming increasingly apparent as business and management adapt to the changing conditions of a world becoming less amenable to traditional expansionist business models. Throughout this book, we maintain an academic stance of not applying prescriptive arguments, such as how to compete or how to make a business more profitable, but a perspective seeking to understand business in relation to various contextual factors in the system, including material and ideational impacts. We hope the theoretical perspective used here, as well as the associated analysis and insights offered, will stimulate readers towards a sustainable paradigm for the business world of tomorrow.

HARUKIYO HASEGAWA
CARLOS NORONHA

Acknowledgements

We are grateful to the anonymous reviewers on the first and also this second edition. The updates and extensive revision of this second edition owe much to their input. We would also like to extend our gratitude to the OMRON Corporation for its financial support. OMRON is a Kyoto-based global company renowned for its good corporate citizenship. It is our great pleasure that its corporate philosophy matches the ethical perspective in this text. In addition we thank Ursula Gavin of Palgrave Macmillan for her encouragement in this project and patience in its progress and to Keith Povey for his excellent professionalism in copy editing the whole book. Last but not least our acknowledgements are also due to Jenny Guan, Lee Byung Hee and Polly Cheong for their great contribution to this project, and Tanmaya Mohapatra, Salam Al Khateeb and Nathan Hirsh for the production of excellent teaching materials: teaching notes made by Salam, PowerPoint slides by Tanmaya and overall proofreading by Nathan. We hope these teaching materials will help lecturers using this book for their courses.

HARUKYO HASEGAWA
CARLOS NORONHA

Introduction

Harukiyo Hasegawa and Carlos Noronha

Asian business in the twenty-first century

> Business schools should aim to produce not just efficient, but also decent human beings whose business life is guided not just by a concern with legal compliance, but with criteria of fairness, which they have worked out themselves and which their conscience makes them want to stick to.
> (**Ronald Dore**, *Asian Business & Management*, 2006)[1]

Despite the serious challenges of the Asian financial crisis of 1997 and the global financial crisis of 2008, Asia as a region continues in its role as a production base for the world. China, Japan and India are the leading economies of Asia and their economic growth for the period 2013–2018 is forecast, by the International Monetary Fund (IMF), to be 10.6 per cent for China, 2.9 per cent for Japan, and 8.6 per cent for India; that of ASEAN as a whole is estimated at 8.2 per cent (International Monetary Fund, 2013).

However, the enormous export-led economies of Asia also generate more negative effects that are familiar to any rapidly developing capitalist economy: questionable performance regarding sustainable development, the environment, social welfare, corruption and unequal wealth distribution. This overview invites investigation of how each economy is structured and run, and how each economy is connected to other economies to create the overall regional development, both through identity and formal institutions such as the Association of Southeast Asian Nations (ASEAN), ASEAN + 3, the China Free Trade Agreement and cooperative arrangements initiated by the Japanese government, as well as various corporate-level links through foreign direct investment (FDI) and supply-chain networks.

Generally speaking Asia's development began with Japan adopting and adapting Western technology from the 1960s through to the 1980s. This pattern was followed successfully by Korea and Taiwan in the period 1980–1990 and by China from 1990 to the present. India, following China, has also shown remarkable economic development. As of 2012, China was ranked second in world GDP rankings with Japan third and India tenth (International Monetary Fund, 2013).

Although these nations constitute the core of economic development in Asia, regional development overall is also generated by other countries, as described in this book. They are interconnected and networked in a variety of ways via capital, human resources, technologies and supply chains. This generates dynamics within and beyond national boundaries. While rapid economic development is, itself, important for enriching lifestyle and culture, its negative consequences should not be ignored, as the balance of the whole system cannot be maintained if the negative consequences become too great. Such negative consequences relate, in our theoretical framework, to the rationale, meaning and issues of ethics. They form the main topic in Chapter 7 and the sections on corporate social responsibility (CSR) in the country chapters of Part II.

Asia self-evidently is currently the most dynamic region of the world economy and can be investigated as an evolutionary fabric of business systems (see Chapter 1 and Figure 1.1). The business system concept used here has been developed by Gordon Redding. We consider it to be a suitable theoretical lens through which to appreciate and understand the complex realities of business in Asia.

Why is a systems theory suitable?

Although various theoretical frameworks – from the fields of economics, political economy, sociology, international relations, Marxism or even philosophy – are available to understand business in Asia, we have chosen a systems approach. As Redding defines it in Chapter 1 it is 'a complex adaptive system in which the business component of a society is analysed against the context of that society'. We consider it to be a suitable framework to examine links between various component factors in a system and their function, and also to compare systems in terms of competitiveness and future trajectories. For this approach we also include contextual conditions such as national history, politics and various external influences such as ideational and material influences. We believe that this systems theory is useful in understanding the complex realities of business in Asia in a nuanced and coherent way.

A system is, in general, composed of various interconnected component factors and the dynamics of such factors generate movement within the system itself. The relative importance of such factors and the way they are connected are fundamental to such movement and the changing trajectory of a system. In natural science and engineering it would be possible to measure quantitatively the relative importance and interrelated movement of the factors in a system, but in social science this is problematic, as such factors reflect constantly changing human activities. What we can do is to understand logically and reflectively how they are connected and how they function as a whole, resulting in overall movement such as performance, or, over a longer time frame, rise and decline. The more factors in a system, the more complex it will be. Underpinning such dynamics are social relations and human activities within a given society, which reflect economic interests, power, preferences, ideologies and social class.

Business systems also interact with external forces, which we call contextual forces. To survive, a system needs to be flexible in relation to such forces. An example of such 'adopt and adapt' processes in human society lies in the shifts of civilization from one region to another, and at a more national level, the drift of economic development from country to country, for example, Japan to Korea, China and India (note that these do not imply physical takeover of one civilization or national development by another). Although we can identify critical component factors in a system, the contextual (external) forces are numerous in types and magnitudes of impacts. In this sense a system needs to be flexible and adaptive in order to maintain smooth running. A system is therefore homeostatic and path-dependent, but with a capacity for constant change and adjustment.

This system concept is shown in Figure 1.1 on page 20. The model can be applied to any country, so that Japan's business system can be discussed in comparison with that of China or Korea, for example. The system logic is therefore functional. The system is conceived to have three layers, each layer having three component factors, making a total of nine factors in the system. Contextual forces will be numerous, but in our system we have two major categories: ideational forces such as globalization and material forces such as technology. Although our system is a consciously constructed logic, it supports the following research aims: (1) understanding complex realities as integrated systems, (2) investigating connections of factors and their mutual influences, (3) comparing the competitiveness of systems, (4) predicting evolutionary rise and fall, and changing trajectories, and (5) identifying challenges and their responses. The limitations are: (1) the importance of component factors and their intensity of influence cannot be quantitatively measured, (2) the selection of factors is subjectively determined,

TABLE I.1 Factors and contextual forces by chapter

Ch.	Factors in business system			Contextual (external) Forces				
	Meaning (culture)	Order (institutions)	Coordination (structure/ systems)	Politics (domestic/ international)	Economy (domestic/ international)	Society/ religion	History/ tradition	Technology/ science
1	*	*	*	*	*	*	*	*
2	***				*		*	
3	*	***	**		*			
4	*	***	*	*	*		*	
5			*	*	*		*	***
6	*	*	***		**			
7	***		***	*	*	*		
8	**	**	**	*	*	*	*	
9	*	*	**	*	*	*	*	*
10	**	**	**	*	*	*	*	
11	**	**	**	*	*	*	*	
12	**	**	**	*	*	*	*	
13	**	**	**	*	*	*	*	
14	**	**	**	*	*	*	*	
15	**	**	**	*	*	*	*	
16	**	**	**	*	*			

NOTE:* = Degree of bearing.

and (3) the dynamics of social relations as manifest in industrial action and social conflicts are not included. Thus, our lens is not all-comprehensive, but assists in a fog of complexities to understand systems in a coherent and comparative way.

Part I consists of seven chapters, and opens with Redding's compact overview, including both an explanation of the theoretical underpinning and its application to major Asian economies. Further chapters focus on specific topics that we consider important not only in research (see Witt, 2012; Witt and Redding, 2013), but also for business practice, and we show how such topics are relevant to factors in business systems. A summary of each chapter's relevance with regard to component factors and contextual forces appears in Table I.1.

Part I: chapters

1. The Business Systems of Asia (Gordon Redding)

2. Asian Cultures and Business Systems (Carlos Noronha and Harukiyo Hasegawa)

3. Accounting and Corporate Governance in Asia (Carlos Noronha)

4. Human Resource Management in Asia (Rosalie Tung)

5. Technology Development in Asia (Leonard Lynn)

6. Regionalism and Production Networks in Asia (Andrew Staples)

7. Sustainable Development and Corporate Social Responsibility in Asia
   (Philippe Debroux)

Chapter 1 provides an overview of Redding's theory and its application. Japan, China, Korea and other selected economies in Asia are investigated and explained from the perspective of the nine key component factors discussed above (on their three conceptual layers of meaning, order and coordination, see Figure 1.1). The bottom layer – 'meaning' – has factors such as such as rationale, identity and authority. The middle layer – 'order', providing institutions – has factors such as financial, human and social capital. The top layer – 'coordination', providing structure and organization – includes ownership, networks and management factors. The message of this introductory chapter is to identify: the importance of the functional structure in a system; the reasons behind variations arising from differences in religion, politics, history, ideas, ethnicity and culture; and the rationale and meaning for their existence.

The importance of cultural understanding in studying Asian business is addressed in Chapter 2. Culture is a foundational component of national business systems. An understanding of culture is also crucial for success in global business, as indicated by the cases cited here: Tata Daewoo Motors and China's Wanda Group in the United Kingdom. This chapter introduces major theories of culture and discusses different Asian cultural systems with their different characteristics and value orientations. These cultural systems interact with respective factors at the order and coordination layers, and culture influences the formation of different types of business system, so that understanding culture is essential to grasp the function of other factors on the order and coordination layers, via the attitudes and behaviours of actors in the business system. Thus, nationally-specific culture (values, norms and socially-constructed realities) will influence a system's institutional and organizational characteristics and *vice versa*, thereby tending to generate increased refinement in the system.

Chapter considers the issues of accounting, finance and corporate governance in Asia which relate to component factors on the order and coordination layers. Through accounting, capital is managed and operating results are communicated to institutions, while the use of capital is monitored by legal and ethical forces through corporate governance mechanisms. Selected Asian cases are provided as examples and are given to highlight these points. Corporate governance differs as a result of differences in ownership and contextual factors, and various institutions emerge to facilitate the complex exchange of resources, including capital itself. Specifically addressed is the development of International Financial Reporting Standards in Asian countries *vis-à-vis* global trends, quality of accounting information, characteristics of corporate governance mechanisms and the importance of business ethics in relation to the financial affairs of corporations.

Chapter 4 explores human capital and its management, which is one of the three factors on the middle layer of the business system. Human resource management (HRM) is key to successful corporate management wherever business takes place, but it needs to be flexible and adaptive to contextual forces if it is to contribute to successful management. Major characteristics of HRM practices in Japan, Korea and China, including similarities and differences across the three countries, receive attention. Although only three countries are subject to detailed investigation, key references for other Asian HRM are provided for follow-up study. Factors (including political, economic and socio-cultural dimensions) in the institutional environment contributing to the evolution of HRM systems and practices in these three countries are then identified, prior to discussion of the challenges ahead for these three countries. The message from this chapter is a concept of 'cross-vergence', which reflects a mixed phenomenon of convergence and divergence as a consequence of flexible adaptation of management to external forces such as globalization. Human capital, and its management (HRM), are directly interconnected with rational factors on the meaning layer and also management factors on the coordination layer. The links and mutual influence between them are critical in the formation of the overall characteristics of a business system, such as liberal market versus coordinated market economies (see Hall and Soskice, 2001).

Chapter 5 investigates the evolution and strength of science and technology in Asian business systems. According to the author, Asia now accounts for around one-third of global expenditure on research and development (R&D). China passed Japan in 2009 and is second only to the United States in R&D spending (see Table 5.1). India has become a centre of global excellence in the knowledge-intensive service sectors and biotechnology. In our theoretical framework, science and technology are considered a major material logic (contextual force) rather than a component factor of the business system. They may however directly influence factors on the top layer and human capital on the middle layer. The chapter starts by studying Asia's rich technological heritage and then moves to ways of thinking about a nation's technological system. The strengths and weaknesses of Asian national technology systems are discussed, leading to an identification of technological challenges facing Asia. The chapter provides insights on technology, which can be easily transferred from one region or business system to another.

The implications of regionalism and regional production networks for a business system are examined in Chapter 6. This topic relates to networks and management at the system's coordination layer. The chapter looks at how firms are organized on a regional basis and how one business system coordinates with other business systems, and considers the case of Toyota's regional production system, suggesting the need for flexible adaptation to contextual conditions in a host economy. From a discussion about adopting a regional perspective prior to an examination of major theories and perspectives, the chapter focuses on regional and Japanese production networks in the automobile sector, ending with the message, 'Regionalized production, therefore, does create an added layer of complexity to our analysis of firms, but the business systems approach remains valid given its capacity to locate that analysis in the broader institutional and societal fabric of the host economy.'

Chapter 7 is an important and insightful chapter that discusses whether we should let economic development proceed as it has been doing, or redirect it with a perspective of sustainability. Thus, the chapter is relevant to ideational logic (corporate social responsibility, CSR) transferred from the West to Asia. Within the framework of a business system it is relevant to factors on the bottom layer. The chapter starts with an interesting proverb: 'give a man a fish and you feed him for a day. Teach a man how to fish and you feed him for a long time.' However, as has been observed, sustainability is not about learning 'how to fish', but about understanding what 'fish' need to grow and reproduce (Ehnert and

Harry, 2012). The concepts of CSR and sustainable development, and the pursuit of policies for sustainable development and CSR, are discussed, as well as how to adjust these two concepts. The chapter ends with alternative approaches for implementing CSR policies.

Part I ends with that discussion of the critical challenge for ourselves and future generations, but all the topics and issues included are key to important functions of the business system. There will be many other issues and topics. They may appear in a different form from the factors chosen for our business system; but when we understand the content and nature of the issues, we can discuss them in relation to factors and contextual forces.

Asian business systems: a variety of complex adaptive systems

Part II switches our focus to Asia's major business systems. Despite distinct political and social histories, a common trajectory today is economic development based upon market principles, albeit under varying political ideologies. There were two criteria for selection of these nine national business systems.

First, they are representative systems showing remarkable economic growth. Other than Japan and Singapore, the countries selected to receive detailed attention have been forecast to expect as high as 8.6 per cent average GDP (nominal) growth for the period 2013–2018 (International Monetary Fund, 2013). For space reasons, we were unable to include Indonesia, Hong Kong and Taiwan, although the latter two are briefly touched on in Chapter 8. We have included India even though it, in reality, belongs to the South Asia region, because of: the size of its GDP (third in Asia and tenth in the world in 2012); its current importance as a hub of the IT and service industry; and its growing importance, after China, as a world manufacturing base.

Second, we consider these business systems to be unique in their component factors, in content and the way they are connected, and also in their contextual forces in terms of geographical, political, societal, religious and international conditions.

Part II: chapters

8. The Business System of Japan (Michael A. Witt)

9. The Business System of China (Robert Taylor)

10. The Business System of India (Vipin Gupta)

11. The Business System of Korea (Martin Hemmert)

12. The Business System of Singapore (Tony Garrett)

13. The Business System of Malaysia (Axèle Giroud)

14. The Business System of the Philippines (Mari Kondo)

15. The Business System of Thailand (Pornkasem Kantamara)

16. The Business System of Vietnam (Nguyen Thi Tuyet Mai and Mai The Cuong)

Chapter 8 tackles the business system in Japan, looking at the shape of the system and then its comparative advantages, continuity and change in the system, international activities and CSR. The chapter ends by considering implications for doing business in Japan. The Japanese business system saw remarkable growth until the mid-1970s and then stable growth until 1990, but subsequently entered a low-growth phase that continues today. Japan's post-war economic development came about through a successful business system that became more sophisticated as development progressed, suggesting a cohesion of component factors at the meaning, order and coordination layers. It is a typical example of a complex adaptive system. Although Japan's performance has declined, it remains Asia's most advanced economy and ranks third in the world in GDP. How can such a tightly woven business system cope with the changing conditions and contingencies from outside? This has been a challenge for Japan over the past two decades and remains a challenge. The chapter explains and discusses the irony and enigma of Japan's experience.

Chapter 9 is about China's business system. China is currently the world's second largest economy in terms of GDP and a factory for many goods sold around the world – the label 'Made in China' is a familiar feature of daily life. What are the characteristics of its business system and what social and economic influence will it have on Asia and elsewhere? The chapter starts with an overview of China's market economy and then moves to the motivation behind its managerial reforms. Also dealt with are Chinese corporate governance and culture, the impact of FDI on Chinese management and CSR in China. Such issues and events can be considered in terms of component factors of the business system and we can see how institutional arrangements differ from elsewhere and why this makes China such a powerful economy in Asia. China is indeed an intriguing opportunity to explore the interaction of meaning, order and coordination factors, creating strength as well as challenges from within. In particular, it is interesting to explore how China's political ideational logic has compromised with the variant ideational logic of market and globalization. Will there be any political and societal forces, either from within or without, that will impact upon the evolving system, and if so how will the system react and adapt?

India, since the mid-1990s, has been one of the world's most successful economies, and in 2012 ranked tenth in the world GDP table and is the subject of Chapter 10. Following a discussion of the culture of one of the most religiously, linguistically and demographically diverse nations in the world, the author looks at India's civil society and institutions before moving on to an in-depth analysis of its business system and changing trends, including the international activities of Indian firms, CSR and ethics. India's business system contrasts sharply with East Asian systems in history, politics and culture. Historically, India has been strongly influenced by the United Kingdom and the Soviet Union. Economic reform (liberalization) since the 1990s and the development of its information technology industry were also key forces that shaped the unique character of its business system. However, like China, India's development faces a dichotomy stemming from the contrasting ideational logics of socialism and capitalism, the former constituting political institutions, and the latter economic institutions. To create economic sustainability, a pressing need whichever direction India leans, pragmatic issues such as wealth disparity, environmental problems, human rights and child labour need to be resolved.

The author of Chapter 11 characterizes Korea's management as 'tiger management' for its speed, aggressiveness, dynamism and bravery. The chapter starts with an overview of the Korean economy and analysis of each period in its economic development, and follows with an analysis of the culture that underpins Korea's business system and an identification of financial, human and social capital as key factors in the system's middle layer. Following this, Korean management, CSR and working and living conditions are discussed. Korea was Asia's fourth largest economy in 2013 and the characteristics not only of its business system and culture, but also of its institutional arrangements, organization and structure make it an attractive and important topic of study.

The business system of Singapore is unique, primarily in its success as a hub for trade and investment in Asia. With one of the region's highest per capita GDP rates (approximately US$50,000), it is becoming one of the world's wealthiest countries, with an infrastructure supporting its successful service and manufacturing industries. Chapter 12 first introduces Singapore's business system and then follows up with the role of the government, the ownership of firms and their management. The chapter closes with a focus on CSR and working and living conditions. Singapore's system is shaped by its geographical location, Confucian culture, human resources, the role of government and other contextual forces, resulting in a hard-working society with a stable economic and political system.

Malaysia's business system is featured in Chapter 13, which begins by describing the system and analysing the institutional environment, politics, capital, inter-firm relationships and labour. An investigation of its competitive advantages and of continuity and change in the business system follows, along with a discussion of the role of international activities carried out by Malaysian firms and MNEs in Malaysia. The chapter ends with a discussion on CSR and implications for expatriates and foreign firms in Malaysia. The key issues for this business system are multiculturalism, government intervention, natural resources, multinational enterprises (MNEs), the position of Malaysia within ASEAN, and how these issues will be managed and influence its current and future business system.

The business system of the Philippines (Chapter 14) reflects the country's struggle with the historical legacies of colonialism. After looking at the macro-economic and social conditions deriving from its post-war development experience, the chapter moves to a detailed analysis of factors in the system and then to its comparative advantages. The second section is about changing trends and international activities, leading to a discussion of CSR in the Philippines. The chapter ends with some implications for expatriates and foreign firms. As the author suggests, the Philippines' business system is unfortunately a typical case of underperformance – while several of its neighbours show an effective combination of development factors, the Philippines ranks only 40th in GDP (2012) and is often ignored in the field as it is neither a big nor an attractive player. Nonetheless, it provides valuable evidence that the performance of a business system depends upon who is running it and for what purpose, thereby suggesting the significance of 'meaning' on the bottom layer of our business system framework.

Thailand, the subject of Chapter 15, is one of Asia's most distinctive and successful systems, placed 31st in world GDP (2012) and sixth among Asian nations. As the author notes, the World Bank now describes Thailand as an upper-middle income economy. The chapter starts with an introduction to the system's macro-economic and social conditions and then moves to an analysis of these and of its comparative advantages. Continuity and change within the system and international activities also come under review, and the chapter ends with CSR and implications for living and working conditions. The uniqueness of Thailand's system lies in its 'meaning' layer, based on Buddhism; its development is led by a model called 'Sufficiency Economy', a philosophy combining values such as moderation, reasonableness, self-immunity and pragmatic issues such as knowledge and morality as a rationale to legitimize the country's economic development.

Chapter 16 turns to the business system in Vietnam, which reflects the country's transformation since 1986 from a strict command economy to a socialist-oriented market economy. Both opportunities and challenges face those running the system. Starting with an introduction to the business system and identifying its competitive advantages, the chapter explains changing trends within the system and international activities of Vietnamese firms. To close, it gives an analysis of CSR and explores working and living conditions in Vietnam. The critical issue facing the country is how to balance differing values such as Confucianism, socialism and the liberal ideology of globalization, and translate them into effective policies and strategies for economic development, while dealing with the negative consequences deriving from the rapid development itself.

In sum, then, Asian business systems show great variety due to their distinctive histories, political ideologies and events, cultural traditions, religions and external ideational influences such as globalization. Such variety suggests great potential for development in the twenty-first century, but development, as always, generates challenges – of environment, sustainable development and socio-economic inequality – both from within and without the system. Such challenges will need to be resolved, for they threaten the very basis of the system being developed.

The ideas and insights throughout this book, plus the stimulating questions raised in each chapter, will help readers deepen their understanding of Asian business, and formulate policies and strategies that will benefit not just short-term objectives, but also long-term sustainable development.

Table I.1 shows how each chapter relates to the function of the relevant business system and also its ideational and material forces. Our approach is thus to put Asia's complex realities into a compact institutional and path-dependent logic to assess how they function as systems.

Features

Several features have been included to help enhance students' understanding of theory, practice and perspective in Asian business.

Companion website: providing rich and up-to-date pedagogic resources for both students and instructors.

Companion teaching notes: a guide for lecturers to enrich teaching for each chapter.

Chapter outline: providing the general topic area, structure and development of information and knowledge in each chapter.

Chapter objectives: a guide for the student to assimilate the key topics and issues raised.

Chapter summary: a useful and compact digest of the information presented, by which readers can understand the relative importance of the content and the author's perspective and insights.

Key concepts: an aid to remembering the definition of terms appearing in the chapter and to assist with clear understanding of the material.

Review questions: questions concerning points raised provide a reference for students to assess and enhance their understanding of the issues in view of business systems theory.

Learning activities: these activities encourage students to engage in their own research and thereby deepen their understanding of relevant issues.

Mini-cases: these stories offer real-life scenarios illustrating issues and theories in the given chapter, and are useful for class discussion of the links between reality and the theory we adopt.

Related web-links: providing supplementary avenues of information for those wishing to explore the issues further.

References: a list of sources/works cited in the chapter, essential for backing up discussion and developing personal perspectives.

Note

1   Ronald Dore (2006) The Important and Unimportant in Business Management. *Asian Business & Management*, 5(1): 9–21, p. 9.

References

Ehnert, I. and Harry, H. (2012) Recent Developments and Future Prospects on Sustainable Human Resource Management: Introduction to the Special Issue. *Management Review,* 23(3): 221–239.

Hall, Peter A. and Soskice, David (eds.) (2001) *Varieties of Capitalism: The institutional foundations of comparative advantage.* Oxford: Oxford University Press.

IMF (2013) World Economic Outlook: Hopes, Realities, Risks, accessed 5 December 2013 at: http://www.imf.org/external/pubs/ft/weo/2013/01/pdf/text.pdf

Witt, Michael A. (ed.) (2012) *Asian Business and Management.* Los Angeles: Sage.

Witt, Michael A. and Redding, Gordon (2013) *The Oxford Handbook of Asian Business Systems.* Oxford: Oxford University Press.

PART I **ASIAN BUSINESS SYSTEMS**
MAJOR ISSUES

The Business Systems of Asia

Gordon Redding

Chapter outline

- Variety in the region and general features
- What a business system is and why they vary between societies
- The business systems of Japan, China and South Korea
- The regional ethnic Chinese, Southeast Asian and IndoChina societies in business

Chapter objectives

After reading this chapter you should be able to:

1 Understand the basic components of the region's variety of business systems.

2 Understand how a business system works.

3 Explain the main features of the business systems of the major economies.

4 Have an initial understanding of the smaller economies of the region.

Introduction

The first thing to understand about business systems in Asia is their variety. This is not ordinary variety, but immense variety; more, for instance, than across Europe. They range from the largest country in the world, China, to some of the smallest (e.g., Singapore), and from some of the richest (e.g., Japan) to some of the poorest (e.g., Cambodia). The area contains a wide range of political systems, ethnic types, religions and historical experiences. So, in order to discuss them, it is necessary to reduce the range by clustering them, with each cluster containing similarities within its membership. This simplification results in losing some of the richness of the differences, but that may be found in the specialized chapters that follow.

The main subdivisions are:

- Japan

- China

- South Korea

- The regional ethnic Chinese

- Southeast Asia

- Indochina

The distinct nature of the Indian sub-continent and its base in quite different traditions of civilization from those of Asia, means that it is better for it to be treated in its own right, which will be done in a chapter devoted to that theme. Otherwise the constant making of exceptions from the patterns further east will interrupt the flow of what is already a complex story.

Regional features

Over millennia the populating of the region tended to be in waves, with people coming in from the north-west and eventually pushing south and eastwards. The result is a layering of different ethnic types, seen very simply as (i) essentially Malay (that is in ethnic terms) to the eastern and southern edges of the region (ii) Sinic (or Chinese) in China itself and penetrating Indochina, (iii) a distinct Japanese ethnic stock, and (iv) a very mixed set of ethnic groups in the Indochina peninsula, most notably the Thai and Vietnamese.

The region encompasses all types of natural environment and contains the active heritages of several great religious and civilizational traditions. Dominant among these is that of China, whose influence lies deep in the formative processes that made Japan, Korea and Vietnam. Elsewhere, and especially in Malaysia and Indonesia, Islam penetrates deep. Thailand is an example of a predominantly Buddhist society and the Philippines has retained the dominance of Catholicism, established during 400 years of Spanish rule.

External influences have historically overlain these traditions in many countries. The British in what was Malaya, Singapore and Hong Kong, the French in Indochina, the Dutch in Indonesia, the Americans in the Philippines (after the Spanish) and the Japanese in the twentieth century in Taiwan, Korea and Manchuria, have all left behind institutions and connections that have marked those countries. Less by way of invasion and colonization, but equally significant has been the influence of India established through trading connections, especially in Southeast Asia. A final wave of influence, similar to that of India, has been the impact of the regional ethnic Chinese who left China in the past 150 years and settled as business people in the countries around the rim of the South China Sea. In more recent decades the influences of multinational corporations on the region have been very strong, not only on management practices, but also on government policies, the importing of technology, and the creation of alliances to link with the markets of the rest of the world. The only country that has remained free from direct foreign influence has been Thailand, protected as it always has been by the strength of its monarchy.

The period from 1945 to 1975 was a period of turbulence as countries tried to establish their new identities and independent political structures. Wars broke out: the Korean War; the American war in Vietnam; a long guerrilla war in Malaya; a bitter civil war in Indonesia; struggles for independence; and a period of *konfrontasi* in Southeast Asia. Other more localized outbreaks of hostility were widespread. In the same period China went through the damaging chaos of the Maoist experiments: the Great Leap Forward and the Cultural Revolution. From that period there remains a fundamental divide between totalitarian states (China, Vietnam, North Korea) and the rest that have moved along the continua of liberal markets and political empowerment.

A second period of relative calm, between 1975 and 1997, followed as the region settled down to the more peaceful pursuits of doing business, and in particular of exporting to developed country markets. This saw a rise in foreign direct investment into the region and also the moving of many factories out of Japan into regional countries with lower labour costs. After Mao's death China went through a major reappraisal of its economic philosophy, coming to terms with the stark facts of the collapse of Communism elsewhere and as a result striking out with its own formula of a 'socialist market economy'. This was the period of the Japanese miracle, and saw also the impressive growth of the South Korean economy.

This long period of stable growth and accumulating success contained within it the seeds of its own destruction as it began to run out of synchronization with the systems of the advanced world. Not in China, but elsewhere, the problem of what had earlier been termed 'ersatz capitalism' lay hidden. This means that inefficient use of capital was covered up by the availability of easy money, either from governments, or from over-optimistic foreigners enchanted by the lure of emerging markets. As the system could not keep up the pretence forever it became increasingly sensitive to a downturn in the economic cycle. That downturn hit the region in 1997, and the Asian Crisis signalled the end of the easy money and the beginning of reforms.

China had been largely insulated from these effects, and so too, to a degree were Malaysia, Hong Kong, Taiwan and Singapore. But everywhere else became an industrial bloodbath, and many companies disappeared. Japan suffered from the huge bubble created in its economy by the inflation of asset values, especially in property, and is still in recovery from that. Korea was hit badly by the logics that flow from borrowing short and investing long. The economies of most ASEAN countries saw heavy losses, currency devaluation and the closing of many firms.

As a result of the crisis the region entered a third phase, a period of reform. Since 1997 this has moved at a different pace in different countries, and recovery has therefore been slow in some cases, notably Japan, Indonesia and the Philippines. Even so the direction of movement has been consistent and has displayed the following broad features:

- Improvements to accountability and disclosure in the financing of industry.

- The reduction of favouritism and corruption caused when officials control access to licences and capital.

- The opening of markets to foreign competition.

- The adoption of international standards in accounting, trading, and intellectual property rights, often via bodies such as the WTO.

- A general rise in professionalism, in both management and administration.

- The adoption of democratic processes in politics.

An important point here is that such trends do not necessarily mean that these countries are converging on a western formula for organizing their societies and economies. They will still find ways of interpreting the core principles in ways that fit local cultures. In other words they will converge to some degree but then remain 'true to themselves'. As a result of that we need to account for the continuing variety of the region's business systems. We must also allow that hybrid systems have been important in achieving progress, even if rarely acknowledged. Singapore could not have progressed without the major contribution of the multinationals. Taiwan owes a great deal to its ties with the United States and to imported technology. China owes much to foreign direct investment, not least from the regional ethnic Chinese via Hong Kong. Hong Kong itself can only be understood by taking account of the global ties that come from its colonial trading history.

What is a business system?

A business system is a complex adaptive system in which the business component of a society is analysed against the context of that society, thus 'the American business system' compared to the 'Japanese business system'. Complex adaptive systems theory is relatively new when applied this way, and the reason it is used is that it allows for the complexity of reality to be considered, whereas some disciplines attempt to reduce that complexity to a simple framework and in the process perhaps miss out things that matter. The core idea is that an economy is a process affected by the logics of economic behaviour, but also by culture, history, and specific societal events and experiences. It is also affected by external influences such as world markets, technology and changes of values. All these forces, economic, technical and social interact in complex ways, and the system evolves to take on a distinct flavour, society by society.

The analysis proposed for use here can be seen in Figure 1.1. The culture is seen as the base layer of **meaning**. Here we analyse how each society constructs its own way of making sense of its surrounding context, and it does so in three main fields. First is that of *rationale*, or the basic reasons adopted by people to explain the way they have chosen to make the economy work: why do they act and in what ways do they prefer to conduct exchange, employment, financing, control, etc.? It is in this sphere that questions of ethics come into play. As Max Weber pointed out, when considering the role of religion in economic development, the business person in running an organization is in a position where ethics become strategic to the firm. To secure a stable relationship with a

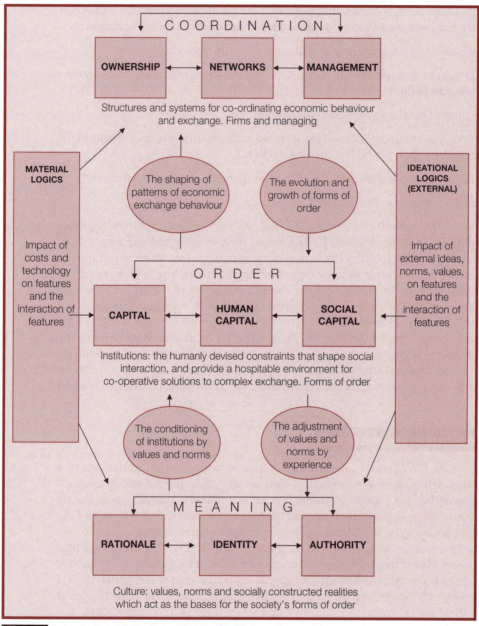

FIGURE 1.1 The elements of a business system

business environment (in a free market) a firm has to behave responsibly in that environment, to act in an honourable manner towards its customers, providing them with goods or services that are respected for their value. The same firm has to treat its personnel with respect and decency if it wants them to be committed. When such matters are handled appropriately, as pointed out by Robert Heilbroner in his study of capitalism, the firm takes on the wider societal duty of providing a benevolent form of dominance. This is more progressive for societies than the earlier forms of dominance by political dogma, military strength or autocratic administration. These 'bourgeois virtues' analysed in detail by Deidre Mc Closkey are major contributors to development. The civilizations of Asia all have in their heritages versions of these ethical ideals available for reinterpretation, as for instance the current concern in China with the harmonious society.

Next is *identity*, or the core ideas in the society about the place of the person in the social structure: is it an individualist or a collectivist system, and in what ways are such ideals interpreted? Next is *authority*, or the way in which power is typically exercised in the society and its organizations, usually enacting the ethics within the rationale. These three aspects of culture have long-lasting and subtle effects.

The middle layer of the model is that of the society's institutions. This is the realm of **order**, and the job of institutions is to standardize and regulate conduct so that it becomes predictable. People can then learn how to act, and can better predict the behaviour of others. The society's economic system can expand and intensify if there is a widespread understanding of the rules of the game and if compliance with those rules is ensured. The main areas in which such order is needed is in the fields where the society's main assets are found and allocated into the system for use. These are its finance *capital*, its *human capital,* and its forms of trust or *social capital*. Capital is about where money is sourced, and how it is allocated for use. Human capital is about where talents and skills are found or encouraged, and how the labour market structures work. Trust is about the relative uses of personal trust (as with personal networks) as against trust in 'the system' (as with reliance on law or bureaucratic process).

The business system itself is at the top of the picture and emerges over time in interaction with the other two sets of influences. It is the field of **coordination**, the pulling together of the resources needed to make economic processes efficient and capable of expansion. This is achieved in three ways: firms come into existence under forms of *ownership,* and these do not follow a universal rule. The Japanese are biased towards *keiretsu*, the Koreans towards *chaebol*, the Chinese tend to favour *smaller personally dominated* firms. These are different ways of holding together sets of assets and controlling their use. Second there are different ways of arranging the *relations between firms* in the economy, with a preference in some cases for alliances, cartels, oligopolies, and in other cases for purer competition. Last, within each firm there are societal preferences for ways of *managing the cooperation* needed to bring together efficiently the human, technical and financial assets. In some societies firms are run with strong top-down discipline. In other societies they are run with much more participation and fair process. Although these responses differ between firms, there is nonetheless much evidence that a societal pattern makes itself felt and produces recognizable differences between national economies. Each society becomes distinct.

The history of a society will also have an effect. Taiwan and Korea bear the imprint of decades of Japanese occupation, and the Philippines its American and Spanish heritages. So too will government policies have an impact on the end result. One cannot understand China without studying the waves of policy change it has gone through. Nor can one understand South Korea (referred to from now as Korea) without acknowledging the series of five-year plans begun under the Park government in the 1960s.

I shall use this framework to describe the business systems of Asia, but before doing so need to advise the reader that much simplification is inevitable in doing so and that it is not intended to substitute for detailed studies of each society. The pictures given are outlines only. It will not be possible to go into every aspect of the model in every case, as this is intended to be an introductory chapter, not a final statement. It serves to make two main points: (1) each society does things its own way; and (2) although they may appear to be drifting closer in some ways, they never meet to make a perfect convergence. The fact that they do not finally converge is what presents international business with its interest and its dilemmas, in both theory and practice.

Japan

The Japanese business system developed as one of the world's most powerful, and especially in industries requiring (a) high levels of technical skill in manufacturing, (b) the building of globally significant brands, (c) complex organizational coordination at high levels of efficiency and (d) an ability to engage workers in product improvement and quality assurance. Typical fields of dominance in global competition are automobiles, machine tools, consumer electronics and communications equipment. How did this dominance come into being? Why is performance in certain other fields such as the service sector less dramatically competitive globally? What is it taking so long to recover the high rates of growth typical of the 1980s? And what is it about the Japanese business system that allows it to deliver wealth per capita at one of the highest levels in the world, and organizations of immense scale and dramatic efficiency?

History and politics

Japan went through a key societal revolution in the early years of the seventeenth century when the Shogun Tokugawa imposed his design on a newly unified nation, in the interests of achieving peace and stability. Key in this were two elements: the decentralization of much decision making into local hands along with an encouragement of participation and the seeking of consensus; the development of a highly effective administrative bureaucracy responsible for strict rules of order, and for keeping the Centre informed about what happened locally. Tokugawa's influence on Japan was massive and lasted for two and a half centuries, only coming to an end when the outside world forced an entry and showed Japan that other countries had left it behind in industry, science, technology and weaponry. The stability had come at the cost of conservatism. The subsequent overthrow of the old regime in 1868 led to the modernization of the state, and the deliberate searching for external models to adopt and adapt.

The subsequent industrialization of Japan happened twice. Up to World War II Japan built huge conglomerate organizations – the *zaibatsu*. World War II destroyed them all and in 1946 Japan began again, but this time under conditions of democracy imposed by the conquering United States. Recovery was fast, especially as the markets of the advanced economies were open. By the end of the 1980s 'Japanese management' had become the world's most respected form, and its economy the most formidable. Deep competences in the managing of technical and organizational complexity, in cooperation within the overall system, and in control of global activities, had made the Japanese company the envy of the world.

However, keeping a business system in perfect balance is never easy and around 1990 Japan entered a period of relative stagnation that lasted through the 1990s and into the new millennium, its capital market never recovering to the crazy peaks of the unreal asset prices that brought it down. Two decades have been lost and the reforms attempted by various governments have not taken hold to the extent needed to return Japan to its dominant position. Certain industries have remained unscathed as they were capable of radical adaptation. Others are victims of the rigidities of a highly inflexible structure, in which ministries, industries, labour unions, banks, and systems of distribution, are all intertwined in bonds of reciprocity, and unable to orchestrate serious change. The absence of flexibility in both labour and capital markets is a handicap in such circumstances, when at earlier periods it was considered a strength.

It would be wrong to exaggerate the weakness of Japan, as much of its strength was retained, but its slowness in growth in recent years has been marked, and so too its apparent inability to adapt. How did this combination of power and inhibition evolve?

Culture

At the centre of Japan's economic culture is the idea that the firm exists to keep people employed, and that return on capital for the advantage of shareholders is not a primary rationale for economic action. Authority came to be exercised under the conditions that subordinate dependence provided reliable workers but only if leadership took responsibility for their care. The underlying moral framework made sense of this mutual vertical bonding. It led also to a tendency to associate the firm as a vertical entity, separate from other entities, and in rivalry with them. A further related cultural legacy was the tradition of decentralized decision making that fostered extensive consensus seeking and that released high levels of creativity and commitment in the workforce.

Institutions

The institutions of finance in Japan – principally the banks, the insurance companies, and the stock markets – are providers of patient capital to industry. They have not been designed to achieve the highest rates of allocative efficiency in the short term. The system has resisted the incursion of outside influences to pursue this, doubtless judging that the short-termism that would result challenges a crucial principle of the overall design.

A similar rigidity occurs in the labour market. The core of the employment system is a set of permanently employed workers – perhaps 40 per cent of the total workforce – and firms invest substantially in their training over years. Those employed on temporary contracts and those employed part-time provide the necessary flexibility in the system. Compared to other societies, the technical skills derive from the firm rather than from the education system and the latter is usually seen as being conservative and centralized, even though standards are high.

Social capital – or forms of trust – is at a level in Japan well above that of other Asian societies and it engenders an unusually high level of cooperativeness between firms, government agencies, subcontractors and supply chain members, unions and management, and members of the elaborate business networks and 'industry clubs' that tie the economy together. The origins of this capacity to cooperate and to trust lie most probably in the centuries-old tradition of seeing the society with a strong sense of shared belonging, and of high quality professional administration. It will also have some connection to the high quality of information, in terms of both quantity and reliability, which the economy is accustomed to.

The business system

The coordination of economic exchange and control is carried out in Japan through the medium of two main types of firm. The heights of the economy are commanded by the very large business groups, known generally as either *keiretsu* or *sogo-shosha* depending on whether they are in manufacturing or trading. The rest of the economy is dominated by small and medium enterprises, often privately owned, and often connected to the large firms through networks of sourcing or distribution. The networking between firms is elaborate and extensive and industry associations flourish. Within firms 'Japanese management' continues to create high levels of employment stability, and to operate with strong mutual dependence between management and workers. The relative stability and long-term nature of employment relations matches the equivalent long term nature of 'patient' capital. In these conditions firms are able to make long-term plans, to invest heavily in technology and training and to build their strategies around product quality based on deep labour skills and incremental product improvements as opposed to constant product-market change. The ability of Japanese firms to handle complex coordination is a distinct strength in global markets and remains a primary reason for the nation's competitiveness. Few societies can handle the mixture of quality, brand-building and adaptivity to the market, at global scale, that the Japanese firms have mastered. But past success can breed inertia, not so much in firms as in the total system in which they are embedded.

China

China and Japan have very different histories despite some shared heritage. In brief terms Japan built itself into one of the world's greatest industrial powers following its opening up in 1868, whereas China suffered relative decline for most of the nineteenth and twentieth centuries, and only began to recover following the reforms begun by Deng Xiaoping in 1980. China's recovery has quite simply been miraculous and high respect is due for the political and economic skills exhibited in the recent transformation of its economy into 'the workshop of the world'. It must however be noted that there was much slack to be absorbed, especially in the huge reserves of labour and via the government's monopoly of land rights. However, China is not yet 'modern' in the sense of achieving global competitiveness on the basis of indigenous inventiveness and large-scale organizational efficiency at international standards.

History and politics

China was a great civilization long before any other now surviving world civilization. It achieved prosperity well ahead of other regions over a thousand years ago. Although it subsequently achieved much in science and inventions, and in state-craft, these were pre-modern achievements, and the industrial revolution passed it by in later centuries, leaving it stranded and isolated by its own wishes. Its system of government has always been highly centralized and has continually displayed the same three components, adapting them to changing surroundings. These are: (1) reliance on a powerful emperor-like figure providing direction; (2) use of an administrative apparatus to extend the will of the central figure into the entire society; and (3) reliance on the family unit as the primary focus of belonging, duty and welfare that also provided the pride that underpins compliance to the rules of proper conduct and the vehicle for the carrying of achieved status. This basic architecture has changed in only two ways. During the Mao experiments the family was temporarily destroyed and the emperor role vastly expanded. And in recent years that emperor role has diffused across a group of technocrats, as the family role expanded again towards its traditional significance.

The Mao period, although giving China back its pride in a reasserted independence, led also to mass destruction of assets and lives. Emerging from the turbulence that followed, a series of controlled experiments posed a radical challenge to earlier orthodoxies, but their instigator, Deng Xiaoping is likely to be judged by history as the true revolutionary saviour of China in its search for a modern condition.

The period since 1980 has seen dramatic shifts in the fortunes of three sectors. The state owned enterprises originally accounting for 75 per cent of the economy have been reduced to about 15 per cent that are mainly the strategic industries that the state needs to control. The sector earlier known as 'the collectives', that once accounted for 36 per cent of the economy, has been partially eroded by the emerging private sector, but remains robust in many cases, having acquired great stimulus in recent years from new opportunities, local support and alliances bringing in new talent, technology and capital. The 'local corporates' this sector accounts for about 20 per cent of the economy. The private sector, of mainly small and medium enterprises, now accounts for about 65 per cent of the economy, and has grown spectacularly from their illegal position in 1980.

A most remarkable political process – a form of quiet revolution – has in recent years seen economic decision-making power pass from the centre to the provinces and cities in a way that leaves them largely autonomous. China's structure is now one in which the local administrations collect the taxes, and spend the major part of them. They are also set up to compete with other local administrations for investment, and to be judged by Beijing on their performance in doing so. To counterbalance this looseness the Party retains tight control of the key positions in the local hierarchies. The effects on the economy are to increase entrepreneurship and to intensify competition. The central government, which allocates development targets and rewards local officials for the achievement of those targets, remains fully aware and firmly in control.

Culture

The Confucian ideal was one in which each family took care of its own members, and was responsible for their social conduct. The role of the state was to ensure that this happened. Compliance to five principles was the basis of order, and these were essentially hierarchies of rights and duties.

Confucianism is not a religion; it is a code of conduct with much advice, but no deity and no notion of heaven. It concerns itself with this world. As a counter-weight to that, other more spiritual religions came and provided the missing component: Buddhism and Taoism, in each of which there is strong emphasis on achieving a balanced relationship with nature. Chinese people tend to hold several such belief systems at the same time. The values that matter most then become (a) respect for authority, (b) reciprocity in relations beyond the family, and (c) identity with family. These are interpreted in daily life through heavy socialization into appropriate role behaviour. The end result is a society in which behaviour is highly predictable and fundamentally stable. The society is also capable of high levels of peaceful interaction.

The cultural features with most impact on economic behaviour are hierarchy and mistrust, and they operate as follows. In this society leadership positions are imbued with moral value; the boss looks after the subordinates in exchange for their loyalty. This means that power is not so much reached by performance-based merit, but by other means such as ownership or connections. The problem of mistrust comes from dependence on personal connections in networking outside the family, so preventing any dealing with strangers on trusting terms.

Institutions

Institutions designed to provide order in China tend still to be legacies of a state with high central control, but low in participation by citizens in adding spontaneously created forms of order. Examples of the latter might be civil society institutions such as freestanding professions, independent control bodies – as for example, over a stock market, or societies like chambers of commerce able to lobby government. Without a rich fabric of institutions providing reliable forms of information and conduct, in addition to government control and law, it is not possible to trust those not known (and bonded) personally. An invisible but significant outcome is the high level of competitiveness between the family-based units for scarce resources.

Capital has until recently been allocated inefficiently in China, as the state banking system had a virtual monopoly on the huge savings of the people and the rights to use them in industrial investment. It has starved the private sector of capital. Foreign banks are recent arrivals and are struggling to obtain a position against a background of changing regulations. The banking system is now under close scrutiny and its efficiency increasing, as is that in the state sector more widely. Much finance for industry is taken from retained earnings and at the smaller scale (still significant in the larger picture) often from informal lending, with start-up capital from friends and relatives.

Human capital is available in colossal quantity as relatively unskilled but trainable labour, and it is this that has until now given China its competitive edge in basic manufacturing. But value-added is greater in higher technology industries, and here China struggles to catch up with the demand for higher skills, and for professional competencies in engineering, accounting and management. Educational infrastructure is expanding at high speed in consequence, but quality of output remains – with some exceptions – below global standards. The organizing of labour markets is still weak, but new legislation has been increasing worker rights, and adding welfare provisions. The most critical determinant of labour costs, however, is location, with Chongqing in the interior offering labour at half the price of Guangzhou on the coast.

Social capital, that is trust, as earlier noted, is weak in China but with the important exception of that available inside the networks of 'clan capitalism' that so typify much industry. Clusters of cooperating firms make up the formula for handling the OEM (original equipment manufacturing) that delivers the workshop of the world. Inside these networks is high trust, flexibility, efficient transaction costs and market responsiveness, and those networks absorb the necessary external contributions of design, technology, brand and market knowledge, and delivery logistics. The resulting economic instrument is China's most powerful asset in world competition at present and largely explains the power of the private sector SMEs.

The business system

China's three business systems comprise its complex economy. The state sector dates from the Communist era of central planning and totalitarian control. Most of it has been sold off in recent years and its remaining industries are those seen as crucial to the national interest. In rare cases, they have become efficient at global standards. They now operate under very close scrutiny, and account for about 15 per cent of GDP.

The second sector, 'local corporates', derives its nature from two events. The first was the building of extensive industry at the local level in the 1950s and onwards when the communes of the Mao era were forced to act as autonomous mini-economies. The second event was the decision, as reform took hold in the 1980s and speeded up in the 1990s, to permit the disposal of these assets to entrepreneurs – often in coalition with local administrators. Many such assets were acquired on very favourable terms, as people decided to 'jump into the sea' and seek wealth. Many of China's new billionaires got their start in what they term now the 'golden years' when such acquisitions were possible.

The third sector is that of private business. China has always had entrepreneurs and a tradition of commerce, and it has also always had a tendency to grow small or medium enterprises under personal control and often connected with a family. Such enterprises would normally have a short life-span and rarely lasted beyond three generations, as family disputes would eventually break them up, or make them inefficient by the time the power of the founder had evaporated among the successors. This is partly because of the inheritance tradition that left equal wealth to all children, a feature in strong contrast with that of Japan and northern Europe, where the assets were passed intact to the principal heir, through succeeding generations, often for centuries.

Since 1980 the private sector has received increasing legal and political support and legitimacy, and now accounts for about 65 per cent of the economy. This phenomenal growth must also be seen against the fact that the funding of such enterprises has been almost entirely by retained earnings or borrowing from friends and relatives. It is predictable that the arrival of foreign banks as lenders to this sector will inject new efficiencies into the processes of capital use. Injections of capital from the regional ethnic Chinese have accounted for the majority of FDI into China since it opened up. As well as capital, however, this same group has brought knowledge of world markets, technology, branding and logistics, and their influence on China's growth has been high.

China's industrial future will be heavily influenced by the growth of its internal market, by the extent to which it prevents outsiders from taking large slices of the cake, and by the organizational challenges of reaching scale and scope while retaining essentially charismatic leadership in many enterprises. Innovation and adaptivity do not flourish at global standards under conditions of centralized control, and it is not certain that China will be ready to meet the implications of this logic when the workshop of the world starts to find its competitiveness challenged, and factories have to run faster and faster to stand still. Some commentators see an emerging pattern whereby China excels as a second-generation innovator in a new world of high global interdependency, but this response comes less from government policy than from entrepreneurial adaptations on the ground.

South Korea

The Korean peninsula was for centuries an autonomous state, but in a tributary relationship with its giant northern neighbour China. It absorbed from China much of its Confucian-style political philosophy. It also closed itself from the outside world, coming to be known at the end of the nineteenth century as the 'hermit kingdom'. That period ended in 1905 when newly expanding Japan invaded and took over the peninsula as an extension of its modernizing economy. Much about Korea in later years can be explained by its years under Japanese rule. It had become another tributary state, this time with foreign ownership of its industry.

The sense of independence among Korean people was not to come into full expression until the 1960s but an early sign of it was the creation in 1443 of a distinct form of writing, and that rare feature in the region – an alphabet. The Korean War in the early 1950s destroyed the country and divided it, and South Korea began after it with minimal assets that were boosted by the drive and skills of its people, and the willingness of the international community to provide it with financial and technical help. The post-war period was marked by a series of five-year plans in which the government took control of the shaping of the economy, and determined upon a strategy of developing the country as a base for manufacturing exports. Entrepreneurs were identified. If they produced the exports they got more support and were allowed to keep the ownership of the companies they had founded.

They built the key instrument of the economy – the *chaebol* – the large conglomerate firm under tight control. There is a large sector of the economy made up of small and medium enterprises, many connected by supply chains into the *chaebol*, but the grip of the latter is firm. Many of them suffered severely in the 1997 financial crisis, as their tendency to borrow short and invest long turned against them. A number of spectacular bankruptcies followed. In the period since there has been much realignment, rationalizing and opening up, and many of the controlling families have retired into the background, giving way to professional managers.

Culture

Korea is a deeply Confucian country and this is evident in the hierarchical nature of many of its organizations, and of its management style. There is also a strong tendency to build personal relations horizontally, often within school groups or place-of-origin networks. An instinct for discipline is perhaps rooted in the experience of military service by many workers and executives, and the constant sense of anxiety about a possible invasion from the unpredictable regime of North Korea. A shared ideal running through the culture, and possibly attributable to the nation's experiences of subjection, and current threat, is a fierce national pride. Firms exist, in the perceptions of many, to strengthen the nation.

Institutions

Several historical legacies have left their mark on the economy's main institutions. First is the respect for the professionalism of the civil service, and the power assigned to it as a consequence. This has deep roots in Confucian ideals and structures of state-craft.

Second is the derivation of much administrative routine and character from the days of the Japanese occupation, during which many society leaders were educated in Japanese. The two features flow together to facilitate what political scientists call a 'strong state'.

In addition, a great deal of new institutional structure, such as law, financial administration and accounting, organizational techniques, and technology itself, has flowed in as Korean companies have successfully interacted with the markets of the developed world, and as those sent abroad for education have returned to apply their learning. A new injection of such ideas and techniques happened as a cost of solving the financial crisis of 1997 and is still resented by many Koreans forced into the market driven rationality of the Washington consensus.

The business system

It could be argued that the great strength of the *chaebol* has come from the ambition and the vision of the owners who ran them, and the availability of government investment to back them, and that as these elements become diluted they will be hard to replace. As these organizations evolve into a new form, many of the earlier ways will be carried with them, and the newly rising professionals and foreigners will be able to perpetuate much of the social psychology of the past, while eliminating its negative effects. It is as yet too early to read these trends clearly but if the recent ascendance of Samsung and LG is anything to go by, the future seems to lie in that direction.

The regional ethnic Chinese

In the nineteenth century Chinese society went through periods of intense strife, with overpopulation, famine, unemployment, civil war, invasion, all exacerbated by a decadent government. In the worst periods people left to find work elsewhere and to support the families who stayed behind. They left mainly from the south, were mainly young men and they went to the countries around the South China Sea – the *Nanyang*. They usually joined their compatriots from specific regions of China, and they found work in the new agricultural and extractive industries being established under colonial rule. Hundreds of thousands went, and after some decades a similar exodus of females took place, and the 'Overseas Chinese' settled down and became part of the fabric of their host societies. After several generations they tend to think of themselves as Malaysians, Indonesians and so on. Their number now in the region is about 35 million, with a further population in Taiwan of around 20 million.

Their organizational pattern was highly consistent. Ownership was tightly held, in either a partnership or within a family group. One person would be the big boss and would take all key decisions and often also many less important decisions. Personal networks of connection with key suppliers, financiers, customers and sources of information would be built as a form of social capital held by individuals. Employees would be treated paternalistically, but discipline maintained. These enterprises had a number of distinct virtues: they were highly efficient in terms of managerial control, and in terms of transaction costs between units in the economy. By concentrating decision power and resources into very few hands they were also able to take opportunities quickly, to adapt as need be and to keep key employees loyal. For the colonial powers they made excellent 'middlemen' in the developing economies, being perceived as diligent, reliable and non-political.

They came to dominate the economies of Southeast Asia, and at the same time to build up the formidable industrial and financial bases of Taiwan, Hong Kong and Singapore. Their 'bamboo network' in the region tied them together as a powerful force and facilitated their taking of opportunities as they unfolded country by country, the most recent aspect of that process being their massive investments in China.

Despite the country differences there are nonetheless certain behaviour patterns that remain typical of the regional ethnic Chinese enterprise as it grows to large scale. Comprehensive regional studies confirm that for those of this type that are publicly listed the transition from the founder to the next generation results in an average loss over the five years around the transition of more than half of stock market value. There is also a strong tendency for accounting practices to conceal sub-unit failures and so to slow managerial responses. Such weaknesses stem from two common features: the retention of family control; and the inability to transfer between generations the tacit knowledge built up via personal relationship obligations. The weakness of professional management is also endemic although in the successful cases this is usually embraced. Mistrust is eventually corrosive. Trust can be highly positive. For the few companies that embrace professional management to the point of giving it strategic influence, their instincts for collaboration allow them to take global markets in fields such as container ports, hotel chains and property investment.

Taiwan was developed by the Kuomintang elite that fled from China having lost the struggle against Communism for dominance. Its development was achieved by a state system of managing the economy, and especially by controlling the major sectors such as banking, steel, transport, and so forth, and then encouraging the growth of entrepreneurship. Especially significant has been the encouragement of technical education and of close ties with the hi-tech industries and research facilities of the United States. This has produced one of the world's most vibrant manufacturing industries in the general field of hi-tech, making own-brand products and components especially for the world's brand names in computing, telecoms, electronics, electrical and machine making.

Hong Kong, now part of China but retaining much autonomy as a Special Administrative Region until 2047, is the core city of the Pearl River delta region of south China containing upwards of 150 million people. It hosts much of the ownership, management, finance, design skill, market access skill and logistics competence needed in its hinterland, and to do so carries forward the skills acquired from its earlier existence as an outpost of the British Empire. For 50 years before the transition in 1997, it developed as one of the world's purest examples of *laissez-faire* economic policy. This gave it an unusual dynamism as the fierce logics of competition, combined with high-quality infrastructure, brought it to developed-country levels of wealth.

Singapore, also earlier British, became autonomous in 1959, and set about building a modern economy by attracting foreign investment, and especially pulling in industry able to respond to the opportunities of both resources and markets in the surrounding region, for which Singapore had traditionally been an *entrepôt*. With very strong government since, it has continued on that path, extending further into industries based in science and high technology and supporting sectors such as banking.

As the business system of the regional ethnic Chinese overlaps extensively with that for the Chinese private sector it will not be described again here.

Southeast Asia

The countries covered here are Indonesia, Malaysia and the Philippines. (Thailand will be included in the final section on IndoChina). The three countries share two features: they were all colonized and bear the traces of that history in their present institutions; and they have all struggled with development during the past 50 years, and been outpaced by their Confucian neighbours. Their current GDP per capita at purchasing power parity is Indonesia US$4,668, Malaysia US$15,589, and the Philippines US$4,140. In Indonesia and the Philippines this is partly a reflection of huge populations, with 215 million in Indonesia and 77 million in the Philippines. Indonesia and the Philippines particularly have displayed unusually high levels of corruption, worsening their administrative weakness. The years of 'reform' that followed the Asian Crisis have seen them move clearly in the direction of greater openness, more rational resource allocation, greater professionalism and more market-based competitive discipline, all sharpened by the arrival of more foreign competition in their own markets.

However, the building of an economy able to attract outside investment, and able to compete in world markets – especially now against China – takes time, and their ratings do not inspire confidence yet. In terms of the World Bank 'ease of doing business' rankings Indonesia is 128th in the world out of 185 countries, and the Philippines is 138th. By contrast on the same scale Malaysia is rated 34th, Singapore first and Hong Kong second.

The Philippines was for centuries a Spanish colony, and the main legacy of that period for the economy is a land-holding 'aristocracy' of a semi-feudal character, that has retained a strong grip on political power, and frustrated many attempts at land reform and the redistribution of wealth. It has been joined by a parallel elite of ethnic Chinese business owners, capable of skilled management, and capable also of co-opting the political support needed in an essentially patrimonial state. These two groups dominate the business scene, and the only other significant players are the foreign companies seeking stable sources of labour skill for manufacturing. The fluency in English of many local people has often attracted many firms from the West. Significant also have been the strong ties with the United States stemming from the period of US protection in the first half of the twentieth century, with its legacies of democracy, law and education.

In Indonesia the legacy was of Dutch colonial control, in place from about the early seventeenth century until the end of World War II, and still visible in many systems such as law and administration. It was not until the fall of military dictatorships, under charges of corruption, that new forms of government could be introduced. Eventually full democracy was reached for the first time and the country has remained stable since. As in the Philippines, ethnic Chinese population numbers are small (about 4 per cent in Indonesia and about 1 per cent in the Philippines), but economic strength is great, amounting to more than half of the ownership of the major local conglomerates in both countries. There are now signs that democracy is eroding the tradition of coopting political support and moving it away from the centre to the local.

In Malaysia, the case is different. It is a much smaller country in population terms, with around 22 million people, although its GDP stands at about 42 per cent of Indonesia's. This stems from its success in developing further the industries taken over after the colonial period and in attracting large amounts of foreign investment. The end result is a powerful set of manufacturing industries bringing in new technology, and management, and making use of not just the relatively low cost local labour, but also lower cost labour imported from Indonesia.

Unlike Indonesia, which is very consciously secular in the political sphere, Malaysia takes religion – or at least ethnicity – into policy making and attempts to protect Malay business against the intense pressures of competition from ethnic Chinese business.

IndoChina

For our purposes, although this region contains Burma, Cambodia and Laos, our attention will be given to the larger economies of Thailand and Vietnam, countries of respectively 63 million and 78 million people. Their different histories have resulted in Thailand being now about four times the weight of Vietnam in economic terms, although the latter is now growing very fast.

Thailand is distinguished from most Asian countries for its comparatively long history of independence from colonial domination. It is a constitutional monarchy, and the role of the king has long been crucial in holding the country together in the face of shifting political alliances and manoeuvres.

In recent years industry has poured in from abroad attracted by a favourable business environment. Manufacturing industry is well established, especially in zones along the east coast and around Bangkok. Again, as in several other regional countries, the ethnic Chinese Thai have established a powerful dominance in local business, and operate on the bamboo network across the region and into China. The first outside company to be registered in China after the Communist era was the CP group, a family owned firm that began in Bangkok selling animal feedstock and seeds.

The other large economy in the IndoChina peninsula is Vietnam and its story is again different. For about a thousand years it was a tributary state of China, until it gained independence in 938. This millennium left an indelible mark in the form of Confucian ideals and centralized government using a mandarin-type system. But for the subsequent thousand years Vietnam was a country under its own government until the interests of France destroyed its autonomy and led to colonial control from 1887. This built upon a long history of French involvement dating back to the 1600s. French colonial policy was even more exploitative than the average around the region and, in the views of some, left the country worse off than when they started. There was however a residual of strong administration and law, and an education system that could be later extended to a greater portion of the population. A series of uprisings in favour of independence marked the twentieth century, culminating in the expulsion of the French after Dien Bien Phu in 1954. Such movements led to what Americans call the Vietnam War (and locals the American War), after which the Vietnamese regained their country. For the next 10 years it was in the grip of hard-liners and dogmatists, but after 1986, an opening up began that has not stopped but could not be described as either fast or clean.

Under the opening up known as *doi moi*, the state sector declined and the private sector grew fast. It is like watching a re-run of the China miracle but in slower motion. The dismantling of a strong state, with a tradition of central planning and interference in the economy, cannot be achieved overnight, but the direction of movement is clear. At present it is ranked the 99th country in the world for 'ease of doing business', much of this handicap stemming from weak property rights and from embedded widespread corruption. Three forms of organization are emerging. The state sector companies, as in China, are succumbing to the forces of the market and being forced to reform their management. The private sector is booming and expanding entrepreneurially using small and medium enterprises. These are flexible enough, as in China, to cope with the uncertainties of their surroundings. The third form is that of foreign investors, attracted especially by the large reserves of low cost and easily trained labour.

Conclusion

The variety of business systems on display here reflects the underlying contrasts in religions, in political preferences, in histories and the injections of ideas they often brought with them, and in ethnicity and culture. But at the same time much continuity is visible: the Confucian family ideal runs through many countries; the strong state is found widely; paternalism in authority systems is widespread; personal systems of trust are widely relied upon; and a powerful work ethic is widespread. But the separating out of these distinct business systems, resulting in virtually every society having its own formula, is due to the rich set of ingredients that goes into each recipe. The variety comes from the combination, and that is why there are so few replications, and why each of these societies needs to be seen in its own right, and with its own reasons for being as it is.

Chapter summary

- Asia is a region of immense variety and contrasts in terms of people, geography, culture, religion, history and so on.

- A business system is a way of looking at a country's economy, a way of understanding how the economy is affected by the unique social and cultural environment thus shaping the type of business system in question.

- Japan's business system and management style are highly influenced by its cultural heritage, strong social trust and the ability to deal with complex coordination.

- China's business system model has evolved after many years of turbulence and changes. Today China's private sector is developing at an astonishing speed and has taken the role of 'the workshop of the world'.

- Korea's originally family-oriented conglomerates have in the past developed into very successful business groups or *chaebols*, which are famous worldwide.

- It is also possible to trace the development of the business systems of the ethnic Chinese who have, due to historical reasons, settled in all over Southeast Asia.

- In fact it can be seen that many Asian business systems are commonly influenced by similar cultural elements such as Confucianism. Nevertheless each Asian business system has its own salient characteristics and features.

Review questions

1 What are the main business systems of the region?
2 What are the principal components of a business system?
3 Give examples of how culture (i.e., meaning) affects institutions (i.e., forms of order) in different societies
4 What are the most representative forms of enterprise in Japan, China and South Korea?
5 What explains the slower growth of Indonesia and the Philippines, compared to Korea, China and Singapore?

Learning activities

1 Draw a diagram like that shown in Figure 1.1 and in the boxes provide one example in each box to show what is meant, describing one society in the region.
2 Draw lines between the boxes to show the complexity of the connections.
3 Add to the diagrams the key facts of the society's history, showing their effects.
4 Consider what kind of firm is likely to be successful in that environment and explain why you think so?

Web links

Organization for Economic Cooperation and Development: www.oecd.org

The World Bank: www.worldbank.org

Central Intelligence Agency: https://www.cia.gov/index.html

The Asia Society: http://asiasociety.org/policy

Asian Development Bank: www.adbi.org

Asian Studies Monitor: www.coombs.anu.edu.au

References and further reading

Asian Development Bank (2011) *Asia 2050: Realizing the Asian Century*. Manila: Asian Development Bank.

Backman, M. and Butler, C. (2006) *Big in Asia*. Basingstoke: Palgrave Macmillan.

Boyer, R., Uemura, H. and Isogai, A. (eds.) (2011) *Diversity and Transformation of Asian Capitalism*. London: Routledge.

Fan, J.P., Wong, T.J. and Zhan, T. (2012) Founder succession and accounting properties. *Contemporary Accounting Research*, 29(1): 283–311.

Guthrie, D. (2006) *China and Globalization*. New York: Routledge.

Heilbroner, R.L. (1985) *The Nature and Logic of Capitalism*. New York: Norton.

Mathews, J.A. (2006) Dragon Multinationals: New Players in 21st Century Globalization. *Asia Pacific Journal of Management*, 23: 5–27.

McCloskey D.N. (2006) *The Bourgeois Virtues: Ethics for an Age of Commerce*. Chicago: Chicago University Press.

Nee, V. and Opper, S. (2012) *Capitalism from Below: Markets and Institutional Change in China*. Cambridge, MA: Harvard University Press.

Orru, M., Biggart, N.W. and Hamilton, G.G. (1997) *The Economic Organization of East Asian Capitalism*. London: Macmillan.

Peng, M.W. and Delios, A. (2006) Conglomerates and Business Groups in the Asia Pacific. *Asia Pacific Journal of Management*, 23(4): 407–417.

Redding, S.G. (1993) *The Spirit of Chinese Capitalism*. New York: de Gruyter.

Redding, S.G. and Witt, M. (2007) *The Future of Chinese Capitalism*. Oxford: Oxford University Press.

Tipton, F.B. (2007) *Asian Firms: History, Institutions and Management*. Cheltenham: Edward Elgar.

Tu, W.M. (ed.) (1996) *Confucian Traditions in East Asian Modernity*. Cambridge, MA: Harvard University Press.

Wade, R. (1990) *Governing the Market*. Princeton, NJ: Princeton University Press.

Whitley, R. (1992) *Business Systems in East Asia*. London: Sage.

Yeung, H.W.C. (2006) Change and Continuity in Southeast Asian Chinese Business. *Asia Pacific Journal of Management*, 23(3): 229–254.

Yeung, H.W.C (ed.) (2007) *Handbook of Research on Asian Business*. Cheltenham: Edward Elgar.

Asian Cultures and Business Systems

2

Carlos Noronha and Harukiyo Hasegawa

Chapter outline

- The importance of cultural understanding in business
- Culture as the foundation of the business system
- Asian cultures and business practices
- Asian cultures, ethics and social responsibility

Chapter objectives

After reading this chapter, you should be able to:

1 Understand the importance of cultural influence on business management.

2 Identify the major theories of values and culture.

3 Identify the leading Asian cultural traits.

4 Identify the major Asian business practices.

5 Understand the Asian views on ethics and social responsibility.

Introduction

Rapid globalization has increased the volume of international trade. Take the case of China as an example. According to the World Bank,[1] China has 1.3 billion people and is now the second largest economy in the world and is increasingly playing an important role in the global economy. More and more foreign capital investments are being drawn into China but this is no one-way traffic. Since China's ascension into the World Trade Organization (WTO) in 2001, the country has actually drawn together many manufacturers in Thailand, Malaysia, Singapore, the Philippines, Indonesia, South Korea and Taiwan, creating a pan-Asia production network. As a result, trade within East Asia has grown at a much faster pace than the region's trade with the rest of the world. As can be seen in Table 2.1, the period 2003–2007 saw a continuous growth of GDP projection in East Asia and developing East Asia with a record double digit increase in 2007. The trend was interrupted by the 2008–2009 financial crisis, but was quickly picked up in 2010 with a stable growth prediction to 2013. The World Bank (2012) expects East Asia to be the strongest performing region.

Like the case of China, we know that globalization is bringing more and more people from different parts of Asia and the world together. In order to succeed in this global arena, it is necessary to have a good understanding of different cultures. International business today demands multicultural interaction, multicultural understanding and multicultural communication. Conventional Western perspectives often view cultural differences in terms of an 'East–West' contrast. In fact, scholars in areas like sociology or cultural anthropology have already pointed out that cultural differences should not be viewed as a polarized system. Rather, we should take the stance of culture being on a continuum. Although some cultures may share certain common traits, every culture is unique. Hence the polarized view is too simplistic.

This chapter has two broad aims. The first is to introduce to the reader the main theories of culture. The second is to present different Asian cultural systems, each with different characteristics and value orientations. Therefore, when these cultural systems interact with the respective business practices, different types of Asian business systems emerge. Understanding them is essential for conducting successful cross-cultural business.

The importance of cultural understanding in business

In order to help understand the importance of cultural understanding in business we will start by looking at a real life example.[2]

In 2001, Daewoo Motors of South Korea ran into financial difficulties and left Daewoo Commercial Motor Vehicles, a subsidiary of the parent, 'owner-less'. In 2004, an announcement was made that Tata Motors, a subsidiary of the Tata Group in India, a gigantic

TABLE 2.1 East Asia and Pacific: GDP growth projections

	2003	2004	2005	2006	2007	2008	2009	2010	2011	2012	2013
East Asia	6.7	7.9	8.0	9/1	10.1	6.3	4.9	9.3	7.0	6.3	7.0
Developing East Asia	8.8	9.0	9.8	10.9	12.3	8.5	7.5	9.7	8.2	7.6	8.0

SOURCE: World Bank (2012).

conglomerate with businesses ranging from automobile to chemicals to consumer products to telecommunication, would be taking over Daewoo Commercial Motor Vehicles. In the beginning the Koreans saw this take over as unacceptable as they considered the Indian motor company inferior in many aspects. Tata Daewoo was established in 2004 despite resistance from the Koreans. Nevertheless, four years later the new company was able to increase its exports five-fold and operating profits by 900 per cent (Oh, 2010); the number of employees increased by 60 per cent (Tata Daewoo, 2011). Today Tata Daewoo is the second largest heavy commercial vehicle manufacturer in South Korea. Cultural awareness played an important part in the successful formation of the new venture. Tata Motors approached the acquisition using a humble attitude instead of a hostile take-over. Tata Motors appointed a native Korean to be the CEO of Tata Daewoo and respected the Korean culture and management style. Tata Motors slowly instilled its Tata Business Excellence Model that differed from the traditional Western emphasis on efficiency but more focused on mutual growth of the company and the community, ethical business practices, the well-being of the various stakeholders and so on. In many respects, Tata Motors was able to gain trust from the employees and the trade union even in times of difficulties, like the financial crisis in 2009, by allocating irregular employees to regular positions. The trade union commented that although Tata was a foreign company, it was able to recognize and respect Korea in many aspects. Today Tata Daewoo has manufacturing plants in India and Pakistan and is exporting to over 60 countries. Understanding Korean culture is the key to business success. The Koreans place a premium on relationships because of their communal nature. Business deals are often concluded through establishing networks rather than employing fact-based management (Chan, 2007).

The above example illustrates cultural influence on business deals and how cultural awareness can affect success. Without cultural consciousness or sensitivity, the acquisition of Daewoo by Tata would not be a success. Clearly cultural knowledge is important but what exactly is culture? In the next section, we will define the meaning of culture and its components.

Culture as the foundation of the business system

In the business system framework that we have adopted for this text, Redding (2005) defined culture as 'values, norms, and socially constructed realities which act as the bases for the society's forms of order' (p. 133). Culture is the foundation layer of the entire framework that underlies the institutions that in turn underlies the business system.

In this section, we will look at different meanings of culture and values. Then the elements of culture under Redding's definition will be analyzed mainly through Hofstede's cultural dimensions with an emphasis on some Asian cultural traits. First, we will look at some basic definitions of culture and value.

The meaning of culture

In the 1950s, American anthropologists Kroeber and Kluckhohn identified no less than 164 definitions of culture raised by anthropologists from 1840 onwards. After carefully analyzing the various definitions of culture, they suggested that:

culture consists of patterns, explicit and implicit, of and for behavior acquired and transmitted by symbols, constituting the distinctive achievement of human groups, including their embodiment in artifacts; the essential core of culture consists of traditional (i.e., historically derived and selected) ideas and especially their attached values; culture systems may, on the one hand, be considered as products of action, on the other, as conditioning elements of future action (Kroeber and Kluckhohn, 1952: 181).

This definition of culture is probably the most commonly cited.

From the above definition, we can identify three main characteristics of culture. First, a culture is shared collectively by members of a group. Hofstede simply defined culture as 'the collective programming of the mind which distinguishes the members of one human group from another' (Hofstede, 1980: 25). Thus, culture enables a group to share and see things in the same way and eventually to shape stable and consistent behaviours. Of course, no single individual will possess all the cultural characteristics of the group since there is a distinction between culture and individual personality.[3] Nevertheless, culture is a concept that rests on human collectivity. Second, culture is a relative concept. There is no so called 'benchmark culture' or 'standard culture'. Every culture is distinct and relative to other cultures' ways of perceiving the world. Third, culture is learned. Kroeber (1917) stated that culture extends above and beyond its biological and psychological bases, having an independent existence at its own level. Culture remains relatively stable and unchanged irrespective of the large turnover in membership that occurs with each new generation. Culture is not genetically instilled. What we accumulate and cultivate to call our culture is transmitted to us, learned by us and shared by members of our group, just like parents pass on to their children their families' particular values.

Next, we will further understand culture by treating it as a system consisting of specific components. Therefore we will simply say that culture is 'a system that contains values, beliefs, attitudes and behaviours shared by a group of people'. Of all these components, values are the most fundamental, the building block of culture. Let us trace the sequence of these components. For example, take filial piety or respect for parents, a salient feature of Asian cultural values. A person with filial piety is likely to cultivate the belief of respect for parents and the elderly. This belief can lead to an attitude of preferring experience to uncertainty. The value, belief and attitude are then manifested in terms of behaviours like ancestor worshipping, cohabitation with the elderly[4] and so on. Of course, due to modernization, many Asians may not manifest all the expected behaviours. However, filial piety remains a core and is expressed to different degrees.

The meaning of value

Kluckhohn (1951: 395) defined value as 'a conception, explicit or implicit, distinctive of an individual or group, of the desirable which influences the selection from available modes, means and ends of actions'. Rokeach (1973: 159–160) defined value as 'an enduring belief that a specific mode of conduct or end-state of existence is personally and socially preferable to alternative modes of conduct or end-states of existence'. Hofstede (1980: 19) defined value as 'a broad tendency to prefer certain states of affairs over others'. From these definitions we can see that value consists of motivational and evaluative elements. It is a person's profound orientation toward something or some matters. Therefore, if we attempt to categorize these things or matters systematically and map them against the person's orientation toward them, a 'value system' or 'value hierarchy' arises.

TABLE 2.2 Classification of Chinese cultural values

Value orientations	Elements of value
Human nature orientation	Harmony with nature, pre-destined fate
Man-to-nature orientation	Abasement, situation orientation
Time orientation	Continuity, past time orientation
Personal activity orientation	Doctrine of the mean, harmony with others
Relational orientation	Respect for authority, interdependence, group orientation, face

Kluckhohn and Strodtbeck's (1961) variations in 'value orientation' concept is a widely mentioned categorization of a value system. By asking five questions, we are essentially categorizing a person's value system into five orientations.[5] They are:

1. Human nature orientation: What is the character of innate human nature? (good, mixed or evil).

2. Man-to-nature orientation: What is the relation of man to nature? (dominant, harmony or subjugation).

3. Time orientation: What is the temporal focus of human life? (past, present or future).

4. Activity orientation: What is the modality of human nature? (doing, controlling or being).

5. Relational orientation: What is the modality of man's relationship to other men? (individualistic, group or hierarchical).

By indicating the possible variations of each orientation, a value orientation framework emerges. This framework gives a clear and broad picture of a person's value system. When the framework is applied to a culture, we can describe the value orientations of a culture and compare values cross-culturally. For example, Yau (1994), in a study concerning Chinese consumer values, presented a classification of Chinese cultural values based on the value orientation framework. Table 2.2 shows the cultural values identified under each orientation. We return to discuss Chinese cultural values in another section. The table serves only as a rough example of how to categorize value orientations.

Rationale

Redding (2005) indicated that a rationale is a society's commonly accepted reasoning for doing things and out of this realm of meaning, a set of means to achieve ends emerges. Rationale is at the base of culture, as constituted by a set of values embraced by the society. Redding pointed out that the rationale determines the purpose of the existence of a firm in the business system. Rationale determines the reason why economic activities are pursued. Rationale underlies business behaviours (Redding, 2002).

We will try to explain rationale in more detail by aligning with Geert Hofstede's cultural dimensions. But before this, a brief explanation of the dimensions is necessary. Hofstede's study of work-related values is undoubtedly the most well known in the literature. He wanted to explore how national culture can influence values in the workplace and to do so he studied data from IBM employees in 40 countries in the period 1967 to 1973. His study was reported in his 1980 classic *Culture's Consequences: International Differences in Work-Related Values*. Since then, innumerable replications and validation studies have been conducted worldwide. In 2001, the second edition of his book extended the findings taken from 74 countries. Due to the mammoth size of Hofstede's project and the stability and consistency of the dimensions uncovered, Hofstede's dimensions of national culture have become the most authoritative. They include Power Distance (PDI), Individualism (versus Collectivism) (IDV), Masculinity (versus Femininity) (MAS) and Uncertainty Avoidance (UAI). For each country, Hofstede calculated indices for each dimension to create country cultural profiles.

Later, as a result of Hofstede's collaboration with psychologist Michael Bond, he added a fifth dimension. In view of the rapid emergence of the 'Five Little Dragons' (Hong Kong, Japan, Singapore, South Korea and Taiwan) and other Asian countries in the world economic arena during the late 1980s to early 1990s, Hofstede and Bond (1988) believed that the 'East Asian Economic Miracle' can only be explained by turning to the domain of culture. Since many of these countries have common cultural roots anchored on the teachings of the great ancient Chinese philosopher Confucius, it became obvious that there is a possible 'Confucian Work Dynamism' dimension in the cultural profile of these countries that may account for, to a certain extent, the East Asian miracle. This dimension was eventually named Long-Term Orientation (LTO) versus Short-Term Orientation (STO).

Hofstede's cultural dimensions continued to be researched and utilized and even criticized by many scholars worldwide (e.g., McSweeney, 2002; Fang, 2003). Most recently, Hofstede collaborated with Michael Minkov and added a sixth dimension (Hofstede et al., 2010) namely, Indulgence versus Restraint (IVR), which is related to the gratification versus control of basic human desires concerning the enjoyment of life.

Next we use two cultural dimensions, namely Long-Term Orientation (LTO) versus Short-Term Orientation (STO) and Indulgence versus Restraint (IVR) to explain the rationale of a culture.

LTO v STO: The long-term orientation dimension can be interpreted as dealing with society's search for virtue. Societies with a short-term orientation generally have a strong concern with establishing the absolute truth. They are normative in their thinking. They exhibit great respect for traditions, a relatively small propensity to save for the future, and a focus on achieving quick results. In societies with a long-term orientation, people believe that truth depends very much on situation, context and time. They show an ability to adapt traditions to changed conditions, a strong propensity to save and invest, thriftiness, and perseverance in achieving results.[6]

IVR: Indulgence stands for a society that allows relatively free gratification of basic and natural human drives related to enjoying life and having fun. Restraint stands for a society that suppresses gratification of needs and regulates it by means of strict social norms.[7]

Confucius' emphasis on stability of the society, the family as the prototype of all social organizations, virtuous behaviours toward others and the virtues of acquiring education, perseverance, thrift, patience and so on are the salient features of many East Asian cultures. East Asian countries high on Confucian dynamism are naturally more long-term and future oriented (Hofstede and Bond's (1988) study revealed that four of the Five Dragons namely, Hong Kong, Taiwan, Japan and South Korea held top positions on the 'Confucian Work Dynamism' scale). Western countries are generally more short-term oriented in that they stress more on satisfying immediate needs and therefore they exercise more social consumption and spending rather than saving and accumulation of funds for long-term investments (Hofstede, 2011). When applied to the rationale of the business system, this dimension explains why it is often said that Japanese firms exist for the sake of the benefits of society and employees while the Anglo-Saxon model often emphasizes shareholder wealth maximization (Witt, 2009). This knowledge makes it much easier to understand why state-owned enterprises in mainland China are taking a lead role in advancing the country's industrial and commercial development since they exist for the interest of the state and the people (Guan et al., 2013). Hofstede (2011) pointed out that the IVR dimension more or less complements the LTO versus STO dimension. For example, in more restrained cultures, less emphasis is put on leisure and more emphasis is on maintaining social order. In more indulging cultures, more emphasis is on happiness, leisure, personal life control and freedom of speech. This again echoes the Asian versus Anglo-Saxon model of the *raison d'être* of the firm in society.

Identity

Redding (2005) recognized identity as an important element in establishing order in society: how do people instinctively owe allegiance? What are the patterns of support and dependence and what choices are available for people to associate themselves with various groups? Only with proper identities established over different groups of people can the stable order of society be advanced into appropriate social and economic structures. This is what Redding (2002) called 'horizontal order' as compared to 'vertical order' as will be seen in the next section.

We will try to explain identity using two cultural dimensions namely, Individualism versus Collectivism (IDV) and Masculinity versus Femininity (MAS).

IDV: The degree to which individuals are integrated into groups. The higher the IDV, the more independent and competitive the people are. People pursue personal goals rather than organizational or national goals. Jobs are designed more for individuals and rewards are based on individual achievement. The lower the IDV (the higher the collectivism) the more emphasis is on collaboration and consultation. People in low IDV organizations are more integrated. Employees' interests are more protected.[8]

MAS: The distribution of roles between the genders to which a range of solutions are found. The higher the MAS, the more assertive and competitive the people are. They emphasize more on material things rather than abstract or spiritual concepts. On the other hand, the lower the MAS (the higher the femininity), the more modest and caring the people's values are. Low MAS organizations emphasize the needs of the employees while those of higher MAS stress individual achievement.[9]

Taking Japan as an example, as an island nation it is geographically isolated. This has made the Japanese people a very homogeneous group. The ecocultural model explains why ancient Japan's isolation together with severe cold weather, frequent occurrence of earthquakes and rice farming agriculture led the Japanese to rely on tight cooperation in order to survive. People lived in small communities and interdependence among these groups is very strong. This has cultivated a culture of social reciprocity (*giri*) or indebtedness that places great importance on taking and returning obligations. So, interpersonal relationships are very delicate and have to be managed carefully. Also, due to the high homogeneity in race, language and way of life, Japanese communication is very 'high-context' (Hall, 1966). Empathy rather than explicit expression is the customary approach. In Japanese-style management, traditional collective decision making (Takamiya, 1972), total quality management, quality circles and other group dynamics activities (Ishikawa, 1985) are managerial manifestations of Japanese collectivism.

Japanese values also have their roots in Shintoism, Buddhism and Confucianism. Locally evolved Shintoism is a religion that reveres nature. It is believed that every element on earth has a deity within. Nature and all things given to men by nature are to be cherished. This has cultivated a culture that prizes social harmony. Also, the Confucian philosophy imported from China over a thousand years ago has been a central tenet of the Japanese way of life. Filial piety, hierarchical social relationships and virtuous behaviours toward others are still salient features of Japanese culture. Nevertheless, Japanese culture is one of the most masculine in the world. Striving for excellence in work and the lack of females climbing the corporate ladder are manifestations of a masculine society. Interestingly, according to Hofstede's survey, Korea scored much lower in terms of the MAS index, pointing to a relatively feminine society. A recent indication of this femininity is Park Geun-Hye becoming the first female president in South Korea (CNN, 2013). More recently, Grant Thornton (2013) released their latest report on women in senior management positions around the world. Top of the list was China with 51 per cent of senior management positions being held by women, as compared with only 7 per cent in Japan. This phenomenon echoes the MAS score of China and Japan as will be seen in the next section which are 50 and 95 respectively.

Authority

Redding (2005) identified authority as a third essential element of culture. This looks at: how power is morally legitimized, defined and exercised; how sensitive society is toward power and hierarchy; and how authority defines how the people, especially the managers and employers, exercise their control over other people, such as the employees and servants. Redding (2002) defined authority as governing the values and norms of the 'vertical order'.

We will try to explain authority using two cultural dimensions namely, Power Distance (PDI) and Uncertainty Avoidance (UAI).

PDI: The extent to which the less powerful members of organizations accept that power is distributed unequally. The higher the index, the more distance is between the less powerful and the powerful. Therefore, leaders in high PDI organizations tend to manage in a more autocratic or paternalistic manner and there is less employee participation. Subordinates actually prefer autocratic management. Also, statuses, titles and formalities are more emphasized. On the other hand, leaders in low PDI organizations tend to be more open to employees and are likely to delegate more.[10]

UAI: A society's tolerance for uncertainty and ambiguity. The higher the UAI, the less people are open to changes. They are more risk averse too. High UAI organizations rely heavily on rules, formalities and standards. Anxiety level at work is also higher. People prefer stability and they tend to remain in the same job for longer periods. Low UAI organizations encourage more unconventional thinking and risk venturing. Anxiety and stress at work also exist but they are not easily expressed outwardly. They are probably more restrained.[11]

For example, Chinese culture is strongly nurtured by the beliefs of Confucianism. In particular, the 'Five Cardinal Relationships' (*Wu Lun*) are most important in connecting responsibilities and superiority of status, thus ensuring the social system functions properly. The five relationships refer to the orderly relationships between lord and servant, father and child, husband and wife, older and younger, and friend and friend. *Wu Lun* emphasizes mutual responsibilities and respect between the two characters in a relationship. Similarly, Korea and Japan are highly hierarchical cultures and business organizations exhibit existential hierarchical inequalities. India is another example of large PDI culture where top down communication and obedience by the subordinate are common. This probably stems from the traditional Indian caste system.

Cultures that exhibit large PDI also tend to exhibit strong UAI. Due to the emphasis on hierarchy, there is strong adherence to clarity and structure and low tolerance for deviant ideas or persons (Hofstede, 2011). For example, Korea has a strong UAI culture that complements with its large PDI. China has a weak UAI culture where ambiguity is much tolerated. It should be noted that in societies where the judicial system is weak and not independent, ambiguity becomes common and this can lead to poor corporate governance and even corruption (Claessens and Fan, 2002).

Cultural dimensions of selected cultures

Now let us examine the cultural profiles of several selected Asian countries in Table 2.3. The scores run from zero, which is the lowest, upwards to higher than 100 in the case of LTO.

In terms of PDI, China scored the highest. This is a reflection of the hierarchical social system in China where relationships at different levels are rigidly structured. Singapore scored also relatively highly, probably due to the existence of a majority of ethnic Chinese and Indians. The caste system in India needs no introduction, hence a PDI score of 77. Japan, rather unexpectedly, scored lower than the other countries. Nevertheless, Japan is also a very hierarchical society where rules and protocols are strictly

TABLE 2.3 Hofstede's dimensions of five countries

	PDI	IDV	MAS	UAI	LTO
China	80	20	50	60	118
Japan	54	46	95	92	80
South Korea	60	18	39	85	75
India	77	48	56	40	61
Singapore	74	20	48	8	48

SOURCE: http://geert-hofstede.com/dimensions.html

obeyed. However, at the same time, Japan is probably the most modernized country when compared to the others. As to IDV, all countries scored rather low, with Korea the lowest. It has been often mentioned Asian people are more collective than Westerners. They tend to be more 'groupistic'. It appears here that the Koreans are particularly so. For MAS, it is needless to mention that the Japanese society is famous for its masculinity. Today, important positions in different walks of life are mainly taken up by males. Compared to Japan, the other countries seem to be more balanced in terms of the battle between the sexes, with Korea championing in this aspect. Concerning UAI, Japan scored extremely highly, which is not difficult to understand since Japanese culture values harmony and stability. On the other hand, Singapore scored extremely low, probably because they are more westernized. However, at the same time, they are also very traditional in the sense that they are very self-restrained, not exposing their emotions casually. Finally, as to LTO, the Confucian dynamism is at work, with China, Japan and South Korea scoring higher than India. The only point of note is the westernization of Singapore renders an LTO score of 48 despite Singapore's Asian outlook.

Asian cultures and business practices

In this section, we will look at a few examples of typical manifestation of underlying cultural values through management systems and practices.

First, in terms of structure, organizations influenced by Asian cultural values tend to be multilayered. This is not difficult to understand due to the Confucian emphasis on proper social relationships between different levels. Especially in large organizations in Japan, the structure resembles the classic hierarchy with line and staff divisions. Michael Porter and colleagues (2000) pointed out that the rigid hierarchical structure common to Japanese corporations can be effective in pursuing operational improvement but it may actually dampen innovative thinking. This is true as new organizational models have gradually been developed in large and successful enterprises such as Sony and Orix.

On the other hand, many Asian countries, especially those with large PDI and weak UAI frequently demonstrate organizational structures resembling 'families' or 'tribes'. In these organizations, the boss adopts a paternal role and subordinates do not have clearly defined roles and responsibilities. Instead, they have social roles. These organizations are characterized by centralized power and personalized relationships (Schneider and Barsoux, 1997). For example, Chinese companies are often family-based, with the founder having centralized power and at the same time acting as a caring father figure.

Since many Asian cultures tend toward the lower end of the masculinity index, being more feminine and ascriptive, organizational policies and procedures tend to be 'high-context'. Compared to Western organizations, organizational processes rely more on social relationships than on written descriptions. For example, Japanese-style management stresses the importance of intensive on-the-job training and small group activities. Chinese-style management emphasizes continuous learning. Therefore, experiences are accumulated through implicit social interactions rather than published company manuals. Knowledge thus becomes company-specific. This is further exemplified by the Chinese and the Japanese's similar cultural distinction between the 'in-group' and the 'out-group'.

The high level of collectivism in Asian cultures also affects the organizational process. As in decision making, the Japanese take a collective approach. The famous '*ringi*' system where a proposal has to be supported and endorsed at all levels before it is sent to the top of the hierarchy is often cited as a manifestation of Japanese collectivism. However, the situation changes when the organizations are highly centralized in terms of power, like small and medium-sized family businesses of Chinese origin such as overseas Chinese or Sino-Thai companies. Here, decisions are made centrally and the number of hierarchical levels can, in effect, be only two.

The emphasis on relational behaviours in Asian cultures can have a great impact on human resource management (HRM) practices. For example, in the selection process and the evaluation process, many Asian practices are labelled as nepotism by the West. This is especially serious in some Asian nations run by highly corrupted governments. The Chinese concept of *guanxi* (personal connection or network) is particularly famous. Nevertheless, *guanxi* here has a positive connotation and does not necessarily touch on corruption. Furthermore, relational behaviours also reflect the traditional concept of 'face', which is central to many Asian cultures. A harmonious situation is created when everyone respects one another's social statuses and relationships. That is, when every-one gives 'face' to everyone, harmony is preserved. Unlike Western cultures, Asian cultures avoid social and personal conflict and believe in fate. Therefore, 'face' given today can become a handsome return in the future. Therefore, in Chinese or other Asian organizations, the personnel recruitment process involves the giving and taking of 'face' due to delicate social relationships. It is not to say here that there is no compe-tition on equal footing, but social connection is extremely important in Asian business encounters.

Schneider and Barsoux (1997) noted that many cultural determinants will affect the corporate strategy adopted. For example, the relationship with nature may influence the adoption of a controlling or adapting strategy. Since most Asian cultures rest on the assumption that man should adapt to nature and not change nature, an adapting strategy appears to be more appropriate. Nevertheless, one should bear in mind that this does not indicate a direct relationship between the kind of culture and the strategy type. As we compete in a globalized arena, a combination of different strategic approaches is often necessary.

One example is reflected in the research of Noronha (2002). He found that many quality management approaches and techniques, which in fact have a Western or Japanese cultural origin, could be implemented effectively in Chinese cultural settings. In accord-ance with Abo's (2007) hybridization theory, 'foreign' management principles and practices, when implemented, will have to be transformed. This transformation is based on the fusion effect of different cultures and a culture-specific management system has to be created. Quantitatively and qualitatively, Noronha's study indicated that the various Chinese values had an influence on the climate, processes, methods and results of a Chinese culture-specific quality system. For instance, many Chinese companies adopt Western management concepts to create a formal organizational system while reinforcing it using Confucian principles. Leadership is created through paternalistic figures giving subordinates positive personal examples. Foreign technologies are imported on a large scale but they are always modified to suit local situations. In oppo-sition to the Japanese approach, small group activities often combine voluntary participation and monetary reward.

Asian cultures, ethics and social responsibility

The final section touches on ethics. Ethics is the philosophical study of values and customs of a group. It involves looking into right and wrong, good and evil, and responsibility. Ethics has three main areas: 'meta-ethics', 'normative ethics' and 'applied ethics'.

'Meta-ethics' is about the origin and meaning of our ethical principles. When put into the Asian perspective, the principal origin of Asian meta-ethics comes from Buddhism and Confucianism. For example, the state of Nirvana where there is no sorrow and pain, the concept of Karma (afterlife) and the belief in not killing any living beings are Buddhist origins of Asian ethics. On the other hand, the Confucian emphasis on social harmony, virtuous behaviours and filial piety are also origins of Asian ethics.

'Normative ethics' involves ethical norms that help us distinguish between right and wrong, good and evil. Many traditional Chinese sayings have become guiding principles as to how one should live an ethical life. For example, 'Reflect on our faults when we take a rest', 'Criticize ourselves before criticizing others' are common Confucian sayings that serve as ethical guidelines for the Chinese as well as other Asians.

'Applied ethics' is the application of ethical theory in real life situations. Examples are issues such as abortion and human cloning.

In the business setting, most Asian businesses embrace the Buddhist or Confucian origin of ethics that emphasizes social harmony and proper relationships among different parties. Unlike the Western practice of having written codes of ethical conduct, Asian businesses generally rely on the underlying cultural values of their organizational members as manifested in daily dealings. These values are often reflected by the emphasis on corporate social responsibility (CSR).

According to a study commissioned by the Centre for Social Markets (2003) and funded by the Department of Trade and Industry, CSR is voluntary and rooted in ethical values and is seen as an important issue by sampled South Asian companies operating in the United Kingdom. The vast majority of companies have engaged in certain socially responsible behaviours; donations to charities, supporting local events, organizations and schools, and environmental initiatives are examples of CSR manifestations. In general, the main spirit of CSR as perceived by these Asian businesses is to 'give something back to the community'.

CSR is currently a hot topic in China (Guan and Noronha, 2013) and other Asian countries. It is important that CSR should go beyond mere donations to charities. Take China for example, the numerous reports of industrial accidents leading to loss of lives and the revelation of hazardous consumer products[12] warrant a closer look at the formalization of CSR policies. With China's membership in the WTO and its advancing into the second place in terms of the biggest economies of the world, CSR will be a dominant issue if Chinese companies wish to maintain competitiveness. This is especially true as China received a corruption perception index of 39 (0 indicating highly corrupt and 100 indicating very clean) according to the 2012 survey conducted by Transparency International. Although corruption does not directly indicate the maturity of CSR, it can give a rough indication. China along with a number of Asian nations will face a long journey in building a healthier environment to foster CSR (e.g., India 36, Thailand 37, Vietnam 31 and Indonesia 32). Nevertheless, some Asian countries or regions such as Singapore

(87), Hong Kong (77) and Japan (74) appear to be on the right track toward sound governance and CSR. A movement to re-emphasize and revitalize the virtuous aspects of Asian cultures is to be awaited.

Chapter summary

- Culture refers to a society's values developed through shared history and experiences over time.

- The value orientation framework classifies cultural values into human nature, man–nature, time, activity and relational orientations. A culture is described by the combination of them.

- Hofstede identified six cultural dimensions namely power distance, uncertainty avoidance, individualism versus collectivism, masculinity versus femininity, long-term versus short-term orientation, and restraint versus indulgence. A culture is characterized by their combination to different degrees.

- Asian values generally have a Confucian origin, which emphasizes social harmony and proper relationships.

- Asian business practices are influenced by their cultural origins such as Confucianism and are manifested in organizational processes, structures, strategies and human resource practices.

- Many Asian nations lag behind in the development of corporate social responsibility despite their traditional cultural roots.

Key concepts

Applied ethics: ethical theory in real life situations.

Confucianism: the teachings of Confucius which stress social harmony, filial piety, virtuous behaviours and proper social relationships.

Culture: a system that contains values, beliefs, attitudes and behaviours shared by a group of people.

Individualism: the extent which individuals are integrated into groups.

Long-term orientation: the extent to which a society is adhering to Confucian virtues like perseverance, thrift and so on.

Masculinity: the distribution of roles between the genders to which a range of solutions are found.

Meta-ethics: the origin and meaning of our ethical principles.

Normative ethics: the ethical norms that help us identify right from wrong.

Power distance: the extent to which the less powerful members of organizations accept that power is distributed unequally

Restraint versus indulgence: The tendency of a society's view toward having fun and enjoyment in life.

Uncertainty avoidance: a society's tolerance for uncertainty.

Value: a broad tendency to prefer certain states of affairs over others.

Value orientation framework: the categorization of value orientations and their possible variations.

Review questions

1 What are the main elements of culture?
2 How do you define value?
3 What are the five value orientations and their variations?
4 What are Hofstede's cultural dimensions and how do they align with the business system framework?
5 What are the characteristics of Confucian-influenced cultures?

Learning activities and discussions

1 There are two famous old Chinese sayings. 'For a gentleman to take revenge, ten years is not too long to wait' (meaning one should bide one's time and wait for the right opportunity to seek revenge) and 'It is not a real gentleman who does not right a wrong' (meaning if you do not take revenge, you are not virtuous). Form two teams and debate these two sayings from a cultural standpoint.

2 Devise a plan to set up a business (e.g., a personnel recruitment agency) with two branches one in Japan and one in the Philippines or another South East Asian country of your choice. Discuss with your colleagues the possible cultural awareness you will need to successfully run the branches.

Wanda expands global footprint with UK plans
Meng Jing and Lyu Chang (*China Daily*, 20 June 2013)

Chinese conglomerate Dalian Wanda Group is to invest more than 1 billion pounds ($1.6 billion) to buy a British yacht maker and to build a top-end hotel in central London, in a bid to expand its overseas presence.

The company said on Wednesday that it will pay about 320 million pounds to acquire a 91.81 percent stake in Sunseeker International Ltd, a Dorset-based luxury yacht manufacturer which is famous for providing yachts for James Bond movies.

The remaining 8.19 percent stake will be acquired by Sunseeker's management team. The deal is expected to be completed by mid-August.

Wanda Group also said it will invest 700 million pounds to build a five-star, 160-room hotel on the South Bank overlooking the Thames River.

The investment marks the company's second major step in its overseas expansion strategy.

Wanda set the current record for the biggest Chinese takeover of a US company when it bought the AMC Entertainment Holdings Inc. cinema chain for $2.6 billion last year.

'We choose the most developed economies in the world, such as the United States and the United Kingdom, as our top destinations for overseas expansion,' said Wang Jianlin, chairman of Wanda Group, which reported revenue of 141.7 billion yuan ($23.1 billion) last year.

'We'll not rule out investing in other developing countries, but we prefer to do our global expansion moves in well-developed markets with well-established laws and regulations,' Wang said, adding the company's overseas operations are expected to contribute to the company's total revenue by 2020.

Wang added that he's very confident about the potential of China's luxury yacht market.

For instance, his company, which bought a Sunseeker Predator 108 Special Edition in 2010, will need to buy at least 30 luxury yachts for the future operations of three yacht clubs in three Chinese coastal cities as part of the company's plans to further develop its tourism and resort business.

He said the company is also considering setting up a manufacturing base for Sunseeker in China to lower the price of luxury yachts in the country. The hefty prices are a result of high import duties, which can be as high as 43 percent.

The booming luxury market in China and Chinese people's growing appetite for luxury goods are only part of reason for Wanda's expansion into the UK. The company's five-star hotel is expected to bring a Chinese touch to London and meet the needs of Chinese tourists, who are increasingly traveling overseas.

According to Wang, the 200-meter-tall hotel, located next to the Palace of Westminster and Battersea Power Station, is expected to become one of London's new landmark buildings. He said the company will build more five-star hotels overseas and plans to expand into eight to 10 major global cities in the next 10 years.

Sebastian Wood, the UK's ambassador to China, said he has seen a surge in investment from Chinese companies in the past few years.

'The UK is the most open economy. As many as 500 Chinese companies operate there,' he said.

In 2011, the UK was the third-largest European Union destination for Chinese investment, after Luxembourg and France, according to the Ministry of Commerce. Chinese direct investment in the country in 2011 was $2.5 billion, it said.

A report released by Rhodium Group, an economic consultancy, in June 2012, predicted that Chinese outbound direct investment will reach $1 trillion to $2 trillion between 2010 and 2020. The report said that a quarter of that will go to Europe through mergers and acquisitions or greenfield investments.

Gary Liu, executive director of the CEIBS Lujiazui Institute of International Finance in Shanghai, said that this is a 'very good time' to invest in Europe due to the current period of economic turmoil.

'Some European assets may be undervalued, but that doesn't mean they're bad, actually they have high potential growth and appreciation value,' Liu said. 'Also, the appreciation of the renminbi makes the cost of acquisitions much lower.'

But Liu also warned of the risks of overseas acquisitions, adding that the completion of a deal does not necessarily mean success.

'The performance of the parent company can be damaged if it's unable to manage the company it buys, which likely has a totally different culture,' he said.

Wang Jianlin said the company will keep Sunseeker's existing management, workforce and production base in the UK.

'We want to have a diverse culture and management style in Wanda Group because our goal is to become a global company,' Wang said.

Questions

1 Liu is aware of the totally different cultures of the Chinese parent company and the UK company being acquired. Can you point out some of the probable cultural differences?

2 Based on such cultural differences, what major difficulties in management do you foresee?

3 Wang mentioned that they wanted to maintain a diverse culture and management style of the Wanda Group by keeping the UK company's existing management and workforce. Do you agree that this is a successful way of creating a really global company?

Web links

Hofstede's cultural dimensions: http://www.geert-hofstede.com

Asian management practices: http://www.apmforum.com/

Global corruption ranking: http://www.transparency.org

Notes

1 http://www.worldbank.org/en/country/china/overview

2 The following case was taken from Oh (2010).

3 According to renowned cultural anthropologist Margaret Mead (1901–1978), an individual is a product of culture that shaped the person in unique ways. Cultural traits are learned by the individual as an infant, and they are reinterpreted and reinforced as the individual goes through different stages of life.

4 It is widely known that Singapore has a housing policy that encourages people to live with their parents.

5 The original Kluckhohn and Strodtbeck orientation framework consists of five dimensions. Some modern writings may include additional dimensions. For example, Lane and diStefano (2000) have added a sixth dimension called 'Man-to-space orientation', which includes three variations: private, public and mixed.

6 http://geert-hofstede.com/dimensions.html

7 http://geert-hofstede.com/dimensions.html

8 http://geert-hofstede.com/dimensions.html

9 http://geert-hofstede.com/dimensions.html

10 http://geert-hofstede.com/dimensions.html

11 http://geert-hofstede.com/dimensions.html

12 For example, the notorious 2008 melamine tainted milk powder that killed six infants and made at least 300,000 others ill and the revelation in 2010 that it was estimated that one in every 10 of all meals in China were cooked using 'sewer' oil scavenged from drains beneath restaurants (Foster, 2011).

References

Abo, T. (ed.) (2007) *Japanese Hybrid Factories: A Comparison of Global Production Strategies*. Basingstoke: Palgrave Macmillan.

Centre for Social Markets (2003) *Giving Something Back: Social Responsibility and South Asian Business in the United Kingdom: An Exploratory Study*. Bangalore: Centre for Social Markets.

Chan, C.P. (2007) Beyond Singapore: Making inroads in Japan and South Korea. *The Edge Singapore*, 28 May.

Claessens, S. and Fan, J.P.H. (2002) Corporate governance in Asia: A Survey. *International Review of Finance*, 3(2): 71–103.

CNN (2013) Park Geun-Hye becomes South Korea's First Female President. *CNN International*, 26 February.

Fang, T. (2003) A Critique of Hofstede's Fifth National Culture Dimension. *International Journal of Cross Cultural Management*, 3(3): 347–368.

Foster, P. (2011) Top 10 Chinese food scandals. *The Telegraph*, 27 April, 2011.

Grant Thornton (2013) *Women in Senior Management: Setting the Stage for Growth. Grant Thornton International Business Report 2013*. Grant Thornton International Ltd.

Guan, J. and Noronha, C. (2013) Corporate Social Responsibility Reporting Research in the Chinese Academia: A Critical Review. *Social Responsibility Journal*, 9(1): 33–55.

Guan, J., Noronha, C. and Tayles, M.E. (2013) Explaining Social Reporting of State-owned Enterprises in China: A Market Economy with Socialist Characteristics. *Proceedings of the 7th Asia Pacific Interdisciplinary Research in Accounting Conference*, Kobe, 26–28 July, 2013.

Hall, E.T. (1966) *The Hidden Dimension*. New York: Doubleday.

Hofstede, G. (1980) *Culture's Consequences: International Differences in Work–Related Values*. Newbury Park, CA: Sage.

Hofstede, G. (2011) Dimensionalizing Cultures: The Hofstede Model in Context. Online Reading in Psychology and Culture, Unit 2, accessed 31 October at: http://scholarworks.gvsu.edu/orpc/vol2/iss1/8

Hofstede, G. and Bond, M.H. (1988) The Confucian Connection: From Cultural Roots to Economic Growth. *Organizational Dynamics*, 16(4): 4–21.

Hofstede, G., Hofstede, G.J. and Minkov, M. (2010) *Cultures and Organizations: Software of the Mind*, revd 3rd edn. New York: McGraw-Hill.

Ishikawa, K. (1985) *What is Total Quality Control? The Japanese Way*. Englewood Cliffs, NJ: Prentice Hall.

Kluckhohn, C. (1951) Values and Value-orientations in the Theory of Actions: An Exploration in Definitions and Classifications. In T. Parsons and E.A. Shils (eds.) *Towards a General Theory of Action*. Cambridge, MA: Harvard University Press.

Kluckhohn, F.R. and Strodtbeck, F.L. (1961) *Variations in Value Orientations*. Evanston, IL: Row, Peterson and Co.

Kroeber, A.L. (1917) The superorganic. *American Anthropologist*, 19(2): 161–213.

Kroeber, A.L. and Kluckhohn, C. (1952) *Culture: A Critical review of Concepts and Definitions*. Cambridge, MA: Peabody Museum.

Lane, H.W. and diStefano, J.J. (2000) *International Management Behavior: From Policy to Practice*, 4th edn. Cambridge: Blackwell.

McSweeney, B. (2002) Hofstede's Model of National Cultural Differences and their Consequences – A Triumph of Faith – A Faith of Analysis. *Human Relations*, 55(1): 89–118.

Noronha, C. (2002) *The Theory of Culture-Specific Total Quality Management: Quality Management in Chinese Regions*. Basingstoke: Palgrave Macmillan.

Oh, H. (2010) Tata Daewoo: An Indian Success Story in Korea, *Asia Pacific Business and Technology Report*, 1 January.

Porter, M.E., Takeuchi, H. and Sakakibara, M. (2000) *Can Japan Compete?* Basingstoke: Palgrave Macmillan.

Redding, G. (2002) The Capitalist Business System of China and its Rationale. *Asia Pacific Journal of Management*, 19, 221–249.

Redding, G. (2005) The Thick Description and Comparison of Societal Systems of Capitalism. *Journal of International Business Studies*, 36, 123–155.

Rokeach, M. (1973) *The Nature of Human Values*. New York: The Free Press.

Schneider, S.C. and Barsoux, J.L. (1997) *Managing Across Cultures*. Hertfordshire: Prentice Hall Europe.

Takamiya, S. (1972) Group Decision Making in Japanese Management. *International Studies of Management and Organization*, 2(2): 183–196.

Tata Daewoo (2011) *Tata is Tata: Tata Daewoo Commercial Vehicle Company Brochure*. Seoul: Tata Daewoo Commercial Vehicle.

Witt, M. (2009) Management in Japan, in H. Hasegawa and C. Noronha (eds.) *Asian Business and Management: Theory, Practice and Perspectives*. Basingstoke: Palgrave Macmillan.

World Bank (2012) *East Asia and Pacific Economic Update 2012 Volume 1: Capturing New Sources of Growth*. Washington DC: World Bank.

Yau, O.H.M. (1994). *Consumer Behaviour in China: Customer Satisfaction and Cultural Values*. London: Routledge.

Accounting and Corporate Governance in Asia

Carlos Noronha

Chapter outline

- The development of accounting standards in Asia
- Accounting information quality in Asia
- Corporate governance in Asia
- Continuing debates and challenges ahead

Chapter objectives

After reading this chapter, you should:

1 Understand the development of International Financial Reporting Standards in Asian countries vis-à-vis the global trend.

2 Assess the quality of accounting information in major Asian economies.

3 Understand the characteristics of corporate governance mechanisms in Asian countries.

4 Understand the importance of business ethics in relation to financial matters in corporations.

Introduction

In the business system framework , adopted for this text, we can see in the middle layer the formal institutions that Redding (2005) defined as 'the humanly devised constraints that shape social interaction, and provide a hospitable environment for cooperative solutions to complex exchange' (p. 133). These institutions have a great influence on the key resources on which business itself depends to operate, for example, shareholders, creditors, unions, pressure groups and other stakeholders may all affect how key actors in business access resources. In terms of resources, Redding identified three forms of capital, namely capital itself (financial), human capital and social capital. This chapter focuses on the first type of capital. We will see how capital is managed and how the operating results are communicated back to institutions through accounting. We will also look at how the use of capital is monitored by legal and ethical forces through corporate governance mechanisms. Examples of selected Asian cases will highlight these main topics.

The development of accounting standards in Asia

International Financial Reporting Standards (IFRS) in Asia

Redding (2005) pointed out that the conditions of accessibility, sources, uses and monitoring of capital differ from society to society and as such financial capital, in particular the communication of it, will require a worldwide common language, especially in this time of globalization. We call this language 'accounting'. Accounting is often broadly defined as an information system that identifies, records and communicates the economic events of an organization to interested users (Weygandt et al., 2011). Here we are stressing the informational role of accounting (Dick and Missonier-Piera, 2010). An indication of how important a common accounting standard for businesses operating in different countries is, is provided by an examination of the Asian financial crisis in 1997 and accounting standards' role in it. According to Rahman (2000), citing a study conducted for the United Nations Conference on Trade and Development, many accounting practices in East Asian countries contributed to the understatement of risk, causing the crisis. For example, he pointed out that actual enterprise debts were hidden by frequent related-party transactions and off-balance sheet financing, foreign exchange risk exposure was not evident, detailed segment reporting was absent, contingent liabilities of financial institutions were not reported and loan loss provisions were inadequate. These were the results of national accounting standards that were not to the level of international reporting requirements or corporations. In some cases the relevant national standards were not followed at all, thus masking poor financial performance and profitability and deteriorating asset quality. Rahman critically pointed out that by adhering to two principles a country's accounting practices will become sound: developing national standards in conformity to International Accounting Standards; and developing proper enforcement mechanisms to ensure national accounting standards are complied with.

Since 2001 the London based International Accounting Standards Board (IASB), (and its predecessor International Accounting Standards Committee IASC set up in 1973) has been working on the development and application of international harmonization through setting financial reporting standards. Accounting standards are guides for the provision of information about the financial performance, position and changes in financial position of an entity so that a variety of users can make informed economic investment decisions (IASB Framework 12). Even under this objective, the guides in each country will have some national differences. Greenwood and Eyles (2006) pointed out that some main factors contributing to such variations included the differences in national legal systems (for example, common law versus continental law), the relationship between tax and reporting systems, the degree of government control and differences in capital markets. The IASB strives to harmonize international differences through the promulgation of International Accounting Standards (IAS) and International Financial Reporting Standards (IFRS). The constitution of the IASB sets out the following objective: 'to develop, in the public interest, a single set of high quality, understandable and enforceable global accounting standards that require high quality, transparent and comparable information in financial statements and other financial reporting to help participants in the world's capital markets and other users make economic decisions' (Alfredson et al., 2009). To date, 41 IAS and 13 IFRS have been issued alongside numerous interpretations and pronouncements. So what are the benefits of having a set of internationally harmonized financial reporting standards?

Improved comparability: financial statements of companies operating in different settings can be compared much more easily thus helping investors and lenders to make better economic decisions.

Reduced information asymmetry: research has indicated that the largest information benefit accrues to voluntary adopters of IFRS while firms that continue to report under local accounting standards may in future face a deficit of information intermediation (Horton et al., 2008).

Reduced cost of capital: research has indicated that the adoption of IFRS, especially in countries where institutional characteristics such as economic freedom, entry regulation, political and governance quality, innovation and legal system (Cherchye et al., 2008) are strong, can significantly reduce the cost of equity capital (Lee et al., 2008).

Stimulated foreign direct investment (FDI): research has indicated that having a set of common reporting standards helps promote cross-border investments and reduce information barriers to FDI (Ding et al., 2010).

Reduced cost of compliance: by following common accounting standards, companies can achieve higher audit efficiency in the long run and thus reduce the costs of audit and statutory reporting.

Better day-to-day operations: standardization allows for better management of resources, financial control and day-to-day operations.

As of 2013 more than 115 countries worldwide require or permit the use of IFRS (Kieso et al., 2011). Member states of the European Union were required, by law, to adopt IFRS as from 1 January 2005 (Soderstrom and Sun, 2007). Though still under discussion, there is a plan for convergence between the US Generally Accepted Accounting Principles (US GAAP) and IFRS in the foreseeable future. Given the situation in the United States and Europe, what is the current situation in Asia? Table 3.1 summarizes the situation of adoption in selected Asian countries.

TABLE 3.1 Progress of adoption of IFRS in selected Asian countries

Country	National standard	Convergence timeline	Notes
People's Republic of China	Accounting Standards for Business Enterprises (ASBE)	ASBEs issued in 2006 were already substantially the same as IFRS.	All listed companies must adopt ASBEs since 2007.
Japan	Japanese Generally Accepted Accounting Principles (GAAP)	Mandatory use of IFRS in 2015/2016.	Listed companies with international operations are permitted to use IFRS since 2010.
India	Indian Accounting Standards (Ind AS)	Originally 2011. Now to be adopted in a phased manner.	All listed companies, banks, insurance companies and large sized entities will adopt the converged standards.
Korea	Korean IFRS (K-IFRS)	Since 2011 K-IFRS are completely identical to IFRS.	All listed companies, state-owned enterprises and unlisted financial institutions must adopt K-IFRS.
Singapore	Singapore Financial Reporting Standards (SFRS)	Since 2008 SFRS are almost identical to IFRS.	Singapore incorporated listed companies are permitted to use IFRS if they are listed in another stock exchange that requires IFRS.
Malaysia	Malaysia Financial Reporting Standards (FRS)	Full convergence with IFRS in 2012.	Some transitioning entities such as agriculture and real estate will be mandated to adopt in 2013.
The Philippines	Philippine Financial Reporting Standards (PFRS)	Since 2005 most IFRS have been adopted, some with modifications.	PFRS apply to all entities with public accountability.
Thailand	Thai Accounting Standards (TAS)	Full adoption of IFRS in 2013.	Phased adoption by all listed companies in 2011, 2013 and 2015.
Vietnam	Vietnamese Accounting Standards (VAS)	VAS based on IAS up to 2003. No plan for full adoption of IFRS yet.	All domestic, listed or unlisted companies have to adopt VAS.

SOURCES: Deloitte IASPlus, PWC IFRS adoption by country, Center of Risk and Regulatory Excellence (2008).

It appears that the progress of adoption of IFRS in Asia is on the right track. Some countries, such as the Philippines and India have yet to resolve many issues before the day full convergence with IFRS can be seen. For example, at a recent IFRS International Forum, Indian standard setters said that they would want to adopt IFRS but at the same time they also wanted some exceptions, which in fact defeat the original purpose of having a single global reporting standard (Gettler, 2011). Other countries like Vietnam have not yet even begun. Phoung and Nguyen (2012) pointed out that IAS, developed in a completely capitalist setting can be less consistent with the needs and the economic structure of a mixed economy known as 'market economy under socialist orientation'. Thus for some Asian countries, convergence with IFRS will require more time and concerted effort.

Characteristics of IFRS

So what are the main characteristics of IFRS as compared to individual national standards and how do they impact on corporate reporting? The following is a brief explanation of the salient characteristics of IFRS.

Principle-based versus rule-based: IFRS are principle-based rather than rule-based that allow flexibility in the preparation of financial statements to interpret transactions and will therefore require much greater disclosure.

Underlying assumptions: IFRS statements are based on the accrual basis and the going concern assumptions. The former stresses that transactions are recognized when they occur, not when cash is received or paid. Thus, users of financial statements are informed of not only past events, but also of future obligations and events useful to their decision making. The latter assumes that business entities continue to operate in the foreseeable future. This assumption affects greatly the disclosure requirements of financial information.

Qualitative characteristics: IFRS statements should possess the following principal characteristics: ease of understanding, relevance, materiality and reliability.

Fair value measurement: IFRS deviates from the traditional historical cost approach and frequently requires fair value measurement for many items, which is defined in IFRS 13 as 'the price that would be received to sell an asset or paid to transfer a liability in an orderly transaction between market participants at the measurement date'.

Financial statements: IFRS statements include a 'statement of financial position', a 'statement of comprehensive income', a 'statement of changes in equity' and a 'statement of cash flows'.

Accounting information quality in Asia

At the beginning of the chapter we noted some drawbacks of the lack of a common set of accounting standards and the lack of rigor in some national accounting standards. It would be expected, then, that the quality of accounting information should have improved with the adoption of IFRS, but has it?

Let's take China as an example. Chen et al. (1999) studied about 50 companies for the period 1994–1997. They found that, on average, the reported earnings based on Chinese standards were 20–30 per cent higher than those based on IAS. Once the earnings were restated from Chinese standards to IAS, they were reduced on average by a minimum of 18 per cent in 1994 and a maximum of 30 per cent in 1995. The authors pointed out that Chinese accounting standards were significantly less conservative, resulting in earnings that were considerably higher than those under IAS. Furthermore, about 15 per cent of the companies changed from a reported profit to a reported loss after restatement to IAS.

None of the companies that initially reported a loss changed into profit after the restatement. Chen et al. (2002) studied a sample of 75 companies over a three-year period (1997–1999). They found that Chinese earnings exceeded IAS earnings in 80 per cent of the sample in 1997, 59 per cent in 1998 and 69 per cent in 1999. In all three years, the mean Chinese earnings were higher than the mean IAS earnings.

Ip and Noronha (2007) performed a quantitative analysis to compare the financial reports of 30 Chinese companies simultaneously listed in Hong Kong (thus following Hong Kong Accounting Standards, which have fully converged with IFRS) and in China (thus following the 1993 ASBE) and found that the harmonization progress of accounting standards had improved significantly. With the exception of results on operating income, all other figures of sales, income before tax, net income, assets, debts and equity prepared under Chinese accounting standards and international standards did not show any significant differences, although some considerable gaps had yet to be eliminated. Ching and Noronha (2011) conducted a further analysis to compare financial statements issued by Chinese listed companies based on the old Chinese Accounting Standards (the 1993 ABSE) and the new ones (the 2006 ASBE). Again, apart from some items due mainly to the requirement of fair value measurement by the international standards, the convergence of ASBE with IFRS had been found acceptable. The financial statements prepared under the new ASBE would be more comparable with those prepared in accordance with IFRS than they would have been previously. Overseas investors and users of financial statements should benefit greatly from this minimized disparity.

Space is limited here to demonstrate the effect of adopting IFRS vis-à-vis using local accounting standards and in fact empirical research in this area concerning Asian countries is very scarce. Nevertheless, interested readers may refer to professional publications that depict the detailed differences between the local accounting standards and IFRS (for example, see PricewaterhouseCoopers (2011) for India) to make assessments on the possible effects on financial reporting results.

The development of corporate governance in Asia

The concept of corporate governance

Corporate governance is the central topic of discussion on how capital market behaviours are monitored in our business system framework. Previously we have explained the informational role of accounting. Here we come to the second role of accounting – the contractual role (Dick and Missonier-Piera, 2010). Accounting data help to control the proper execution of explicit and implicit contracts between the firm and its various business partners and stakeholders, maintaining their relationships based on the peculiarities of the firm. Proper execution will depend on the corporate governance mechanism of the firm.

In the award-winning 2003 Canadian documentary film 'The Corporation', we can see an excerpt from an old US educational movie where a character states that he did not want to be personally liable for a personal mistake he might make in a partnership. His advisor immediately suggested him to 'incorporate' his business. By doing so, the business itself turns into a legal person and therefore he would get the protection he needed through 'limited liability'. Therefore instead of a group of persons being liable, it becomes the corporation itself that would become liable. That was probably the attitude of business operators in the past, trying to maximize profits while avoiding any personal liabilities, regardless of whether they were financial or moral. In view of the meltdown of many large US corporations (for example, Enron, Worldcom) causing catastrophic repercussions to the world economy, the importance of corporate governance has become dramatically clearer since 2002 (Monks and Minow, 2004). Building on the foundation of Donaldson's (1982) notion on the corporation as a moral agent, Freeman's (1984) stakeholders' theory and those of many other earlier and later business 'ethicists', modern corporate governance is a set of regulatory and market mechanisms underpinning the relationships between the firm, the board of directors, its shareholders and stakeholders with an objective of governing how the corporation is being directed and controlled and therefore to mitigate conflict of interests among the various parties involved.

The OECD (2004) has emphasized that there is no single good corporate governance model for all companies but some common principles from successful corporate governance experiences have been identified:

Ensuring the basis for an effective corporate governance framework: the corporate governance framework should promote transparent and efficient markets, be consistent with the rule of law and clearly articulate the division of responsibilities among different supervisory, regulatory and enforcement authorities.

The rights of shareholders and key ownership functions: the corporate governance framework should protect and facilitate the exercise of shareholders' rights.

The equitable treatment of shareholders: the corporate governance framework should ensure the equitable treatment of all shareholders, including minority and foreign shareholders. All shareholders should have the opportunity to obtain effective redress for violation of their rights.

The role of stakeholders in corporate governance: the corporate governance framework should protect the rights of stakeholders established by law or through mutual agreements and encourage active cooperation between corporations and stakeholders in creating wealth, jobs and the sustainability of financially sound enterprises.

Disclosure and transparency: the corporate governance framework should ensure timely and accurate disclosure is made on all material matters regarding the corporation, including the financial situation, performance, ownership and governance of the company.

The responsibilities of the board: the corporate governance framework should ensure the strategic guidance of the company, the effective monitoring of management by the board, and the board's accountability to the company and the shareholders.

Models of corporate governance

Most countries' corporate governance models fall on either one of three models: the Anglo-US model, the Japanese model or the German model. The major characteristics of each model are briefly provided here. Then the corporate governance situations in several major Asian countries will be discussed.

The Anglo-US model

A corporate governance triangle made up of shareholders, management and the board of directors characterizes the Anglo-US model. The model of having the chief executive officer as the chairman of the board of directors as the same person, which had led to abuse of power is no longer common in the United States and the United Kingdom. Separation of ownership and management is the salient feature of corporate governance and the Anglo-US model is now introducing an increasing number of 'outsiders', such as non-executive directors, to the board in order to bring more independent and objective views to the decisions of the board. The United States, being the world's largest capital market, has the most corporate governance regulations on disclosure of corporate and board member information. Nevertheless, because the shareholders and management do have varied interests, and managers are acting as agents for the principals, there are opportunities for managers to attempt maximizing their own interests. For example, in positive accounting theory (Watts and Zimmerman, 1986), the opportunistic view allows the view that managers would use earnings management to make accounting figures look rosy so as to maximize their own executive compensation.

The Japanese model

Under the *keiretsu* system, the bank, management, the board of directors and the government are the main players of Japanese corporate governance and their interactions are mainly for relationship development. This model, more of a coalition of stakeholders, differs from the Anglo-US model, which is shareholder-based (Aoki, 2000). A typical Japanese corporation is affiliated to a main bank, which is the largest shareholder of the corporation, an efficient fund provider, a monitor and controller of the corporation on behalf of all shareholders and a rescuer if the corporation should fall into financial distress (Okabe, 2004). The bank also, solely, provides various services that would be provided by different institutions such as commercial banks, investment banks and consultancy firms in the United States. Non-affiliated and foreign investment is marginal. The board of directors consists of almost no non-executive directors. Government industrial policies are very important and retired government officials often sit on boards. Like in the United States, Japanese regulations also require a high level of corporate, shareholder and board member information disclosure.

The German model

Similar to the Japanese model, banks play various significant functions in German corporate governance. But unlike the situation in Japan, corporate and foreign shareholders are common. The most famous feature of the German corporate governance model is the two-tier board system. There is a management board, which consists of 'insiders' and a supervisory board, which consists of entirely 'outsiders', often including labour representatives. For separation of management and supervision, no one can sit simultaneously on the two boards. This supervisory board oversees and advises the management board and the board compositions are fixed by law. Recently, there has been a trend in Germany to include more 'outsiders', especially minority shareholders to complement the stakeholder-based approach to corporate governance (Odenius, 2008).

Corporate governance in China

China also follows a two-tier board system with Company Law requiring the formation of a supervisory board. The board of supervisors are supposed to monitor the board of directors in many aspects but the problem is that they are not given the power to vote on executive decisions and the election of directors, managers and finance officers, thus making their role purely supervisory (Yang et al., 2011).

Bai et al. (2004) pointed out that ownership is concentrated in listed firms in China, thus making it possible to channel resources out to parent or related parties' accounts. There have been many counts of unconstrained large shareholders misuse of firm resources because in China dispersed ownership is scarce. In developing economies like China, corporate ownership is highly concentrated in the hands of a single investor associated with the central or local government or government-controlled institutions such as state-owned enterprises (Gul et al., 2010).

When the state is the controlling owner, the situation becomes more complicated. Claessens and Fan (2002) pointed out that the state as agent of the ultimate owner, that is the people, faces a lot of conflicts of interests since it enforces the law, regulates the banking industries and has incentives that may be different from those of the people. Claessens and Fan reported empirical research that concluded that firm accounting performance is negatively related to the level of state ownership. Liu (2005) also reported that China's corporate governance model could best be described as control-based in which the controlling shareholders, usually the state, employ governance mechanisms to tightly control the listed firm. Focusing on the period 1999–2001, Liu's empirical findings indicated that the largest shareholders held on average 44.8 per cent of the shares and one-third of the CEOs were chairmen of boards of directors. Although surprisingly more than 70 per cent of the board members were outside directors they were frequently appointed by the controlling state and are communist party secretaries (Yang et al., 2011, There were very few professionals such as lawyers sitting on boards.

In 2001, a mandatory guideline was issued to require at least two independent directors on the board by 2002 and one-third of the board members to be independent directors by 2003 (Yang et al., 2011). This can be seen as an attempt to improve the poor corporate governance situation in China. Some empirical studies also reported that independent directors are an effective corporate governance mechanism in developing countries. In the long run, to better China's corporate governance, there must be further reduction of the state's participation in the firm and an independent judicial system.

Corporate governance in Korea

In Korea, the controlling shareholders or owners of *chaebols*, which in for example 1996 owned 23 per cent of the outstanding shares but effectively controlled 68 per cent of the voting rights through cross-shareholdings, often used 'tunnelling' schemes (Bae et al., 2002) to expropriate corporate value from their minority shareholders (Kim and Kim, 2008). However, after the Asian financial crisis, serious reform in corporate governance mechanism was implemented. Kim and Kim (2008) illustrate the characteristics of today's Korean corporate governance. First, in terms of internal mechanism, merit-based executive compensation is now more and more common in Korean firms as opposed to the traditional seniority-based system. By aligning managerial compensation and shareholder value, executives and managers are less likely to engage in tunnelling schemes. Another change in internal mechanism is through better internal monitoring. After the crisis, the percentage of required independent directors changed from 25 per cent to 50 per cent. In terms of external measures, legal tools are the most important. Laws permitting securities and derivatives suits can deter false disclosures, insider trading, market manipulation and negligent external audits. Finally, the Korean media also contributes by exposing corporate scandals more frequently.

Corporate governance in Asian countries

Family control remains the most dominant form of ownership in East Asian countries. Carney and Child (forthcoming) reported that in 2008 the Philippines witnessed the largest increase in family controlled firms. Pyramid and cross-shareholding varied in different Asian countries. For example, in Korea cross-shareholding is popular but in Thailand less than 20 per cent of corporations use cross-shareholdings (Claessens and Fan, 2002). Over 60 per cent of the 500 largest companies in India are family-run business groups in which tunnelling activities have been reported (Chakrabarti et al., 2008). Clause 49 of the Listing Agreement in India now requires half of the board of directors to be independent directors and two-thirds of the audit committee to be external members. State control is also important in Malaysia, Singapore, Indonesia and Thailand. Separation of ownership and control remains relatively unchanged as a whole for this region. The OECD has identified similar problems with Asian corporate governance and called for urgent reform of governance mechanisms. A recent OECD (2011) report highlighted six major priorities:

1. Private and public sector institutions should continue to make the business case for good corporate governance among various parties.

2. All jurisdictions should strive for effective corporate governance laws and regulations.

3. The quality of financial and non-financial disclosure should be enhanced in a timely and transparent manner.

4. Board performance must be improved by training and evaluation and the board nomination process should be transparent and include full disclosure.

5. The legal and regulatory framework should ensure that non-controlling shareholders are protected from expropriation by insiders and controlling shareholders.

6. Shareholder engagement should be encouraged and facilitated.

Continuing debates and challenges ahead

Asian countries still face a long journey in the accounting standards harmonization process. Some countries like Vietnam have not even started to adopt IFRS. They are facing difficulties in introducing these global standards due to their own special social, economic and political systems. The adoption of IFRS requires a complementary change in the economic and legal framework of the country. The case of China is indeed a successful implementation of IFRS as a result of the changes in Company Law and changes in the sociopolitical setting, which have complemented the adoption. Advanced adopters of IFRS such as Japan, Korea and Singapore will continue to take a leading role and act as exemplars.

However, the weak corporate governance problem in many Asian countries remains the Achilles' heel of corporate Asia. Again, amendment of securities laws and having an independent judicial framework are essential in improving corporate governance mechanisms. Large controlling shareholders are still dominating Asian firms while the interest of minority shareholders is being sidelined. The lack of accountability of executive directors, the insufficient number of independent non-executive directors on the boards, the lack of transparency on directors' remuneration and related-party transactions are still troubling many Asian firms. In fact, cultures, both local and corporate and social morality or ethical standings are also very important factors affecting the overall level of corporate governance in a place. The 2012 Corruption Perception Index issued by Transparency International (http://cpi.transparency.org/cpi2012/) still see many South East Asian countries including China with an average score of nearly 35 over a scale from 0 (highly corrupted) to 100 (very clean) (China 39, Indonesia 32, the Philippines 34, Thailand 37, Vietnam 31, India 36).

In recent years, many Asian countries including China, have had an immense interest in non-financial reporting. Through the support of the state, national and international organizations, non-financial disclosure in the areas of environmental protection (green accounting, carbon accounting), sustainability and CSR have been greatly encouraged. Some countries such as those in Europe have laws mandating this kind of disclosure. Currently, in Asia, these disclosures are still largely voluntary. In fact, there are also well-recognized global standards for CSR reporting, which can be referred to. For example, the Global Reporting Initiative (GRI) on sustainability reporting, the SA8000 on labour matters, the AA1000 on stakeholder engagement, the ISO26000 on CSR, the UN Global Compact on human rights, environment and labour and the Carbon Disclosure Project (CDP) on carbon emission reduction strategies.

Some Asian countries, for example Japan, have been doing quite well in CSR reporting for some years. For example, the top three all-time reporting countries according to the Corporate Register Reporting Awards are the United Kingdom, the United States and Japan (Cohen, 2011). China is still at the beginning of this journey. In light of the numerous corporate scandals in China in recent years (such as the notorious 2008 Sanlu milk powder scandal), the people are becoming more and more aware of their basic rights as stakeholders of companies and members of a community (Noronha et al., 2013). They are demanding more and more disclosure of companies' affairs, in both financial and non-financial matters. In order to catch up with the global trend, firms in Asia must legitimize their profit-making activities by enhancing higher transparency and disclosure.

Chapter summary

- Various stakeholders have influence on how business actors in the business system obtain financial capital.

- Accounting is the language to communicate a firm's financial and non-financial performance back to the stakeholders.

- There is a need for a standardized set of accounting standards to be applied all over the world, and therefore the development of International Financial Reporting Standards (IFRS).

- Various Asian countries are at different levels of adoption of IFRS with some countries still having a lot to work to do before full adoption is achieved.

- Accounting data reports on the results of implicit and explicit contracts between the stakeholders and the firm and the specificities of their relationships depend on the respective corporate governance mechanism.

- There are three main models of corporate governance: the Anglo-US model, the Japanese model and the German model. No one model or framework is best.

- Many Asian companies have concentrated ownership and have weak corporate governance leading to tunnelling of resources from firms to major shareholders.

- Family-controlled and state-controlled firms in many Asian countries also have corporate governance problems.

- Many Asian countries will still be challenged by accounting standards harmonization and corporate governance difficulties and more efforts and resources should be invested in these areas together with the cooperation of the governments, professional bodies and international organizations.

- Asian countries will have to continue to develop in many financial as well as non-financial reporting areas like green accounting, sustainability reporting and corporate social responsibility reporting.

Key concepts

Accounting: an information system that identifies, records and communicates the economic events of an organization to interested users.

Accounting standards: guides for how to provide information about the financial performance, position and changes in financial position of an entity so that a variety of users can make informed economic investment decisions.

Corporate governance: the system by which companies are directed and controlled (Cadbury Committee, 1992).

Fair value: the price that would be received when an asset is sold or is paid to transfer a liability in an orderly transaction between market participants at the measurement date.

Insiders: people inside the company such as members of the board of directors.

Outsiders: people outside the company such as independent non-executive directors, labour and government representatives.

Principle-based standards: standards that allow financial statement preparers flexibility to interpret transactions and will therefore require a much larger amount of disclosure.

Quality of accounting information: the degree of the reflection of the real financial realities of the firm.

Two-tier board system: a corporate governance mechanism that consists of a board of directors and a supervisory board which supervises the directors' decisions and actions.

Review questions

1 Why do we need a standardized set of accounting standards worldwide?
2 What are the advantages of adopting IFRS?
3 What are some characteristics of a good corporate governance system?
4 What are the characteristics of the Anglo-US, the Japanese and the German models of corporate governance?
5 What weaknesses in corporate governance do some Asian countries suffer from?

Learning activities and discussions

1 Browse the internet and select one Asian country. Collect information on its accounting standards and corporate governance mechanism and prepare a short country-specific report.

2 'Unlike Asian countries, the United States is still reluctant to harmonize their accounting standards (US GAAP) with IFRS'. Discuss with your classmates the above statement.

Olympus projects annual loss of $412m, missing estimates
(*China Daily*, 2 February 2012)

TOKYO – Olympus Corp, the camera maker that admitted to accounting fraud and lost 59 percent of its value last year, predicted an annual loss of 32 billion yen ($412 million), which was worse than analysts' estimates.

The scandal, which broke in October, had no major effect on Olympus's business, the Tokyo-based company said in a statement on Monday. Analysts from Barclays Capital and Deutsche Bank Group estimated a 25.5 billion-yen average loss.

Olympus is considering ways to boost capital after it restated past securities reports and took a $1.3 billion cut in net assets in December.

The world's biggest maker of endoscopes plans a special shareholder meeting on April 20 for investors to vote on new management.

Any decision on a strategic alliance will be determined by a new board, President Shuichi Takayama said last month.

The Tokyo Stock Exchange last month allowed Olympus to keep its stock market listing by fining the company 10 million yen and telling it to submit reports on efforts to improve management.

The exchange put Olympus on a watchlist last year after the company admitted to inflating fees to advisers on the $2.1 billion acquisition of the London-listed Gyrus Group PLC in 2008 and overpaying for three Japanese companies.

The company still faces criminal probes and shareholder lawsuits against executives including Takayama even after purging executives including ex-chairman Tsuyoshi Kikukawa, whom the company found to have been involved in the 13-year loss cover-up scheme.

The company has been reeling since Michael Woodford disclosed inflated takeover costs after he was fired as chief executive officer on Oct 14.

The allegations forced the company to reveal a $1.7 billion scheme to conceal soured investments dating back to the 1990s, which raised concerns among investors and lawmakers over Japan's corporate governance rules.

The company's operating profit will probably decline 62 percent to 36 billion yen while its revenue may increase 0.8 percent to 854 billion yen. While the revenue forecast matched estimates, the operating-profit forecast misses the average estimate of 41 billion yen.

Olympus closed 0.4 percent higher at 1,282 yen in Tokyo trading. The stock is down 48 percent since Woodford's dismissal.

Questions

1 What could be some possible impacts to the various stakeholders if Olympus were delisted from the Tokyo Stock Exchange?

2 From the case of the Olympus scandal, what do you think are the biggest problems in terms of corporate governance of large Japanese corporations today?

Web links

Deloitte IASPlus http://www.iasplus.com

OECD corporate governance: http://www.oecd.org/corporate

Olympus scandal: http://en.wikipedia.org/wiki/Olympus_scandal

References

Alfredson, K., Leo, K., Picker, R., Loftus, J., Clark, K. and Wise, V. (2009) *Applying International Financial Reporting Standards*, 2nd edn. Queensland: John Wiley & Sons Australia, Ltd.

Aoki, M. (2000) *Information, Corporate Governance and Institutional Diversity: Competitiveness in Japan, the US and the Transitional Economies*. Oxford: Oxford University Press.

Bae, K.H., Kang, J.K. and Kim, H.M. (2002) Tunneling or Value Addition: Evidence from Mergers by Korean Business Groups. *Journal of Finance*, 56(7): 2695–2740.

Bai, C.E., Liu, Q., Lu, J., Song, F.M. and Zhang, J. (2004) Corporate Governance and Market Valuation in China. *Journal of Comparative Economics*, 32: 599–616.

Cadbury Committee (1992) *Report of the Committee on the Financial Aspects of Corporate Governance*. London: Gee & Co. Ltd.

Carney, R.W. and Child, T.B. (forthcoming) Changes to the ownership and control of East Asian corporations between 1996 and 2008: A primacy of politics. *Journal of Financial Economics*, accessed 31 October 2013 at: http://dx.doi.org/10.1016/j.jfineco.2012.08.013

Center of Risk and Regulatory Excellence (2008) *Comment Piece: IFRS Adoption in Asia Pacific and Japan*. Belgium: FRSGlobal.

Chakrabarti, K., Megginson, W. and Yadav, P.K. (2008) Corporate Governance in India. *Journal of Applied Corporate Finance*, 20(1): 59–72.

Chen, C.J.P., Gul, F.A. and Su, X.J. (1999) A Comparison of Reported Earnings under Chinese GAAP vs IAS: Evidence from the Shanghai Stock Exchange. *Accounting Horizons*, 13(2): 91–111.

Chen, S., Sun, Z. and Wang, Y. (2002) Evidence from China on Whether Harmonised Accounting Standards Harmonize Accounting Practices. *Accounting Horizons*, 16(3): 183–197.

Cherchye, L., Gaeremynck, A. and Verriest, A. (2008) Institutional Characteristics and Firm Profitability, accessed 31 October 2013 at: http://ssrn.com/abstract=1013143

Ching, L.C.H. and Noronha, C. (2011) The Impact of the New Accounting Standards for Business Enterprises (ASBE) on Financial Results of Mainland Chinese Listed Companies. *Advances in Accounting incorporating Advances in International Accounting*, 27(1): 156–165.

Claessens, S. and Fan, J.P.H. (2002) Corporate Governance in Asia: A Survey. *International Review of Finance*, 3(2): 71–103.

Cohen, E. (2011) Why don't Japanese REPORTS WIN AWARDS? CSR-reporting, accessed 31 October 2013 at: http://csr–reporting.blogspot.com/2011/04/why–dont–japanese–reports–win–awards.html

Dick, W. and Missonier-Piera, F. (2010) *Financial Reporting under IFRS: A Topic Based Approach*. Chichester: John Wiley & Sons Ltd.

Ding, Y., Chen, C.J.P. and Xu, B. (2010) Convergence of Accounting Standards and Foreign Direct Investment. Later presented at: Finance and Corporate Governance Conference Paper 2011, accessed 31 October 2013 at: http://dx.doi.org/10.2139/ssrn.1703549

Donaldson, T. (1982) *Corporations and Morality*. Englewood Cliffs, NJ: Prentice Hall.

Freeman, R.E. (1984) *Strategic Management: A Stakeholders' Approach*. Boston, MA: Pitman.

Gettler, L. (2011) IFRS debate heats up in Asia. Institute of Chartered Accountants Australia, accessed 31 October 2013 at: http://www.charteredaccountants.com.au/News–Media/Charter/Charter–articles/Reporting/2011–10–IFRS–Debate–Heats–Up–in–Asia.aspx

Greenwood, R. and Eyles, D. (2006) *International Financial Reporting Standards*, 2nd edn. Guangzhou: Sun Yat-sen University Press.

Gul, F., Kim, J.B. and Qiu, A.A. (2010) Ownership Concentration, Foreign Shareholding, Audit Quality and Stock Price Synchronicity: Evidence from China. *Journal of Financial Economics*, 95, 425–442.

Horton, J., Serafeim, G. and Serafeim, I. (2008) Does Mandatory Adoption of IFRS Improve the Information Environment? London School of Economics Working Paper.

Ip, C.K. and Noronha, C. (2007) The Progress of Accounting Harmonisation in China: A Comparison of A-share and H-share Financial Results, *Managerial Auditing Journal*, 22(6): 620–640.

Kieso, D.E., Weygandt, J.J. and Warfield, T.D. (2011) *Intermediate Accounting: IFRS Edition*. Hoboken, NJ: John Wiley & Sons Ltd.

Kim, E.H. and Kim, W. (2008) Changes in Korean Corporate Governance: A Response to the Crisis. *Journal of Applied Corporate Finance*, 20(1): 47–58.

Lee, E., Walker, M. and Christensen, H.B. (2008) Mandating IFRS: Its Impact on the Cost of Equity Capital in Europe. ACCA Research Report 105. The Association of Chartered Certified Accountants.

Liu, Q. (2005) Corporate Governance in China: Current Practices, Economic Effects and Institutional Determinants. *CESifo Economic Studies*, 52(2): 415–453.

Monks, R.A.G. and Minow, N. (2004) *Corporate Governance*. Oxford: Blackwell.

Noronha, C., Si Tou, M.I. and Guan, J. (2013) Corporate Social Responsibility Reporting in China: An Overview and Comparison with Major Trends. *Corporate Social Responsibility and Environmental Management*, 20(1): 29–42.

Odenius, J. (2008) Germany's Corporate Governance Reform: Has the System become Flexible Enough? IMF Working Paper. WP/08/179.

OECD (2004) *OECD Principles of Corporate Governance*. Paris: OECD.

OECD (2011) *Reform Priorities in Asia: Taking Corporate Governance to a Higher Level, Asian Roundtable on Corporate Governance*. Paris: OECD.

Okabe, M. (2004) The Financial System and Corporate Governance in Japan. Policy and Governance Working Paper Series No. 17. Graduate School of Media and Governance. Keio University.

Phoung, N.C. and Nguyen, T.D.K. (2012) International Harmonization and National Particularities of Accounting: Recent Accounting Development in Vietnam. *Journal of Accounting and Organizational Change*, 8(3): 431–451.

PricewaterhouseCoopers (2011) *Decoding the Differences: Comparison of Ind AS and IFRS*. PricewaterhouseCoopers India.

Rahman, M.Z. (2000) Accounting Standards in the East Asia region. Paper presented to the Second Roundtable on Corporate Governance, OECD and World Bank. Hong Kong 31 May–2 June 2000.

Redding, G. (2005) The Thick Description and Comparison of Societal Systems of Capitalism, *Journal of International Business Studies*, 36: 123–155.

Soderstrom, N.S. and Sun, K.J. (2007) IFRS adoption and Accounting Quality: A Review. *European Accounting Review*, 16(4): 675–702.

Watts, R.L. and Zimmerman, J.L. (1986) *Positive Accounting Theory*. London: Prentice-Hall.

Weygandt, J.J., Kimmel, P.D. and Kieso, D.E. (2011) *Financial Accounting: IFRS Edition*. Hoboken, NJ: John Wiley & Sons Ltd.

Yang, J., Chi, J. and Young, M. (2011) A Review of Corporate Governance in China. *Asian Pacific Economic Literature*, 25(1): 15–28.

Human Resource Management in Asia

Rosalie L. Tung

Chapter outline

- Confucianism and HRM
- HRM in Japan, Korea and China
- The challenges ahead

Chapter objectives

After reading this chapter, you should be able to:

1. Understand the major characteristics of HRM practices in Japan, Korea and China, including similarities and differences across the three countries.

2. Identify the factors in the institutional environment (including political, economic and sociocultural dimensions) that have contributed to the evolution of HRM systems and practices over time in Japan, Korea and China.

3. Gain an appreciation of the challenges ahead for Japan, Korea and China in the area of HRM.

Introduction

The wide variety of business systems described in Chapter 1 contributes to the diversity in human resource management (HRM) policies and practices in Asia Pacific. Given the differences in political, economic, and sociocultural systems in the broad range of countries that comprise Asia, it is not possible to cover the HRM systems and practices in all economies in this region. Rather, the focus will be on Japan, South Korea (Korea, in short) and China, three countries in East Asia that have been clustered together as 'Confucian Asia', that is countries that have been influenced by the teachings of ancient Chinese philosopher, Confucius. Brief references will be made to other southeast and southern Asian countries, where relevant.

Cumulatively, the three 'Confucian Asian' countries account for a sizable portion of that region's economic wealth and development. If one were to include southern and southeast Asia, this region becomes even more salient, both in terms of population and potentials for further economic growth. Both Japan and Korea are members of the Organisation for Economic Co-operation and Development (OECD) and hence categorized as developed countries. While China surpassed Japan as the second largest economy in the world in 2010, it is still a developing country. In addition, Japan and Korea are both free market economies while China continues to operate on mixed-market principles.

Apart from the aforementioned differences between Japan and Korea, on the one hand, and China, on the other, it is important to note that there are significant variations within each country, especially China. In Japan, there are subtle yet longstanding and notable differences in dialect and business culture between Kansai (Osaka) and the Kanto (Tokyo) regions. In Korea, despite the remarkable homogeneity of its population, there are centuries-long differences between the southeast (Gyeongsang region) and the southwest (Jeolla region) in economic development and political attitudes. In the case of China, there are 55 recognized ethnic minority groups alongside the Han majority. The language and cultural customs of the ethnic minorities are very different from those of the Han Chinese. In addition, there are substantial differences in per capita income and business styles across China, even among the developed regions. For example, even though Beijing, Shanghai and Guangzhou are all economically developed, there are significant differences in business negotiation styles and practices across these three major business hubs. Furthermore, business negotiation styles and practices in the less developed regions in western China are again very different from that in the coastal provinces. In addition, Hong Kong is now part of China and HRM practices there are very different from that in China per se with state-owned enterprises (SOEs) operating very differently from privately owned firms (non-SOEs). Also, given the substantial foreign investment in China, the operations and practices in foreign-invested enterprises (FIEs) are different from those in non-FIEs. Even in the case of India, the most populous democracy in the world, studies have shown that there are big differences in HRM practices between firms in the private and public sectors.

Besides variations in HRM systems across countries, there can also be significant generational differences. A 2012 survey by Pricewaterhouse Coopers of over 4,000 graduates from 75 countries around the world born between 1980 and 2000 (referred to as 'millennials') – a group that will comprise one-half of the global workforce by 2020 – found that 'millennials want more "just a job"'. Their aspirations, values, expectations and needs differ from that of their predecessors in some important ways. These differences have tremendous implications for HRM of the younger generation worldwide, including Asia. Where relevant, these differences will be discussed in this chapter.

While there are intergenerational, cross-national and intranational differences, it is important to note that globalization and cross-border investments, with their accompanying phenomena of benchmarking and best practices, have contributed to 'cross-vergence' or 'bounded convergence', that is, convergence along certain dimensions while differing on others. For example, while most countries in this region recognize the importance of pursuing best practices, such as the implementation of High Performance Work Systems (HPWS), studies on export-oriented industries in both Malaysia and Sri Lanka have shown that there is often a mismatch between avowal of these principles and actual practice. Where relevant, 'bounded convergence' in HRM practices will be alluded to in this chapter.

The characteristics and evolution of HRM system and practices of each country are presented in the context of four major HRM functions: (1) staffing and employment security; (2) training and development; (3) compensation and performance appraisal; and (4) industrial relations.

Confucianism and HRM

Confucianism is a philosophical tradition that guides human behaviour and relations between people or groups of people in society. Some of the principal tenets of Confucianism that have a lingering effect on HRM practices in these countries are:

- Strong work ethic – this explains why employees are willing to put in long hours of work beyond their prescribed nine-to-five job and often forego their allotted annual vacation.

- Education and learning – this explains the value placed on education, training and development.

- Hierarchical ordering of relationships and obedience to authority – Confucius prescribes the appropriate behaviour that governs different categories of relationships. The father–son relationship demands absolute obedience to the father's dictates with the reciprocal obligation of the father to look after his son. In the corporate context, this translates into high power distance, authoritarianism, unquestioning compliance with directives of one's superiors and respect for age/seniority. Since the father–son bond is a permanent one, it leads to long-term commitment by both employers and employees in the form of lifetime employment.

- Gender role differentiation – one of the five relationships prescribed by Confucius pertains to husband–wife. The husband is the breadwinner and attends to all matters external to the household while the wife has primary responsibility for their children's education and household affairs. This accounts for the low representation of women in managerial/professional ranks and why women traditionally leave the workforce once they bear children.

- Emphasis on the family – Confucianism emphasizes the sacrificing of one's self-interest to the general welfare of the family. This explains for the collectivistic orientation ascribed to East Asian societies. To a certain extent, one's coworkers are regarded as members of an extended family. Hence it is common for employees to be known by the company for which they work, such as a 'Mitsui man' or 'Samsung man'.

While countries in southeast and southern Asia may not subscribe to Confucian principles per se, in reality, the multicountry study of leadership styles and cultural values (known as the GLOBE project) has shown that the distinguishing features of the southern Asian countries are very similar to those exhibited in Confucian societies, albeit with differences. These include group and family collectivism, high power distance and emphasis on humane leadership.

HRM in Japan

Human resources have been recognized as a key to the success of Japanese organizations as the country is devoid of natural resources. As a result of this importance line managers typically regard HRM as one of their primary responsibilities. As such, the HRM department plays a relatively modest role in a firm's overall HRM activity.

Traditionally, the characteristics of Japanese HRM are: lifetime employment, continuous on-the-job training, seniority-based pay and harmonious labour-management relations. These characteristics were prevalent in the first four decades of continuous economic growth after World War II.

Staffing and lifetime security

This system favours the recruitment of male college graduates upon completion of their university education and promotion from within. Lifetime employment (LTE) is extended to this core group of employees, known as career staff. LTE is essentially a psychological contract between the employer and an employee that the former will take care of the latter for life; in return, an employee identifies strongly with the company and is extremely dedicated to organizational objectives. This system engenders loyalty and commitment on the part of the core employees who are willing to work long hours, seldom take their full allotment of annual vacation and endure personal sacrifices to facilitate the attainment of organizational objectives. As such, job-hopping and recruitment at middle- and senior-management levels are rare.

In reality, most large organizations have a parallel system of employment for non-core employees, primarily women who leave the workforce after they have children. In addition, under the *keiretsu* system in Japan, there is an intricate supply of contractors and subcontractors who are not protected by LTE – this complex network provides systemic flexibility that enables the firm to gain access to surplus labour to cope with periods of economic expansion and eliminates the need to lay off core employees during recessionary times.

Most large organizations have adopted a system of temporary transfers (*shukko*) that serves a dual purpose. On the one hand, it can be used to fast-track career staff with high potentials in the form of temporary assignments to one of the company's subsidiaries at a grade or two higher than their current position. If they perform well, they will be transferred back to the parent organization at a higher level. On the other hand, it is a mechanism for 'losing' career staff with below-average performance.

Recruitment of career staff is primarily based on the candidate's relational abilities (that is, how well the recruit can get along with others in the organization) and degree of fit with the company's values. There is intense after-hours socializing to inculcate the fresh recruits in the company's organizational culture. The traditional practice of recruiting new university graduates means that job-related skills are de-emphasized in the selection criterion.

Training and development

Apart from the Confucian influence, this emphasis on learning is reinforced by the Zen philosophy of enlightenment that stresses continuous improvement. Given LTE, companies can afford to invest in extensive training of their career staff, both classroom- and experiential-based learning. Since the emphasis of training is on the development of generalists rather than specialists, job rotation within and across functions is widely used. In general, most Japanese firms offer a single career ladder toward line managerial positions.

To meet the demands of outward foreign direct investment (OFDI) by Japanese multinationals, high potential career employees are often sent overseas to attend graduate programs, acquire knowledge of foreign cultures and languages, and/or further develop their skills and global orientation while receiving their salaries. These activities represent a substantial investment on the part of the sponsoring organizations. In some large Japanese multinationals, these overseas training programs can extend for four years where the first year is devoted to language training, followed by two years in a post-graduate program (such as a MBA), and ending with one year of work in the overseas subsidiary. The reason for such extensive training is premised on the belief that in order to be good producers (that is, produce goods/services that are in demand in a foreign country), one has to be, first and foremost, a good consumer of that country's culture.

Japanese expatriates are used extensively at the top levels of their overseas operations. To meet localization requirements in many foreign countries, even though host country nationals (HCNs) may be hired as senior managers, to ensure adequate control, Japanese expatriates are often deployed as advisors. Extensive training is provided to the locals, including bringing those with high potential to headquarters for further development.

Compensation and performance appraisal

In light of LTE and the Confucian influence of respect for age, compensation is largely a function of an employee's seniority or organizational tenure. In the 1970s, Japanese firms adopted a skill-grading system designed to encourage employees to acquire new skills; in practice, however, the link between skills attainment and remuneration was virtually non-existent. In other words, the skill-grading system became synonymous with seniority-based pay and has been characterized as mono-dimensional with a single career ladder. Under this system, pay increases are more or less automatic and promotion is slow. In general, it takes seven years for a new career recruit to be advanced to the rank of 'person-in-charge' and 14 to15 years before promotion to 'group manager'. There is little variation in pay for employees at the same organizational rank regardless of performance.

Under this system, performance appraisal is primarily on a person's managerial and/or supervisory capabilities. These attributes are deemed essential for advancement to the managerial ranks.

Industrial relations

Japanese companies are organized on the basis of enterprise unions that cover fulltime employees only. There is an annual collective bargaining process between management and the unions (*shunto*) that traditionally focused on salary increases in each rank. In times of economic expansion, there is usually little disagreement between labour and management over these issues resulting in a generally harmonious industrial relations' scene.

After four decades of continuous economic growth; the appreciation of the yen that inflated the cost of Japanese products and services abroad; the overall ageing of the Japanese workforce (Japan has one of the world's oldest populations); rising competition from other newly industrialized and emerging markets in the manufacturing and service sectors (notably, Korea and China); the hollowing of industry in Japan (offshoring of manufacturing to mitigate some of the aforementioned trends); and the onset of the Asian financial crisis in 1997 (many Japanese financial institutions were heavily exposed to bad loans) have all contributed to the faltering of the Japanese economy that began to surface shortly after the early 1990s. The so-called 'lost decade' where economic growth is very slow or negative is now entering into its third decade. The devastation caused by the 2012 earthquake and tsunami compounded the economic plight.

In light of the aforementioned challenges, both external and internal, there have been changes to Japanese business systems, including its HRM practices. It is important to note that these changes are still evolving and uneven across industries/sectors and firms. Furthermore, there is disagreement among experts on the nature and extent of such changes. The evolving changes are presented in the order presented in the preceding section.

Staffing and employment security

In general, there is agreement that LTE has been retained although it has undergone major transformations, including the substitution of the term, 'lifetime' with 'long-term'. Consistent with the trend in Western organizations toward downsizing and flatter organizations (that is, fewer organizational levels within a division, known as 'delayering'), long-term employment now applies to a smaller group of employees. Downsizing and delayering are accomplished through: (a) encouraging early retirement (in some cases, people retire as early as age 45); (b) a dramatic reduction in intake of new college graduates; (c) greater reliance on subcontracted or temporary employees; and (d) the greater magnitude (numbers of people affected by such transfers) and frequency of *shukko*. For managers aged 50 to 60 who are still guaranteed employment, they may lose their status and benefits through such transfers.

A new development is the emerging trend to hire outsiders at the mid-career level with more specialized and/or professional skills. The changes described above coupled with those outlined below, have resulted in a breakdown of the psychological contract that prevailed in the era of economic boom.

To comply with the Equal Employment Opportunity law enacted in 1986, women college graduates are now hired on a 'minor career course' with substantially inferior terms and are not covered by LTE and seniority-based pay.

Training and development

In the past, the heavy corporate investment in training and development benefited companies as personnel turnover was negligible. With the erosion of the psychological contract, companies stand to lose as highly trained personnel (talent) may choose to leave. However, because the 2012 PwC survey found that millennials value training and development and work–life balance more than bonuses, Japanese organizations have little choice but to continue to provide extensive training for their career staff.

Compensation and performance appraisal

There is growing recognition among Japanese firms that the practice of seniority-based automatic pay increases is incompatible with their revised strategy to build leaner and more efficient organizations. Many progressive companies seek to fast-track employees with strong potentials in the form of speedier progression up the hierarchical ranks and higher remuneration (mostly in the form of bonuses). To accomplish this, more frequent performance appraisals are undertaken to track a person's progression. Statistics show that salary differentials have widened in many large organizations that give more emphasis to competence and skills over the traditional criteria of age and organizational tenure. While the skill-grading system is intact in most organizations, greater account-ability has been stressed. A 1999 survey revealed that for promotion to the level of sub-section manager, over 80 per cent of companies considered ability and actual performance as important criteria.

In addition, some firms have established a multitrack career ladder to replace the traditional single career path. Under this new model, it is easier to advance to senior management either as generalists or specialists.

The aforementioned changes are more in tune with the values and expectations of millennials. For example, the 2012 PwC survey found that young people 'expect rapid progression, a varied and interesting career and constant feedback'.

Industrial relations

Downsizing and the growing trend toward individualization of remuneration have meant that the unions can no longer 'guarantee' job security or across-the-board wage increases. In 2002, the Japanese Trade Union Confederation (*Rengo*) dropped its traditional demand of uniform basic monthly pay increases. However, *Rengo* has urged the Government to provide a stronger social safety net for the unemployed to match those of other industrialized countries.

Furthermore, with the move toward individualization of remuneration and performance appraisal, employees have filed more grievances with their unions. This is a new role for the enterprise unions as their mechanisms are designed for collective bargaining under conditions of communal solidarity.

HRM in Korea

As is the case in Japan, human resources have played an important role in Korea's economic development. After the Korean War (1950–1953), the country was divided into North and South. Heavy industries were concentrated in the North while the South is rich in agricultural land. The role of HR cannot be ignored in the South's remarkable transformation from a tattered agrarian economy after the Korean War where per capita GDP was only US$87 to its ascendancy to the ranks of OECD (industrialized country status) in 1997.

As a result of the Confucian influence and the legacy of the Japanese occupation of Korea for four decades, the HRM system in Korea bears many similarities to that of Japan. In general, Korean HRM systems can be divided into two major time periods: pre-1987 and post-1987. The year 1987 marked the Declaration of Democratization in Korea that affected all aspects of Korean society, including the introduction of a presidential election and the implementation of autonomous collective bargaining. The characteristics of Korean HRM system in pre-1987 era are outlined below.

Staffing and employment security

Prior to 1987, the Korean HRM system can be characterized as paternalistic, seniority-based and promotion from within. The employer took care of virtually all aspects of their employee's life; in return the former expected unswerving loyalty and commitment from the latter. Hierarchical ordering is perhaps even more visible than that in Japan for at least two reasons: (1) strong militaristic tradition – even today, there is mandatory military service for all young men; and (2) the owners/families of the founding fathers of the three largest *chaebols* (Hyundai, LG and Samsung) are still actively involved in management of their respective companies. Many leading Korean *chaebols* were established in this period.

Since the primary objective of the government after the Korean War was economic growth, a series of five-year development plans were implemented. Unlike the situation in Japan, the Korean Government, rather than market forces, was very influential in all aspects of the country's economic development.

Similar to Japan, the core employees in Korean firms were recruited directly upon graduation from university. Employment tests were used extensively in recruitment. Similar to the Japanese HRM system, previous work experience was de-emphasized.

Training and development

In the pre-1987 period that favoured the recruitment of new college graduates, the company provided intensive training in job-related skills. On joining the company, new recruits undergo several months of 'socialization' camps where they learned about the corporate culture and developed camaraderie and team spirit. Extensive training was provided for the career staff at all levels while little training was given to temporary or contingent workers (also known as irregular workers) and below-average performers. Job rotation was used extensively as the emphasis was on developing generalists rather than specialists.

Compensation and performance appraisal

Similar to *shunto*, there is an annual wage negotiation in Korea where the government-sponsored Federation of Korean Trade Unions (FKTU), in consultation with the Ministry of Labour, negotiate with various firms. In practice, in the pre-1987 era, remuneration was essentially on the basis of seniority rather than performance. Similar to the situation in Japan, college recruits who joined the company at the same time received more or less the same pay.

Industrial relations

In the pre-1987 era, workers' rights were ignored as the national priority was economic growth.

The Declaration of Democratization in 1987 coincided more or less with the 1988 Seoul Olympics. By then, the country had made sufficient economic progress to showcase the country's achievements to the world when the media spotlight was on Korea's hosting of the Olympics. The late 1980s also coincided with a rapid rise in the value of the Korean Won that rendered Korean exports less competitive worldwide. By then, China had embarked on its open door policy and its cheap and abundant labour led many manufacturers from the industrialized countries to shift their production facilities there. Two major milestones in the post-1987 period were the outbreak of the Asian financial crisis in 1997–1998 and Korea's advancement to OECD ranks. In the post-1987 period, Korean HRM practices evolved toward a market-based model and many companies adopted a pluralistic approach in their search for greater efficiency and international competitiveness.

Staffing and employment security

Beginning in 1987, consistent with the goal of greater efficiency, the more progressive companies used internships, blind interviews and recruitment specialists to assist with hiring decisions. In addition, employees with outstanding performance were fast tracked for promotion.

In the first decade after 1987, job security was more or less guaranteed as the Labour Standard Act prohibited the sacking of employees except with just cause. However, performance appraisal was used extensively to weed out those who were non-promotable. The latter were psychologically pressured to leave the company.

The Asian financial crisis in 1997 that resulted in the collapse of many less-efficient *chaebols* presented an opportunity for many Korean employers to legitimize their adoption of: (1) greater flexibility in labour market reforms that included dismissing below-average performers and recruiting talent from external sources – according to the Korea Labour Institute, between 1997 and 1998, 43.7 per cent of the workforce was shed by the 300 companies surveyed, twice the number of the preceding year; and (2) incentives linked to performance. With downsizing and delayering, as in the case of Japan, the psychological contract that formerly existed between employers and employees was broken. In a 2002 survey by Hyundai Research Institute and *Korean Joongang Daily* of 436 managers at 100 large companies, over two-thirds of the respondents felt that the Asian financial crisis signalled the end of LTE. Accordingly, approximately half of the respondents indicated that they planned to leave their organization within the next five years.

With the dismantling of the psychological contract, job-hopping became more common. As such, companies had to compete for talent and, more importantly, undertake initiatives to retain them. The war for talent is particularly intense in the telecommunications/internet sector, where external recruitment (including recruiting from abroad) is common. Among the larger companies and firms in the high tech sector, growing attention is paid to global talent management.

The post-1987 period also witnessed an increase in the use of irregular workers where there is no guarantee of continued employment beyond the completion of a specified job.

In 1995, the Korean Assembly passed the Equal Employment Act to eliminate discrimination against the hiring of women. However, women are still severely under-represented in managerial ranks. In fact, Korea ranked lowest among OECD countries in gender equality.

Training and development

As Korea transitioned from low-cost to higher value-added manufacturing and high tech industries, extensive training was provided to all career employees, particularly to high performers. This period also coincided with the first overseas expansion by Korean multinationals. Similar to the practice at Japanese multinationals, Korean firms sent their promising employees abroad for further education to learn foreign languages and culture/customs to prepare them for eventual work in their company's overseas subsidiaries.

Despite the continued use of expatriates at senior management in overseas subsidiaries, there is a trend among the successful Korean MNCs to recruit and train HCNs with high potentials, including bringing them to headquarters for development. This represents an important component of their global talent management program.

Compensation and performance appraisal

In the period 1987–1997, in an attempt to promote greater efficiency, companies attempted to link remuneration more closely to competencies and performance. The use of 360° feedback (multiple raters feedback), was introduced. According to the annual pay surveys by the Korea Ministry of Employment and Labour, 57.4 per cent of companies have adopted some performance-based scheme compared to 1.6 per cent of companies in 1996. In some companies, profit sharing linked to performance, can account for one-half of an employee's remuneration. There were wide variations across firms, however. For example, at Hyundai, only 7 per cent of its employees are entitled to stock options.

Industrial relations

With democratization, unions and strikes are no longer outlawed. In 1987 alone, the number of labour strikes surged to approximate the cumulative number of industrial strikes in the preceding quarter century. Union membership peaked at 18.6 per cent in 1989 and after the Asian financial crisis has fallen to 12 per cent. Union membership is concentrated in key industries such as automobiles, shipbuilding and public utilities. When labour disputes arise, they tend to be highly confrontational, high profile and on a large scale.

HRM in China

As the world's most populous nation, China's leaders recognize that its people are both a bane and a boon to the country's fortune. On the downside, it is a major challenge for any government to feed and provide employment for over a billion people. On the upside, where properly harnessed and trained, it can provide a cheap and abundant source of labour. By leveraging its huge labour force, China has succeeded in becoming the 'manufacturing workshop of the world' that catapulted it to rank as the second largest economy in the world in 2010, after the United States.

Broadly speaking, HRM in China can be divided into two phases: the Mao era (pre-1976) and the post-Mao era. Mao refers to Mao Zedong, Chairman of the Chinese Communist Party and founder of the People's Republic of China. The characteristics of HRM systems in state-owned enterprises (SOEs) in the Mao era are outlined below. SOEs formed the industrial backbone of China prior to 1976.

Staffing and employment security

In China, this is referred to as the 'iron rice bowl' and 'cradle-to-grave' systems. Under socialism, the government takes care of all aspects of a person's life from birth to death, including the designation of one's job and place of work, whom they marry, how many children they will have, and so on. Under the 'iron rice bowl' system, firings were rare and labour mobility was virtually non-existent.

As far as recruiting is concerned, the system of hereditary inheritance of jobs in SOEs was in place until the late 1980s. The use of 'redness' (political correctness) versus 'competence' (job skills) oscillated as the primary criterion in hiring between periods of political thought reform in China. During the Cultural Revolution (1966–1976), a calamitous period where the stated objective was eradication of traditional and capitalistic elements from society to attain full communism, 'redness' was emphasized.

Training and development

In the absence of labour mobility in the Mao era, training focused on developing the skills and abilities necessary to perform the job assigned to the person. Under central planning, the universities and post-secondary education were, in general, designed to train people for specific fields/jobs, such as engineering, shipbuilding, and so on. Thus, many of the post-secondary education institutes are industry/sector specific.

Apart from the study sessions organized by the trade unions described under industrial relations below, most training was on-the-job.

Compensation and performance appraisal

Following the Soviet model, an eight-grade wage scale was enforced. As egalitarianism was the norm, there was little deviation in compensation for people in each of the wage scales. During times when competence was emphasized over redness, bonuses were used to reward workers for outstanding performance. However, because the amounts involved were small, the primary motivator to spur higher performance was designation as model workers. The latter's pictures were prominently displayed throughout the factory. For exceptional model workers, their pictures and stories of outstanding contribution were featured in the national media for emulation across the country.

The primary reliance on non-material incentives (or moral suasion) to enhance performance has its limits, however. An anonymous quote best captures the essence of this problem: 'they pretended to pay us [the workers] and we pretended to work'.

Industrial relations

While all SOEs had trade unions, strikes and workouts were non-existent as under socialism, the factories belonged to 'the whole people'. Therefore, in principle, employees do not strike against themselves.

The trade unions were, in essence, an extension of the Chinese Communist Party. They played an important role in conducting study sessions to upgrade workers skills, indoctrinate employees on the principles of working for the common good and emulating model workers. In addition, they made housing and childcare arrangements, organized social activities, hosted marriages and arranged funerals/burials.

After Deng Xiaoping consolidated his power base to become China's supreme leader in 1978, the country embarked on an 'open door' policy where pragmatism and economic growth took precedence over political ideology. This policy was implemented along with the 'Four Modernizations' program to pursue development in science and technology, industry, agriculture and national defence. In 2001, China joined the World Trade Organization (WTO), under the terms of which it had to liberalize its economy. For three decades, China's economy grew at double-digit rates.

In the area of HRM, after 1992, a series of laws was enacted that: (1) gradually replaced personnel administration with human resources management; (2) phased out the system of the 'iron rice bowl'; and (3) paved the way for the implementation of market forces to coincide with China's evolution from a centrally-planned socialist to a 'mixed' economy. SOEs that once accounted for almost 80 per cent of the country's GDP now comprise only 20 per cent of China's economy. In the post-Mao era, privately-owned firms, foreign-invested enterprises (FIEs) and joint ventures (JVs) now account for the majority of China's GDP.

Every year since 2002, according to the A.T. Kearney Foreign Investor Confidence Index, China has been consistently ranked as the most attractive destination of foreign direct investment (FDI) by CEOs and CFOs from around the world. As foreign investors have a tremendous influence on their Chinese operations, there is a wide diversity of HRM approaches and practices as these often adopt the policies and programs of their respective parent companies. It is not possible to discuss all of these variations.

Staffing and employment security

To raise efficiency and compete internationally, SOEs that collectively employed over 100 million workers, underwent substantial restructuring. A major step towards this effort was downsizing since underemployment (that ended in redundancies) was widespread. To avoid social unrest, workers cannot simply be fired; rather they were laid off but continue to receive some benefits from their previous employers. To supplement their income, many of these SOE workers had to seek re-employment or wait for employment, euphemisms for seeking new employment or unemployment, respectively.

There is wide variation in HRM practices in China, however. On the one extreme are the below-average performers, where HR directors essentially continue to function as personnel managers even though their titles have changed. These continue to view their jobs as enforcing rules and policies to regulate employee behaviour. At the other extreme are high-performing FIEs whose HR policies and programs resemble international best practices with Chinese characteristics. The latter term, 'Chinese characteristics', refers to the reality that all companies in China, including FIEs that are wholly-owned subsidiaries of foreign multinationals, have to comply with Chinese labour laws and local norms.

In general, in the post-Mao era, selection and recruitment have shifted from state allocation to more market-based mechanisms, including the use of professional recruiters for hiring at the managerial level. Much emphasis is placed on a candidate's educational background and work experience. In other words, competency is stressed although personal connections (*guanxi*) continue to play a role in selection decisions.

The year 1986 witnessed the introduction of fixed-term employment contracts. The new labour law of 1994–1995 prescribed two types of employment contracts, one for the individual and another on a collective basis. The latter primarily applied to large SOEs and international joint ventures.

Job-hopping for career progression purposes is common – Chinese millennials in the 2012 PwC survey indicated that career progression is more important than competitive salaries in their decision to join an organization and only 18 per cent planned to work for the same employer on a long-term basis.

Compared to Japan and Korea, China has the best record in terms of gender equality given Mao's slogan, 'women hold up half the sky'. However, similar to the experience of other former socialist countries in Central and Eastern Europe, gender equality has regressed with economic liberalization in China.

Training and development

To upgrade the skills levels in the country, Chinese companies (both SOEs and non-SOEs) are fully cognizant of the need to train and educate workers, particularly in terms of developing managerial talent. Numerous reports suggest that there is still an extreme shortage of qualified managerial talent.

There is wide variation in types of training programs provided. In general, training emphasized the development of technical and people-oriented skills through coursework and on-the-job training.

Beginning in the 1990s, MBA programs and lower-level management courses proliferated throughout the country, particularly in the coastal regions. Like Japan and Korea, as China embarks on outward foreign direct investment (OFDI), many Chinese companies have begun to send their employees with high potential to study abroad. In addition, China has succeeded in attracting many overseas Chinese who have studied and/or worked abroad to return to China to disseminate best practice. The case of Dr Kai-Fu Lee (see the mini case at the end of this chapter) is an outstanding example of this development.

Compensation and performance appraisal

To improve efficiency, widespread evaluation of employees was introduced in both SOEs and non-SOEs and remuneration became more closely tied to performance. Merit-based compensation has become the standard for progressive SOEs, non-SOEs and FIEs. Since it is fairly standard for employers in China to provide housing or housing allowances, most non-SOEs and FIEs have to adopt similar practices.

With economic reforms, a wide wage gap emerged between SOEs and FIEs. Furthermore, there is the general belief that FIEs provided more comprehensive training to their employees. As such, many college graduates, particularly women who perceive that FIEs practice more gender equality in their employment practices, prefer to work for leading FIEs.

The wide income disparity between employees in various types of organizations and the multitude of compensation schemes has led to a surge in 2010 of China's Gini coefficient to 0.7 (1.0 being maximal inequality). China's income inequality is now among the highest in the world.

Industrial relations

Employee relations are enterprise-based although employees of SOEs and, to a lesser extent joint ventures and foreign-invested enterprises, are allowed to join one trade union only, the state-sponsored All-China Federation of Trade Unions (ACFTU). At present, members do not have the 'right to strike' as this clause was removed from the 1982 Chinese Constitution. Where grievances and conflicts arise, arbitration and conciliation occur at the enterprise level.

For reasons stated at the beginning of the chapter, while it is not possible to delve into different aspects of HRM practices in southern and southeast Asian countries, the 1997 Asian financial crisis, continued globalization of the world economy and the desire for rapid/sustained economic growth have meant that most countries in this region have tried to emulate best practices. However, studies have shown that (1) there continues to be a divergence of HRM practices between local subsidiaries of foreign-invested enterprises and domestic firms, and organizations in the private and public sectors; and, (2) challenges in implementing some of these best practices, such as HPWS. These challenges stem, in part, from deeply ingrained cultural values and attitudes, stage of economic development, and labour market inflexibilities.

Challenges

While Japan, Korea and China have all accomplished a remarkable job in leveraging their respective countries human resources to attain very rapid economic growth, challenges remain. Specifically, these pertain to the (a) ageing of the workforce, (b) a looming war for talent, and (c) HR issues associated with OFDI. Each of these challenges is outlined below.

Ageing of the workforce

Japan and Korea enjoy the dubious distinction of having the oldest populations among OECD countries. The success of the one-child policy in China has also contributed to the rapid ageing of its population – in Shanghai, a major commercial city in China, the fertility rate is 0.83 (the natural replacement rate is 2.1). An ageing workforce affects productivity and constrains economic growth as there are insufficient young employees to replace those retiring. The payout of retirement benefits, higher medical expenses and decreased tax revenues resulting from lower employment can impose enormous strains on a country's expenditure. Japan already suffers from a huge budget deficit (200 per cent of its GDP in 2012).

In general, countries can rely on four mechanisms to circumvent this trend: (1) increase birth rate, (2) extend working age, (3) immigration, and (4) greater deployment of women. Despite incentives, the downward trend in fertility has yet to be reversed. In terms of extending the working age, there is a limit. Toyota Motor Company, for example, is actively recruiting its retirees to return on a part-time basis. Furthermore, older workers may not have the skills to perform some jobs created by new technologies.

As far as immigration is concerned, both Japan and Korea have very low rates of immigration, stemming in part from the difficulty in integration of non-ethnic Japanese or Koreans into these respective societies. Only 1.6 per cent (Japan) and 2 per cent (Korea) of legal residents are foreigners. In the case of Korea, approximately half of the 'foreigners' are ethnic Koreans from China. In the light of the homogeneity in both Japanese and Korean societies, immigration presents a challenge. Resulting from the presence of ethnic minorities in China and of the large inflow of FDI, of the three countries under consideration here, China has developed a more open attitude toward foreigners.

As far as the greater use of women, this requires a very fundamental shift in societal attitude. In Japan, Korea and China, while women account for almost one-half of university graduates, there is a persistent and severe under-representation of women in managerial ranks in Japan and Korea. Again, China has a better record in this regard. Even with the election of the first woman President in Korea (Park Geun-Hye) in December 2012, many do not expect a dramatic change in attitude toward women in the workforce as Park's popularity stems largely from the fact that she is the daughter of former General Park Chung-hee, the longest-ruling dictator of Korea from 1961–1979. General Park is generally credited as the architect of Korea's economic miracle.

War for talent

In light of the ageing of the workforce in most developed and emerging countries (except India), the growing 'boundarylessness' nature of careers, and the greater relaxation of immigration/emigration barriers to movement of peoples across international boundaries, there is a growing war for talent worldwide. That is, to compete internationally, companies are willing to recruit talent from anywhere in the world regardless of country of origin and/or citizenship. 'Boundaryless' careers refer to the emerging trend where employees are willing to move from company to company and even across countries. These attitudes were borne out in the 2012 PwC survey of millennials. This attitude is also evident in the case of Dr Kai-Fu Lee at the end of this chapter.

Outward foreign direct investment

With the success of the Chinese economy, Chinese firms have now joined Japanese and Korean multinationals in OFDI. Despite the longer histories of overseas investment, Japanese and Korean multinationals continue to experience challenges abroad. A first challenge is the difficulty in recruiting the best and brightest HCNs to work for them when the job market is good – this stems, in part, from the perception by locals that a 'rice paper ceiling' exists, namely it is difficult for them to be promoted above a certain level and/or ascend the organizational ranks of corporate headquarters of these MNCs. The same challenge will most probably apply to Chinese MNCs as well – in surveys of university students in Canada and Denmark, many HCNs indicated that they would only work for Chinese MNCs if there were no better job opportunities elsewhere because many could not separate Chinese MNCs from the Chinese government.

A second challenge pertains to the perceived discrimination of women in the workplace. Sumitomo Shoji America Inc., Honda of America and Hyundai Electronics of America Inc., were targets of high profile sexual discrimination suits in the United States. Similarly, there have been allegations of sexual harassment at Japanese and Korean MNCs, such as Hyundai Motor Manufacturing Alabama. The gender-role differentiation in these two countries may have resulted in practices that can be perceived as constituting harassment in some host societies. As Chinese MNCs step up their OFDI, it remains to be seen as to whether they will also be the subjects of such suits.

The continued economic success of Japan, Korea and China depends, to a large extent, on their ability to deal with the aforementioned challenges.

Conclusion

Changes in the institutional environment have contributed to the evolution of business systems posited in Chapter 1 and, in turn, led to transitions in HRM policies and practices in Japan, Korea and China. Similar changes, albeit different in magnitude and scope, have occurred in other southeast and southern Asian countries. The evolution in staffing decisions, employment security, compensation, performance appraisal and industrial relations in the three Confucian Asia countries have been described in this chapter. To compete internationally, progressive companies in these countries have adapted the world's best practices to suit their respective countries' contexts, thus supporting the assertion made in Chapter 1 that a business system is a 'complex adaptive' mechanism. Emphasis on efficiency and the need to compete internationally that have resulted from globalization have led to greater emphasis on competence-based selection and promotion decisions and performance-based compensation schemes – these represent 'bounded convergence' with that in the West. Yet, as noted throughout the chapter, divergence continues along other dimensions in accordance with the unique circumstances and cultural traditions of these countries.

Chapter summary

- Confucianism has left its mark on many aspects of HRM practices in Japan, Korea and China, including a strong work ethic, respect for age and gender-role differentiation.

- The 'lost decade' in Japan has provided the impetus for change in different HRM practices and policies.

- The democratization of Korean society has contributed to reforms in its HRM system.

- Asian values generally derive from Confucian origins, which emphasize social harmony and proper relationships among different parties. Even countries in south-east and southern Asia that are not influenced by Confucianism share many of these values and attitudes, albeit with differences.

- The post-Mao era has witnessed seismic changes in China's HRM policies and practices.

- Many Asian nations are far behind the mature development of corporate social responsibility despite of traditional cultural roots.

Key concepts

Boundaryless careers: the emerging global trend where people are willing to move from company to company and even across countries in pursuit of career goals/ objectives.

Bounded convergence (also referred to as cross-vergence): with increased contacts among people from different countries, there is convergence along certain cultural dimensions while divergence on other cultural dimensions continues.

Confucian Asia: Asian countries that have been influenced by the teachings of ancient Chinese philosopher, Confucius.

Guanxi: personal connections.

'Iron rice bowl' (also known as 'cradle-to-grave' system): Under socialism, the Chinese government took care of all aspects of a person's life from birth to death, including

the designation of one's job and place of work, whom they marry, how many children they will have, and so on.

Lifetime employment: a psychological contract between the employer and an employee that the former will take care of the latter for life; in return, an employee identifies strongly with the company and is extremely dedicated to organizational objectives.

Millennials: people born between 1980 and 2000. They will comprise one-half of the global workforce by 2020.

'Redness' versus 'competence': the use of 'redness' (political correctness) versus 'competence' (job skills) as the primary criterion in hiring oscillated between periods of political thought reform in China.

'Rice paper ceiling': the perception by local nationals that it is difficult for them to be promoted above a certain level and/or ascend the organizational ranks of corporate headquarters of these MNCs.

Shukko: a system of temporary transfers (*shukko*) in Japan that serves a dual purpose. On the one hand, it can be used to fast-track career staff with high potentials. On the other hand, it is a mechanism for 'losing' career staff with below-average performance.

Shunto: annual collective bargaining process between management and the unions with regard to wage increases and other terms of employment in both Japan and Korea.

Talent poaching: in the looming war for talent, organizations recruit talent (i.e., highly qualified people) from competing organizations through the use of a variety of incentives.

War for talent: the competition among companies and nations to recruit talent (i.e., highly qualified people) from anywhere in the world regardless of country of origin and/or citizenship.

Review questions

1   Identify and discuss how the institutional environment (political, economic and sociocultural) has affected the evolution of HRM policies and practices in each of the East Asian countries of Japan, Korea and China.

2   Do you share the sentiments expressed by millennials contained in the 2012 PwC survey? Why or why not?

3   Do you think that Japan, Korea and China will be able to contend with the three major HR challenges that confront them? Why or why not?

4   In the light of the limited deployment of women in the managerial ranks in Japan and Korea, what are some challenges associated with sending women to work in these countries? Be specific.

1 Draw a matrix that compares and contrasts the various dimensions of HRM policies and practices in Japan, Korea and China.

2 Based on what you know about HRM policies and practices in Japan, Korea and China, if you were to work in one of these countries, which country would you choose? For the selected country, would you prefer to work for a domestic or foreign-invested enterprise? Please state the reasons for your choice.

MINI CASE

Talent poaching – the case of Dr Kai-Fu Lee[1]

Dr Kai-Fu Lee was born in Taiwan and emigrated to the United States at the age of 12. Upon graduation with a PhD from Carnegie Mellon University in computer science (specializing in speech recognition technology), he worked briefly at his alma mater and spent six years at Apple Computer. In 1998, Lee joined Microsoft and was relocated to Beijing (China) where he was responsible for establishing Microsoft Research Asia. In 2000, he returned to the United States as Microsoft's VP of Interactive Services. In 2005, Lee's departure from Microsoft for Google was the subject of a legal suit between these two technology giants.

Microsoft sought to enforce a one-year non-compete clause that Lee signed when he became VP of Interactive Services. In July 2005, Washington State Superior Court Judge Gonzalez, pending trial set for January 2006, issued a ruling that allowed Lee to work for Google but prevented him from engaging in projects that may use the proprietary information that he developed at Microsoft. At the end of December 2005, Microsoft and Google settled out of court. Lee became the founding president of Google China and oversaw Google's expansion in China.

In September 2009, Lee resigned from Google to establish his own company, Innovation Works, a $115-million venture capital fund to assist Chinese start-ups in the mobile Internet business. In a 2009 interview that appeared in *Business Week*, he explained his latest career move as follows: 'Now is really the perfect timing because of the confluence of three things. One is the tremendous talent in China that is more willing to try exciting things. Second is the growth of cloud computing, mobile internet, and e-commerce in China. We're at an inflection point for these three areas. Third, the venture space has a vacuum with no "angels" in China. That leads to a dry deal flow for mid- to late-stage funds, which have a lot of money and are unable to invest.'

Lee now lives in China. In addition to running Innovation Works, he has written an autobiography, writes a personal blog with a large following, and runs a popular website to assist Chinese youth in their studies and careers.

Questions

1 Using specific concepts learned in this chapter, how does the case of Dr Kai-Fu Lee illustrate the war for talent among firms and countries?

2 Should Microsoft have gone to court over Dr Lee? Why or why not?

3 Do you agree with the ruling made by Washington State Superior Court Judge Gonzalez that Lee should be prevented from engaging in select projects that may use proprietary information that he developed at Microsoft? Why or why not?

Web links

Managing tomorrow's people: Millennials at Work. 2012. Pricewaterhouse Coopers, accessed 31 October 2013 at: http://singapores100.com/download/PwC-Gary_Chua.pdf

Women matter: An Asian perspective. 2012. McKinsey & Co. accessed 31 October 2013 at: http://www.mckinseychina.com/2012/07/02/women-matter-an-asian-perspective/

Notes

1 Chao, L. (2010) Ex-Googler aims for China's mobile users. *Wall Street Journal.* September 6, accessed 31 October 2013 at: http://blogs.wsj.com/chinarealtime/2010/09/06/ex-googler-lee-aims-for-chinas-mobile-users; Escolar, R.E. (2008) Google conquers China: An interview with Kai-Fu Lee, 11 June, accessed 31 October 2013 at: http://www8.gsb.columbia.edu/articles/node/309

2 Hof, R. (2009) Interview: Google China's Kai-Fu Lee debuts Innovation Works. *Business Week.* September 6, accessed 31 October 2013 at: http://www.businessweek.com/the_thread/techbeat/archives/2009/09/post_18.html (Accessed January 15, 2010).

References and further readings

Aycan, Z., Kanungo, R., Mendonca, M., Yu, K., Deller, J., Stahl, G. and Kurshid, A. (2000) Impact of Culture on Human Resource Management Practices: A 10–Country Comparison. *Applied Psychology*, 49(1): 192–221.

Bae, J. (2011) Self-fulfilling Processes at a Global Level: The Evolution of Human Resource Management Practices in Korea, 1987–2007. *Management Learning*, 43(5): 579–607.

Bae, J., Chen, S.-J. and Lawler, J.J. (1998) Variations in Human Resource Management in Asian Countries: MNC Home-country and Host-country Effects. *International Journal of Human Resource Management*, 9(4): 653–670.

Benson, J. and Debroux, P. (2004) The Changing Nature of Japanese Human Resource Management. *International Studies of Management and Organization*, 34(1): 32–51.

Budhwar, P. and Boyne, B. (2004) Human Resource Management in the Indian Public and Private Sectors: An Empirical Comparison. *International Journal of Human Resource Management*, 15(2): 346–370.

Caspersz, D. (2006) The 'Talk' versus the 'Walk': High Performance Work Systems, Labor Market Flexibility and Lessons from Asian Workers. *Asia Pacific Business Review*, 12(2): 149–161.

Debrah, Y.A., McGovern, I. and Budhwar, P. (2000) Complementarity or Competition: The Development of Human Resources in a South–East Asian Growth Triangle: Indonesia, Malaysia and Singapore. *International Journal of Human Resource Management*, 11(2): 314–335.

Dobbs, R., Lund, S. and Madgavkar, A. (2012) *Talent Tensions Ahead: A CEO Briefing* (November). Washington, DC: McKinsey & Company.

Gupta, V., Surie, G., Javidan, M. and Chhokar, J. (2002) Southern Asia Cluster: Where the Old Meets the New? *Journal of World Business*, 37(1): 16–27.

Miah, M.K. and Bird, A. (2007) The Impact of Culture on HRM Styles and Firm Performance: Evidence from Japanese Parents, Japanese Subsidiaries/Joint Ventures and South Asian Local Companies. *International Journal of Human Resource Management*, 18(5): 908–923.

Morris, J., Hassard, J. and McCann, L. (2006) New Organizational Forms, Human Resource Management and Structural Convergence? A Study of Japanese Organizations. *Organization Studies*, 27(10): 1485–1511.

Rowley, C., Benson, J. and Warner, M. (2007) Towards an Asian Model of Human Resource Management? A Comparative Analysis of China, Japan and South Korea. *International Journal of Human Resource Management*, 15(4–5): 917–933.

Tung, R.L., Paik, Y. and Bae, J. (2013) Korean Human Resource Management in the Global Context. *International Journal of Human Resource Management*, 24(5): 1–17.

Warner, M. (2012) Whither Chinese HRM? Paradigms, Models and Theories. *International Journal of Human Resource Management*, 23(19): 3943–3963.

Technology Development in Asia

Leonard Lynn

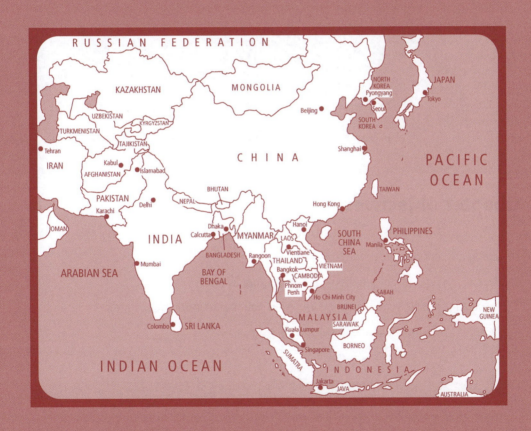

Chapter objectives

After reading this chapter you will have an understanding of:

1 Asia's rich technological heritage.

2 Ways of thinking about a nation's technological system.

3 The strengths and weaknesses of the Asian national technology systems.

4 The technological challenges now facing Asia.

Introduction: opportunities and challenges posed by Asian technology

In the twentieth century and in the first decades of the twenty-first century Singapore, Malaysia, Thailand and, most notably, the giant nations China and India, were joining Japan, South Korea and Taiwan as major centres of technological strength. In 2009 China passed Japan, becoming second only to the United States in R&D spending (see Table 5.1). India, while less impressive in R&D spending, was rapidly becoming a centre of global excellence in the knowledge-intensive service sectors and in biotechnology. Overall, Asia now accounts for around a third of global expenditures on R&D.

This growth in Asian technological strength poses opportunities and challenges for business people, policy makers, and citizens of Asian and other countries. People around the world benefit from technological advances created in the new centres of innovation where new products are created and new features are added to existing products. Increasing technological sophistication allows an improved approach to problems such as: disease, poverty and environmental degradation. Multinational enterprises, a major source of technological advance, are exploiting new opportunities to draw on rich stocks of human resources in science and engineering in China, India, Thailand, Indonesia and other parts of Asia. Lower costs in these countries allow firms to engage more people in the search for answers to technical problems than would otherwise be feasible. Sometimes researchers in different societies offer different perspectives or have different interests, which enrich approaches to the development of technology. A pharmaceutical company, for example, may find more people with expertise in infectious diseases in India than in North America or Europe. More generally, different countries tend to develop particular strengths in different fields of science or technology. In different parts of the twentieth century, for example, Germany led the way in chemical technology, the United States and the United Kingdom in aeronautics and the development of computers, and Japan in industrial robotics and manufacturing technology. Recognizing the

TABLE 5.1 Gross R&D expenditures by country 1998, 2003, 2008, 2009 (millions of purchasing power parity US dollars[1]) and as percentage of GDP (in parentheses)

	1998	2003	2008	2009
China	16.3 (0.65)	47.1 (1.13)	120.8 (1.47)	154.1 (NA[3])
India[2]	NA (0.78)	NA (0.80)	NA (0.88)	NA
Japan	91.1 (3.00)	112.3 (3.20)	148.7 (3.44)	137.9 (NA[3])
South Korea	14.6 (2.26)	24.0 (2.49)	43.9 (3.36)	NA[3]
US	226.9 (2.58)	292.0 (2.62)	403.7 (2.82)	401.6 (NA[3])

NOTES:
1 Purchasing power parity (ppp) exchange rates are based on the relative costs of certain goods and services in different countries. When wage and other costs differ greatly between countries ppp rates provide a better indicator of comparative R&D 'inputs' than market exchange rates;
2 Comparable ppp expenditures are not available for India. R&D expenditures as percentage of GDP were not available for 2009;
3 Not available.
SOURCES: Adapted from Appendix Table 4.43 in National Science Board (2012); India data from Department of Science and Technology (2009), Table 2, p.76.

need to gain access to new sources of S&T human resources, US multinationals, for example, drastically increased their R&D spending in Asia between 1998 and 2008 – from 52 million to more than one-and-a-half billion dollars in China and from 23 million dollars to more than half-a-billion dollars in India.

The rise of technological strength in India, China, and some other Asian countries, has also caused uneasiness in both Asian and Western countries. Some of this unease is based on the close relationship between technological capability and military strength. Three of the large Asian countries, China, India, and Pakistan now have nuclear capabilities.

Some Westerners see the rise of Asian technology as posing an economic threat. One widely circulated report a committee of the US National Academies of Sciences (2007) said it was 'deeply concerned that the scientific and technological building blocks critical to our [US] leadership are eroding at a time when many other nations are gathering strength … we fear the abruptness with which a lead in science and technology can be lost … It doesn't matter whether you're a lion or a gazelle – when the sun comes up, you'd better be running'. Concerns were expressed that China and India had more science and engineering graduates than the United States (see Table 5.2) and the European Union, leading to fears that the rise of Asian technology would result in the loss of well-paying jobs and innovative capacity in the west. In the past the twin forces of technological progress and globalization destroyed low-paid relatively unattractive jobs in the rich countries, but also resulted in the creation of at least as many attractive and highly-paid jobs. Now the situation may be different.

Two factors primarily accounted for the privileged position enjoyed by European and US workers in the nineteenth and twentieth centuries: they were better educated than their counterparts in Asia and elsewhere, and they were backed by greater levels of investment in technology. By the early twenty-first century these advantages were rapidly disappearing – the education gap was closing and globalization meant that capital and technology flowed freely across national boundaries. Today it is not just western blue collar workers who worry about the loss of jobs to Asia, it is also university graduates in fields like computer science, medical technology and engineering.

TABLE 5.2 Science and engineering first university degrees, in selected Asian countries (thousands)

	2000	2004	2008
China	359	672	1,143
India	NA[1]	462[1]	NA[1]
Japan	353	351	337
South Korea	97	119	130
Taiwan	40	79	93
US	399	459	496

NOTES:

1 Not available;

2 Latest year available for India was 2003.

SOURCES: Adapted from National Science Board (2012) Appendix Tables 2.32 and 2.33; Indian data from Table 25, National Science and Technology Information System, Government of India, *Research and Development Statistics* 2007–2008. Original data from University Grants Commission University Development in India, *Basic Facts and Figures*.

There have also been losers in the Asian countries entering the global technology system. Local businesses and local governments are sometimes swamped by powerful multinationals. There is a loss of local control. Older skills become obsolete. The pace of change is sometimes faster than the ability of people to adapt. Traditional values are challenged in the home and community. New technologies sometimes have negative environmental impacts.

Although they have profited from the globalization of technology development, western multinationals are concerned about the rise of powerful new competitors. Just as the earlier rise of Japan, Taiwan and South Korea presented new competitors in the automotive (Toyota, Nissan, Hyundai), home appliance (Sony, Panasonic, LG) and electronics (Samsung, Hyundai) industries, the rise of the newly emerging Asian economies of India, China and others are generating firms in biotechnology (Ranbaxy), personal computers (Lenovo), and software (Wipro, Infosys). A risk is that some of the western multinationals out of concern about their new competitors will pressure their home governments to adopt protectionist policies, thus initiating destructive trade wars.

Asian legacies in science and technology

Until the European Renaissance (fourteenth to seventeenth centuries) and the Industrial Revolution (eighteenth century), the civilizations of China and India led the world in science and technology. Japan and Korea, also were advanced in many science and technology sectors, as were some of the Southeast Asian civilizations. The first Chinese mechanical clock appeared some 600 years before its European counterpart. Chinese technologists led the world in studies of optics, acoustics and magnetism. Iron and steelmaking technology was far ahead of that in the West. Gunpowder and explosive weapons were developed in China some 300 years before they appeared in Europe. China may have led in the development of the drive belt and chain drive. The Chinese are also credited with inventing paper, block-printing and movable type, as well as porcelain. The Chinese may have been the first to use biological means to control insect pests. Vaccinations were used in China since the beginning of the 16th century and possibly several centuries earlier.[1]

India was also a world leader in science and mathematics. Indeed many of the advances in Chinese astronomy, medicine and mathematics were based on knowledge transmitted to China from India by Buddhist monks. Indian scholars developed heliocentric models of the solar system before the Greeks, and India is often credited with originating such fundamental mathematical concepts as zero, the decimal system, the algorithm and the square root. An Indian mathematician utilized differential calculus in the twelfth century.

European missionaries in the late sixteenth century were surprised by the advanced levels of technology they found in Japan. Movable type was first put to extensive use in Korea during the early fifteenth century, perhaps earlier than elsewhere in the world. The 'turtle ships' used by Koreans in fighting a Japanese invasion in the late sixteenth century, were among the world's first iron-clad warships.

Why did Asian science and technology fall behind that of the West? At one time it was thought that Asian technology had stagnated because of an innate conservatism in Asian social institutions. Now it is more widely believed that the West moved ahead because of a sudden acceleration in the development of Western science and technology, the 'scientific revolution'. During the Renaissance Europe began importing scientific and technical knowledge from Islamic civilizations. Some of this knowledge had been developed by the Greek and Roman civilizations, then lost to Europe and preserved by Arabs, Turks and Persians. Some had been created by the Islamic civilizations, and some had been transmitted by them from India, China and other civilizations. This infusion of knowledge coincided with the development of experimental science and increased application of mathematics to scientific analysis, accelerating the development of European science and technology.

The Industrial Revolution, beginning in eighteenth century United Kingdom, combined important technological advances including the use of new basic materials (especially iron and steel), sources of energy (coal, steam engines, electricity, petroleum), machines (such as the power loom and spinning jenny), transportation equipment (steam locomotives and ships), and communications equipment (telegraph). The effective use of these new technologies enabled the West to achieve economic and military dominance over much of the world, including the great civilizations of Asia.

Early Asian responses to the Western technological challenge

The Asian civilizations initially reacted to the rising technological challenges from the West with complacent self-confidence. This is exemplified in a famous letter written by the Emperor of China to the King of England in 1793. The Emperor refused to expand trade with Britain, explaining: 'As your Ambassador can see for himself, we possess all things. I see no value on objects strange or ingenious, and have no use for your country's manufactures.' In a follow-up communication the Emperor added: 'Our Celestial Empire possesses all things in prolific abundance and lacks no product within its own borders. There was therefore no need to import the manufacturings of outside barbarians in exchange for our own produce' (Blackhouse and Bland, 1914).

Beginning in the early seventeenth century the Japanese government banned Westerners from entering Japan – except for a small Dutch trading post in Nagasaki harbour. Korea was similarly isolated from the West. India, divided and weak, did not have the option of isolation. It was not able to develop a unified response to the Europeans. After a century of gradual incursions India became a British colony.

Concerns about a Western technological threat erupted in Japan with the arrival of Commodore Perry of the US Navy when Perry's flotilla arrived near Edo (modern Tokyo) in 1853. Perry demanded permission to deliver a letter from the US president. The clear military superiority of Perry's 'black ships' convinced the Japanese to allow Perry to deliver the letter and to return a year later to sign a trade treaty. Perry's crew members demonstrated such achievements of Western technology as the steam engine and telegraph. The military implications of this technological superiority were clear to the Japanese and in the mid nineteenth century China was being militarily humiliated by the British in the Opium Wars.

Leaders in both China and Japan were increasingly alarmed by these events and by the Western colonization of much of Asia. Reformers in both countries wanted to introduce Western technology as a means of maintaining independence from the West. Japan's greater political unity and stronger tradition of learning from other civilizations allowed these efforts to take effect much more quickly than was the case in China.

The Japanese government sent young Japanese abroad to study western technology and the institutions involved in creating and disseminating technology. The Japanese hoped to establish a strong national technology system, but one based on Asian values. A new government drawing on the traditional authority of imperial power, but dominated by military leaders, was established in 1868. Thousands of foreign technical experts were brought to Japan. Industrial technology was imported through joint ventures and other forms of technical links with European and US companies. In the years before World War II, Japan also successfully developed world-class technologies of its own. By the early twentieth century Japan was able, militarily, to challenge Russia, a major European power. In the 1930s Japan was itself a world power with colonies in Asia and the Pacific.

The creation of institutions and arrangements to foster technological development was much spottier in the other Asian nations. In the late nineteenth and early twentieth centuries Chinese reformers were thwarted by entrenched interests. China was torn apart by foreign powers supporting various regional war lords into the 1930s, then by Civil War and the Japanese invasion. Virtually all the other Asian countries were colonies until the late 1940s.

The revival of Asian technology

In the last half of the twentieth century most Asian countries gained greater freedom of action. They sought to develop policies and institutions that would lead to rapid industrialization and greater technological strength. Throughout Asia there were strong debates about the best way to achieve technological strength. Some thought it best to foster the development of domestic capabilities by keeping out foreign companies and refusing to pay seemingly exorbitant fees for foreign intellectual property. Some believed that opening the doors to foreigners would result in the Asian countries falling back into a quasi-colonial status. Others favoured more exposure to international flows of technology and the challenge of foreign competition.

Japan

After World War II Japan was handicapped by widespread destruction at home, a lack of foreign exchange, and poor access to international flows of scientific and technical information. Under the terms of its surrender Japan was not allowed to develop certain strategic industries such as aviation and nuclear energy.

To fully utilize scarce domestic resources Japanese policy makers concentrated on the development of industries such as electrical power generation, steelmaking and shipbuilding as these were seen as key to the development of other industries. Advanced technologies were imported for *these* industries but, because of Japan's balance of payments problems, the government tightly controlled technological imports. Japanese firms were prevented from purchasing technologies that did not seem critical to Japan's economic development. Foreign firms were discouraged from moving into Japan, even when they might have brought technology with them.

Japan quickly developed its technological capabilities. Its technological advance was supported by a strong education system and a favourable global political and economic environment (including strong United States support to build up Japanese industry during the Korean War, and later during the Cold War, and also by the liberalization of international trade).[2]

China

Once the Chinese civil war effectively ended in 1949, the Chinese government sought to promote the advance of science and technology. Initially, China relied on its Communist ally, the USSR, as it tried to build a modern technology system. Soviet technology, know-how and technical experts were imported on a large scale. The Soviet system also provided a model for the Chinese during this period.

The former Academia Sinica was re-established as the Chinese Academy of Sciences (CAS) and new R&D institutions were set up. The new system emphasized the integration of research and production, with research expected to have immediate practical applications. In 1956 the government announced a 12-year science and technology plan aimed to make China an industrial leader. The basic research institutes were controlled by the CAS, the applied and military research institutes were controlled by industrial ministries. Training was the responsibility of the universities. In 1960 China's relations with the Soviet Union cooled, increasing China's isolation and its attempt to move to technological autonomy.

Two decades later, under Deng Xiao-ping, China initiated a series of reforms, increasingly opening the economy to foreign investment (and actively seeking it in some areas), and shifting activities to the private sector. In 1985 science and technology at public research institutes was separated from the production activities of state-owned enterprises.[3]

India

After India gained its independence in 1947 it established a system of national research laboratories based on the French model. Under the Council for Scientific and Industrial Research there were some two dozen institutes with scientists encouraged to develop new products for Indians. New engineering schools were established, including some of the now-famous Indian Institutes of Technology.

Policy emphasized indigenous technical capability. Prime Minister Jawaharal Nehru reportedly believed that 'if an item of equipment was imported from abroad, all one got was that particular instrument. But if one built it oneself, an all-important lesson in expertise was learnt as well'.[4] India's Scientific Policy Resolution of 1958 emphasized sustainable and equitable development. In a Technology Policy Statement in 1983 the Indian government declared science and technology to be the basis of economic progress. The Resolution advocated making the maximum use of Indian resources and to develop technological self-reliance. Traditional skills and capabilities were to be used so as to ensure maximum development at minimum cost. The policy stated that: 'Fullest support will be given to the development of indigenous technology to achieve technological self-reliance and reduce the dependence on foreign inputs ... Support must therefore be provided ... in favor of products made through indigenously developed technologies.'[5] As in Japan proposed technology imports were critically evaluated, and often discouraged, as was the establishment of R&D facilities by foreign firms. Many of India's best scientists and engineers left for more attractive career opportunities in the United States or Europe.

India's spending on scientific research was only 0.1 per cent of gross national product (GNP) in 1947. A decade later this had increased to 0.5 per cent (still far below the 2–3 per cent common in most developed nations).

National innovation systems

A highly influential tool for understanding a nation's technological strength has been the 'national innovation systems' (NIS) framework. This framework first gained widespread prominence when Freeman (1987) used it to explain Japan's spectacular economic success in the decades immediately following World War II. The NIS framework was later used as an analytic tool (and guide for policy makers) by the Organisation for Economic Co-operation and Development (OECD) and has been used as a model in many Asian countries.

The NIS has been variously defined, but is generally taken to include the network of interconnected institutions within a country that create, store, disseminate and exploit technologies. These institutions include universities, government laboratories, think tanks, corporate research laboratories, professional associations and other organizations. They also include management practices and patterns of interfirm relationships.[6] The NIS framework has been used to evaluate the innovative strength of various economies, and to suggest 'leverage points' where policy interventions might increase the effectiveness of a system.

Figure 5.1 summarizes some of the elements attributed to the Japanese NIS in the late twentieth century. The Japanese government, most notably the Ministry of International Trade and Industry (reorganized into the Ministry of Economy, Trade and Industry in 2001), but also other Ministries as well as trade associations and academics, played a coordinating role in the Japanese NIS. The government issued visions based on projections of technological trajectories. Based on the visions, and with government support, firms organized research consortia to avoid redundancies of effort and bring together complementary strengths. The Japanese government pressured foreign firms to share technology as a condition of entering the Japanese market and assured that major firms in key industries had money to invest in R&D, and in new plant and equipment.

In Japan firms were often organized into 'keiretsu'. Keiretsu are groups of firms centred on banks and other financial institutions, but including general trading companies, large manufacturing companies in key industries, and networks of smaller firms that supply the manufacturing companies with components and services. Keiretsu members supported each other and engaged in collective long term planning, including investment in large scale technology projects. Being financed by loans from affiliated financial institutions, rather than equity and debt markets, keiretsu firms could invest heavily in R&D with minimal concern about short term results that might drive down stock or bond prices.

Japanese employment practices were also credited with contributing to Japan's technological successes. Since the regular employees of major firms typically spend their careers at

Government
Brings together industry, government, academic experts to determine future industrial and technological needs
Coordinate Japan's advance to vanguard in these trends

Corporate system
Keiretsu groups with members in finance, trade and industrial supply chains to jointly develop technology and invest for long term

Financial system
Provides 'patient capital'to firms

Education system
Provides good basic education in mathematics and science for factory workers
Trains large numbers of engineers

Employment system
Career-long employment – allowing centrally controlled career paths
Large investment in employees

FIGURE 5.1 A stylized model of the Japanese national innovation system

a single firm, the firm could invest heavily in their development. There was little concern that the investment would be lost when employees took jobs at other firms. Engineers at major Japanese firms were rotated between R&D, manufacturing and customer service. This gave them a holistic view of technology and customer needs, which was thought to enhance the ability of Japanese firms to commercialize technology.

The Japanese NIS was widely credited with helping Japan reach the frontier in industrial technology. Governments and international organizations such as the OECD closely studied the Japanese NIS seeking lessons for improving the innovative capacity of other countries. Some other Asian countries began modelling their innovation systems on Japan's.

As the Japanese economy faltered in the 1990s, however, the limitations of Japan's technology policies became apparent with its need to extend its technological frontiers. While some technological breakthroughs are predictable, others, such as the Internet and cell phones, are less so. While the Japanese financial system allowed firms to plan for the long-term, it also allowed firms to continue investing in technologies that were not succeeding. Japan's powerful technology companies such as Fujitsu, Hitachi and Sony might have fared better in competition with fast rising firms like Samsung if they had been pressured by shareholders to move more quickly out of less promising businesses. Further, while *keiretsu* firms can participate easily in joint technology development projects with fellow group members, they are less free to work with other, new none group, partners.

The Japanese education system (like that of some other Asian countries) was criticized for emphasizing rote learning at the expense of creativity. While the Japanese employment system allowed firms to invest more in the technological expertise of their employees, it was less efficient in the allocation of human resources. Some Japanese firms, for example, 'stockpiled' electrical and electronics engineers in the 1980s, and then found they did not need them. The engineers kept their jobs, but their training was wasted.

Finally, in Japan (as in South Korea) the emphasis on supporting large firms entailed a de facto discrimination against small and medium sized enterprises. These firms found it hard to obtain the capital they needed to develop and entrepreneurship was stunted.

It should be noted that the NIS framework has its critics. Some say it does little more than to list the institutions and practices involved in the development of technology. It sheds little light on the creation and dissolution of institutions. Others say that in a world of increasing globalization it may make less and less sense to focus on national innovation systems. Firms and intellectual property now flow freely across national boundaries. A focus on national innovation systems can also lead to techno-nationalism, a sense that nations are in a zero sum competition with each other in which technological successes in one country are taken as threatening other countries, rather than providing a potential resource for them.[7]

Current challenges[8]

Many Asian economies have made important progress in developing their national innovation systems in recent years. This is reflected by such indicators as patent counts, publications in top scientific journals, R&D spending (see Table 5.3), and numbers of science and technology personnel (see Table 5.4). While recognizing the achievements reflected in these indicators, it should be kept in mind that each of them has limitations when comparing the S&T strength and evaluating the growth of different national innovation systems. Firms may acquire large numbers of patents for strategic purposes such as blocking other firms from controlling key technologies, so numbers of patents may not reflect the actual creation of new technology. Some technological advances are difficult to patent, or may be more easily protected by secrecy rather than by the disclosures required by patents. English language technical and scientific journals are dominant, giving an advantage to English-speaking scientists. R&D spending reflects the *effort* to create new technology, not the actual creation of new technology. And, different accounting practices may result in some things being counted as R&D expenses in one country that would not be in another (is the salary paid to a janitor who cleans a lab a research expense?). A country may train large numbers of engineers and scientists, but not use them effectively. Countries also vary in what some scholars call 'absorptive capacity': the ability to identify and commercialize new technology wherever the technology might come from. Not all S&T advances are beneficial to society. Some contribute only to the military strength of one country compared to its neighbours or the commercial strength of one multinational against its rivals.

Japan

In Japan the central challenges facing science and technology policy makers in the early twenty-first century was how to make the country a leader, as opposed to simply being a follower and incremental improvers. Other Asian economies were becoming as skilled as the Japanese as fast followers and incremental improvers. Moreover their costs were lower. Japan was not closing the gap with the United States in reaching the frontiers of technology development. At the same time policy makers in Japan believed that a strong NIS was needed to help Japan cope with the problems of an ageing populating and shrinking work force.

TABLE 5.3 Gross domestic expenditures on R&D as percentage of GDP (large Asian countries)

	2000	2004	2007
India	0.77	0.77	0.80 (estimate)
China	0.90	1.23	1.44
Japan	3.04	3.17	3.44
South Korea	2.30	2.68	3.21
Pakistan	0.13	NA[1]	0.67
Indonesia	0.07	NA[2]	NA[2]
Philippines	NA[3]	NA[3]	NA[3]
Thailand	0.25	0.26	NA[4]

NOTES:
1 Pakistan's was 0.44 in 2005, the 2000 percentage is based on partial data;
2 Indonesia's percentage was 0.05 in 2005;
3 The Philippines' percentage was 0.15 in 2002 and 0.12 in 2005;
4 Thailand was estimated at 0.25 in 2006;
5 Data unavailable for Bangladesh.
SOURCE: UNESCO Institute for Statistics as reported in UNESCO (2010).

TABLE 5.4 Total researchers and per million inhabitants 2002 and 2007 (large Asian countries)

	2002		2007	
	Total	Per million	Total	Per million
India	115,936	111	154,827	137
China	810,525	630	1,423,380	1,071
Japan	646,547	5,087	709,974	5,573
South Korea	141,917	3,023	221,928	4,627
Pakistan	12,689	77	26,338	152
Indonesia	42,722	205	NA	NA
Philippines	5,860	71	6,896	81
Thailand	18,114	281	20,506	311
US	1,342,450	4,566	1,425,550	4,663

NOTE: Data unavailable for Bangladesh.
SOURCE: UNESCO (2010).

Wide ranging criticisms have been made of the Japanese system. Bureaucratic barriers have kept its universities from contributing new technologies as effectively as their United States counterparts. Japan's employment and industrial systems have made it difficult to establish entrepreneurial firms and its technological resources have been concentrated in large companies.

Reforms were initiated to address these problems. University professors were given greater freedom to work on technological development projects with companies, and between 2002 and 2007 the number of joint industry-university research projects doubled. Changes were made in financial markets to provide more venture capital. It is not clear how successful these reforms will be in enhancing the creativity of Japanese technology. Some fear, for example, that the Japanese are blindly remaking their system of higher education based on the US model without considering how suitable that model may be for Japan.

As Tables 5.1 to 5.4 show, many indicators of technological strength show Japan continues as a world leader. Yet, Japan has still not entirely opened itself up to potentially beneficial foreign inputs of technology. It continues to have the lowest levels of import penetration, inward foreign direct investment and foreign workers of any member of the OECD.[9] Between 2002 and 2007 the numbers of patents issued to the Japanese dropped, as did Japan's share of scientific publications.

China[10]

Over the closing decades of the twentieth century China continued its integration into the global economy. It joined the WTO in 2001 and encouraged foreign investment. In 2005 the Chinese State Council released medium- and long-term science and technology plans to cover the period until 2020. The plans call for China to increase R&D spending to 2.5 per cent of the country's GDP by 2020, around the level of the advanced economies, and to move China into the top rank of countries in terms of patents and highly-cited scientific papers. China's R&D spending had grown from 0.60 per cent of GDP in 1996 to 1.23 per cent by 2003. As Table 5.1 shows, it reached nearly 1.5 per cent in 2008. During these years Chinese spending on R&D was increasing at around 20 per cent a year. Other policies included government procurement programmes, tax incentives, measures to encourage foreign firms to transfer technology to China and policies to encourage expatriate Chinese scientists and engineers to return to China. Recognizing the environmental problems industrialization was bringing to China, the government set goals to reduce per capita energy consumption and the emission of pollutants.

China is now behind only the United States and Japan in the numbers of its scientific publications, though the rate of citations per paper is only about one-third that of the United States and less than half that of Japan, Germany and France. In 2003 China became the third country, after the United States and the USSR to send astronauts into space. Some Chinese multinationals, including Huawei, Lenovo and Geely are setting up R&D facilities in the West and also gaining R&D capabilities by making foreign acquisitions.

Despite these impressive successes, China still faces a number of challenges as it improves its NIS. While China's education system has greatly improved, the percentage of its young people receiving higher education is still relatively low, and only a relatively small number of its universities are of high quality. The Chinese system of intellectual property rights protection has been hotly criticized and may be a barrier to R&D in China. It makes foreign firms reluctant to conduct high-level technology development activities in China and it reduces the incentive for Chinese to invest in the creation of new technology. Further poor intellectual property rights protection has made it difficult for Chinese firms to license foreign technologies. This has sometimes posed problems. It might be noted, however, that China had no patent laws at all before 1985, and there are signs the Chinese government now takes intellectual property seriously.

India

Reforms in the early 1990s substantially opened up the Indian economy, and since then the country has successfully built hi-tech and knowledge-intensive industries. Through the 1990s the Indian economy grew at an average rate of 8.1 per cent a year, with some of the growth attributed to the software industry – revenues of which grew from $197 million to $8 billion. Software exports over this period increased from $100 million to $6.3billion.[11]

In 2003 a new Science and Technology Policy was announced under which Indian R&D spending was targeted to rise from the 0.8 per cent of GDP in 2003 to 2.0 per cent of GDP by 2007 (the ratio actually only reached 0.88 per cent). India's Eleventh Five-Year Plan (2007–2012) had provisions intended to strengthen India's NIS. It called for massive increases in public spending on science and technology and for enlarging the pool of science and technology personnel. In 2005 India revised its patent laws to bring them into compliance with WTO agreements on intellectual property rights.

Government policies also increasingly encouraged foreign R&D activities in India. By the end of 2009 there were 750 foreign R&D centres in India. General Electrics (GE) invested more than $80 million in the John F. Welch Technology Center in Bangalore. The centre features state of-the art laboratories and more than 2,500 engineers and scientists. Senior officials at GE and other multinationals describe their facilities in India as equalling those in the United States. As Indian technology has globalized official policy statements have shifted from concerns about foreign control of technology to the need for India to strengthen its protection of intellectual property rights. India's national laboratories are highly regarded, and its institutes of technology are among the best technical universities in the world.

India was also moving outward in its participation in technology development networks. From around 2005 Indian multinationals aggressively began to acquire technology-based foreign firms. Sixteen Indian firms acquired major western firms to gain access to technology. The number of Indian scientific publications nearly doubled between 2002 and 2008.

The Indian technology system, too, however, is faced with daunting challenges. The country's basic education system and most of its higher education system are still weak. One study found that a quarter of the teachers in public elementary schools were absent, and half of those present were not actually teaching at any given time. The percentage of India's workers with a higher education is somewhat lower than China's and R&D spending is much lower.[12] Critics also point out that only a small percentage of the Indian population has so far benefited from the advance of Indian high technology.

Other Asian countries

In the first decade of the twenty-first century South Korea regarded science and technology as core to its national aspiration of becoming an 'advanced country' and a world power. South Korea hoped to reach a target of R&D expenditures amounting to 5 per cent of GDP by 2012 with low carbon green growth. Investments in R&D doubled between 2001 and 2007. The number of patents registered overseas tripled and the number of scientific articles published more than doubled. Taiwan and Singapore also have become 'advanced economies' with regard to national innovation systems.

Many of the Southeast Asian states have become integrated into the global technology value chains of multinational firms. In part this is driven by the intensification of globalization through the WTO and other international bodies that have made it increasingly difficult for countries to maintain autonomous technology policies. In part it is driven by countries seeking opportunities for economic development though cooperation with foreign multinationals. The smaller economies, however, lack the bargaining power of China, India and Japan, and doubts have been raised about the degree to which globalization is helping them to increase their indigenous technological capabilities and the degree to which they can distribute the benefits of technological globalization to their citizens. Some research suggests that while Singapore has done well in this regard, Malaysia, Thailand and other countries have been less successful.[13]

Two of the large Asian countries are struggling to find roles in the emergent global technology system. While Pakistan, as shown in Table 5.3, is a little behind India in spending on R&D as a percentage of GDP and leads slightly in number of researchers per million of population (Table 5.4), it has not been a popular R&D host for foreign investment. Indonesia lags in spending on R&D.

Chapter summary

- The Asian economies, particularly China and India, have recently increased their technological capabilities to world class levels. This poses both challenges and opportunities for the world's rich countries.

- Before the Industrial Revolution of the eighteenth century, the civilizations of China and India led the world in science and technology.

- The technological rise of the West posed severe challenges for the major Asian civilizations, but (with the notable exception of Japan) most of the Asian civilizations were unable to respond until the late twentieth century.

- One way of understanding a nation's technological capabilities is to think of it in terms of national innovation or national technology systems, though this framework has limitations that must be considered.

- Japan was the first modern Asian country to catch up with the West technologically, and so provided a model that has been followed (in part) by other Asian countries.

- China initially tried to adopt a Soviet model of technological development, but eventually discarded this.

- India attempted unsuccessfully to foster its technological capabilities by keeping out foreign firms.

- Today Japan still sees itself as lacking sufficient technological creativity. China and India, despite their recent advances have problems related to the protection of intellectual property, insufficient private sector spending on R&D and education.

Key concepts

Absorptive capacity: the ability of a company or country to use technology developed elsewhere.

Intellectual property rights: rights the creator of intellectual property (inventions, books, music, etc.) holds. They may be protected by patents, copyrights or secrecy.

National innovation system (NIS): a framework for thinking about how various institutions contribute to a nation's ability to create new technology.

Techno-nationalism: the notion that technology development is a zero sum game between nations in which one nation's success is detrimental to the well-being of other nations.

Review questions

1 The rapid increase in the technological strength of large Asian countries poses both challenges and opportunities for businesses and governments both in the West and in Asia. What are these challenges and opportunities for those in the West? What are they for those in Asia (including the smaller Asian nations)? Which challenges and opportunities are common to the West and Asia?

2 After centuries of leadership why did Asia fall behind the West in science and technology? Why might it be useful to understand the reasons for this?

3 Japan's NIS was considered to be wildly successful after World War II and into the last two decades of the twentieth century. Aspects of it were imitated by other countries both in Asia (e.g., South Korea, Malaysia, Singapore) and the West. What is a 'national innovation system'? Describe the major components/characteristics of Japan's NIS. In the past few decades there has been considerable scepticism about the efficacy of the Japanese NIS. Why?

4 China, India and Japan all face significant challenges with regard to their technological capabilities. What are the major challenges facing each of these countries, and how likely are they to be overcome over the next 20 years?

5 Many Asian countries are attempting to sharply increase their spending on R&D. What are the costs and benefits of a country investing heavily in R&D?

Learning activities and discussions

1 Use the internet to find out how different Asian countries now compare in spending on R&D.

2 China and India both have a history of announcing national innovation systems plans. Use the Internet to see how the plans of the two countries compare. Which country is more successful in implementing the plans? Why do you think this is the case?

Technology policy and broader social issues
Apple versus Samsung Electronics – the 'patent battle of the century'

In April 2011 Apple sued Samsung Electronics alleging that Samsung had infringed design patents for the iPhone, iPad and iOS operating systems. Apple demanded approximately $2.5 billion in damages from Samsung. Samsung countered with allegations that Apple had infringed Samsung patents, including two of which were essential to 3G technology.

Apple then broadened its claims, saying Samsung had blatantly copied the look and feel of Apple's devices in the Samsung's Galaxy smartphones and tablets. Apple presented pictures showing that pre-iPhone Samsung Smartphones looked substantially different from the iPhone, while those marketed after the iPhone looked like iPhones. Apple said that Google and other companies had warned Samsung that certain Samsung tablets looked too much like copies of the iPad, and asked Samsung to provide a more 'distinguishable design'.

Samsung argued that it had started designing smartphones that resembled the iPhone before the iPhone was released. Samsung released an internal design presentation from September 2006 that featured GUI layouts and adjustable orientations. Samsung argued that with the iPhone design Apple had actually copied Sony. Samsung said that before the iPhone design had been conceived, an Apple executive sent an article about Sony designs for portable electronic devices to Steve Jobs and other Apple executives. Shortly after an Apple industrial designer was asked to prepare a 'Sony-like' design for an Apple phone.

Apple responded by saying it had an earlier prototype of the iPhone called 'Purple' dating back to 2005.

Regarding the Samsung 3G patents, Apple claimed that Samsung had deceived the international body responsible for creating 3G mobile cellular systems for networks standards, slipping Samsung patents into the standards, thus illegally monopolizing technology markets. Samsung accused Apple of using its lawsuit to stifle legitimate competition so as to maintain 'its historically exorbitant profits'. Samsung asserted that the Android phones made by Samsung and other firms offer a more flexible open operating system with more product choices than the Apple phones, and said Apple was trying to restrict market access for these phones. Over the following months the battle between the two corporate giants took on global dimensions, being placed before more than 30 courts on four continents.

Intellectual property

Patent laws are intended to promote technological progress. The patent holder is given exclusive rights to the invention for a limited period of time. During this period s/he can realize monopoly profits. This provides an incentive for inventors to invest time and money developing new products. To secure the patent, however, the inventor cannot keep the invention secret, but must give a detailed description of it. This contributes to the technological advance of society.

How much should intellectual property laws protect and benefit the creator of intellectual property? Too little and few will bother continuing development of new and improved products. Too much and the new technology will be so expensive that it will be under used. What really represents enough of an advance to constitute legitimate intellectual property? Some patents may represent a trivial or obvious advance. In effect the patent may slow progress by forcing the payment of royalties when none are deserved. Additionally, many businesses engage in 'defensive patenting'. They might register patents, for example, just so they can counter-sue if they are accused of violating someone else's patent. Defensive patents can also be used to prevent others from applying for similar patents.

Apple Inc. and Samsung Electronics

Apple Inc., a US multinational corporation, is famous for designing and marketing consumer electronics, computer software and personal computers including the iPod, iPhone, iPad iTunes media browser and the iOS mobile operating system. Apple operates more than 300 retail stores in 10 countries, and an online store selling hardware and software products. It has around 50,000 employees and worldwide annual sales of more than $65 billion. *Fortune* magazine named Apple the most admired company in the United States in 2008, and in the world in 2008, 2009 and 2010. However, the company has also been widely criticized for its contractors' labour, environmental and business practices.

In 2001 Apple introduced the iPod portable digital audio player – over 100 million units were sold within six years. In 2003, Apple's iTunes Store was introduced, offering online music downloads and integration with the iPod. The service quickly became the market leader in online music services. Apple became the third-largest mobile handset supplier in the world due to the popularity of its iPhone. In 2010 Apple released the iPad, a large screen, tablet-like media device. The iPad runs the same operating system as the iPhone, and many iPhone apps are compatible with the iPad. This instantly gave the iPad a large app catalogue. On the day the iPad was launched in the United States it sold more than 300,000 units. In 2010, Apple also released the fourth generation iPhone and refreshed its iPod line of MP3 players.

Samsung Electronics was founded in 1969 as a division of South Korea's Samsung group. By 2012 Samsung Electronics had annual sales of more than $140 billion, more than 200,000 employees in 61 countries and was rated as the twelfth most powerful brand in the world. Samsung is the world largest mobile phone manufacturer and the world's largest technology firm by sales. Samsung launched the Galaxy line of mobile phones in 2010, challenging the dominance of the i-Phone.

'The patent trial of the century'

After Apple sued Samsung and Samsung counter-sued, a German court granted Apple a preliminary injunction against the sale and marketing of the

Samsung Galaxy Tab 10.1 across most of Europe (the ban was later temporarily lifted in the European Union, outside Germany). Meanwhile Samsung filed a claim with the Federal Court of Australia accusing Apple of infringing on seven Samsung patents in the iPhone and iPad.

Efforts to negotiate a settlement between the companies failed, and in August 2012, a US jury ruled that Samsung should pay Apple over one billion dollars in damages. Samsung said they would appeal against the court ruling. A week later the Tokyo District Court gave Samsung a partial victory, ruling that Samsung's mobile devices did not violate an Apple patent that allows mobile devices and personal computers to share data. In October Samsung filed a new lawsuit against Apple in a US court, contending the iPhone 5 infringed Samsung patents.

Questions

1 A good patent system should reward inventors so that they have strong incentives to invent, provide desirable new products and encourage the flow of new knowledge. How well did the current system function in the Apple–Samsung patent war?

2 From the standpoint of consumers would it be better if Apple or Samsung wins? Why?

Web links

Technology development in Japan: www.mext.go.jp/english/

Technology development in China: www.most.gov.cn/eng/

Technology development in India: http://dst.gov.in/

Technology development in South Korea: http:/english.moe.go.kr/enMain.do

Notes

1   The history of Chinese science and technology is extensively documented by Joseph Needham in numerous works. See, for example, Needham (1969). Also see Graham (1973).

2   A good source on the evolution of technology policy in Japan until the late 20th century is Samuels (1994).

3   See, for example, Simon (1988) for events in China during this period.

4   Greenstein, G. (1992). A gentleman of the old school: Homi Bhabha and the development of science in India. *American Scholar*, 61, (3), 417 as cited in Guha (2007).

5   Government of India, Department of Science and Technology website: http://dst.gov.in/

6   Key sources on national innovation systems include Freeman (1987) and Nelson (1993).

7   See for example, Lynn and Salzman, (2006) and Lynn et al. (2012).

8   The following section draws extensively on UNESCO (2010).

9   OECD statistics cited in *The Economist*, 1–7 December, 2007, Special Report on Business in Japan.

10 Some recent sources on China: Segal (2002), Sull (2005) and Popkin and Iyengar (2007).

11 For a readable account of the rise of one of the major Indian software companies, see Hamm (2007). Also see Popkin and Iyengar (2007).

12 To learn more about the challenges facing the Indian technology system see National Research Council (2007).

13 See, for example, Doner and Ritchie's (2003) discussion of hard drive production in Southeast Asia.

References and further reading

Blackhouse, E. and Bland, J.O.P. (1914) *Annals and Memoirs of the Court of Peking*. Boston: Houghton Mifflin.

Department of Science and Technology (2009) *R&D Statistics*. New Delhi: Government of India.

Doner, R.F. and Ritchie, B. (2003) Economic Crisis and Technological Trajectories, in W. Keller and R. Samuels, R. (eds.) *Crisis and Innovation in Asian Technology*. Cambridge: Cambridge University Press, pp. 187–225.

Freeman, C. (1987) *Technology Policy and Economic Performance: Lessons from Japan*. London: Pinter Publishers.

Graham, A.C. (1973) China, Europe, and the origins of modern science. In Nakayama, S. and Sivin, N. (eds.) *Chinese Science: Explorations of an Ancient Tradition*. Cambridge, MA: MIT Press, pp. 45–69.

Guha, R. (2007) *India after Gandhi: The History of the World's Largest Democracy*. New York: Harper Collins.

Hamm, S. (2007) *Bangalore Tiger: How Indian Tech Upstart Wipro is Rewriting the Rules of Global Competition*. New York: McGraw-Hill.

Lynn, L. and Salzman, H. (2006) Collaborative Advantage, *Issues in Science and Technology*, Winter, 74–82.

Lynn, L., Meil, P. and Salzman H. (2012) Reshaping global technology Development: Innovation and Entrepreneurship in China and India, *Journal of Asia Business Studies*, 6(2): 143–159.

National Research Council (2007) *India's Changing Innovation System*. Washington, DC: The National Academies Press.

National Science and Technology Information System, Government of India, *Research and Development Statistics 2007–2008*, accessed 4 November 2013 at: http://www.dst.gov.in/about_us/ar07-08/ar07-08index.htm

National Science and Technology Information System, Government of India, *Research and Development statistics 2007–2008*.

National Science Board (2012) *Science and Engineering Indicators*: National Science Foundation (NSB 12-01).

National Science Foundation, Division of Science Resources Statistics (2007) Asia's Rising Science and Technology Strength: Comparative Indicators for Asia, the European Union and the United States. NSF 07-319. Arlington, VA.

Needham, J. (1969) *The Grant Titration: Science and Society in East and West*. Toronto: University of Toronto Press.

Nelson, R.R. (ed.) (1993) *National Innovation Systems: A Comparative Analysis*. New York: Oxford University Press.

Organisation for Economic Co-operation and Development (1999) *Managing National Innovation Systems*. Paris: OECD.

Organisation for Economic Co-operation and Development (Various years) *Main Science and Technology Indicators*. Paris: OECD.

Popkin, J.M. and Iyengar, P. (2007) *IT and the East: How China and India are Altering the Future of Technology and Innovation*. Boston: Harvard Business School Press.

Samuels, R.A. (1994) *Rich Nation, Strong Army*. Ithaca, NY: Cornell University Press.

Segal, A. (2002) *Digital Dragon: High-Technology Enterprises in China*. Ithaca, NY: Cornell University Press.

Simon, D.F. (1988) *Technological Innovation in China*. Cambridge, MA: Ballinger.

Sull, D.N. with Wang, Y. (2005) *Made in China*. Boston, MA: Harvard Business School Press.

UNESCO (2010) *2010 UNESCO Science Report*., Paris: UNESCO Publishing. Accessed 4 November 2013 at: http://www.unesco.org/new/en/natural-sciences/science-technology/prospective-studies/unesco-science-report/

US National Academies of Science/National Academy of Engineering/Institute of Medicine (2007) *Rising Above the Gathering Storm: Energizing and Employing America for a Brighter Economic Future*. Washington, DC: National Academies Press.

Regionalism and Production Networks in Asia

Andrew Staples

6

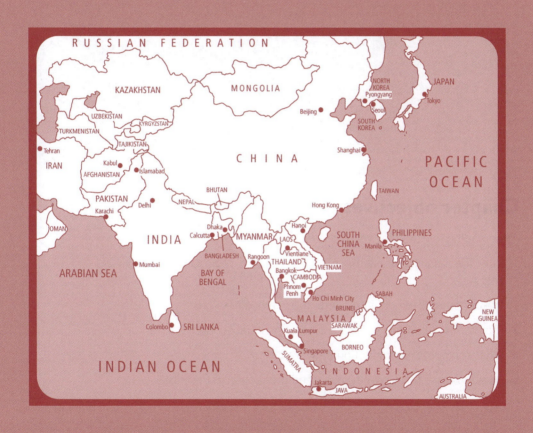

Chapter objectives

After reading this chapter, you will understand:

1 How the business systems model relates to regional production in East Asia.

2 The importance of adopting a regional perspective.

3 The broader relevance of the East Asian political economy.

4 What constitutes a production network.

5 How Japanese firms have regionalized production in East Asia.

Introduction

Redding notes that the business system is embedded in the institutional fabric and that both rest on societal culture meaning that 'each society does things in its own way' (2009: 12). Simply put, this is what makes Toyota a Japanese firm and Apple an US firm. Yet at the same time firms are not confined to their domestic (institutional and societal) settings and indeed it may be said that globalization is fundamentally about firms seeking resources, production sites and markets *outside* their national boundaries. What, then, are the implications of globalization for the business systems approach? Moreover, if business systems are complex adaptive systems 'in which the business component of a society is analysed against the context of that society' (Redding, 2009:10), how can the reality of international business be captured and effectively analysed by the model?

Part II of this book considers the business systems found in individual Asian economies but the central aim of this chapter is to examine the implications of *regionalism* and *regional production networks* for the business systems approach with particular reference to the coordination layer of the model – that is, how firms are organized on a regional basis. This chapter is organized as follows: the remainder of this section outlines the importance and relevance of adopting a regional perspective before we turn our attention in the second section to the concept of the regional production network by locating it within major theoretical approaches to international production. In the third section we become more familiar with the context of East Asia before subsequent sections provide examples of such networks in Asia utilizing an industry and firm level perspective. We conclude by returning to the question posed by globalization for the business system model.

Global to regional

Globalization continues to forge a more interdependent and interrelated world resulting in 'global shifts' in the geography of economic activity (Dicken, 2010). Rather than slowing down in response to the (on-going) global financial crisis, which emerged in 2008, the pace of change may have instead accelerated and the direction is clear; economic and political power is flowing east. Global shifts have been led by the multinational enterprise (MNE) and facilitated by rapid advances in information and communications technology (ICT) and the prevailing, if contested, hegemony of neo-liberal ideology.[1] At the same time it is increasingly clear that a regional disaggregation of these processes is necessary for us to grasp the complex realities of the contemporary international division of labour. Indeed, while the globalization debate continues to stimulate and inform mainstream discourse, the regionalization of production, trade and investment continues apace. When considered alongside concomitant regionalism[2] the increasing importance of the region becomes clear.

Three factors support this assertion: first, global economic activity is overwhelmingly located in three regional nodes of East Asia, Europe and North America and all exhibit greater or lesser degrees of economic integration, with Europe's single market, currency and parliament (political integration) at the most advanced stage[3] while North America (through NAFTA[4]) and East Asia follow, although care should be taken to avoid overstating the depth and cohesion of these latter two regions. Second, our allegedly 'global' multinationals have been shown, in fact, to be overwhelmingly regional in nature in terms of both markets and organizational structure (Rugman, 2005[5]). Toyota, for instance, may be globally recognized but just under 75 per cent of sales and 90 per cent of production in 2012 took place in Asia Pacific (including Japan) and North America with the respective figures for Europe at just over 10 per cent and 5 per cent. Additionally, Toyota's global operations are managed by regional headquarters in Europe (Belgium), North America (the United States) and Asia (Singapore, Thailand and China in addition to home operations in Japan) (Toyota, 2012). Third, in recent years the multilateral trading system under the World Trade Organization (WTO) has stuttered to a halt as repeated attempts to conclude the Doha 'development' round of further trade liberalization have failed. As a result of this multilateral vacuum the world has witnessed a huge expansion in bilateral and regional free trade agreements (FTAs), not least in East Asia (see Figure 6.1).

The regional nature of much global activity, then, suggests the appropriateness of adopting a regional approach and methodology and as stated above, the aim of this chapter is to examine the business system model from this regional perspective. It is at this point that our attention turns to consider the regional production network both as an organizational structure and in terms of how it relates to its regional environment. As will be examined the continued organizational evolution of the MNE, in response to a fast paced and highly competitive economic environment, poses significant challenges for traditional firms, and location-based explanations of international activity. Accordingly it is suggested here that the complex reality of contemporary transnational production may only be grasped through the utilization of a conceptual framework that is able to analyse effectively the ways in which regions and networks of firms interact.

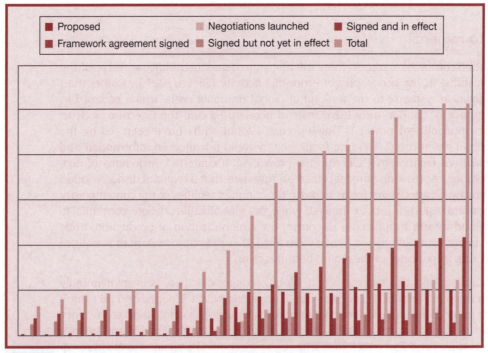

FIGURE 6.1 Growth in free trade agreements in Asia, 1995–2013

SOURCE: Asia Regional Integration Center Free Trade Agreement database available at: http://www.aric.adb.org/ftatrends.php.

What then are regional production networks and why do they deserve our attention? Although a working definition will be provided shortly a satisfactory answer to this question may only be gained through a review of the major theoretical approaches to internationalized production and perspectives on the regionalism/regionalization dynamic. This will be attempted but to allow us to continue this introductory section we may initially define a regional production network as *a series of vertical and horizontal linkages between economic actors in a geographically defined space* (the region). The precise nature and extent of these linkages will vary with industrial sector, geographic region and also the cultural embeddedness of the firm or firms in question. With regard to the second part of the question, these networks deserve our attention as they constitute the contemporary reality of production as it is rarely the case that any single firm retains within itself in one location all aspects of its value chain.

Finally our investigation into the regional production network is focused on East Asia for a number of reasons, not least the remit of this book. The nature of regionalism in East Asia, the degree of regionalization and the variety of business systems observable offers a rich empirical source. At the same time the reader is urged not to limit his or her investigation of regional production networks (RPNs) to East Asia alone as further examples may be found elsewhere, particularly in North America and across the European Union.

Theories and perspectives

This section is presented in two parts. The first traces the development of theories of international production (the 'why' questions), which seek to explain the cross-border activities of firms while the second focuses more on the emergence and development of the regional production network.

Foreign direct investment and international production

Foreign direct investment (FDI) is the term used to describe the phenomenon of firms investing in foreign countries and is defined in contradistinction to portfolio investment[6] as long-term in nature and exerting a degree of managerial control. When, say, Toyota builds a new production facility in Thailand it is engaging in FDI. Although defining FDI may be relatively straightforward, the question of *why* firms engage in the practice is more complicated. Why, for instance, do firms go through the expense and trouble of building overseas production capacity rather than utilizing other more arms-length forms of international interaction such as exporting and licensing? What is it that drives firms overseas and that has led to the organizational form of production that we will study (the production network)?

Something of an evolutionary record exists with regard to attempts to answer these questions. Contemporary approaches to FDI can be traced back to the era of classical economics and its concern with comparative advantage and international capital movements. Marxist theorizing, which continues to inform critical approaches to FDI and development, regarded such international capital flows as an inevitable consequence of the capitalist world system. Later work on international trade theory, particularly that of Heckscher and Ohlin, focuses on a nation's factor endowments and subsequent comparative advantage as an explanatory factor. However, the rapid growth of FDI in the post-war period highlighted deficiencies in these approaches and necessitated the development of new analytical models that could take into account the increasing relevance of the multinational company. In response, perhaps three broad themes have emerged that focus on the firm, trade and location, and internalization.[7]

While these approaches certainly progressed our understanding of internationalized production a considerable distance from classical economics and Marxist analysis, Dunning noted that 'no single hypothesis offers a sufficient explanation of non-trade involvement [FDI]' (1977: 297) (see Table 6.1 for a summary of theoretical approaches to internationalized production). That is, while the firm-based, trade and location, and internalization approaches all offered insights into the motives for FDI, no one single theory existed to unify the field. To fill this lacuna Dunning sought to combine existing approaches into a paradigm that identified ownership, locational and internalization (OLI) advantages. His aptly named Eclectic Paradigm of International Production states that 'the extent, form, and pattern of international production [is] determined by the configuration of three sets of advantages as perceived by enterprises' (Dunning, 1987:2). In other words, the eclectic paradigm hypothesized that some combination of these advantages must exist for firms to undertake FDI. Dunning's paradigm has made a significant contribution to our understanding of FDI and the MNC and is widely regarded as offering a 'unifying framework for determining the extent and pattern of foreign owned activities' (Mudambi, 2002: 263). At the same time we must also note that this has not gone unchallenged and before we move on to consider the regional production network we should first take into account an alternative model that has particular relevance for East Asia.

This macro-level approach originated in Japan and relates FDI to a sequential model of development based on comparative advantage, and the 'unique' features of Japanese firms. Commonly referred to as the flying geese paradigm[8] the model initially emerged

TABLE 6.1 Summary of theoretical approaches to internationalized production

Approach	Scale or focus	Features
Circuits of capital	Global	• FDI as inevitable outcome of capitalist system
Firm specific advantages	Micro	• Firm has certain advantages that allows it to overcome the 'cost of foreignness'
Product life cycle	Location	• The product life cycle determines location of production. Locational advantages
Internalization	Micro	• Firm's internalize transactions to reduce costs and/or protect intellectual property
The electic paradigm	Multi	• Ownership specific advantages • Location specific factors • Internalization advantages
Japanese tradition	Macro	• Sequential regional 'catch-up' development based on comparative advantage • Japanese firms as qualitatively distinct from western firms

in the 1930s (Akamatsu, 1962) as analysis of Japan's pre-war pattern of development through interaction with advanced (Western) economies. It has since, however, become much more commonly associated with post-war Japanese FDI and economic development in East Asian countries. Some Japanese analysts questioned the applicability of theories developed from the study of Western firms (such as described above) to the experience of Japanese firms and their operations in East Asia. Kojima and Ozawa (1984) in particular took exception to two aspects of firm-based theories of FDI. First, the microeconomic focus on the individual firm (thus excluding FDI cooperation among firms or networks of firms such as Japanese business groups or keiretsu[9]), and second the disregarding of macroeconomic issues including the impact of FDI on late developing economies. As a consequence they felt that the Western tradition as examined above focused disproportionately on negative aspects of FDI and overlooked the developmental potential of Japanese FDI. While some considerable criticisms of this approach exist[10] it does nevertheless anticipate to some degree the more recent development of global production chain and network analysis and the flying geese analogy has provided a powerful, if historically contingent, visualization of East Asian development.

Regional production networks

The literature as briefly reviewed above offers explanations as to why firms undertake internationalize production and 'horizontal'[11] FDI in particular but says much less about 'vertical' FDI and the emergence of the regional production network, although the flying geese paradigm hints at it. This section then considers why such networks have emerged before narrowing our focus onto the East Asian experience.

One useful concept for us to consider is that of 'fragmentation'. Simply put, if a firm can realize a reduction in production costs by breaking up operations into discrete sections and locating those sections in places best suited for them, then fragmentation may occur. As an example, head office functions tend to be located in urban areas where proximity to important features of the business environment, such as communications, financial and legal services, marketing and so on, override the high cost of land. Manufacturing operations, however, have a different set of locational demands such as ease of transportation of inputs and outputs. Large factories tend to be built where land is cheaper and trade easier. As long as the cost of coordinating or servicing these dispersed activities is lower than keeping them in one location, fragmentation may take place. So far this simple example has been kept within national borders but the next logical step is to consider locating certain components of the value chain overseas. By doing so, labour intensive operations, for instance, could then be located where the cost of labour is lower than the home location. Again, as long as the benefits of fragmentation (i.e., lower production costs) outweigh the costs (i.e., transportation, international management) then a rationale exits to fragment the value chain.

In fact, globalization has propelled and accelerated fragmentation as barriers to trade fall, governments liberalize trade and investment regimes and the cost of communications (taken here in its broadest sense to include telecommunications and logistics) drops. Moreover, certain industries or products, such as consumer electronics, may be particularly suited to fragmentation and the rationale to do so increases when intense competition shortens the product life cycle and narrows profit margins, as has happened in recent years.

Fragmentation also leads us to consider the concept of the value chain which is defined here as a process whereby 'technology is combined with material and labor inputs, and then processed inputs are assembled, marketed, and distributed. A single firm may consist of only one link in this process, or it may be extensively vertically integrated' (Gereffi et al., 2005: 79). Value chain analysis focuses on the extent to which the MNC identifies and manages core competencies internally (that is, to integrate vertically) or chooses to coordinate linkages with those external actors who are better able to perform certain aspects of the value chain (i.e., outsourcing). The reality, of course, tends to lie at some point between these extremes. Indeed, Gereffi et al. (2005) identified five global value chain governance types that move from a *market*-based type (where simple, codified products are purchased through arms-length transactions from the market) through to the *integrated* firm where transactions take place predominantly, if not exclusively, in-house. These governance types are seen as falling on a scale that measures the degree of explicit coordination of the value chain running from low (market type) to high (integrated firm). The governance of value chains also has implications for the business systems model as a greater reliance on the market mechanism may be more prevalent in Western firms while Japan has been described as a 'network economy' where firms maintain close links with one another and other actors.

To briefly recap, fragmentation theory presents a rationale for firms to engage in vertical FDI and the concept of the value chain offers insights into the coordination and control of these structures. Our next task is to consider why regional production networks appear to be so prevalent and advanced in East Asia. To do so, the following section introduces the broader context of the East Asian political economy before examining how regional economic integration drives, and is driven by, regional production networks.

Regional economic integration in East Asia

The political economy of East Asia

A number of important issues should be kept in mind when examining East Asia's political economy. First, East Asia is currently the world's most economically dynamic region and accounts for an increasing share of global GDP, which reached almost 40 per cent in 2012 (World Bank, 2012). The region is also home to rapidly emerging and expanding markets and a growing number of leading MNEs (179 in the Fortune Global 500 in 2012, up from 116 in 2001).[12] Moreover, rather than standing in simple contrast to the current financial and economic difficulties faced by Europe and North America, East Asia's economic vim and growing geopolitical importance reflects a fundamental shift in the global economy.

Second, as this book explores, the region is economically, politically, socially and culturally diverse meaning that no single model can explain the region's continuing economic development. An early attempt to distil the lessons of the East Asian experience of development was made in 1993 with publication by the World Bank of the East Asian Miracle report, which tackled the question of whether the 'miracle' of East Asian economic development could be attributed to, on the one hand, the 'developmental state' or, on the other, 'market friendly' strategies (Thompson, 1998).[13] This issue has not yet been satisfactorily resolved and was given further impetus by the events of the 1997/8 Asian financial crisis (Jomo, 2003). China's 'socialism with Chinese characteristics' model of economic development offers a further alternative to consider.[14] Yet in spite of these sometimes politicized debates the reality remains that the region has experienced tremendous economic gains over the past four or more decades, which have lifted millions out of poverty. Japan served as the key driver of this growth in the 1960s, 1970s and 1980s but more recently has been eclipsed by China's rapid ascent (see Chapter 9) and China replaced Japan as the world's second largest economy in 2010.

Third, in contrast to the 'top-down' or *de jure* experience of politically led regionalism[15] observed in Europe, the process in East Asia is more 'bottom-up' or *de facto* in that deepening intra-regional trade (including, importantly, intra-firm trade) and investment activity has created a rationale for closer political integration. While this binary view is somewhat misleading – regionalism and regionalization are, in reality, two sides of the same coin and closely interdependent – the description is a useful and valid way of highlighting a distinctive feature of the development of a regional economic entity in East Asia. Moreover, both processes have accelerated in recent years resulting in an ever deeper degree of economic integration. The intra-regional trade ratio for East Asia, for instance, has grown from approximately 35 per cent in the early 1980s to around 53 per cent by 2011 (see Figure 6.2), which is less than that observed in the European Union (at approximately 73 per cent) but ahead of NAFTA at approximately 48 per cent and other formal groupings such as Mercosur in South America (Paprzycki and Ito, 2010; World Trade Organization, 2012).

Intra-regional trade

Much of this intra-regional trade is accounted for by the movements of intermediate goods, particularly machinery parts and components and notably in ICT related goods. The share of these kinds of intermediate goods in manufactured goods in ASEAN, for instance, is over 60 per cent (International Monetary Fund, 2008). The composition of

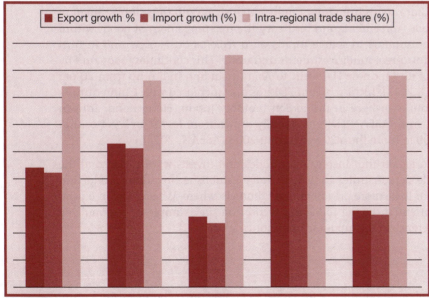

FIGURE 6.2 Trade in East Asia, selected years

SOURCE: Asia Regional Integration Center Trade and Investment database available at: http://www.aric.adb.org/trade_investment.php

this intra-regional trade, which is distinct from that in Europe and North America where finished products feature more strongly, is a crucial factor as it provides 'clear evidence of the development of international production networks within East Asia' (Kimura and Obashi, 2011: 3). When intermediate goods are shipped between countries it demonstrates that they are part of a production process that has been dispersed within a defined geographic space which, as introduced above, corresponds with our working definition of a regional production network.

Intra-regional FDI

We have seen how intra-regional trade points to the existence of regionalized production in East Asia. Further evidence for this may also be found in intra-regional foreign direct investment and indeed trade and FDI often go hand-in-hand. Since the mid-1980s Japan in particular has been an important source of investment in East Asia. As the yen strengthened in response to the Plaza Accord of 1985,[16] Japanese exporters sought to mitigate their declining competitiveness by relocating operations, particularly labour intensive operations, from Japan to lower cost countries elsewhere in East Asia. Initially the destinations for this form of FDI included Korea and Taiwan but as these economies experienced their own period of rapid economic growth (see elsewhere in this text), Japanese firms increasingly targeted Southeast Asian economies such as Thailand and Malaysia. These investments created 'export platforms' where the final destination for finished goods, such as consumer electronics, might be the rich consumer markets of North America and Europe.

Once a factory is established it needs to be supplied with intermediate goods such as components, which in many cases would have been supplied from Japan itself thus further stimulating intra-regional trade. However, in response to pressure from host governments, and in an attempt to reduce dependence on high-cost Japan, firms sought to 'localize' their procurement. This was given further impetus by the Asian Financial Crisis when local currencies plummeted in value relative to the yen making imports of intermediate goods from Japan more expensive. With the establishment of the ASEAN Free Trade Agreement, and in theory the free movement of goods within member states, the rationale to source inputs on a *regional* basis grew and in turn stimulated further intra-regional investments and trade. This continues today and by 2011, 34 per cent of all Japanese FDI went to Asia (including India) up from 20 per cent in 2001 (JETRO, 2013). Intra-regional FDI has also increased with China attracting investments from elsewhere in the region, notably Japan, Hong Kong, Taiwan and Korea. Finally, Intra-ASEAN FDI has steadily grown from less than 2 per cent of total inflows in 2000 to more than 20 per cent in 2008 (ASEAN, 2012).

East Asia, then, is a region that increasingly trades and invests within itself and the nature of that trade demonstrates that firms have established regional production networks that appear to be more prevalent there than elsewhere. We are now in a position to focus our attention in the following section on an example of regionalized production with reference to the Japanese automotive sector.

Keiretsu

Networked or a collaborating family of firms, *keiretsu* (系列), are a characteristic feature of business organization in Japan. *Keiretsu* emerged in the early post-war period as either the re-incarnations of former pre-war *zaibatsu* (財閥) conglomerates including Mitsubishi, Mitsui and Sumitomo that had been broken up by legal reforms demanded by the occupying Allied forces; or newly emerged manufacturing firms, including Sony and Honda. Interestingly, the Chinese characters for *zaibatsu* are the same as those for present day Korean family owned conglomerates, the *chaebol*.

The prevailing (severe) economic conditions of post-war Japan and other historical factors presented a rationale for close cooperation between firms across the value chain rather than their vertical integration into one entity. These practices became institutionalized over the following years of Japan's rapid economic recovery and growth as the firms themselves expanded in size and (international) scope. In trying to understand this growth and global expansion, foreign analysts in the 1980s identified the *keiretsu* structure as a source of competitive strength for Japanese industry. They identified some 'family resemblances' across the various groups, which included the practice of cross-shareholding, financing secured from a group, or main, bank rather than the stock-market, long term commercial relationships with suppliers, and personal ties, often cemented through regular meetings of company presidents and personnel exchange. In this analysis these features afforded *keiretsu* groups a number of strategic advantages over Western firms including stability in ownership, shared risk, long-termism and, in the case of the manufacturing groups, the opportunity to pursue quality and the elimination of waste through investment in human resources.

Keiretsu are conceptualized as being either horizontally (financial) or vertically (manufacturing) orientated, although examples do exist where both forms co-exist. The Mitsubishi group, which includes a bank, a general trading company, heavy industry and automobile production, is often cited as an example of a horizontally organized *keiretsu*. In total, the Mitsubishi group is made up of over 500 companies. Toyota, on the other hand, is a classic example of a vertically organized *keiretsu* with Toyota Motor Corporation, at the apex of a huge number of directly and non-directly controlled suppliers.

Finally, we should note that some debate exists over the extent, relevance and uniqueness of the *keiretsu* and further, the impact of the economic downturn in the 1990s and concomitant challenges of globalization. One of Carlos Ghosn's priorities when Renault effectively took control of Nissan in 1999 was the deconstruction of Nissan's *keiretsu* of suppliers, which were regarded as uncompetitive, costly and of decreasing relevance.

Japanese auto maker production networks in East Asia

Japanese auto makers have established a dominant position in East Asia both in terms of number of units produced and total sales (Busser and Sadoi, 2003). This is particularly true in ASEAN economies. A combination of historical, geographical, and market factors explain this situation. Local demand was originally met through exports and local assembly of knock-down kits[17] exported from Japan. This is a common feature in the auto sector where the development of local production capacity can take years to achieve and is even more challenging in developing economies. However, increasing demands by host governments for localization throughout the 1980s forced Japanese firms to develop local production capacity. This was restrained not least by the relatively small scale of national markets and, in an industry where minimum scale economies are achieved with the production of 150,000 plus units, a rationale emerged for the development of regional networked capacity.[18] In other words, by organizing production on a regional scale, Japanese auto firms were able to compensate for locational *disadvantages*. Attempts by ASEAN governments to counter these scale economy issues centred on facilitating intra-ASEAN trade in components and a number of schemes emerged over the years.[19] Yet national priorities consistently trumped regional development and until the late 1990s most schemes had only a limited effect. By 1997, then, auto production in ASEAN was still labouring under fragmented national policies and priorities although the investment environment was certainly more conducive than in previous years as governments in the region increasing switched from local content requirements and tight regulation of inward investment (local equity stakes, for example) to active promotion of FDI and liberalization. Figure 6.3 shows Toyota's regional production network in terms of AICO (intra-company component trade) agreements.

A decisive moment came with the Asian financial crisis, which had an immediate and negative impact on the region in general and more specifically on the production and sales of autos. While currencies and economies crashed Japanese auto makers found themselves with excess capacity, a severe drop in demand and increasingly expensive Japan-based supply chains. Paradoxically, the crisis is now regarded as having acted as a catalyst for the transformation of the regional economy and auto sector, which has bounced back with surprising resilience. Table 6.2 documents the most significant responses to the crisis by Japanese automakers.

Perhaps more important, though, are the deeper responses to the crisis that continue to shape markets and structures today, for instance, member states agreed to accelerate AFTA implementation, which limits tariffs to 0–5 per cent between member economies and a later lead-in time for newer member states. This formalized a single, regional

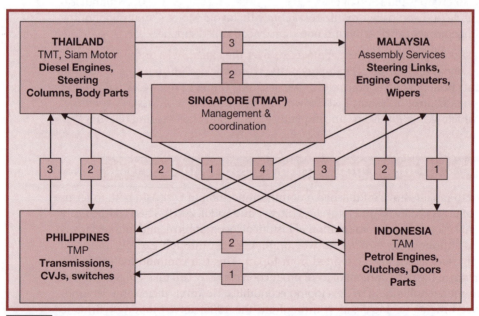

FIGURE 6.3 Toyota's ASEAN production network under AICO agreements (CKD packs), 2003

SOURCE: Based on data compiled from ASEAN Secretariat Toyota Annual Reports.

TABLE 6.2 Immediate responses to the Asian financial crisis

Issue	Response
Market orientation	• From domestic to export
Excess capacity	• Suspension of operations • Retooling • Rapid expansion of exports
Excess human resources	• Increased training in country and Japan • Reduction of shifts
Crisis hit affiliates	• Increase equity stake
Network	• Maintain

market and allowed Japanese auto makers to rationalize and reorganize their regional production networks. Freed of the implicit expectation that trade in components and kits should balance between member states, firms were instead able to organize networks on the basis on economic and market factors, rather than political expediency. Second, a clear push towards localization has taken place, which is reflected in the establishment not only of regional management headquarters but also research and design facilities and the development of regional models or 'Asian cars'. Toyota has also established a Global Production Centre in Thailand that acts as a regional node for personnel training and development in a move designed to localize operational management further and to ensure consistent quality. In this way, regional production networks have expanded in terms of breadth and depth.

Additionally, the relationship between firm and state has experienced a significant shift. As noted above the investment environment greatly improved due to changing attitudes towards inward investment. More specifically in Thailand this led to tax exemption on imported machinery, a repeal of local content requirements, the granting of majority stakes in joint ventures and a reduction in corporate tax. The bargaining power of firms also increased in more subtle ways. Toyota, for instance, was able to secure a lower tax rate for its double-cab Hilux pickup truck, which would normally have attracted a much higher Sports Utility Vehicle (SUV) rate, by suggesting that it would refrain from making a previously advertised huge investment in new production plant. Moreover, it was able to secure from the Thai government tax incentives that reduced the cost of the investment by 30 per cent. This issue of bargaining power and asymmetric power relations is returned to in the final section.

A decade after the crisis tore through the region, the auto industry in Southeast Asia – and the Japanese regional production network in particular – was in a strong and competitive position. Thailand has been particularly successful in hosting Japanese firms and has emerged as a hub for regionalized production. The proposed ASEAN Economic Community (AEC)[20] aims to deepen regional economic integration by further enhancing the attractiveness of the region as a single market and production base. Such efforts create and sustain a strong rationale for regionalized production and we can expect Japanese automakers to remain in the forefront of this trend.

Conclusion

This chapter has examined the concept of the regional production network in the context of East Asia and with reference to Japanese auto makers in particular. We have seen why and how firms have moved beyond their own borders in pursuit of competitive advantages and how there is a symbiotic relationship between trade and investment. That is, deepening trade and investment linkages serve to promote regional economic integration, which in turn presents a more favourable business environment more conducive to regionalized production – a virtuous circle. In the introductory section of this chapter we also raised the question of how the business systems approach can capture the reality of regionalized production. The key to answering this question lies in understanding the 'adaptive' nature of the business system. By necessity and design, firms move beyond their national borders and are confronted by systems quite different from those found at home and the central managerial concern becomes the extent to which the firm adapts to these new surroundings or attempts to apply familiar (home) practices in spite of the new environment. Toyota, for instance may seek to apply its production system in Southeast Asian countries while simultaneously adapting to the norms and requirements of the host economy. Regionalized production, therefore, does create an added layer of complexity to our analysis of firms but the business systems approach remains valid given its capacity to locate that analysis in the broader institutional and societal fabric of the host economy.

Chapter summary

- The complex nature of contemporary international production necessitates the development of better analytical tools, including a focus on the value chain and production network rather than the individual firm.

- Globalization has led to a fragmentation of the value chain and the emergence of global production networks, which present increasingly elaborate geographical and organizational structures.

- East Asia as an economic entity is distinct from those found elsewhere due to its particular experience of development.

- Japanese firms have played a central role in 'networking' the region.

- Japanese auto makers have regionalized production in Southeast Asia in response to national policies and are rationalizing them in response to regional polices.

- The business systems approach remains a valid tool for the analysis of regionalized production.

Key concepts

Eclectic paradigm: an analytical tool used to identify the reasons for the overseas activities of a firm.

Foreign direct investment: where firms invest overseas and retain some degree of managerial control.

Fragmentation: the splitting up of the value chain.

Horizontal FDI: establishing factories overseas where similar products are produced as in the home country.

Keiretsu: a Japanese term denoting a networked or relational group of firms.

Production networks: a set off inter-firm relationships that bind a group of firms into a larger economic unit (Sturgeon, 2000: 2).

Regionalism: a political process that seeks to more closely integrate a defined regional space.

Regionalization: some degree of economic integration in a defined regional space.

Value chain: the sequence of productive (i.e., value added) activities leading to and supporting end-use (Sturgeon, 2000: 2).

Vertical FDI: establishing factories overseas where different stages of the value chain are located by a firm overseas.

Review questions

1 'Regional production networks appear to be more prevalent in East Asia than elsewhere'. Identify factors that support this assertion.

2 Horizontal FDI essentially refers to the phenomenon of firms relocating production from one country to another but how does this differ from vertical FDI? Illustrate your answer with reference to either the production of cars or consumer electronics.

3 Is the business systems approach a suitable model with which to analyse regional production networks? If yes, why? If not, why not?

Learning activities and discussions

1 Select a major multinational company in an important industrial sector (e.g., electronics or auto manufacture) and use the company website and other resources to build up a picture of its overseas production networks. Analyse these networks in terms of 'push' (out of the home location) and 'pull' (into the host location) factors.

2 Apply Dunning's 'eclectic paradigm' to the firm's overseas operations. Can these be explained in terms of (O) ownership advantages, (L) locational advantages and (I) internalization advantages?

MINI CASE

Toyota has moved to link a regionalized production network with global markets and in doing so has achieved a degree of localization previously unseen in emerging markets.

Toyota's innovative international multipurpose vehicle (IMV) project

Although planning for the IMV project began in 1999, soon after the Asian financial crisis, its genesis is not solely attributable to this event. Sales of the Hilux pickup truck had been steadily declining in Japan, Toyota was (and remains) committed to increasing overseas production, and a strategic decision was taken to design affordable yet high quality pickup trucks and multipurpose vehicles (MPVs) for growth markets, mainly in emerging economies including East Asia. This was further compatible with the overall strategy of increasing Toyota's global market share of auto production and sales. The crisis did, however, force a critical re-evaluation of Toyota's traditional strategy of local assembly using components, particularly more complex intermediate products such as engines, from Japan. Toyota's leitmotif is *kaizen* and consistent quality and this explains why the company had been initially reluctant to relocate overseas from Japan the highly efficient production capacity that had been built up over decades. The challenges associated with replicating the Japanese model overseas are well documented

(Abo, 2007) and are magnified in developing economies, such as those found in Southeast Asia. Moreover, Toyota's application of lean manufacturing is dependent on closely coordinated supplier networks. Yet the collapse of regional economies and the drop in the value of the Thai Baht in particular, presented an urgent economic rationale to increase localization of component sourcing. Additionally, the previous model of offloading older models in developing economies was coming under pressure from competitors, particularly Korean firms. The challenge, therefore, was twofold; to offer attractive models utilizing the latest technology but still suitable for developing economies, and to do so while maintaining a competitive price. Toyota's response to this is found in the IMV project, the stated aim of which is to 'realise global optimal production and supply networks' (Toyota Annual Report, 2003).

IMV vehicles, of which there are five models with three body styles (pickup, SUV and multipurpose vehicle), share a common platform, which reduces design and production costs and is becoming a common feature in auto production. This platform is also specifically designed for the sometimes challenging driving environments found in developing economies. The choice of these models reflects diverse consumer demand in developing countries. Thailand, for instance, is the world's second largest market for one-ton pickups while Indonesian consumers prefer the MPV style. The IMV vehicles also act as entry level models that familiarize consumers in emerging economies with Toyota's competitive strengths and, the intention is that these consumers will be favourably disposed towards Toyota's mainstay sedans as middle classes expand and consumer tastes become more sophisticated. A similar line of reasoning can be identified at Honda with regards to power products (generators, outboard engines, agricultural tools) and motorcycles.

Production is centred on Toyota's Thai and Indonesian plants but assembly also takes place in Argentina and South Africa (see Figure 6.4). Crucially, all production occurs outside Japan and localization rates are high, reportedly 97 per cent in Thailand, which means that production does not have to rely on components sourced, expensively, from Japan. This is where the ASEAN advantages comes into play as Toyota, along with other Japanese auto makers, have been developing their supplier networks on a regional basis for the past two decades. It is this historical investment and development of local suppliers that allows Toyota to realize the advantages of low-cost labour while maintaining quality. Due to intense scrutiny of the supply chain and high localization rates, cost savings are reported to be around 30 per cent, allowing Toyota to compete therefore

both on cost and quality. Yet operating in emerging economies can also bring associated risks, particularly with regards to disruption of the supply chain. To mitigate this, Toyota has built-in some flexibility to the demands of just-in-time production by requiring plants to maintain a two-week supply of components on site. The initial production target at the project's launch in 2002 was for 500,000 units with Thailand as the key player allocated an annual target of 280,000 units of which 140,000 designated for export markets. The Thai plant further produces and exports diesel engines. However strong demand following commencement of the production line in 2004 saw the overall target for the project revised upwards to 700,000 units. By comparison, Toyota's total consolidated production in 2006 was approximately 8 million units.

IMV production is also supported by the presence of Toyota's regional HQ, Toyota Motor Asia-Pacific (TMAP), in Singapore (established in 2001), which is 100 per cent owned by TMC. In contrast to the more straightforward activities of regional management structures in North America and Europe, Toyota's organization in East Asia has emerged from the necessity of dealing with the complex nature of the regional division of labour and of a need for better coordination of supply chains and parts complementation under AFTA. Additionally, the establishment of a Global Production Centre (an advanced, globally integrated training facility) in Thailand in 2003 supports the development of human resources in the region, further facilitating localization while maintaining quality. Finally, Toyota established its first R&D centre in an emerging economy, Thailand, in 2005 further underlining its commitment to localization of design. (See Table 6.3 for details of production bases in 2012.)

The IMV project thus represents an innovative response to competitive global markets and localized demand. By drawing on an existing regional production network in (ASEAN) and production and assembly facilities in other emerging economies Toyota is successfully linking spatial scale and organizational structure.

This has been facilitated by localization of production, investing in the development of regional supply chains, a commitment to local staff, and regional management. Given surging demand in emerging markets (45 per cent of Toyota's total sales in 2011) the IMV project can be regarded as a successful model of global/regional production organization and by March 2012 over 5 million units had been produced under the scheme.

SOURCE: Toyota promotional material, 2012.

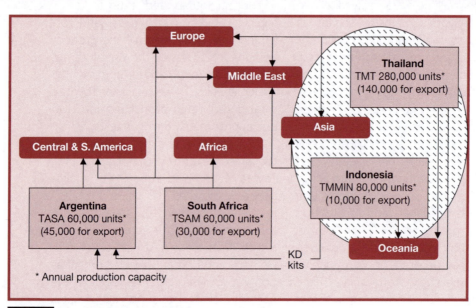

FIGURE 6.4 The IMV supply network at launch

NOTES: TMT – Toyota Motor Thailand Co., Ltd; TMMIN – PT. Toyota Motor Manufacturing Indonesia; TSAM –Toyota South Africa Motors (Pty.) Ltd; TASA –Toyota Argentina S.A.
SOURCE: Toyota promotional material, 2003.

Questions

1 Why did Toyota establish a regional production network in Southeast Asia? Identify three key drivers.

2 Once you have identified these drivers, consider what managerial and operational challenges a regional production network presents. Identify three key issues.

3 How can host economies capture value from foreign direct investment? Illustrate your answer with reference to Toyota in Thailand.

TABLE 6.3 Main IMV production bases in 2012

Country	Affiliate	Production vehicle	Start of production	Annual Production	Export destination
Thailand	TMT	Pickup truck (Hilux VIGO)	August 2004	350,000 units (Including 202,000 units for export in 2011)	Europe, Asia, Oceania
		Sport utility vehicle	2005		The Middle East
Indonesia	TMMIN	Minivan	September 2004	100,000 units (Including 38,000 units for export)	Asia, the Middle East
South Africa	TSAM	Pickup truck	2005	120,000 units (Including 87,000 units for export)	Europe, Africa, etc.
		Sport utility vehicle	2005		
Argentina	TASA	Pickup truck	2005	92,000 units (Including 47,000 units for export)	Latin America
		Sport utility vehicle	2005		

NOTES: TMT – Toyota Motor Thailand Co., Ltd; TMMIN – PT. Toyota Motor Manufacturing Indonesia; TSAM –Toyota South Africa Motors (Pty.) Ltd; TASA –Toyota Argentina S.A.

Web links

Toyota Motor Corporation: http://www.toyota.co.jp/en/index.html

Toyota's IMV project: http://www.toyota-global.com/investors/ir_library/annual/pdf/2012/feature/

International business resource site: http://globaledge.msu.edu/

World Investment Report: http://www.unctad.org

World Trade Organization (Regional Trade Agreement Gateway): http://www.wto.org/english/tratop_e/region_e/region_e.htm

Global production networks research group at the University of Manchester, U.K.: http://www.sed.manchester.ac.uk/geography/research/gpn/

Notes

1   Neo-liberal ideology is taken in this context to refer to the pursuance of free-enterprise liberalism characterized by, for example, deregulated markets, declining state involvement in economic activity through the privatization of national assets and a commitment to global trade liberalization.

2   Regionalization is understood here as the deepening of regional economic integration through trade and investment while regionalism refers to a more political process such as observed in the European Union.

3   After a period of intense speculation that the currency would collapse in response to severe economic difficulties in Greece and elsewhere in Europe throughout 2012, the Euro remained in operation in early 2013. However, tremendous tensions remain and the future of the Euro in its current form cannot be taken for granted in the longer term.

4   The North American Free Trade Agreement.

5   Rugman suggests that of the world's 500 largest MNEs, which account for 90 per cent of the world's stock in FDI and over half of world trade, only 9 can be categorized as truly global and that the vast majority (320) 'are home region based and derive an average of 80 per cent of their sales inter-regionally' (2005: 224).

6   Portfolio investment refers to the electronic movement of highly liquid capital for investment. Fund managers in one country may decide to invest capital in a foreign country on behalf of the investors and this process plays a vital function in capital formation. However, such funds are also seen as highly volatile and prone to herd-like behaviour and for this reason have been variously described as 'hot' or 'mad' money. The East Asian financial crisis of 1997–1998, for instance, was precipitated by massive outflows of portfolio investments from developing economies.

7   Firm based models (see in particular Hymer, 1976) seek to identify the specific advantages (brand, technology, management) that firms hold, that allow them to compensate for the presumed cost of foreignness, while trade and location analysis (see in particular Vernon, 1966) links the product life cycle with the location of production. Internalization approaches (Buckley and Casson, 1976) stem from transaction cost economics (i.e., the cost involved of making an exchange) and suggest that FDI is inevitable where a firm seeks to internalize its activities as opposed to operating through licensing or subcontracting.

8   Akamatsu conceptualized economies as flying geese (*gankou keitai*) in a 'V' formation. In the original analogy Western economies, particularly those of the United Kingdom and the United States, were the lead geese and through interaction with these economies Japan, as a following or 'catch-up' economies experienced a sequential process of economic development. This process included the progression through industrial sectors, the shift from imports to domestic production and finally exports. In a further extension of the model exports are replaced by overseas production.

9   See *'keiretsu'* section.

10 See in particular Hatch and Yamamura (1996) who criticize Japanese FDI as 'embracing' developing nations, which leads to a form of dependency on Japanese firms, capital and technology. It should also be noted that some economies, notably Korea and more recently China, have resisted this form of investment from Japan in pursuit of their own models of economic development.

11 Horizontal FDI is where firms set up production plants in overseas markets rather than exporting from home. It is contrasted with 'vertical' FDI whereby a 'firm establishes manufacturing facilities in multiple countries, each producing a different input to, or stage of, the firm's production process', (Deardorff, 2013).

12 More dramatically, the number of Chinese firms has rapidly expanded in this list and whereas the top six Asian firms were all Japanese in 2005, by 2012 the top three positions were all taken by Chinese firms (accessed 4 November 2013 at: http://money.cnn.com/magazines/fortune/global500/).

13 The World Bank report points out that 'the diversity of experience, the variety of institutions, the great variation in policies among the high-performing Asian economies means that there is no East Asian model of rapid growth with equity. Rather, each of the eight economies we studied used various combinations of policies at different times to perform the functions needed for rapid growth' (World Bank, 1993: 366).

14 Sometimes referred to as the 'Beijing Consensus', which stands in stark contrast to the 'Washington Consensus'.

15 A deeper examination of regionalism in East Asia is beyond the scope of this chapter but revolves around free trade agreements such as the ASEAN Free Trade Agreement (AFTA), regional intergovernmental meetings such as the East Asian Summit and other initiatives in financial cooperation and security issues.

16 Where the governments of the then G5 (France, West Germany, Japan, the United States and the United Kingdom) agreed to coordinated market interventions to depreciate the value of the US dollar relative to the yen. The yen subsequently strengthened by approximately 50 per cent over the following two years.

17 Localization of auto assembly and production proceeds from the import and assembly of completely knocked down (CKD) kits to semi-knocked down (KD) kits and then through limited local production to complete local production. CKD assembly commenced in Thailand in the 1960s, moved into the KD stage in the 1970s and 1980s and achieved local production in the 1990s. Complete local production is the current goal for most Japanese auto makers (see also Yamashita, 1998: 61–79).

18 Toyota, for example, was producing the Corolla sedan in small numbers in five different countries.

19 The ASEAN Industrial Complementation Scheme (AIC) in 1981, Brand to Brand Complementation (BBC) in 1988, ASEAN Industrial Cooperation (AICO) in 1996 and the Common Effective Preferential Tariff Scheme (CEPT) which was superseded by the establishment of the ASEAN Free Trade Area (AFTA) in 2003, although Malaysia delayed full implementation of this scheme in an attempt to protect its ailing national car projects.

20 To be implemented by 2015.

References

Abo, T. (ed.) (2007) *Japanese Hybrid Factories: A Worldwide Comparison of Global Production Strategies*. Basingstoke: Palgrave Macmillan.

Akamatsu, K. (1962) A historical pattern of economic growth in developing countries. *The Developing Economies*, 1(1): 3–25.

ASEAN (2012) ASEAN Statistics, accessed 4 December 2013 at: http://www.asean.org/resources/2012-02-10-08-47-55

Buckley, P.J. and Casson, M.C. (1976) *The Future of the Multinational Enterprise*. London: Homes & Meier.

Busser, R. and Sadoi, Y. (eds.) (2003) *Production Networks in Asia and Europe: Skill Formation and Technology Transfer in the Automobile Industry*. London: Routledge.

Deardorff, A. (2013) Deardorffs' Glossary of International Economics, accessed 4 November 2013 at: http://www-personal.umich.edu/~alandear/glossary/intro.html

Dicken, P. (2010) *Global Shift: Mapping the Changing Contours of the World Economy*, 6th edn. London: Sage.

Dunning, J.H. (1977) Trade, Location of Economic Activity and the MNE: A Search for an Eclectic Approach, in O. Bertil et al. (eds.) *The International Allocation of Economic Activity, Proceeding of Noble Symposium*, Stockholm. London: Macmillan.

Dunning, J.H. (1987) The Eclectic Paradigm of International Production: A Restatement and some Possible Extension. *Journal of International Business Studies*, 19: 1–31.

Gereffi, G., Humphrey, J. and Sturgeon, T. (2005) The Governance of Global Value Chains. *Review of International Political Economy*, 12(1): 78–104.

Gruenwald, P. and Hori, M. (2008) Intra-regional Trade Key to Asia's Export Boom, IMFSurvey Magazine: Countries & Regions, accessed 4 December 2013 at: http://www.imf.org/external/pubs/ft/survey/so/2008/car02608a.htm

Hatch, W. and Yamamura, K. (1996) *Asia in Japan's Embrace*. Cambridge: Cambridge University Press.

Henderson, J., Dicken, P., Hess, M., Coe, N. and Yeung, H. (2002) Global Production Networks and the Analysis of Economic Development. *Review of International Political Economy*, 9(3): 436–464.

Hymer, S.H. (1976) *The International Operations of National Firms: A Study of Direct Foreign Investment*. Cambridge, MA: MIT Press.

JETRO (Japanese Trade and Investment Statistics) (2013) Online database, accessed 4 December 2013 at: http://www.jetro.go.jp/en/reports/statistics/

Jomo, K. (2003) Reforming East Asia for Sustainable Development. *Asian Business and Management*, 2(1): 7–38.

Kimura, F. and Obashi, A. (2011) Production Networks in East Asia: What We Know So Far. ADBI Working Paper 320, Tokyo: Asian Development Bank Institute, accessed 4 November 2013 at: http://www.adbi.org/working-paper/2011/11/11/4792.production.networks.east.asia/

Kojima, K. and Ozawa, T. (1984) Micro- and Macro-Economic Models of Direct Foreign Investment: Toward a Synthesis. *Hitotsubashi Journal of Economics*, 25(1): 1–20.

Mudambi, R. (2002) The Location Decision of the Multinational Enterprise, in P. McCann (ed.) *Industrial Location Economics*. Cheltenham: Edward Elgar, pp. 263–385.

Paprzycki, R. and Ito, K. (2010) Investment, Production and Trade Networks as Drivers of East Asian Integration. Global COE Hi-Stat Discussion Paper Series gd09-117, Institute of Economic Research, Hitotsubashi University.

Redding, G. (2009) The Business Systems of Asia, in H. Hasegawa and C. Noronha (eds.) *Asian Business and Management*. Basingstoke: Palgrave Macmillan, pp. 7–30.

Rugman, A. (2005) *The Regional Multinationals: MNEs and 'Global' Strategic Management*. Cambridge: Cambridge University Press.

Sturgeon, T. (2000) How Do We Define Value Chains and Production Networks? MIT IPC Globalization Working Paper 00–010.

Thompson, G. (ed.) (1998) *Economic Dynamism in the Asia-Pacific*. New York and London: Routledge.

Toyota (2003) *Annual Report*, Nagoya: Toyota.

Toyota (2012) Production Companies Outside Japan, accessed 4 December 2013 at: http://www.toyota-global.com/company/profile/facilities/pdf/2013/overseas_production_base.pdf

Vernon, R. (1966) International Investment and International Trade in the Product Cycle. *Quarterly Journal of Economics*, 80: 190–207.

World Bank (1993) *The East Asian Miracle*. Oxford: Oxford University Press.

World Bank (2012) *Capturing New Sources of Growth*, East Asia and Pacific Economic Update, Vol. 1, accessed 4 December 2013 at: http://data.worldbank.org/sites/default/files/eap-update-may-2012-full-report_1.pdf

World Trade Organization (2012) World Trade Developments, accessed 4 December 2013 at: http://www.wto.org/english/res_e/statis_e/its2012_e/its12_world_trade_dev_e.pdf

Yamashita, S. (1998) Japanese Investment Strategy and Technology Transfer in East Asia, in H. Hasegawa and G.D. Hook, (eds.) *Japanese Business Management: Restructuring for Low Growth and Globalization*. London and New York: Routledge, pp. 46–60.

Corporate Social Responsibility and Sustainable Development in Asia

Philippe Debroux

Chapter outline

- Concepts of corporate social responsibility (CSR) and sustainable development
- Positioning in the pursuit of sustainable development and CSR policies
- Required adjustment to the two concepts
- The different approaches of implementing CSR policies

Chapter objectives

After reading this chapter, you should be able to:

1 Understand the meaning of the CSR and sustainable development concepts in Asia.

2 Identify the environmental and social problems in Asia that require a CSR and sustainable solution.

3 Understand the different policies followed by the private and public actors in applying the concept of CSR and sustainable development.

4 Devise scenarios about CSR and sustainable development and assess their plausibility.

Introduction: corporate social responsibility (CSR) and sustainable development – concept and phenomenon

The growing importance of CSR and sustainable development in Asia

CSR includes the economic, legal, ethical, and discretionary (philanthropic) expectations that the organizations' stakeholders have of organizations (Carroll, 2004) in a business environment based on market principles and the rule of law. Society is not homogeneous, but is made up of various stakeholder groups, each with its own interests and expectations of corporate behaviour. Moreover, societal norms and values are in a constant state of flux, the complexities of which raise problems for organizations that require social legitimacy (Roper, 2012). CSR was associated from the start to the idea of sustainable development, as identified as development that 'meets the needs of the present without compromising the ability of future generations to meet their own needs' (United Nations, 1987).

As the proverb says: 'give a man a fish and you feed him for a day. Teach a man how to fish and you feed him for a long time'. However, as was pointed out sustainability is not about learning 'how to fish' but about understanding what the 'fish' need to grow and reproduce (Ehnert and Harry, 2012). Agriculture, forestry and fishery can be depleted or abundant. Likewise, workers can be impoverished, undertrained and disgruntled, or financially secure, skilled, dynamic and highly engaged. In this respect, along with their objective of generating profit companies have an ambivalent position inside the societies in which they are integrated. They produce goods and services, create employment, contribute to the state income, and to some extent participate to development through philanthropic and local development-related initiatives. However, they also generate negative externalities: over-exploitation of natural resources, pollution, destruction of bio-diversity, exploitation of human resources or violations of human rights.

The shift toward green growth and green economy

It is argued that the business model, which privileged efficiency and output and helped to make Asia the most dynamic economic zone, can no longer be relied on for designing and evaluating new broader policies, or for measuring a country's overall performance. The approach based on export, cheap labour and neglect of the social, political and ecological environment is no longer an option in developing Asia. However, developed Asia is also on an unsustainable path in terms of use of natural and human resources (United Nations Environment Programme, 2011). This calls for a business system based on a 'green economy' concept resting on sound regional, state and corporate governance, inclusive of all types of human resources, while using natural resources in a sustainable manner.

For the United Nations Environment Programme (UNEP) there is no inherent contradiction between economic growth, social equity and environmental protection. A green economy would result in improved human well-being and social equity, while significantly reducing environmental risks and ecological scarcities. It can be thought of as one that is low carbon, resource efficient and effective, and socially inclusive. It should be understood as a means to achieve the objective of sustainable development (UNEP, 2011). The holistic framework developed by Redding (2005) is useful for the purpose of addressing those issues in their socio-economic and cultural contexts. Green economy requires a shift of focus from the formulation of legal systems to the construction of schemes supporting the effective integration of regulatory regimes, development of required infrastructure and stabilization of the recycling economy. Business, public authorities and the representatives of the civil society in Asia now consider CSR and sustainable development as key elements of the transformation of economies and societies that have to be part of any business and public economic or welfare policy.

It is not only a question of norms enacted by the state and administrative and legal frameworks aiming to implement them. In the perspective described by Redding it means the production and activation of the 'rules of the game', more or less formal and explicit, guiding the actions of businesses and structuring the relationships they have with their stakeholders (Redding, 2005). Those rules are the product of negotiation, alliances and network building, and power relationships among stakeholders whose interactions are both constitutive of those rules and structured by them.

Although intrinsically linked, three forms of environmental, societal and governance-related (ESG) rules can be identified. There are public rules through which the state constrains and incentivizes business through public policies, laws and regulations, systems of incentive, control and sanction, and administrative and legal management of the litigations that oppose business and stakeholders; civil rules through which the civil society exert a pressure through industrial relations (strikes, collective bargaining), protest actions (demonstrations, information campaigns, boycotts), or court actions; and self-rules, through codes of conduct, certifications, or governance-related initiatives.

The nature of the complexities and organizational responses of business to the challenges of these rules of the game are transcribed typically in the name of 'stakeholder engagement' (Freeman, 1984). However, Roper (2012) argued that the definitions of stakeholders' engagement often imply that the relationship between business and society is discussed in those terms – business and society. Implicit is a separation of 'business' from 'society' that induces a concept of social responsibility often seen as 'doing good' rather than a complex and enduring process of generating simultaneously mutual benefit in ESG terms. Sustainability and stakeholder engagement are the two sides of the same coin. Sustainability cannot be achieved without a type of stakeholder engagement that encompasses all dimensions at the same time.

The growing involvement in CSR and sustainable development in Asia

Both developed and developing Asia have embraced the concepts of CSR and sustainable development during the past decade. A key dimension of sustainable development is the link with technological and social innovation. Developing Asia, first of all China, intends to shift from low-end assembly sectors that are the least profitable and the most polluting. The move towards higher value-added products and services is a key element in maintaining world competitiveness. Just following rules prescribed by someone else may put Asian business at a disadvantage. So, developed Asia aims to become a rule-maker in the green economy. Backed by government Japanese companies have developed a variety of products, for example, in the auto manufacturing sector with electric vehicles (battery powered, fuel cell and hybrid) to electronic and housing industries with products consuming less energy, use less material and a greater percentage of recyclability (Nakamaru, 2010). South Korean (referred to as Korea from here for convenience) and Chinese companies have followed suit. The Korean initiatives led to an increased volume of investments by leading companies, such as Samsung Electronics and LG, in the environmental sector. A report by the Ministry of Knowledge Economy (MKE) indicates that sales of green products increased from $1 billion in 2007 to $6.7 billion in 2010 (MKE, 2011). Many public and private investments, related to sustainable development, have been directed to energy efficiency improvement and renewable energy development with a long-term perspective. China is building the equivalent of a 1-GW thermal power station every 10 days, and burning vast amounts of coal. As a result, by 2050 the revenue per capita is projected to be four times higher and the CO_2 and air pollution index three times higher. Its per capita CO_2 emissions equals European levels, and China will continue to account for about 30 per cent of global emissions until 2030 (Economist Intelligence Unit, 2012). At the same time it is building a 'green' energy system faster than any other country. The Chinese government is convinced that China can become a technological and economic leader in this transition to the green economy without sacrificing growth. China is already the biggest investor in renewable energy in the world: it has the largest installed wind power capacity of any country and its companies have gone from supplying 1 per cent to supplying 49 per cent of the world's photovoltaic solar panels in the last decade (Economist Intelligence Unit, 2012), taking market shares away from their Western and Japanese rivals.

Sustainable development is therefore already a central policy principle for Asia and integrated in business strategy. However, it has many facets and is very complex, ambiguous and fluid. It often requires significant trade-offs. China suffers from significant air pollution problem but cannot get away from coal as a key energy source for the foreseeable future. Japan's public opinion is reluctant to see government restart nuclear facilities only a few years after a major nuclear disaster and history of grave nuclear accidents. But the high cost of energy is impeding the attempt to revive the Japanese economy and a large majority of Japanese SMEs cannot compete at the current energy cost. The difficulty to operationalize the concept of sustainability is compounded by the absence of a single mechanism that could be utilized to take into account all short-, medium- and long-term economic costs and benefits.

The tools and approaches that can be experienced such as full cost accounting, policy mix analysis and multi-stakeholder processes are now widely used in China and Japan. The Japanese miscellaneous eco-city projects are considered promising in a number of other countries. However, caution is needed in applying them to individual countries, cities and situations. The contexts are different from one to another. The ESG model of sustainable development (see later) is indeed attractive. However, it may be difficult to operationalize in countries suffering from severe governance problems, as it the case in many Asian countries (as will be seen afterwards). These conceptual difficulties should not negate, however, the importance of the concept as a key principle that underpins the conservation of the environment and the improvement of living standards. As the nature of sustainability-related issues becomes more complex, combinations of different policy tools are increasingly utilized to achieve various policy goals. A wide mix of regulatory measures, framework approach, market-based measures, voluntary agreements, procedural measures and information measures are adopted in all countries in the region. Particularly in the context of developing countries such as Indonesia, China and Vietnam, public authorities are aware that their capacity for implementation of complex instruments is limited. Flexibility is required, and many Asian countries place more and more emphasis on multi-stakeholder and participatory approaches. They are essential as the increasing number of stakeholders is involved in social and environmental decision-making and implementation. However, multi-stakeholders' frameworks must treat fairly *all* stake-holders. This is not always the case. In most countries they are skewed in favour of a small number of specific stakeholders. Therefore, they cannot be operationalized without a clear framework of norms and standards. Otherwise they could easily be used for manipulation in decision-making and the policy implementation processes. Thus, institutional strengthening and capacity development are important to ensure that the various stakeholders are genuinely and effectively engaged in such processes for better ESG management.

Required adjustment to the two concepts

Limits of the current business model

The favoured efficiency-driven model has led to a rise of environmental standards and contributed to economic growth. However, it has not induced a downward spiral in the overall use of resources – quite the opposite. The Asian economy is shifting towards a resource intensive structure. Per capita material use is now around the world average and could triple by 2050 under the same growth trajectory (Kojima, 2011). Moreover, the fruits have not been equally shared. True, growth has led to the emergence of a large middle class all over the region. During the 1990 to 2007 period, the number of people living on less than $1.25 a day decreased by 0.4 billion from 1.8 billion to 1.4 billion in most Asian countries – but the trickle-down effect is insufficient. Of the chronically food insecure people in the world 500 million live in Asia. Rural poverty has receded but a considerable number of Asian urban inhabitants live in slums with poor access to safe drinking water and to sanitation services (Asian Development Bank, 2012). In the past 25 years, Asia has lost 50 per cent of its forests and one-third of its agricultural land has been degraded. Asia's rivers contain a much higher quantity of pollutants than the world average. Of the world's 15 most polluted cities, 13 are in Asia. It is projected that 2.4 billion Asian people will suffer from water stress by 2025 (Asian Development Bank, 2012).

The green growth strategy, if pursued as currently planned, has a high probability of experiencing the Jevons' Paradox (Alcott, 2005), which states that as the efficiency with which a resource is used increases, the use of the resource tends to increase as well because consumers find that they can afford more of it. For the time being Asian countries environmental rankings are not very high. In the Environmental Performance Index ranking Japan is ranked 23, Singapore 43, Korea 52, Indonesia 74, Vietnam 79, China 116, and India 125 (Yale University, 2012) . Under a scenario that considers no major changes in environment and development policies, the cost to achieve environmentally sound development is estimated at $ 12.9 billion a year. Under a scenario in which the goal for developing countries of Asia is to achieve the best practices of OECD countries by 2030, the cost would be $70 billion/year. In addition, it is estimated that repairing the damage done to the land, water, air and living biotope in Asia would require $25 billion a year (ADB, 2006).

Reluctance to shift toward a green economy

Moving toward sustainable resource circulation and management will be required in order to move towards a less-resource intensive development pattern. However, this will not be easily achieved. In countries facing unemployment of low skill workers such as

India, Indonesia and Vietnam the idea that damage to the environment is an unavoid-able by-product of growth is still prevalent. The price on the world markets for many of their products is either stagnant or decreasing but the demands for, and the costs of, social and environmental compliance is increasing. For instance, virgin material tax or taxing for inefficient use of resources in industrial sectors may raise concerns of competitiveness that can induce a move out of the country by multinationals. The pulpwood and palm oil industries in Indonesia are good examples. The implementation of corporate certification schemes for forestry is strongly impeded and its efficacy reduced because of the government's dependence on those industries (Bartley, 2003). The resulting squeeze on profits that such governance programs are perceived to be associated with make local companies (and their governments) reluctant to engage in those schemes.

An insufficient use of human capital

Few Asian companies can be said to yet utilize fully their human capital potential despite progress in this respect (discussed later). When they engage with a category of employees it is often at the detriment of others. The presence of foreigners and especially women in managerial positions remains low, especially in Japan and Korea (McKinsey and Company, 2012). There are still few channels to develop engagement with the local workers in Japanese and Korean multinationals' subsidiaries in Asia (Debroux, 2011b). The use of atypical workers that are given little or no training and are paid salaries below that which the ILO considers a 'decent wage' (ILO, 2010) remains widespread. The numerous labour actions in Vietnam, Indonesia, China and India indicate a growing frustration with the current development pattern. However, developed Asia, from Singapore to Korea and Japan, also suffers from growing labour instability, and social and economic alienation of some parts of their population (Ofreneo, 2008).

The current informal labour arrangement and underpaid, undertrained non-permanent formal employment represents a huge pool of under-utilized human capital, a source of low productivity as well as persistent poverty (Kuriyama, 2009). This under-utilized group includes a large number of workers and a growing number of young qualified people and affects both developing and developed Asia. The lack of integration opportunities for these workers alongside poor working conditions could significantly and structurally hinder economic and social development and also become a source of political instability (OECD, 2012). This situation is unsustainable in economic terms as is also unacceptable socially and ethically unacceptable, not only by NGOs but also by groups representing business interests (ETI, 2012).

The challenges ahead

The need for governance changes

Better governance is said to allow more efficient policies in ESG terms (OECD, 2008). This is carried out through the rules of law that insist on respect for human rights, clear separation between the three powers, existence of mechanisms of evaluation of government action and a degree of autonomy of local powers. From an institutional perspective, the key question is whether institutional or structural changes could accelerate the achievement of the sustainable development agenda. A multistakeholder approach requires the right framework of norms and standards for institutional strengthening and capacity development. Improved governance is vital in achieving global goals, and no amount of incremental reform at the global level can substitute for: more robust reform at the regional and national level; greater empowerment of communities and other stakeholders; and more innovative approaches to enabling factors such as welfare and labour, and financing and policy reform.

The question is whether the old governance arrangements that focused on efficiency-driven policies and practices can be transformed so that Asian economies can move toward a green economy, or if more radical reform is required. Governments in developing Asia have problems of implementation of regulations, due to: a lack of regulatory enforcement resources; uncertain laws with few penalties for non-compliance; corruption; and inadequate infrastructure and human resources to collect evidence for law breaking by companies (ADB, 2006). Ranking in terms of level of corruption is not impressive with Japan (17), Korea (45), China (80), India (94) and Vietnam (123). Singapore in fifth place is the only Asian country in the top 10 (Transparency International, 2012).

With the exception of the ISO norms and guidance (for the SR26000 – social responsibility standards) the overall presence of Asian companies in transnational governance schemes remains subdued in the Global Reporting Initiative (GRI), the Global Compact (GC) (see Table 7.1), the World Business for Sustainable Development and the Ethical Trade Initiative (ETI), among others. Many companies have their own codes of conduct but the presence is also weak in industry-based transnational schemes. It should be added, however, that if a relatively few Asian companies are yet formal members of the transnational schemes many more often utilize the concepts as guidance. It is notable in the GRI.

In the GC scheme Japan is overtaken by Korea and the presence of non-business concerns is insignificant. China is the leader in Asia, but it is overtaken by India for the non-business participation (NGO, academics and cities). In total, both are largely ahead of Japan. Socially Responsible Investment (SRI) funds in Asia are rising (see Table 7.2) (ASrIA, 2012) but they are still smaller than in the United States and the United Kingdom. This seems to reflect the limited interest by Asian companies to be listed on the socially responsible financial market indices that have been developed to measure corporate sustainability: the Dow Jones Sustainability Index (DJSI) and the FTSE4Good. Except for Japan, only a few Asian companies have so far been included in these evaluations.

TABLE 7.1 Participants in the United Nations Global Compact (2010)

Country	Business	Other	Total
Japan	110	7	117
Korea	117	56	173
China	166	29	197
India	154	71	231
France	615	77	692
Germany	140	43	183
United States	269	148	417
Total	6113	2378	8491

SOURCE: United Nations (2010).

TABLE 7.2 Asia-based sustainable investment funds (total: $75 billion)

Region	Total identified SRI Assets funds under Management market	Total Asset management (in $billion)	Percentage of total market
Asia ex-Japan	64	2,200	2.90
Japan	10	4,400	0.20
Asia total	74	6,600	1.10
Global	13,338	61,600	21.60

SOURCE: ASrla Research Local sustainable investment funds (as at the end of 2011).

The need for a new social compact

The distributional impacts of policies related to the green economy are important, including for competitiveness. The vision should promote innovation, as well as skills and inventiveness. Exclusion and widening inequalities can damage long-term welfare. Quality of life should be recognized as a desirable and measurable outcome of policy. Secure and meaningful employment providing adequate purchasing power is necessary in a sustainable and socially cohesive economy. Also required is a growing economic system. One that increasingly satisfies human needs and wants without enlarging the ecological footprint needs an adequate supply and quality of human capital, especially if those human needs must be satisfied through more effective use of resources.

This explains why the debate on social protection has been at the centre of the evolution of the forms of capitalism in Japan, Korea and China during the past three decades. This development raises questions concerning the dialogue that companies and labour have to engage in. Alongside business and government, labour unions have been part of tripartite arrangements, notably in Japan, Singapore and Malaysia that allowed employment relationships to sustain a dynamic growth. However, it is more difficult to keep the tripartite system alive in labour systems characterized by increasingly heterogeneous working conditions and contractual relationships. Moreover, the neglect (particularly in Japan) by labour unions of the temporary workers in developed Asia, and of informal labour in developing Asia is now unsustainable and must be corrected to create new sustainable and inclusive labour systems. Finally, the financing of welfare (including pension) systems in ageing societies will necessitate difficult political decisions on cost sharing. The debate started in Japan, Korea and Singapore about long-term pension and social security systems, so far with no conclusive results. In China, developments in the domain of welfare and well-being are likely to become key factors to assure the stability of the regime (Li, 2011).

Positioning in the pursuit of sustainable development and CSR policies

The rise of civil society in Asia

Long-term sustainable development supposes the involvement and acceptance of the actions by local people. For instance, energy and water supply-related projects require the delegation of management responsibility to local communities and the strong commitment generated among local managers by an incentive system. The voices of local people must be heard when basic rights are not respected. For example, one pressing problem is the protection of forests and the people living in or around them. The development of large-scale monocrop plantations in countries such as Indonesia and Malaysia (see the case study at the end of the chapter) often neglects the rights and concerns of local people. They are also the source of environmental damage with the use of irrigation. The use of pesticides damage ecosystems. Successful community forests require secure land tenure, a voice for marginalized groups and strong institutional support. It can only be achieved with the help of NGOs as part of a multistakeholder structure.

A positive development has been an increase in court activism, with the creation of 'green benches' and the training of judges and prosecutors to hear environmental cases. In India and the Philippines, the supreme courts have issued instructions to the national environmental agencies to enforce the law and clean up the environment. It is argued that companies' participation in voluntary programs often depends on local advocacy and that the low participation of Asian companies in transnational governance initiatives could be explained by the presence of closed regimes in which civil society is less influential than in the West (Drezner and Lu, 2009). Nevertheless, community protests are now abundant and have included demonstrations, including in China, over the construction of chemical plants, in the Philippines over plantation expansion plans, Malaysia over palm oil production, land grabs in China and Cambodia and the environmental impacts of mines in Indonesia. The movement is so large and diversified that business will have to cope with the issue, including development of stakeholder engagement with the advocacy NGOs.

From philanthropy to integration of CSR in business policy

Asian corporations were not oblivious to their social responsibilities but they have traditionally been fulfilled as implicit obligations embedded in business practices and culture-bound institutional frameworks (Fukukawa, 2009). Responsibility was in the hand of the owners and it did not imply the creation of organizational mechanisms. In both Chinese and Japanese social hierarchy the position of the merchant and entrepreneur is traditionally low. Their roles had to be socially legitimized and it led to business cultures where a benevolent attitude towards employees, business partners and customers, and the surrounding community is expected (Economist Intelligence Unit, 2005; Ho, 2006). The core of values that appear in the statements of business leaders in Japan is 'faith' and 'trust', drawn from Buddhism and Confucianism. Doing something 'good' for society is regarded as a symbol of being a 'successful person' who deserves respect and is distinguishable from the 'money-seekers'. It is in following such precepts that Japanese companies promote partnerships with local communities in educational projects, infrastructure building and poverty alleviation (Tanimoto, 2009).

Zinkin (2007) identifies overlap between the tenets of Islam and the principles of the Global Compact. Likewise, the revival of Confucianism in China and in Hong Kong is typical of the perceived necessity to give moral legitimacy to social and economic order (Ho, 2006). The Hong Kong based businessman, Li Ka-Shing, has established a foundation and together with the Chinese Ministry of Civil Affairs he launched the Pediatric

Hernia Rehabilitation Program in 2009 to provide free surgery for children. Likewise, through initiatives related to Alibaba.com, its founder, Jack Ma supports Chinese small and medium enterprises (Credit Suisse, 2010). The Indian Tata group supports community development, health and safety, and cultural activities. The Infosys Foundation runs orphanages, hostels, hospitals, libraries, relief shelters and homes for destitute and mentally ill women, and invests in tribal welfare (Raja, 2004). The same trend is observable in Southeast Asia. For example, Putera Sampoerna, a successful businessman in the tobacco business, founded the Putera Foundation to improve entrepreneurial education in Indonesia, a country marred with high youth unemployment (Credit Suisse, 2010).

The nature of activities is often unrelated to their core business although there are also examples of engagement linked to business activities. This is notable in the case of Base of the Pyramid (BOP) projects aimed at the development of low-income markets that are cultivated in Japanese, Korean, Indian and Chinese companies. However, even in the case of unrelated activities it does not preclude stakeholder engagement as exemplified by the projects of Japanese companies and some Korean companies (Lee, 2005) carried out in conjunction with NGOs and international organizations. For instance, Toyota participates in reforestation projects in China, which is external to the company's activities, but the projects involve a number of employees, require managerial decisions, require technological transfers, are potentially scientifically developing and have an impact on the level of skills and knowledge of employees and locally involved manpower (Toyota, 2006).

Therefore, those philanthropic activities play a role in building societal well-being. They sometimes imply investments that have a significant economic and social local impact. The examples given show that they can also foster entrepreneurship and management guidance in the absence of venture capital industry and comprehensive public programmes that help small and new businesses. These initiatives are based on interpersonal trust – a keystone of relationships in the region. The initiatives taken by business leaders are not only expected but they have a strong societal legitimacy.

A shift towards an explicit type of CSR

However, an increasing number of Asian companies acknowledge that philanthropy is not a substitute for an assessment of and development of a program of CSR policies. Their activities share common characteristics with what is observed in European and US companies in the sense that they require changes in the internal dynamics in the organization. They have regular discussions with suppliers and the public authorities, they try to structure their engagement with key stakeholders through advisory panels, hold focus group interviews, and perform employee and customer surveys in order to receive constant feedback on their actions. CSR is part of HRM, as well as being part of corporate governance and risk management (Debroux, 2011a).

In organizational terms, in the most advanced large companies the tendency is to have a formal structure to govern the CSR agenda at the headquarters and in the subsidiaries, and to have managing directors preside over CSR committees. They want actively to engage in social development programs. They also engage more actively with their stakeholders on projects related to disease, biodiversity, or other issues requesting broad and diversified knowledge and experience (Debroux, 2011b).

Asian companies disclose more detailed non-financial information related to social and environmental issues. In adopting the triple-bottom-line concept, they recognize the necessity of adopting a kind of 'implicit' CSR that has features in common to the US-style 'explicit' CSR. The willingness to go beyond altruistic contribution appears more clearly in the CSR reports. Asian companies intend to advertise openly their activities to a larger public, an attitude that goes against cultural traditions that give prevalence to 'being and doing good anonymously'. Although considered as morally commendable this type of implicit CSR, dictated by the value of modesty could also reduce the overall efficacy of CSR diffusion in the whole society. The emerging explicit type of CSR allows advocacy where companies set the example in terms of CSR best practices. This is important, especially in developing Asia, where a large part of the social and environmental externalities originate from small companies that show little respect for formal social and environmental norms.

Many large Asian companies nurture strategic human resources and develop long-term sustainable relationships. Care is taken to ensure external and internal equity in recruitment, reward and promotion. Enablers are utilized to remove bias in recruitment and evaluation processes that could lead to race, gender or other types of discrimination. Evaluation of individual performance goes with training opportunities but also recognizes the difficulties involved in maintaining deadlines and work intensity. It is necessary to maintain space in the HRM system for programs of regeneration for managerial staff that enables them to participate in CSR activities. Corporate cultures are expected to maintain and encourage CSR values. The awareness of (mainly environment-related) CSR issues enables CSR values to become part of the mechanisms of prevention and improvement that include sustainability indicators linked to the employees' evaluation and reward systems (Debroux, 2011b).

Currently, CSR social dimensions are often still viewed as a necessary cost of doing business, especially concerning non-core and foreign employees. Environment-related CSR policies are considered easier to manage because they do not affect companies' internal dynamics to the same extent and progress can be advertised. The growing success of eco-products also means that environmental issue-driven CSR responds directly to the market demand. However, pressure from Western companies, business organizations and NGOs is mounting to raise human rights issues and increase labour standards. A comprehensive CSR policy on those matters would require closer relationships with the advocacy NGOs than most Asian companies have currently. Asian companies are self-sustaining and self-contained and are fearful of the direct intervention of outsiders in their management practices. For instance, Japanese companies actively collaborate with NGOs with whom they can manage projects on a business-like manner but they are uneasy in dealing with NGOs that advocate causes (Debroux, 2011b).

The different approaches of implementing CSR policies

The management of the value chain

As the result of the cost and the difficulties experienced in developing relationships with very small concerns, companies tend to narrow the number of suppliers with whom they work on CSR policy (Welford and Frost, 2006). Problems concern the verification of information. It is almost impossible to know what happens in remote factories, especially in fields where the value chain is complex. The intention is to create a critical mass of suppliers with whom a dialogue can be sustained, and to engineer ripple effects reaching the levels below. In this respect, the sophistication of the external and internal monitoring systems that Nike (Lim and Phillips, 2008) has put in place show that it is possible to transform a competitive, arms-length market structure into an economically secure relationship with the buyer in the global value chain. The Nike approach goes beyond the mere request of applying a code of conduct. It requires a constant flow of information, incentives and knowledge transfer in order to obtain a superior compliance of the code of conduct and, eventually, have key suppliers develop an independent ethical commitment to CSR (Lim and Phillips, 2008). To reach levels below the first layers in the supply chains, co-opting traditional community sources of power with the help of NGOs may be more effective than a top-down policy. In most developing Asian countries the development of NGOs as grassroots organizations may offer an alternative response to the need for community level contacts.

Regulation and market incentives

A mix of stick and carrot type policies is preferred. Enforceable rules are devised such as the obligation of publishing ESG reports. It exerts pressure while giving publicity for sound policies. In doing so, business could be compelled, indirectly, to perform adequately. An increasing number of countries are enacting laws that require environmental impact assessment (EIA) for all major projects. Volunteer initiatives are also promoted such as PROPER in Indonesia, Eco-Watch in the Philippines, Green Rating Project in India and Green Watch in China (Kathuria, 2008). The PROPER scheme was introduced in Indonesia in 1995. Companies agree to be rated by the government; this rating can lead to penalties for inferior environmental performance. If a company receives a significantly bad rating for two consecutive years, financial institutions or banks must halt financial loans and other aid to the company. The scheme is said to have helped companies in complying with environmental standards. Other countries such as the Philippines and Vietnam are introducing similar mechanisms (Lopez et al., 2009).

The eco-town program (Global Environment Centre Foundation, 2005) is an example of putting policy into action to develop industrial and technical infrastructure in order to sustain the development of a sound resource efficient society. An effective approach to improve the capacity of local governments is networking between cities for knowledge sharing and mutual learning. The Kitakyushu initiative for a clean environment (CITYNET) is one example. The Promotion Council for Low-Carbon Cities was formed in 2008 from 13 eco-model cities, other cities and ministries, research institutions and private companies. They are now committed to becoming low carbon, sustainable cities, and are working with national and prefectural governments, the private sector and the general population to achieve their aims.

A few Asian countries have introduced policies enhancing the awareness of consumers to purchase more environmentally sound goods and services. Japan enacted the Law on Promoting Green Purchasing in 2000, requiring the national government, its affiliated organizations and local governments to purchase products that are environmentally sound. Korea followed suit in enacting a 'Green Purchase Act'. A Green Purchasing Network (GPN) was established in 1996 in Japan. It consists of small and large corporations, local governments and consumer organizations, and provides information on environmentally friendly products. Korea formed its GPN in 1999, Malaysia in 2003, and Taiwan and Thailand in 2005 (Green Purchasing Network, 2012).

It was observed (Green Purchasing Network, 2012) that in terms of consideration of eco-friendliness when buying products China comes first with 80.5 per cent, followed by India (75.6 per cent). Japan is far behind with 38.4 per cent, a figure in line with Western countries. In terms of the number of manufacturers of eco-friendly products, another survey indicates that the Korean Eco-Label comes top followed by the Japanese Ecomark, ahead of the EU Ecolabel and the American ENERGY STAR (Hak, 2012). The adoption of environmental management system (EMS), such as life-cycle assessment (LCA), environmental reporting, environmental accounting, and the application of ISO 14001, has also grown rapidly. Japanese companies are well ahead in term of ISO 14001 certificates issued, followed by Chinese and Korean companies. They rank in the top ten countries in the number of ISO certificates issued. Taiwan, India and Thailand have also increased their number of certified companies and the growth rate in Asia tends to be higher than elsewhere (ISO World Inc., 2012).

CSR and sustainable development at the regional level

There is no overarching regional environmental or sustainable development institution in the Asia-Pacific region, although regional arms of global institutions such as UNEP Regional Office for Asia and the Pacific, UNDP, WHO, FAO, and UNESCAP, use their convening powers. They provide a unified 'voice' for the community represented. The creation of the Mekong River Basin ecosystem based inter-governmental body is a good example of regional collaboration. It has set a prototype for effective ecosystem-based, natural resource management and an alternative sustainable livelihood development, in a region where few rivers and water bodies have been governed by legally binding agreements. It is a difficult challenge to create a sustainable channel of trade and prosperity in the Mekong River basin that contains 70 million people and encompasses the 230 million people of Cambodia, China's southern province of Yunnan and Tibet province, Myanmar, Laos, Thailand and Vietnam. Diverse interests are represented, from agriculture, fisheries, energy and transportation. The project needs to be envisioned from broad perspectives recognizing the symbolic and pragmatic dimensions of the river development from being more than a transportation route or source of commodity water, to seeing it as an ecosystem worthy of preservation and protection for future generations. Balanced, sustainable development is pitted against pure economic objectives with difficult trade-offs in and between the countries involved.

Conclusion

There is a consensus in most Asian countries on the point that CSR should be both voluntary and regulated. On the one hand companies claim that they should be given the possibility to develop innovative CSR and sustainable development-related policies and practices. As a result of the importance given to the shift toward a green economy public authorities tend to agree with them. They attempt to nurture the right business environment to allow this to happen. The use of a mix of regulatory measures, market-based measures, voluntary agreements, education and information measures is expected to give results in time. On the other hand, significant results cannot be expected without more stringent enforcement of the existing laws and regulations to ensure that companies become highly responsible and avoid free riding.

It is observed that blending considerations of efficiency and energy supply security with low-carbon and low-pollution systems, as well as a commitment to social equity require a dramatic revamp of the current growth regime. The problem is that the benefits of the shift remain unconvincing for many companies and countries. For the time being, the incentive not to comply to ESG requirements often outweighs the incentive to do it in an uncertain regulatory environment. The eradication of monopolies, corruption and preserve subsidies will remain difficult and politically challenging. Long periods of authoritarian regimes have created rooted vested interests in some countries. It means that despite more formalization of the rules in the region, the regulatory environment is likely to remain unstable and less responsive to centralization and rationalization, especially in developing Asia. It calls for a pragmatic approach of the issue of environmental sustainability.

The shift to a green economy is not only a question of technology it also requires more autonomy and more resources for civil society. The most formidable challenge will be to create a sustainable business and welfare system that is inclusive of all inhabitants in the region. The debate on all those issues has just begun.

Chapter summary

- There is a growing recognition that solutions to CSR and sustainable-related problems require the involvement of people and organizations down to the local level.

- Asian civil society is increasingly assertive and challenges the environmental, social and consumption-driven status quo and the vested interest of public authorities and business concerns in the region.

- Asian countries develop problem resolution mechanisms at national, sub-regional and regional levels involving private and public organizations but the level of institutionalization of the schemes remains lower than in the West.

- The model of sustainable development based on economic efficiency has reached its limit but the conditions are not yet ripe to shift smoothly toward the green economy concept.

- Economic nationalism and fear of losing the battle in the transition to green economies is a powerful driver of the initiatives currently taken by leading Asian economies.

Key concepts

Business case: the concept of having a non-technical reason for a project or task. In CSR language it means that responsible behaviour can be financially sound.

Code of conduct: a set of rules outlining the responsibilities of, or proper practices for, an individual or organization.

Corporate social responsibility: a concept whereby organizations consider the interests of society by taking responsibility for the impact of their activities on customers, employees, shareholders, communities and the environment in all aspects of their operations.

Eco-labelling: A labelling system for consumer products (including foods) that are made in a way that limits detrimental effects on the environment. All eco-labeling is voluntary.

Global Compact: an initiative from the UN to encourage businesses worldwide to adopt sustainable and socially responsible policies, and to report on them.

Global Reporting Initiative: the world's de facto standard in sustainability reporting guidelines.

Green economy: a sustainable economy and society with zero carbon emissions and a one-planet footprint where all energy is derived from renewable sources, which are naturally replenished

Philanthropy: the act of donating money, goods, time, or effort to support a charitable cause, usually over an extended period of time and in regard to a defined objective.

Social labelling: labelling that is put on a number of products informing the purchaser that they have been produced in places that respect international social and labour norms.

Socially responsible investment: an investment strategy that combines the intentions to maximize both financial return and social good.

Stakeholder engagement: voluntary relationships between stakeholders in order to facilitate the achievement of objectives related to CSR and sustainable development

Sustainable development: a socio-ecological and economic process characterized by the fulfilment of human need while maintaining the quality of the natural environment indefinitely.

Tripartite system: a system under which government, management and labour are considered as equal social partners discussing and negotiating social, business and labour relationships respectful of all the parties interest

Triple bottom line: reporting of companies measuring organizational (and societal) success; economic, environmental and social.

Review questions

1 Do you think that Asian countries can develop original solutions to the current issue of green economy, in terms of ideas, concepts and policy? If so, which and how should they be implemented?

2 How do you explain the success of the ISO norms among Asian companies compared to the relative lack of interest in transnational governance schemes?

3 How do you appraise the philanthropic activities of Asian companies?

4 What would be required for Asian companies to establish more fruitful relationships with the advocacy NGOs?

5 How do you appraise the Eco-town project developed in Japan? Do you think that it fits well with the concept of green economy?

Learning activities and discussions

1 Imagine you are a business operator (producer or service provider) and select three key issues that you consider relevant in establishing a stakeholder dialogue based on ESG principles. Establish a priority list of the stakeholders with whom you think you have to establish a dialogue to solve the issues. List the crucial points that have to be discussed and agreed upon and explain how you intend to proceed to find a long-term solution.

2 Collect information on your competitors' CSR and sustainable-related activities from the publications of relevant programmes, and from company websites or news coverage accessed via the Internet – about four similar companies from four different Asian countries in a given industry. Try to find common patterns and differences. Explain the patterns and differences you find.

MINI CASE

The Roundtable on Sustainable Palm Oil (RSPO)

The RSPO was formed in 2004 with the objective of promoting the growth and use of sustainable palm oil products through credible global standards and engagement of stakeholders. RSPO is a not-for-profit, market-led association that represents palm oil producers, palm oil processors or traders, consumer goods manufacturers, retailers, banks and investors, and NGOs representing environmental and social interests. It has been set up to bring the sector together in order to develop and implement standards for sustainable palm oil. All stakeholders have equal rights and can raise issues. The decisions are taken by consensus. So far only principles and criteria for sustainable palm oil production have been discussed and loosely agreed upon. It allows flexibility but no permanent institutional support mechanisms or appropriate financing mechanisms have been established for implementing policy measures and activities that are collectively supported by the countries concerned in the region (Crow, 2006).

Decisions require complex multi-stakeholder engagement because the palm industry is at the nexus of issues that are of different relevance for each stakeholder. It is very important to Indonesia and Malaysia and to local companies because it creates a large number of jobs, brings foreign currency to the state and is very profitable. Plantation owners have greatly increased the productivity in utilizing genetically modified organisms and developing new seeds. The industry presented itself as a hi-tech innovative sector whose development is in line with the country's strategy toward high quality and high value-added products. Palm oil is utilized in thousands of products in the food and cosmetic industries. Producers would be unable to make a large range of their products without palm oil because there is no adequate substitute in most of the cases. It can also be utilized as biofuel.

However, the impact of palm oil plantation expansion on the orang-utans population in Indonesia is likely to lead to its extinction within 20 years. The destruction of tropical forest for the plantation expansion threatens some of the richest spots of biodiversity in the world. It is established that land rights of indigenous people and small owners are most often not respected because of bribery and fraud. Labour conditions in the plantations do not respecting core labor standards of the ILO in terms of safety, wage and other working conditions. It also utilizes child labour and illegal immigrants on a large scale and provides almost no employees' development opportunities. A number of proposals have been made to make the industry sustainable. Money could be provided to local government in order to cover the costs of the projects aiming to protect the environment and improve labour conditions. Green palm certificates are already on sale that would guarantee the soundness of the products to the buyers and their customers. The scheme is a typical example of what is developing in Asia in regard to environmental, social and governance sustainability. Although some progress is recognized no member is really satisfied with the outcome of the roundtable so far. Criticisms are made, notably by NGOs for reasons that reflect the conflicts of interest among the parties. Suggestions are also made to improve the system. Some buyers have decided to stop relationships with a number of suppliers but others also work together (with the help of NGOs) in order to improve the system. In that sense, it exemplifies the difficulties and potentialities of the use of the multistakeholders' approach.

Questions

1 Do you think that the Green Palm Certificate provides a long-term solution to the issue of sustainability of the palm oil industry? If not what kinds of incentives do you think would be more effective?

2 Which stakeholders will be the most interested in the issue of the orang-utan and how do you think that a retail business should deal with the issue?

3 What do you think is the most sensible way of dealing with the issue of child labour in the palm oil industry?

Web links

International Labour Organization: www.ilo.org

OECD: www.oecd.org

CSR Asia: http://www.csr-asia.com

References

Alcott, B. (2005) Jevons' Paradox. *Ecological Economics*, 54: 9–21.

Asian Development Bank (ADB) (2006) *Asian Environment Outlook Report*. Manila: Asian Development Bank

Asian Development Bank (2012) *Asia Water Watch 2015*. Manila: Asian Development Bank.

(ASrIA)Association for Sustainable and Responsible Investment in Asia (2012) *Annual Report on SRI in Asia*, accessed 4 November 2013 at: www.asria.org/

Bartley, T. (2003) Certifying Forests and Factories. *Politics and Society*, 31: 433–464.

Carroll, A. (2004) Managing Ethically with Global Stakeholders: A Present and Future Challenge, *Academy of Management Executive*, 18(2): 114–120.

Credit Suisse (2010) Strategic Philanthropy: Unlocking Entrepreneurial Potential, White Paper 1. Report written by CSR Asia for Credit Suisse.

Crow, L. (2006) Business and NGOs – A Force for Change? *CSR Asia Weekly*, 2: 20.

Debroux, P. (2011a) Human Resource Management and Employment Systems in Asia: Directions of Change and New Challenges, in R. Bebenroth and T. Kanai (eds.) *Challenges of Human Resource Management in Japan*. London: Routledge.

Debroux, P. (2011b) Survey in Japan, Vietnam and Korea on CSR and HRM policy in Local Companies (unpublished manuscript).

Drezner, D. and Lu, M. (2009) How Universal are Club Standards? Emerging Markets and Volunteerism, in M. Potoski and A. Prakesh (eds.) *Voluntary Programs: A Club Theory Perspective*. Cambridge, MA: MIT Press, pp. 181–206.

Economic Intelligence Unit (2005) *The Way of the Merchant, Corporate Social Responsibility in Japan*. London: Economist Intelligence Unit.

Economist Intelligence Unit (2012) *A Greener Shade of Grey*. A special report on renewable energy in China. London: Economic Intelligence Unit.

Ehnert, I. and Harry, H. (2012) Recent Developments and Future Prospects on Sustainable Human Resource Management: Introduction to the Special Issue. *Management Review*, 23, (3): 221–239.

Ethical Trading Initiative (ETI) (2012) Annual Report, accessed 5 November 2013 at:. www.ethicaltrade.org

Freeman, R. (1984) *Strategic Management: A Stakeholder Approach*. Marshfield, MA: Pitman.

Fukukawa, K. (2009) Global Crossroads – Corporate Social Responsibility in Asia, in K. Fukukawa (ed.) *Corporate Social Responsibility in Asia*. London: Routledge, pp. 1–22.

Global Environment Centre Foundation (2005) Eco-Towns in Japan, accessed 5 November 2013 at: www.gec.jp/

Green Purchasing Network (2012) About GPN, accessed 5 November 2013 at: www.gpn.jp/English/aboutgpn.html

ISO World Inc. 2012. (2012) *World-Wide Number of ISO 14001*, accessed 5 November 2013 at: www.iso.org/

Hak, Joo–Hyun (2012) Winning Eco-product Strategies. *SERI Quarterly*, October, 95–99, accessed 5 November 2013 at: www.seri quarterly.com

Ho, B. (2006) Confucian Businessmen. *CSR Asia Weekly*, 2(43).

ILO (International Labour Organization) (2010) *The Concept of Decent Work*. Geneva: ILO

Kathuria, V. (2008) Public Disclosures: Using Information to Reduce Pollution in Developing Countries. *Environment, Development and Sustainability*, 11(5): 955–970.

Kojima, S. (2011) Reduce Policy Towards Sustainable Society. *Proceedings of Research on Environmental Economic and Social Impacts of Resource Circulation Systems in Asia and the Pacific*. Manila: Asian Development Bank.

Kuriyama, N. (2009) The Role of Business in Asian Living and Working Conditions, in H. Hasegawa and C. Noronha (eds.) *Asian Business and Management: Theory, Practices and Perspectives*. Basingstoke: Palgrave Macmillan, pp. 151–171.

Lee, K-H. (2205) Why and How to Adopt Green Management into Business Organizations? The Case Study of Korean SMES in Manufacturing Industries. *Management Decision*, 47(7): 1101–1121.

Li, M. (2011) The Impact of China's Aging Population. *SERI Quarterly*, October, 25–33.

Lim, S.J. and Phillips, J. (2008) Embedding CSR Values: The Global Footwear Industry's Evolving Governance Structure. *Journal of Business Ethics*, 81: 143–156.

Lopez J.G., Sterner, T. and Afsah, S. (2009) Public Disclosure of Industrial Pollution – The PROPER Approach for Indonesia? University of Gothenburg, School of Business, Economics and Law, *Working Paper in Economics*, No. 414.

McKinsey and Company (2012) *Women Matter: An Asian Perspective*. Author.

Ministry of Knowledge Economy (Korea) (2011) *Report on Environment-related Investments*, accessed 11 November 2011 at: http://mke.go.kr/language/eng/

Nakamaru, H. (2010) Trends and Future Issues of Environmental Management in Japan. *Asian Business and Management*, 9(2): 189–208.

OECD (2008) *OECD Principles of Corporate Governance*. Paris: OECD.

OECD (2012) *Employment Outlook*. Paris: OECD

Ofreneo, R. (2008) Rights for Asia's Invisible Majority, Social Justice for all Working Women and Men. *Asian Labor Law Review*, 7(5): 4–11.

Raja, M. (2004) *Asia Times*, September 30, 2004, accessed 5 November 2013 at: www.atimes.com

Redding, G. (2005) The Thick Description and Comparison of Societal Systems of Capitalism. *Journal of International Business Studies*, 36(2): 123–155.

Roper, J. (2012) Stakeholder Engagement: Concepts, Practices and Complexities, in Kigyo Shakai Forum (ed.) *Jizokukanona Hatten to Multistakeholders [Sustainable Development and Multistakeholders]*. Tokyo: Chikura Shobo.

Tanimoto, K. (2009) Structural Change in Corporate Society and CSR in Japan, in K. Fukukawa, (ed.) *Corporate Social Responsibility in Asia*. London: Routledge, pp. 45–66.

Toyota (2006) *Sustainability Report 2006*. Jidosha Kabushiki Gaisha.

Transparency International (2012) *Corruption Index 2012*, accessed 5 November 2013 at: www.transparency.org/

United Nations (1987) *Our Common Future, Report of the World Commission on Environment and Development*.

United Nations (2010) *United Nations Global Compact* accessed 5 November 2013 at: www.unglobalcompact.org

United Nations Environment Programme (2011) *Towards a Green Economy: Pathways to Sustainable Development and Poverty Eradication*. UNEP accessed 5 November 2013 at: www.unep.org/greeneconomy

Welford, R. and Frost, S. (2006) Corporate Social Responsibility in Asian Supply Chains. *Corporate Social Responsibility and Environmental Management*, 13: 166–176.

Yale University (2012) Environmental Performance Index, accessed 5 November 2013 at: http://epi.yale.edu/

Zinkin, J. (2007) Islam and CSR: A Study of the Compatibility between the Tenets of Islam, the UN Global Compact and the Development of Social and Natural Capital. *Corporate Social Responsibility and Environmental Management*, 14: 206–218.

PART II VARIETIES OF BUSINESS SYSTEMS IN ASIA

The Business System of Japan

8

Michael A. Witt

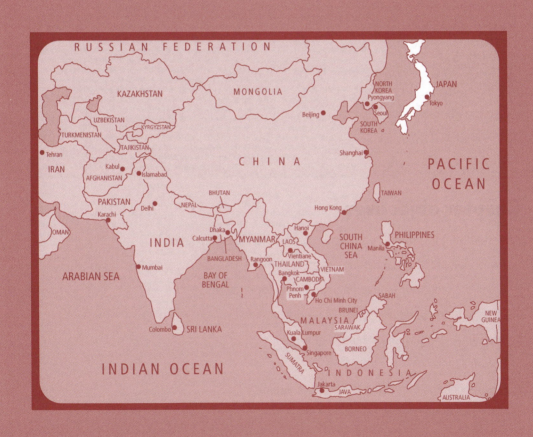

Chapter outline

- The Japanese business system
- Comparative advantage
- Continuity and change in the Japanese business system
- International activities of Japanese firms
- Corporate social responsibility (CSR) and Japanese business

Chapter objectives

After reading this chapter, you should have an understanding of:

1 The shape of the Japanese business system.

2 Areas of comparative advantage and their foundations.

3 Change in the business system over time.

4 International activities of Japanese firms.

5 CSR in Japan.

6 Key implications for doing business in Japan.

Introduction

Japan's economy is Asia's most developed and its second-largest. It is a densely populated country of 128 million people living in an area about the size of Germany (82 million people) and somewhat smaller than California (36 million people). Japan was the first Asian nation to industrialize.

Japan's modern economic development began in the second half of the nineteenth century, almost one century ahead of the Asian 'Tiger' states. It blended features of Japanese society with Western know-how. Knowledge transfer was selective and adaptive, so Japan did not become a clone of the West but evolved its own unique ways of doing things. In this, it has been so successful that despite slow growth for most years since 1990, it still accounts for about 30 per cent of nominal economic output in Asia-Pacific (including China).

As a consequence, Japan's influence on Asia and the world economy has been considerable. Japan's development approach became the model for many emerging markets in Asia-Pacific, with South Korea and Taiwan at the forefront. Japanese managerial innovations have had a major impact on business worldwide, and their influence can today be found in any modern factory.

Despite its impact on the world, to many Japan remains somewhat of an enigma. The objective of this chapter is to take some of the mystery out of Japanese business.

The Japanese business system: culture and key historical influences

Rationale

Like most firms outside the Anglo-Saxon countries, Japanese firms do not see the maximization of shareholder value as their ultimate purpose. Rather, Japanese firms exist to serve society in general and their employees in particular.

Consider these statements, taken from informal interviews conducted with senior executives of leading Japanese firms (Witt and Redding, 2010):

> As an individual manager, I think the most important thing is it has to be a company that can continue to contribute to society in its own way.
> I think [most important] is the employees. … Pay the shareholder a dividend within tolerable bounds.

Implicit is a reversal of Anglo-Saxon and business school thinking that firms should maximize shareholder value, subject to the constraint of not alienating other stakeholders such as society and employees. Japanese firms instead aim to generate benefits for society and employees, subject to the constraint of keeping shareholders from revolting. While pressure from international investors has led Japanese firms to pay more attention to shareholders, the overall formula has proved resilient.

Even owner-managed firms exhibit a relative de-emphasis of owner interests. For instance, during Japan's lost decade of low economic growth in the 1990s and the early 2000s, many owner-managers went into debt instead of firing employees.

Understanding why Japanese business emphasizes the concerns of society and employees requires an appreciation of key historical events and their impact on Japanese business. One such key event occurred with the beginning of the Tokugawa period in Japan in 1603. After centuries of civil war, Japan was united and at peace. The new government under *shogun* (literally meaning 'general', here meaning 'military ruler') Tokugawa Ieyasu implemented a number of measures to ensure this unity and peace would last.

One step was the introduction of a Confucian social order, which is generally biased against business activities, as handling money matters is considered vulgar. The introduction of a Confucian-style four-tier social caste system reinforced this. This structure sees scholars (a role assumed by the samurai) at the top, followed by farmers and artisans. Merchants were the bottom class, as Confucius had argued that trading was a parasitic activity adding no value to society. Business under this system was closely circumscribed, with rule violations meeting severe punishment. The lasting impact on Japanese business has been to anchor in the collective mindset the necessity of firms to justify their existence to society.

Despite government hostility to business, merchants generally thrived, in some cases amassing large fortunes. This proved useful when two later key historical events compelled Japan to commence rapid industrialization. In 1853, Commodore Matthew Perry and his black ships (so called for the colour of their hulls) arrived in Japan to demand that the country open to foreign trade. Japan had imposed severe restrictions on foreign trade from 1635 onward in order to counter Portuguese and Spanish religious and colonial ambitions. Perry's arrival had several effects beyond reopening trade. One was to demonstrate how far Japanese technology had fallen behind the West. Another was to revive the fear of colonization. The United States and other nations imposed so-called Unequal Treaties on Japan, and the Japanese realized that much of the world, including China, had fallen to Western imperialism.

The ineffective Tokugawa government of the time was overthrown in 1868 in the Meiji Restoration. The name of the event stems from the official pretence that it returned real power over Japan to the Emperor Meiji. In reality, the Meiji Restoration replaced one select group of rulers with another. Concluding that Japan could only remain independent if it learned to play the Western game of international politics, the new rulers initiated rapid reforms. Their objective was encapsulated in the slogan rich country, strong army (*fukoku kyôhei*): independence and security for the nation required a strong army, which needed a strong economy. Serendipitously, the merchant class had funds and business experience to propel Japan towards industrialization. Business had become useful to society.

Two further key developments occurred following Japan's World War II defeat in 1945. First, national strategy was shortened to 'rich country'. This shift is evident in the Yoshida Doctrine (after Prime Minister Shigeru Yoshida), which emphasizes economic growth while leaving international politics and defence essentially to the United States. This focus on the economy further elevated the importance of business.

Second, the US occupation imposed a democratic constitution. Democracy in the Japanese interpretation became associated with equality in economic outcomes. Before the war, inequality was the norm; when, for instance, a section chief working for one of the major firms allegedly could have bought a villa from a single annual bonus. In contrast, post-war Japan evolved a system that distributed economic wealth through universal male employment, which has developed into a goal of its own over time.

In sum, the purpose of the firm is the generation of benefits for society and employees. In our discussion of the purpose, we have already encountered the key means for meeting this purpose. One is an important role for government in providing general direction for the country and in maintaining social and economic order. This implies an important role for government regulation – liberalization is seen as leading to chaos – as well as cooperative relations between government and business. Cooperation with other firms, including competitors, is appropriate for maintaining order and creating synergies, especially when Japanese firms need to catch up with foreign competitors. Further implied are measures to limit the influence of (especially foreign) investors and the acceptance of education as a means of social mobility and establishing hierarchy.

Identity

The Japanese have a relatively collectivist sense of identity that puts the interests of the group above those of the individual. Counter to what Westerners tend to expect, the available data show no clear trend towards individualism over time. For instance, the Survey on Social Consciousness by the Prime Minister's Office shows people putting national over personal benefit, with the proportion of people doing so practically unchanged in recent decades. With collectivism comes conformity pressure; as the Japanese say, 'the nail that stands out gets hammered in'. Consequently, few Japanese insist on doing things their way, which contributes to low levels of entrepreneurship in Japan.

Different Asian societies emphasize different kinds of collectives (groups). The most important group for Japanese males, and in Japanese economic life generally, is the firm. This is to be interpreted in the context of lifetime or long-term employment, with many employees spending more hours with their colleagues than with their families. Even outside work, employees tend to socialize with co-workers.

Besides the company, school ties represent an important source of identity. Graduates from the same schools are expected to help one another for the rest of their lives.

Authority

Japanese society is fairly hierarchical, with authority relations structured along Confucian lines. Traditionally, Confucian hierarchies have a strong paternalistic element, with subordinates owing unconditional obedience in exchange for help and protection from their superiors. In Japan, a strong sense of community, a desire for harmony and consensual decision making combine to soften this element. It is rare for superiors to impose their views.

The Confucian influence is evident in the determinants of the hierarchy, with the most important being sex, age and education. Today, both sexes enjoy equal status under the law. However, the notion of a division of labour between the sexes persists, with women in charge of household and children and men in charge of providing an income. In reality, the role of women in the workplace is considerable, though mostly in non-managerial positions. Career women have become more common but remain rare in middle and upper management.

Minimal age differences are sufficient to establish hierarchy. In twins, the difference in time of birth establishes a hierarchy of older/younger brother/sister. In school and work, belonging to a different intake establishes hierarchy, expressed in the terms *sempai* and *kohai* (senior and junior). *Sempai–kohai* relations tend to persist even after people have graduated or retired.

Education establishes hierarchy on the basis of the Confucian ideal that social position should be a function of educational attainment. Confucius advocated a universal education system, with attainment evaluated through state examinations. The best and brightest were to run the country as the top bureaucrats. The Japanese education system still follows this approach. The school or university attended largely determines an individual's career perspectives – top-tier firms hire from top-tier schools, second-tier firms, from second-tier schools and so on.

The government

The role of the Japanese government in the economy is to provide stability and guidance. The Japanese generally do not share the Western, and especially Anglo-Saxon, faith that the economy is essentially stable and self-sustaining and thus best left to its own devices. Market forces are perceived as potentially harmful, requiring restraint. Nor is there a strong belief that market forces alone are sufficient to guide the economy into the future, for example, by inducing the development of new technologies.

The government plays this role in a number of ways. One is to limit – not eliminate – competition. The underlying rationale is that too much competition will weaken the viability of firms and increase the risk of bankruptcies. Bankruptcies mean unemployment so too much competition runs counter to the purpose of the firm. The government imposes limits through formal regulations, but also through informal directives known as administrative guidance. Where regulations and guidance fail to prevent bankruptcies, the government tends to arrange for bank bailouts or mergers with healthy competitors.

A second tool is industrial policy, which aims at inducing firms to move into industries with higher value added. After the war, industrial policy was straight-forward: observe more advanced countries to identify the next industry to develop, then provide incentives to a select group of companies to enter that industry, for example, through preferential access to capital and subsidies.

This model had become obsolete as Japan caught up with the West in the late 1970s. Being a developed nation means uncertainty about what industries to develop next; technologies that look promising may fail, while others may unexpectedly emerge and succeed.

The Japanese industrial policy has thus switched to promoting basic research and encouraging firms to experiment with new technologies. A common policy tool is R&D consortia. In these consortia an average of about 20 firms conduct collaborative research on new technologies for some 6 to 10 years. This collective approach reduces the associated risk for firms, which is also reduced through government funding that covers part of the costs. For instance, the 10-year micromachine technology consortium of 23 firms received about US$250 million in government support (Witt, 2001).

Unlike most Asian governments, the Japanese government generally does not impose its will from above. Japanese politics involves high levels of societal coordination. This means that policymaking involves extensive consultations of government officials, business representatives and often other parties such as academics. Avenues for these consultations include deliberation councils within ministries (*shingikai*) as well as thousands of industry associations. Societal coordination takes considerable time, and if no consensus emerges, policy gets stuck (Witt, 2006). At the same time, this process helps to avoid policy mistakes and ensures that once policy is decided, implementation is typically swift and thorough.

The Japanese business system: business environment

Financial capital

The key characteristic of the financial system is its reliance on indirect finance, that is, bank loans. Though Tokyo is a major international financial centre, Japanese firms use banks to meet about two-thirds of their external funding needs (Witt, 2006).

Banks' lending decisions are based on a mixture of market criteria, strength of existing business relationships and government input. The relative importance of these has changed over time. In the immediate post-war era, banks essentially did as government told them. Since then, market criteria have gained importance.

Most loans are long-term loans. Even in the case of debtors verging on bankruptcy, banks rarely recall their loans; instead, especially large firms may receive new loans to keep them afloat. This is partially explained by the importance of preventing bankruptcies in order to maintain employment, but also by a sense of mutual obligation from years of business relationships.

Human capital

The education system generally produces very good results. Schooling through high school is practically universal, and the 2010 gross enrolment rate in tertiary education was 60 per cent (Witt, 2014). Attainment tends to compare favourably with that in most other advanced industrialized nations. In a 2009 OECD study of 72 nations (OECD, 2010), Japanese students were fifth in natural sciences, eighth in reading and ninth in mathematics.

Despite these good results, the system has shortcomings. First, it emphasizes memorizing facts over critical and creative thinking. This is linked to Confucianism, in which standardized examinations on classical texts determined scholarly standing. Second, given the importance of education in determining one's career prospects, getting into good schools is crucial. This requires passing entrance examinations, which puts a lot of pressure on students to prepare. Many children attend private cram schools after regular school ends in the afternoon, returning home late in the evening only to spend several more hours doing homework.

The Japanese education system is relatively weak in two areas: tertiary education and vocational training. Tertiary education suffers from low motivation of students. Once students pass the entrance examinations, they are virtually guaranteed to graduate and get a job in line with the status of the school. As a consequence, most Japanese college students know more when they enter than when they graduate. The Japanese public vocational training system is weak, with most training taking place inside firms. The fact that employees typically stay for a long time allows firms to make major investments in training.

About 20 per cent of the labour force is organized in unions, predominantly at the company level. The strength of such company unions is difficult to gauge, because their interests are closely aligned with those of the company. Management tends to see unions as partners in running the company. Strikes occur mostly as a ritual component of the annual 'spring offensive' (*shunto*), during which employees may stop work briefly in support of the wage bargaining process.

While only a small proportion of workers, mostly at large firms, have the informal promise of lifetime employment, most male employees are employed for the long term. Counter to predictions of the demise of long-term employment, average tenure of male employees has risen from 10.8 years in 1980 to 13.8 years in 2010 (Inagami & Whittaker, 2005; Ministry of Health, Labour and Welfare, 2011). Job tenure for women tends to be shorter. Many women stop work upon marriage, then re-enter the workforce on a part-time basis once the children have left home.

The number of non-regular workers (mostly workers on temporary contracts) in Japan has been on the rise for at least the past three decades, reaching 34 per cent in 2010 (Witt, 2014). Careful analysis suggests that this phenomenon does not represent a breakdown of the existing employment structure but the rise of a complementary employment system. Key drivers include an increase in the female workforce, often in newly created lines of employment such as home-care; a higher propensity of retired seniors to go back to work; and a larger number of tertiary education students working while still in school (Witt, 2014).

Social capital

Social capital is what allows people to cooperate without fear of being taken advantage of – in other words, trust. Japanese levels of trust are generally very high. At the personal level, the Japanese tend to build strong reciprocal relationships. At the systemic level, the Japanese generally believe that society helps ensure outcomes are fair. An expression of this latter point is that written employment contracts are rare. Punishment for breach of trust typically involves social sanction, such as exclusion from the group. Recourse to the legal system is possible, though relatively rare.

Strong trust enables high levels of social networking. One indicator of this is the number of industry associations, which, standardized by population size, is twice as high in Japan as in the United States and some 50 per cent higher than in Germany (Witt, 2006).

The Japanese business system: the business system

Ownership

Most major Japanese firms are listed corporations. On average about 52 per cent of outstanding stock is owned by other firms. Perhaps one-tenth of these shares represent cross-shareholdings, in which firms own each other, and about half are long-term shareholdings. Within business groups (see 'Networking' section) cross-shareholdings are usually considerably higher. Holdings by foreign investors were 29 per cent in 2009, although foreign shareholdings move quickly with market sentiment (Witt, 2014).

As mentioned, most Japanese do not support shareholder value, but believe that the purpose of the firm is to serve its employees and society. A key implication is that corporate governance mechanisms giving shareholders control are undesirable, as shareholders may pursue their interests at the expense of employees and society. Japanese firms are insulated from shareholder pressure by having a majority of their shares owned by usually friendly firms. This makes it difficult for any shareholder to gain a controlling stake or even attempt a hostile takeover. Recently, many firms have also adopted poison pill defences against takeovers, with government encouragement. For instance, Japan's Bull-Dog Sauce Company in 2007 invoked a poison pill defence to ward off a hostile takeover bid by a US investment fund. As a consequence of these and related measures, shareholders have little leverage, few hostile takeovers happen.

Networking

Japan's is a network economy. Firms routinely exchange information, coordinate and cooperate with a number of actors, such as other firms and government agencies.

One prominent type of network is the business groups.[1] These are collections of firms in different industries, about 30 to 40 on average, that maintain close ties with one another in the form of information exchange, but also in areas such as cross-shareholdings, interlocking directorates and intragroup purchasing. In the post-war period, there were six major groups, namely, Daiichi, Fuyo, Mitsubishi, Mitsui, Sanwa and Sumitomo. In 1999, the last year for which data are available, they accounted for 13.2 per cent of capital, 11.2 per cent of assets and 10.8 per cent of sales in the Japanese economy (Japan Fair Trade Commission, 2001). The early twentieth century saw mergers across group boundaries, bringing the number of business groups effectively to four (Witt, 2014). Coherence in these groups seems to have weakened but has not fully disappeared.

Many Japanese manufacturing firms maintain dense networks with suppliers and distributors, known as *keiretsu*. These networks have received much attention in the automotive industry as an important source of competitive strength. Business relations in these networks are typically for the long term rather than by arm's-length contracting. If a supplier is temporarily uncompetitive, its customer will normally maintain the account and offer help to correct the problem. Recent trends seem to have somewhat weakened the *keiretsu* in favour of more market-based exchange relationships.

In intra-industry loops (Witt, 2006), firms informally exchange information ranging from technological matters to market conditions. Partners in this exchange include other firms in the same industry, the respective industry association, government and other actors connected to the industry such as researchers, banks and journalists. Through these intra-industry loops, firms keep abreast of developments in their industry and influence joint initiatives such as standards setting. The first step towards entering intra-industry loops is normally to join the respective industry association. Figure 8.1 shows a conceptual representation of the three different network types.

Management

Decision making in Japanese firms is collective. Especially major decisions, such as a fundamental strategy change, involve extensive consultations with the various stakeholders of the company – including, where appropriate, production workers – until an

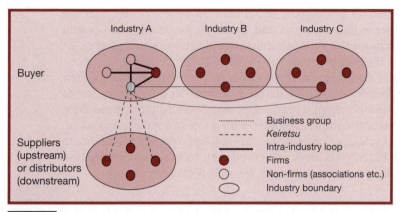

FIGURE 8.1 Conceptual representation of different types of networks

SOURCE: Adapted from Witt (2006).

overall consensus emerges. This process can be extremely time-intensive, and in recent years, some Japanese firms have sought to streamline and centralize these processes. However, once everyone agrees on what to do, implementation is usually quick and thorough.

The traditional criterion for promoting people has been seniority, that is, the number of years worked in the company. Though some firms seem to have begun to deviate from it, the overall evidence suggest that this seniority principle is alive and well (Witt, 2013). Counter to conventional wisdom, this system does account for performance variations. Of every annual intake of fresh graduates, good performers are promoted earlier than average. Those seen as less capable are sidelined over time through mechanisms such as formal promotion with no new, or less, responsibility, seconding to subsidiaries or associations and early retirement.

Comparative advantage

Japan has its strongest comparative advantages in car manufacturing and in the production of machinery and equipment (OECD, 2012). Japan's biggest comparative disadvantage is in travel, with far more Japanese traveling abroad than foreigners visiting Japan.

In general, Japanese firms excel in industries relying on incremental innovation. Incremental innovation occurs where the same kind of product becomes better and better through continuous improvement (*kaizen*). The long-term character of outside finance and the weakness of corporate governance allow firms to keep employees for the long term. This enables firms to invest in training employees to produce high-quality products, as they can be sure that people will remain with the firm long enough for the investment to pay off. At the same time, long-term employment makes employees willing to acquire skills that are useful only for their present firm, as they do not have to worry about their job market value. The result is a qualification pattern that is conducive to continuous improvement and high-quality production.

Japanese firms also tend to perform well where standardization of parts and processes enable high product quality. This mode of production benefits from the integration of shop-floor workers in quality management, which has had a great impact on the development of production management worldwide. For instance, production line employees are organized in small groups (quality control circles) who take responsibility for continuous improvement of the quality of work processes, products and services. In addition, close cooperation with suppliers, often in the context of *keiretsu*, helps improve product quality and is a key enabler of just-in-time (JIT) production, in which inventories and associated costs are minimized. Cooperation among firms in the same industry, facilitated by intra-industry loops, aids standard setting.

Continuity and change in the Japanese business system

The Japanese way of business has proved highly resilient to change. This is most visible in economically bad times, such as the 'lost decade' of low economic growth in the 1990s. Normally, economic pain leads to structural reforms. For example, the US business system underwent a fundamental transformation as the country encountered economic problems in the 1970s and 1980s. In the case of Japan's lost decade, however, there is little evidence of truly fundamental changes (Witt, 2014).

One cause of this rigidity is that the system is more flexible than it looks. For instance, labour costs are highly adaptable. Bonuses account for a large part of take-home pay. In bad years, companies can cut them, thus reducing labour costs significantly without firing employees. Participatory management means employees can see why the cuts are needed, which prevents disaffection. If cutting the bonus proves insufficient, firms may offer early retirement packages or transfer some employees to subsidiaries with lower pay.

However, these measures are insufficient in times of fundamental change, such as the present. The world economy is in transition from the industrial to the information technology age, and previous transitions have necessitated a thorough reform of business models. In addition, globalization has intensified cost pressures, and societal ageing paired with a shrinking population is reducing the size of the workforce.

Japan has been slow to respond for several reasons. Most Japanese are fairly content with the present system and are willing to bear the costs of maintaining it. In addition, comparative advantage of Japanese firms is dependent on the present way of doing business, as described earlier.

Most important, though, is that change requires societal coordination and, as discussed earlier under the role of government, this takes time and can get stuck. As unsolved problems accumulate, the associated economic costs should give firms an incentive to look for their own solutions by working around or ignoring the existing way of doing things. This would help firms avoid the costs of non-change and would put pressure on the coordinated decision-making process to produce results. However, in Japan, the social deviance this implies is socially unacceptable and the dense social networks in the economy increase the risk of discovery and sanction. Everyone needs to wait until societal coordination has run its course.

International activities of Japanese firms

Japanese firms are active players in the world economy. One main avenue of Japanese involvement is international trade. In 2011, Japan was the world's fourth largest merchandise exporter (4.5 per cent share by value) and importer (4.6 per cent) it was also the world's sixth largest commercial services exporter (3.4 per cent) and fifth largest importer (4.2 per cent). Counter to perception abroad, the Japanese economy is not highly dependent on exports, with 2010 exports accounting for about 15 per cent of GDP. This is about on par with the United States (13 per cent), but low compared with China (31 per cent) and Germany (47 per cent).[2]

The main destination for Japanese merchandise exports is East Asia, which in 2011 received about half of Japan's exports. Within that region, most trade went to China, Hong Kong, Taiwan and South Korea. The United States follows at about 15 per cent and the European Union (EU), at about 12 per cent. As mentioned earlier, the greatest strengths in Japanese exports are automobiles and machinery.

The second main avenue of international activity is foreign direct investments (FDI) In 2011, Japan accounted for about 6.7 per cent of new FDI worldwide and held about 4.5 per cent of the existing worldwide stock of FDI. While the recent strength of the Japanese yen has helped the country re-emerge as a major source of FDI, its present position is fairly minor, especially considering its economic size. In 2011, the United States and Germany held 21.3 per cent and 6.8 per cent of the existing FDI stock. Among the Asian economies, Japan was second to tiny Hong Kong, which held a slightly larger proportion of worldwide FDI stock (4.9 per cent) than Japan.[3]

Major areas of Japanese investment are the United States, Western Europe and East Asia. Of the 2011 stock of Japanese outward FDI, 29 per cent was in the United States, 27 per cent in Asia and 23 per cent in Western Europe. In terms of new Japanese FDI during the period from 2009 to 2011, Asia received about 33 per cent of Japanese FDI, Western Europe 29 per cent and the United States 14 per cent. Manufacturing accounts for about half of new investments, with a focus on chemicals and pharmaceuticals. Services account for the other half, with an emphasis on finance and insurance.

Trade and investment patterns of Japanese firms are interconnected in complex ways (Westney, 2001). One is that part of Japanese FDI has occurred in order to facilitate trade, for example, following the opening of Japan to international trade in 1868, Japanese general trading companies as well as other service firms providing trading infrastructure (banks, transport services) opened branches overseas, predominantly in Asia. Following Japan's defeat in 1945, the pattern repeated itself.

A second interconnection is that some of Japan's FDI has occurred to reduce or forestall trade frictions. For instance, Japanese car-makers have made major investments in the United States from the 1980s onwards. A major reason for doing so was to reduce Japanese car exports to the United States, which threatened to trigger US protectionism, closing a major market for Japanese producers. Similarly, Japanese firms invested in the European Union, especially in the United Kingdom, in the 1990s, as they feared that the completion of the European Common Market might lead to a protectionist 'Fortress Europe' shutting out others.

Third, a significant part of Japanese trade involves shipments to and from subsidiaries abroad. For instance, Japanese firms investing in China often source their equipment and ship components and subassemblies from Japan. A substantial part of the finished products of Japanese subsidiaries in China is exported back to Japan.

Counter to expectations that firms everywhere converge on the same 'best practices', Japanese multinational enterprises (MNEs) maintain distinct characteristics in their overseas investments. In particular, they tend to implement Japanese-style organizational patterns abroad and employ relatively high proportions of Japanese expatriate managers. In addition, Japanese MNEs often take many of the suppliers in their existing Japanese *keiretsu* with them to new markets.

Corporate social responsibility (CSR) and Japanese business

The CSR record of Japanese firms is mixed. On the one hand, service to society is, as discussed, in the DNA of Japanese business. Firms are typically concerned with the well-being of their stakeholders, including employees, society at large, customers, suppliers and also shareholders. Larger firms in particular contribute significantly to society in areas such as the arts, education and sports. The environment has received attention from the 1960s, with Japan now occupying a leading position among high-density population countries in terms of environmental sustainability. Corruption is relatively low, both at home and in the activities of Japanese firms abroad.

Other aspects of CSR seem less developed. Japanese firms have a tendency to attempt to cover up even major problems when they occur, such as nuclear accidents or food poisoning cases. This seems to be related to efforts to protect the firm against expected sanction from society at large. Among other areas with weaknesses, as mentioned in the literature (e.g., Wokutch and Shepard, 1999; Robins, 2005), are privacy policies for customers, CSR standards for suppliers, improving employability of personnel, opportunities for women and friendliness towards families, opportunities for minorities in Japan (for example, ethnic Koreans) and elsewhere (for example African Americans in US plants), publication of sustainability reports, joint work with non-government organizations (NGOs), and transparent corporate governance.

Bearing in mind our earlier discussion, the causes of limited progress on some of these dimensions are clear. The implied values run counter to existing social norms and business practices. CSR is a Western product, reflecting Western thinking of what the world should look like. This overlaps only partially with Japanese views. For instance, why should Japanese firms focus on increasing employability of personnel if their focus has been on maintaining lifetime or long-term employment? And if firms do not pursue shareholder value, why would they need transparent corporate governance?

In other areas, there may be overall agreement in Japan that change is desirable, but change in Japan takes time. For instance, many Japanese would agree that women should have better career opportunities. While more firms may now hire women for the career track, the seniority system means it will take years for the new recruits to reach management positions.

Chapter summary

- Japan's economy is the second-largest and most developed in Asia.

- Japanese firms are controlled by their employees and run for the benefit of employees and society as a whole. Cooperation within and across firms and with other organizations is pervasive. This sets Japanese business apart from firms in Anglo-Saxon and other Asian nations, but is similar to business in Europe.

- Japanese firms are world leaders in industries featuring incremental innovation as well as standardization and attendant high quality. They are at a disadvantage in industries with radical innovation and non-standard processes.

- The government plays an important role in ensuring order and guiding the economy. Liberalization is considered tantamount to chaos.

- Change in Japan is typically slow because of high levels of societal coordination. However, once change is agreed, implementation can be quick and universal.

- Japanese firms are major players in international trade and investment.

Key concepts

Business groups: collections of firms in different industries that have close ties with one another while remaining formally independent.

Company unions: groups representing the interests of labour, organized at the level of each individual firm; one of the 'three sacred treasures' of Japanese management.

Industrial policy: government policy aimed at guiding and promoting the development of specific industries and technologies.

Intra-industry loops: social networks connecting firms as well as non-firm organizations (for example, associations) in the same industry.

Keiretsu: strictly speaking, production and distribution networks; the term is often also applied to business groups.

Lifetime employment: informal promise to provide continuous employment for the duration of one's career; one of the 'three sacred treasures' of Japanese management.

Quality management: a system of means for ensuring quality standards in the production of goods and services.

Seniority principle: the practice of promoting employees based on the length of tenure with the firm; one of the 'three sacred treasures' of Japanese management.

Societal coordination: the practice of using collective consultation, deliberation and cooperation to change rules and practices.

Review questions

1 Describe the rationale, key historical influences, identity and authority in the Japanese business system.
2 Explain the characteristics of financial capital, human capital and social capital in the Japanese business system.

3 Describe the aspects of ownership, networking and management in the Japanese business system.

4 In what kinds of industries does Japan excel? Why?

5 Why is change in Japan so difficult?

6 How are Japanese firms integrated in the international economy?

7 Why is the CSR record of Japanese firms mixed as viewed from a Western perspective?

Learning activities and discussions

1 Japanese firms are slow to change. What does this imply in the present age of globalization and rapid technological change?

2 In most Asian countries, firms rise and disappear quickly. What is the situation in Japan? Use the internet to explore the level of entrepreneurial activity as well as the age of major Japanese firms. Explain what you observe.

3 Even though foreign firms tend to make good profits in Japan, the country receives little inward FDI. By contrast, while foreign firms have had difficulties making money in China, China in a good year probably receives more inward FDI than Japan has in total since 1945. How do you explain this?

MINI CASE

Bull-Dog Sauce and Steel Partners

Bull-Dog Sauce is a Japanese manufacturer of ready-made sauces and other food products. It is best known for its *tonkatsu* sauce, which is a type of thick Worcester sauce used as a condiment for *tonkatsu* (Japanese-style deep-fried pork cutlet). Founded in 1902, it is headquartered in Tokyo and employs about 200 people. It is listed on the Tokyo Stock Exchange. In its business year ending in March 2007, its return on total sales of about US$140 million was 4.3 per cent, with an operating income of about US$6 million.

Its largest shareholder in 2007, with a holding of 10.25 per cent of outstanding shares, was Steel Partners, a privately owned, New York based hedge fund. Steel Partners tends to invest in stocks of small publicly listed companies it considers to be under-priced. The company is known for intervening actively in the management of companies it controls to bolster their share prices and thus increase shareholder value. Among the measures commonly used by activist hedge funds are headcount reductions, asset sales and spin-offs of parts of the business not considered to be essential to the core business. Often, acquired companies would also be expected to take on large amounts of debt to reimburse the acquiring hedge funds for at least part of the acquisition price.

On 18 May 2007, Steel Partners announced to Bull-Dog Sauce's other shareholders that it sought to acquire all the shares of the company at ¥1,584 per share.

Unconvinced by the post-acquisition plans presented by Steel Partners, the leadership team of Bull-Dog Sauce announced on 7 June that it opposed the takeover bid because it would not be in the interest of shareholders. It called for a general shareholder meeting to be held 17 days later to decide the fate of the company.

At the meeting, 83.4 per cent of the shareholders – in essence everyone but Steel Partners – approved a plan to issue stock warrants to existing shareholders as of 10 July, with the express exception of Steel Partners and its affiliates. These warrants would enable shareholders to purchase three additional shares at a price of ¥1 per share, in effect quadrupling the number of their shares for ¥3.

A mechanism was adopted to make the exercise of these options automatic.

Steel Partners, on the other hand, was to be compensated with ¥1,188 (75 per cent of its offer price) per share it held. The effect would that Steel Partners' ownership share in Bull-Dog Sauce to be diluted to less than 3 per cent. Steel Partners' share would in effect become insignificant.

Steel Partners took to the courts to combat these measures, which it felt to be discriminatory, unfair and unnecessary. The Tokyo District Court dismissed the request for an injunction, noting that a majority of shareholders had approved the measure and that Steel Partners had received equal economic benefits relative to the other shareholders. In rejecting Steel Partner's appeal, the Tokyo High Court went so far as to label Steel Partners an 'abusive acquirer' aiming at short-term profits at the expense of the long-term viability of the company. The Supreme Court affirmed dismissal of the suit, echoing the views of the District Court.

On 18 April 2008, Bull-Dog Sauce announced that Steel Partners had sold its remaining stake in the company.

Questions

1 Why did Steel Partners fail to win its hostile takeover bid of Bull-Dog Sauce?

2 Could Steel Partners have won? If so, how?

3 What are the implications for foreign businesses in Japan? For foreign investors?

Sources

Bull-Dog Sauce company website, accessed 6 November 2012 at: www.bulldog.co.jp

Chen, S.J. (2007) Japan high court keeps Bull-Dog Sauce from Steel Partners' jaws, accessed 6 November 2012 at: http://www.forbes.com/2007/08/08/bulldog-steel-partners-markets-equity-cx_jc_0808markets03_print.html

Hall, K. (2008) Steel Partners off the sauce in Japan, accessed 6 November 2012 at: http://www.businessweek.com/stories/2008-04-18/steel-partners-off-the-sauce-in-japanbusinessweek-business-news-stock-market-and-financial-advice

Milhaupt, C.J. (2009) Bull-Dog Sauce for the Japanese soul? Courts, Corporations, and Communities – A Comment on Haley's View of Japanese Law. *Washington University Global Studies Law Review*, 8: 345–361.

Osaki, S. (2007) The Bull-Dog Sauce Takeover Defense. *Nomura Capital Market Review*, 10(3): 2–20.

Web links

Economic statistics, information on doing business in Japan and government support: http://www.jetro.go.jp

Worldwide comparisons of the ease of doing business: http://www.doing-business.org

FDI statistics: http://stats.unctad.org/fdi

Trade statistics: http://stats.unctad.org/fdi

Notes

1   Confusingly, these are known in the West mostly by the Japanese word '*keiretsu*', which in Japanese is typically used to refer to the supplier and distributor networks discussed in the next paragraph.

2   Statistics in this and the following paragraphs are available on the websites of JETRO, the World Bank, and WTO.

Investment statistics are available on the websites of JETRO and UNCTAD. Links are given at the end of the chapter.

3   Hong Kong numbers include investments from Taiwan to China channelled through Hong Kong and Chinese funds disguised as inward FDI to take advantage of government incentives.

References and further readings

Beinhocker, E.D. (2005) *The Origin of Wealth: Evolution, Complexity and the Radical Remaking of Economics*. London: Random House.

Inagami, T. and Whittaker, D.H. (2005) *The New Community Firm: Employment, Governance and Management Reform in Japan*. Cambridge: Cambridge University Press.

Japan Fair Trade Commission (2001) 企業集団の実態について 第七次調査報告書 [Concerning the Actual State of Business Groups: Report on the Seventh Survey]. Japan Fair Trade Commission.

Ministry of Health, Labour and Welfare (2011) 賃金構造基本統計調査 [basic survey on wage structure], accessed 6 November 2013 at: http://www.mhlw.go.jp/toukei/list/52–22.html

OECD (2010) *Pisa 2009 Results: What Students Know and Can Do – Student Performance in Reading, Mathematics and Science*, Volume I. Paris: OECD.

OECD (2012) OECD. Statistics, accessed 6 November at: http://stats.oecd.org

Robins, F. (2005) The Future of Corporate Social Responsibility, *Asian Business & Management*, 4(2): 95–115.

Schvaneveldt, S.J. (2002) Just-in-Time, in A. Bird (ed.) *Encyclopedia of Japanese Business and Management*. London: Routledge.

Westney, D.E. (2001) Japan, in A.M. Rugman and T.L. Brewer, (eds.) *The Oxford Handbook of International Business*. Oxford: Oxford University Press.

Witt, M.A. (2001) Research Cooperatives, in A. Bird (ed.) *Encyclopedia of Japanese Business and Management*. London: Routledge.

Witt, M.A. (2006) *Changing Japanese Capitalism: Societal Coordination and Institutional Adjustment*. Cambridge: Cambridge University Press.

Witt, M.A. (2014) Japan: Coordinated Capitalism between Institutional Change and Structural Inertia. In Witt, M.A. and Redding, G. (eds.) *The Oxford Handbook of Asian Business Systems*. Oxford: Oxford University Press, (in press).

Witt, M.A. and Redding, G. (2010) *The Spirits of Capitalism: German, Japanese, and US Senior Executive Perceptions of Why Firms Exist*. Fontainebleau/Singapore: INSEAD Working Papers.

Wokutch, R.E. and Shepard, J.M. (1999) The Maturing of the Japanese Economy: Corporate Social Responsibility Implications, *Business Ethics Quarterly*, 9(3): 527–540.

9

The Business System of China

Robert Taylor

Chapter outline

- Overview of China's market economy
- The command economy: the Soviet mentor
- Managerial traditions and a new managerial mind set
- State enterprise managerial autonomy, working conditions and labour mobility
- Property rights, corporate governance and the private sector
- Corporate social responsibility and living and working conditions in China

Chapter objectives

After reading this chapter, you should:

1 Have an overview of China's market economy.

2 Understand the motivation for China's managerial reforms.

3 Comprehend Chinese corporate governance and culture.

4 Be aware of the impact of FDI on Chinese management.

5 Recognize the global impetus behind corporate social responsibility in China.

Introduction: the evolution of China's business system

This chapter discusses how the Chinese business system has been evolving since the initiation of the economic reforms by China's then paramount leader, Deng Xiaoping in 1978, a contrast with the previous period after the Communist accession in 1949. During the years following the accession the urban industrial sector, under the command economy was dominated by state enterprises, funded by the central government, which in turn set production targets. In a sense these industrial enterprises or *danwei* were not only places of work but communities providing benefits in areas like health and education. Lifetime tenure of employment, however, stifled personal initiative and entrepreneurship, crucial if Chinese industry was to be globally competitive in the wake of the open door policy implemented in the early 1980s. While greater autonomy has been granted to state enterprise managers as incentives to improve performance, private enterprise has been encouraged and now accounts for most industrial output. Government policy, since the 1990s, has been to create conglomerates or multinationals from major state enterprises that since the year 2000 have increasingly been engaged in outward investment in both developing and developed countries. In summary, it could be said that, in terms of corporate governance, China's business system reflects a number of influences: the personal loyalties and obligations characteristic of Confucian culture, vestiges of the command economy and Anglo-American managerial traditions that have impacted human resource management. The changing nature of the Chinese business system teaches how corporate governance evolves, as it increasingly manifests a hybrid form rather than, for instance, a replica of Western values and norms.

Overview of China's market economy

Since 1978, the date of the accession to power of China's paramount leader, Deng Xiaoping, macroeconomic reform has impacted the structure and style of industrial management. Such change has resulted in a greater awareness of corporate social responsibility. The following summary provides the market economy perspective against which contemporary Chinese management will be viewed.

China vies with India as the most populous nation on earth and has long been seen as the world's greatest potential market. China's exponential foreign trade growth and the massive inflow of foreign direct investment (FDI) since 1978 attest to the country's emergence as a global economic player, which in turn impacts on corporate governance, as discussed in the main body of this text. The input of foreign capital, technology and managerial expertise has contributed to unprecedented economic growth rates. In 2011 China's economy grew by 9.2 per cent compared with 10.4 per cent in 2010 (Businessweek, 2012). Standards of living have improved, with a significant rise in disposable income, especially for urban households (Censky, 2012). China's foreign trade grew by 22.5 per cent in 2011, including a rise in exports of 20.3 per cent, compared to the previous year, to reach a total of US$3.64 trillion, indicating China's continuing ascent as a major trading nation. There seem no limits to China's growth potential (China Daily, 2012).

Such growth reflects continuing macroeconomic and managerial reform, including industrial restructuring. The first priority of reform was the state industrial sector which, in a bid to create globally competitive multinationals, still plays a major role. To enhance state enterprise competitiveness, changes in management and corporate governance were undertaken, with simultaneous encouragement of private enterprise. The move from plan to market continues; the share of industrial output originating in the state-owned and collective sectors fell from 81.7 per cent to 11 per cent between 1993 and 2008 (Rawski, 2011). The presence of the foreign invested sector has led observers to describe China as the world's workshop but yet much FDI has been devoted to assembly or light manufacturing rather than technological innovation. Moreover, in these sectors, China faces increased competition from low wage economies like Vietnam and Indonesia, and so official policy promotes hi-tech products. In fact, the key to future competitiveness is indigenous innovation, which is now being accorded high priority.

In addition, however, rapid economic growth has incurred costs: environmental degradation and social inequality, the latter addressed by the 11th Five Year Plan (2006–2011) and its 12th counterpart (2011–2015). Included in the plans is the call to create a harmonious society, reflecting the values of Confucianism, which places a premium on stability and the reciprocal rights and duties of ruler and subject. Social and income inequality is being reduced through labour legislation, wages being raised and domestic consumption consequently increased. Significantly, the disposable income of China's growing middle class, especially in the southeastern cities but even in the countryside, is growing, providing opportunities for foreign and domestic companies alike thus stimulating consumption rather than exports (Censky, 2012).

Simultaneously, the 2008 Labour Contract Law has targeted foreign investor employers, often suspected of exploitation, and is also designed to accommodate hi-tech manpower who, by virtue of the nature of their work, must be accorded greater initiative and higher salary (Taylor, 2011).

The above policies and trends are a spur to further reform towards hi-tech enterprise scientific management, to which foreign expertise will contribute. This is proceeding on two fronts: state initiative in corporate governance, and technological infusion through foreign investment. One example of corporate governance reform is Netcom, the telephone company, where 7 out of 13 directors are outsiders; there is thus potential for increasing managerial accountability, hitherto unusual for a state controlled enterprise. The company party secretary's task is still to ensure that state policy is upheld but shareholder interests are nevertheless protected, given CCP concerns with broader social and economic issues (Dean, 2006). Examples of technological infusion through foreign investment are Nanjing Automobile's acquisition of part of MG Rover and the Japanese car manufacturer, Toyota's, manufacturing presence in China, designed to produce environmentally friendly vehicles for both Chinese domestic and global markets (Bolger, 2006; O'Connell, 2006).

The previous discussion provides background information within which Chinese industrial management has been conducted. I have discussed the consequences of China's impressive economic growth, the continuing pursuit of industrial restructuring and managerial reform, and attempts to reduce social inequality through increased domestic consumption. In turn, labour legislation impacts wage costs incurred by foreign investor manufacturers. Chinese and foreign global players alike are affected by China's reformed corporate governance. The following sections examine China's post-1978 managerial reforms.

The command economy: the Soviet mentor

The major theme of this text is contemporary Chinese management. First it is necessary to examine managerial norms and values under the pre-1978 command economy, a mind set at variance with Western business practice. On their accession to power in 1949 the CCP leaders were faced with the enormous tasks of national reconstruction and economic rehabilitation; they were dedicated to transforming China into an advanced industrial country. Not only had years of warfare and civil strife taken their toll on China's infrastructure but sources of experienced managerial cadres were lacking. While technical competence was crucial, the issue of political reliability was paramount.

In the early 1950s, state sector industries were being created under the command economy, for which the mentor was the Soviet Union, whether in terms of industrial plant, managerial expertise or a higher education system geared to rapid economic development. At the same time, China began to produce its own graduates, as the universities were reorganized on Soviet lines, with specialists trained in a number of fields, especially engineering. Notably, graduates were to be assigned, without exercise of personal choice, to managerial positions in industry. The deployment of management and labour to the newly constructed state enterprises necessarily reflected the priorities of central planning devised along Soviet lines, and many Chinese technologists and engineers were also trained in Russia.

Soviet managerial structures and styles were introduced, especially in northeast China, where much heavy industry, the main priority of the First Five Year Plan, (1953–1957) was established. Central planning and macroeconomic governance meant a vertical hierarchical chain of command between ministries in Beijing and individual industrial enterprises. The allocation of raw material inputs and capital, as well as the despatch of products, was conducted through state distribution, a system that essentially remained until the reforms of the 1980s, which were intended ultimately to grant state enterprise managers the kind of autonomy enjoyed by their counterparts in the Anglo-American tradition. I now discuss the reforms initiated after 1978.

Creation of a new managerial mind set

The Third Plenum of the Eleventh Central Committee in 1978 was a crucial watershed in that it addressed the fundamental issues of managerial reform implemented during the 1980s and beyond. In industrial reform, the intention was to make state enterprise directors and managers, who were on the lowest rungs of ministerial bureaucratic hierarchies, more accountable in the new market economy. Incumbent managers had been socialized in a risk-averse environment and had interests to defend. The pace of reform was slow; the reforms did not have a detailed plan but a general sense of direction in which commercially oriented practices would be injected into the state sector to make it more domestically and globally competitive. It had been concluded that while spectacular economic gains had accrued from earlier five year plans, in terms of factor productivity and increasing living standards China had lagged behind other newly industrializing countries in Asia. Before the 1980s China had played a minimal role in the global economy; its foreign trade had been a supplement to 'make good' domestic deficiencies. By the early 1980s, Chinese economic planners had realized that there were limits to autarchy, and the generation of capital for development from within China and the wherewithal for sustained growth would only come from foreign trade and investment. In turn, achievement of competitiveness demanded a change of managerial mind set, now increasingly being driven by both market competitiveness and the recruitment of returned Chinese MBA graduates trained in the West.

State enterprises were controlled by administrative fiat, not economic levers, and the acquisition of scarce supplies by directors, for instance, was secured via personal relationships within the hierarchical chain of command. Egalitarian remuneration rates applied within the managerial cadre and between shop floor workers inhibited risk taking and entrepreneurship as well as innovation. The ideological role of enterprise party committees and their secretaries did not favour the individual initiative of managers. Additionally, soft skills like marketing were the province of central ministries, which had the best information concerning the overall business environment.

State enterprise managerial autonomy, working conditions and labour mobility

Managerial autonomy of the state enterprises

Accordingly, in September 1982, the 12th Congress of the CCP unveiled a series of measures including abolition of lifetime tenure for managerial cadres, as well as attempts to raise their educational levels and reduce their average age, in the interest of greater commercial accountability, entrepreneurship and soft skills. These reforms, however, were initially difficult to implement and in the 1980s contracts were often renewed on expiry of the cadre's term. In fact, such policy regarding term contracts was much more successful when applied to workers in general. These initiatives were an integral part of the more fundamental reforms designed to increase autonomy of individual industrial enterprises. Experimental reform, first implemented in state enterprises in Sichuan Province, was extended to those throughout the country in the early 1980s; eventually they were to become responsible for their own profits and losses. Certain rights were granted: enterprises could retain a limited amount of profit under the state plan, with an even greater percentage to be kept if derived from above quota production. This was permitted after national plans had been fulfilled. The intended uses for retained profit were technological innovation and the development of new products, in addition to spending on welfare and workers' bonuses, the latter being distributed on the basis of performance. More depreciation funds could be kept by the enterprise. Moreover market outlets were now diversified outside state commercial departments. There were problems, however, with the reforms both in terms of ineffective implementation and their extent. Bonuses lost their motivational value because they were traditionally distributed to all workers. Responding to market demand and diversity placed a premium on improved auditing and accounting. Finally, profits derived from increased productivity and market segmentation would only be meaningful if state-led pricing mechanisms were liberalized (Laaksonen, 1998: 231–238).

Thus, in 1984, the on-going reforms were consolidated, being intended to increase the autonomy and decision-making power of state enterprises. Prices were, to an extent, allowed to float for goods produced in excess of state quotas. Prices could be set in a band within 20 per cent of their state equivalents. Certain strategic goods, however, were excepted. Moreover, that state enterprises could select their sources, from both within and outside the central planning system, effected the emergence of horizontal relationships between customers and suppliers. Significantly, enterprises were given greater freedom in recruitment; while directors and party secretaries were still appointed by their respective outside hierarchies, workers could now be engaged through formal examinations, even if under the guidance of state labour agencies. The system of the unified assignment of graduates was not abolished until the 1990s but for the first time directors had the right to reject those assigned. In line with moves towards performance related pay, enterprises were allowed greater leeway in wage setting (Laaksonen, 1998: 239–241).

Working conditions and labour mobility

The managerial reforms discussed above were designed to induce greater competitiveness, but China's state enterprises also discharged responsibilities not generally incumbent upon Western companies. This is because the state industrial enterprise or *danwei* until the 1990s was a community as well as an employer, reflecting aspects not only of the Soviet style command economy but traditional Chinese familial type relationships and values, redolent of Confucianism. The *danwei* was responsible for a range of services: schools for workers' children, health provision in the form of hospitals and clinics on site, housing adjacent to the enterprise, recreational facilities and, importantly, pensions and other types of welfare. Expenses were borne by the work unit even though ultimately monies came from the state treasury. Thus, in contrast to Western companies where the employer–employee relationship was contractual, workers' allegiance to the *danwei* was social and psychological (Naughton, 1997: 169). In fact, managers would be frequently consulted by workers on purely personal matters.

By the 1980s two major consequences suggested that the *danwei* was ripe for reform. First, given increases in longevity, the number of beneficiaries had grown and this, coupled with the fact that the sons and daughters of existing employees were engaged, often regardless of the unit's need, placed additional financial burdens on the enterprise, which carried surplus labour as a result. Second, while in pre-reform days the *hukou* or residence system reduced physical movement and contributed to political control of the urban population, by the 1980s, the lack of earlier mobility was impeding adjustment to changing markets. Labour could not move, even if it wished, because of loss of welfare and housing. In addition, the central and local assignment of university graduates and secondary school leavers meant that after the late 1950s, with the exception of the Great Leap Forward period from 1958 to 1961 when industry was partially decentralized, there was virtually no labour market.

Labour mobility, however, was one objective of reform and the market was creating new opportunities. In the face of competition, state enterprises sought to cut costs by employing more temporary workers, such as rural migrants, but not according them welfare benefits. Moreover, with the increased incidence of the officially encouraged foreign-invested sector and the permitted revival of private enterprise from the 1980s onwards, new employment systems were emerging. Sino-foreign joint ventures and wholly owned foreign enterprises might offer provisions such as housing and be subject to the national insurance rules discussed later in relation to the state sector, but they also introduced new Western contractual arrangements, which contrast with the *danwei* social contract. In addition, private enterprises, which often are run on family lines, have not been in a position to confer *danwei* style benefits. Furthermore, with an increasingly competitive labour market, state enterprise employees have become more mobile and some are destined to move the foreign and private sectors, which offer less security of tenure. Such influences are reinforcing state sector labour reform (Solinger, 1997: 195–222).

Undoubtedly, *danwei* links have been seen as impediments to enterprise efficiency and labour mobility in response to the market. At a macroeconomic level, reformers have instituted a national social insurance system, mandated by labour legislation in 1995, as the key to labour mobility.

The benefits that the *danwei* formerly conferred were a crucial element in the management of China's state enterprises but the reform of areas like pensions and housing have altered the relationship between manager and employee, which is also being affected by the practices of the foreign-invested sector. While the latter may also offer on-site housing and pension provision via private insurers, they are also subject to Chinese labour legislation, and their human resource management practices are more contractual and in direct contrast to the former features of China's state enterprises. The separation of ownership and management, the subject of the next section, will have an even greater impact on the evolving role of the *danwei*.

Property rights, corporate governance and the private sector

Property rights and corporate governance

The inauguration of market socialism after Deng Xiaoping's southern tour in 1992 represented a compromise between the maintenance of political monopoly by the CCP and moves towards privatization in the interests of greater domestic and global competitiveness. The earlier granting of greater managerial autonomy and the loosening of *danwei* controls had not effected the separation of ownership and management in the state sector. To achieve this there were two main prerequisites. First, a managerial cadre responsible to a Board of Directors and simultaneously disciplined by the dividend demands of shareholders and second, a legal infrastructure including the clear delineation of property rights. The objective of creating a new system of corporate governance was set down by General Secretary Jiang Zemin in his political report at the Fifteenth CCP Congress in September 1997, even though it legitimized a number of changes already in motion. Some state enterprises had already been listed on the Shanghai Stock Exchange, founded in 1990, and that in Shenzhen, established in 1991, even though in many cases the state remained the major shareholder, with a high percentage of shares not being traded. This consolidated moves from budgetary allocation, initially towards bank lending and latterly through equity. Such measures were intended to reduce the state's liability for enterprise debt, since there were now other shareholders who could theoretically discipline management (Yabuki and Harner, 1999: 121–129). Thus, joint stock companies were being created and corporations had legal person status but, while equity would play a greater role, no true privatization immediately ensued. The latter demands the creation of property rights that did not formally exist under the command economy since they were exercised through state administrative fiat. As Steinfeld (2000: 27–44) pointed out, it is not a question of property rights transfer but their creation in the first place. Moreover, legal infrastructure, still in the making in China, must provide adjudication and redress if property rights are challenged. In turn, what is needed is a corporate governance system, including shareholding, which can provide incentives for investment, monitor management and ensure the optimal use of resources (Chen, 2005: 16–29).

The ideal typology discussed above reflects the Anglo-Saxon model where shareholders monitor management on the basis of transparent auditing procedures and there exists a competitive market for mergers and acquisitions through enterprise performance (Chen, 2005: 16–29). To date, however, it cannot be said that the emerging Chinese corporate governance structure has consistently replicated this model. The Chinese attempt to create *jituan* or conglomerates as multinationals, advantaged by economies of scale, serves as an illustration. During the early 1990s, the Chinese government launched the policy of 'grasping the large and letting go the small'; successful enterprises would be retained by the state with the smaller and less competitive hived off to private interests. Larger state enterprises were subject to incorporation, characterized by clear governance and transparent accounting (Hannan, 1998: 62–104; Newfarmer and Liu, 1998: 8–13).

In this context, the Company Law, implemented in 1994, enshrined the creation of a modern enterprise system. Firms would become legal entities with their own profit and loss. Mergers and acquisitions, again in the interests of economies of scale, would be based on economic considerations alone. By 1997, 120 enterprise groups or *jituan* had been established in pillar industries such as automobiles, electronics, pharmaceuticals and steel. There have, however, been barriers to the emergence of a modern enterprise system. One company type envisaged by the Company Law was the joint stock company, permitted to raise capital through public offerings on stock exchanges. Nevertheless, an impediment to the establishment of new corporate governance, including property rights, is that many state enterprises have been incorporated since the 1990s as wholly state-owned firms rather than shareholding companies. Thus the state is likely to remain a major institutional shareholder, even though increased public offering of shares should in time make enterprise management more accountable to external monitoring of performance (Hannan, 1998: 62–104; Newfarmer and Liu, 1998: 8–13; Shieh, 1999: 50–54; Sutherland, 2003: 39–66; Yabuki and Harner, 1999: 130–133).

In summary, it could be argued that continuing Chinese state involvement in corporate governance is more redolent of the post-war Japanese system, characterized by institutional cross-shareholding within the *keiretsu* group, even if the latter have always operated within an ostensibly free market economy.

Finally, the creation of a more effective legal infrastructure and transparent corporate governance are seen by Chinese and foreign commentators alike as the best means of eliminating corruption in business where, for instance, relations with corrupt government officials and bribery can expedite the conclusion of contracts. Another aspect of legal regulation concerns health and safety: exports of dangerous Chinese products highlight the need for more consistent law enforcement in China.

China's private sector

While the institution of a modern enterprise system has been one means of disciplining China's state sector, a second involves the encouragement of the private sector, which played a minimal role during the period from 1949 to 1978, but was legitimized as an important organizational part of China's socialist market economy with legal status at the Sixteenth Congress of the CCP in 2002 and granted equal rights at the Tenth National People's Congress in 2004. There is, however, a range of entities within this sector and definition is contentious, given that in the 1980s and 1990s private enterprises were heavily reliant on local government for facilities and, in some cases, funding (Sanders and Chen, 2005: 231–245).

Private firms, varying in size, in both services and manufacturing, include former collective enterprises run by local governments but handed to private entrepreneurs to manage, as well as companies funded and run by individual owners or in partnership. Some now have limited liability while others have also diversified into high technology sectors as *jituan*, the conglomerates, or as shareholding firms. There remain, however, both exogenous and endogenous barriers to the growth of the private sector. Enterprises have often had to rely on private borrowing, the so-called social finance, rather than funds from banks, which have been reluctant to lend, preferring instead the state sector. They have also been subject to double taxation, that is, on the enterprise and the individual owner in addition to miscellaneous fees exacted by local governments. Furthermore there are market barriers to specific industries, involving complex approval procedures favouring state firms. Finally, to date the private sector has often been advantaged by not paying state national insurance contributions but these charges will be increasingly difficult to evade, especially with diversification into higher wage cost, technology intensive areas (Fu, 2004: 166–177; Garnaut and Song, 2004: 1–14; Krug and Polos, 2004: 72–96; Meng, 2004: 146–165).

In fact, the issue of technological diversification impacts on the management of the private sector. To date such enterprises have been heavily concentrated in labour intensive industries like textiles in East China but, as they diversify, limitations in terms of corporate governance come into focus. Invariably ownership and management have been combined in family control, which restricts growth. Technology and product differentiation demand more specialist managers not necessarily present among family members (Garnaut and Song, 2004: 225–235). There is now evidence, clear in Chinese economic and industrial journals, that human resource deployment is being given greater attention, with scientific recruitment of those with soft skills like marketing and accounting. Private enterprise is increasingly subject to labour legislation, which in turn has a bearing on the retention of employees, maintained, for example, through assessment-based training provision. Outside recruitment, scientific management and the reduction of direct family control are leading to the separation of ownership and management, with increasing incidence of companies limited by shares. Commercial bank loans are becoming an option as the banking system is reformed. The appointment of boards of directors and a greater dispersal of shareholding have the potential to effect closer monitoring of managerial performance in the private and the state sector (Child and Pleister, 2004: 195–198; Fu, 2004: 170–174).

Corporate social responsibility

Corporate social responsibility: environmental protection

Changes in corporate governance and property rights have been designed to maintain domestic and global competitiveness but China's success has nevertheless had its costs in economic overheating, environmental degradation and trade deficits sustained by China's trading partners. These managerial issues are addressed next.

Corporate social responsibility (CSR) is a feature of civil society, mainly characteristic of Western advanced industrial nations, and Chinese reformers, whether intentionally or not, have created new centres of economic power, increasingly represented by associations, nominally at least, independent of government. Moreover, a number of these bodies, such as environmental lobbies and consumer groups, have emerged in reaction to such costs of economic growth as atmospheric pollution, land degradation and imperfect market practices. In fact, in China's Eleventh Five Year Plan (2006–2010) and Twelfth Five Year Plan (2011–2015), the country's leaders have sought to address the negative consequences of growth by calling for the creation of a harmonious society. Regional differentials, income inequality and environmental degradation are to be reduced, with global trade surpluses lessened by encouraging greater consumption of products at home.

These objectives are only achievable through the joint action of industry and government but the focus here is on the discharge of corporate responsibility in the wider social and microeconomic contexts, using case studies of environmental protection and human resource management. Given the passage of environmental legislation since the late 1970s, the CCP leadership has shown its commitment to sustainable development, acknowledging that the country's energy efficiency and pollution reduction measures still fall far short of those in developed countries (Dollar, 2007). Such trends call for industrial restructuring towards hi-tech production, both to diversify export products and adjust to greater market segmentation and consumer discernment at home. While government seeks to direct enterprises to clean production through technical guidance and financial assistance, moves by manufacturers are constrained by the conflict between environmental protection and economic profit, especially in the high-polluting, labour-intensive sector, which will still play a part in economic growth. Nevertheless, strategic targeting of new niche markets, created by greater consumer discernment regarding green issues, may facilitate cost internalization, an example being the Chinese textile and garment industries that are using less polluting, genetically variegated cotton, energy saving technology for washing wool and computer-led printing and dyeing skills (Taylor, 2007: 81–99). Such cost internalization, however, demands new expertise, which large rather than small and medium-sized enterprises can afford. Capital Steel's corporate strategy has addressed the issue of environmental protection by relocation of facilities outside Beijing and moves towards production of high-grade steel based on quality, variety and service (Taylor, 2007: 81–99). The consumer also shows responsibility in the case of car ownership, set to increase, and vehicles are a major source of pollution in China's cities. In the wake of government initiatives in 2000, like the fuel tax designed to encourage such energy saving technology as electric batteries and the creation of a market for small vehicles with low petrol consumption, manufacturers have conducted research into the use of liquefied petroleum gas (LPG) and compressed natural gas (CNG) and experimented with improving battery performance to further the commercial viability of electrically-powered cars (Hildebrandt, 2003: 16–21; Turner, 2003: 22–25; Taylor, 2007: 81–99).

In summary, sustainable development may only be achieved by a socially responsible strategic management responding to segmented market-led industrial restructuring.

CSR: human resource management, recruitment, training and localization

Corporate social responsibility, however, is directed not only to the wider community but relates to satisfying the personal and professional needs of the workforce within the enterprise. Human resource management is nevertheless derived from Anglo-American practice and alien to the state-directed unified assignment of managers and workers as well as to the Marxist-Leninist assumptions characteristic of the command economy. Since the 1990s, state enterprises have enjoyed greater freedom in labour deployment, and the introduction of hi-tech industries, often through the medium of Sino-foreign joint ventures, demands that employees, particularly when given greater initiative, be subject to more scientific and sophisticated means of control, a characteristic of a more complex modern economy, given the increases in white-collar staff. Human resource management, which considers labour as capital rather than cost, may be defined as directing a motivated workforce dedicated to a company's success. Thus, a corporate mission unites individual and company interests (Child, 1994: 157–158). As Chinese companies embrace Western managerial styles, human resource management is being regarded as a complete process encompassing recruitment, remuneration, evaluation, training, retention of employees and social welfare. By the 1990s, managerial positions in state enterprises were being increasingly advertised, with technical specialists especially being employed through the market, in some cases directly from science and technology departments in universities, and even through headhunting.

Scientific recruitment, in the form of systematic testing and interviewing techniques, is being introduced. Given that remuneration is one motivator, pay and promotion are increasingly based on educational level, responsibility, performance and innovation rather than age and seniority. As important in motivation as remuneration, however, are job satisfaction and career advancement, to which training through apprenticeship for the shop floor workforce and courses both internally and externally, especially in the fields of soft skills like accounting and marketing, for managers, contributes. Nevertheless the provision of targeted training requires a credible evaluation process, more common in foreign multinationals in China, which in turn are influencing state enterprises (Child, 1994: 172–180; Tang and Ward, 2003: 81–82; Taylor, 2005: 5–21; Warner, 1986: 326–342).

Training, however, may prove a mixed blessing. On the one hand its incentives may facilitate the retention of managers and technical experts; on the other, unless the skills acquired are company specific, employees in search of higher pay may carry their knowledge to company competitors. But, as a hedge against defection, companies may insert clauses in labour contracts requiring employees to repay training costs if they leave before the end of a stated period (Melvin, 2001: 30–35, 43).

Recruitment of managers and their training discussed above brings into focus the localization of human resources as opposed to the secondment of staff to China by multinationals. Such localization has been a growing trend. In general, there have been two stages in localization. In the 1980s and 1990s basic employment training was provided for Chinese workers in labour intensive industries involved in processing and services, while technological personnel and higher management were seconded from the home country. During the second stage, from the year 2000 onwards, senior management ranks have been filled locally, being recruited from master's and doctoral degree graduates, educated in famous Chinese universities and institutes, as well as Chinese trained overseas. Thus, in many multinational companies, a high proportion of top management has been locally sourced (Wu, 2009).

Apart from cost advantages where, for instance, local managers are paid less in terms of salaries and benefits, localization confers certain other advantages, especially in marketing areas. Local staff are knowledgeable of Chinese cultural values and market trends, and can target consumer tastes better, particularly when they have been trained in-house in marketing techniques or in some cases through secondment in the multinational's home country (Wu, 2009; Wang and Liang, 2000).

The localization process may in turn facilitate the emergence of a new corporate culture, especially in foreign invested enterprises in China.

CSR: corporate culture, FDI and business networks

Essentially, the above aspects of human resource management are designed to effect identification between individual employees and company interests. Similarly, the provision of social welfare by enterprises is an inducement to employee commitment and an area where foreign-invested companies have taken the lead. The *danwei* is being replaced by nationally legislated welfare; the private insurance benefits and assistance with mortgages increasingly provided by foreign-invested ventures may well be emulated by the state sector, as service providers from overseas enter China under the terms of the World Trade Organization (WTO) (Melvin, 2001: 30–35, 43). Finally, loyalty in Western settings has been instilled through the establishment of corporate culture; again, foreign companies are the pioneers but it is possible that the familial type solidarity of the *danwei* may be harnessed to respond to a competitive market, forming a hybrid of Chinese tradition and Western practice.

In conclusion, corporate social responsibility in China is emerging in relation to both the wider domestic community and within the enterprise. Reference has been made to the influence of FDI on Chinese managerial practices. However, China's conglomerates, the *jituan*, both state and private, are increasingly engaged in globalized operations as multinationals through outward investment, and this is likely to have an even greater impact on managerial areas like corporate social responsibility. Initially, during the 1990s, China's outward FDI was motivated by the industrial need for minerals and oil, witness current Chinese relations with countries as diverse as the states of Central Asia, Africa and South America. Increasingly, however, two concerns have dictated company policy: the imperative to circumvent trade barriers, for example, in the European Union, and the search to obtain high technology from overseas companies via merger and acquisition in order to expand into new markets through regional and global networks in the European Union and the United States as well as Asia. Instances of the latter that may be cited include the purchase by Lenovo of a controlling stake in IBM's personal computer business in 2004, Shanghai Automobile Industry Corporation's acquisition of an almost 50 per cent stake in South Korea's Ssang-yong Motor Company and Haier, the white-ware manufacturer's construction of a production base in the United States (Smith and Rushe, 2004).

In fact, Chinese outward investment in the United States and the European Union has accelerated in recent years, the objectives being to upgrade technology, to move up the value chain and to improve managerial skills in the interest of greater competitiveness. By the end of 2011 China's global FDI amounted to US$365 billion. In the same year Chinese firms invested $4.5 billion in the United States and $10 billion in Europe. Currently, Chinese companies in Europe employ 54,000 EU workers (China Business Review, 2012; Rosen and Hanemann, 2012).

Consequently, Chinese companies' corporate social responsibility and their commitment to ethical standards will necessarily evolve as they become major players in global management.

Working and living conditions in China

Since the year 2000 China has been undergoing accelerated socioeconomic change, affecting the living standards of both Chinese and foreign expatriates, with implications for corporate strategy. Hitherto regarded as a hardship posting, China's southeastern cities now enjoy living standards approaching those of metropolises in Western countries with, for example, advanced medical facilities.

With economic growth has come consumer discernment and diversification of taste. A consumer culture, aided by social media, has made Chinese more aware of rights and the possibility of litigation in the context of an emerging civil society, factors which foreign investors must take account.

These changes have a bearing on corporate strategy. China, formerly regarded as the world's workshop, specializing in labour intensive industries, is now moving up the hi-tech chain. This is leading to upward pressure on wages and demands for better working conditions, underlining the importance of human resource strategies. Additionally, foreign ventures are facing intensified competition from Chinese multinationals' domestic and overseas enterprises. In conclusion, socioeconomic change in China is influencing the lifestyle of expatriates and foreign enterprises' corporate strategy.

Chapter summary

- China is a country with a population of over a billion but only since the 1990s has it played a major role in world trade.

- From 1949 to 1978 China had a command economy characterized by an uncompetitive state industrial sector, governed by central planning.

- The reforms of the 1980s were designed to create a new managerial culture by granting more autonomy in decision making to state enterprises.

- In the 1990s new systems of corporate governance were introduced. The separation of ownership and management in state enterprises was initiated, with the private and foreign-invested sectors cited as examples for emulation, as China moved from a command to a market economy. China's outward investment may in turn facilitate technological and managerial learning.

- Western managerial traditions have brought awareness of corporate social responsibility to Chinese enterprises in areas like environmental protection.

- The creation of new Chinese corporate cultures is motivational, enhancing the competitiveness of Chinese companies as Asian regional and global players.

Key concepts

Soviet-style command economy: A system where the state planned production and distribution.

Danwei: Both an employer and an agency looking after employee welfare.

Hukou: What determines one's residence in China. It acts also as a means of political control.

Jituan: Conglomerates formed from state and, increasingly, private enterprises.

1 Why were the existing sources of managers seen as inadequate for the command economy?

2 What do you consider were the main defects of China's command economy?

3 How is the delineation of property rights crucial for the creation of a new system of corporate governance in China?

4 What are the political impediments to the discharge of corporate social responsibility in China and how may they be overcome?

5 What impact will China's outward investment in the United States and the European Union have on Chinese corporate governance and human resource management?

Learning activities and discussions

1 It has been assumed that the Chinese should adopt Western managerial practices. In this context, and in the light of your own experience, examine the strengths and weaknesses of Western management and its suitability for emulation by the Chinese.

2 Examine, through examples drawn from media reports and the internet, the extent to which Chinese companies are discharging corporate social responsibility.

3 In all countries government plays a role in the economy. Consider the changing role of the Chinese state in the economy and its impact on management in the light of the transition from a command to a market economy.

MINI CASE

Guangzhou Honda: human resource management

It is against the background of commitment to the creation of a harmonious society that the discussion of Japanese human resource management in China should be viewed. In the early years of China's open door policy Chinese workers sought employment in Japanese invested companies that were seen as sources of high income and a good working environment. But as the market economy has deepened and state and private domestic enterprises offer higher wages and better working conditions, employment in Japanese enterprises has seemed less attractive, and labour disputes have increased (Liu, 2007). Accordingly, Japanese companies in China have been developing long-term strategic labour relations, drawing from different Western models, with greater emphasis, for example, on achievement related pay (Zeng and Su, 2009).

To illustrate such modification, Guangzhou Honda, the joint venture car company, will serve as a case study, even though human resource practices necessarily differ among Japanese companies in China. Focus will be on a number of features: employment tenure, performance assessment, training and managerial hierarchies. Finally, the extent of localization will be assessed.

In December 2007 managers and workers signed three to five year contracts with the company that in principle would be extended indefinitely on completion (Zhang, 2007). While initially at a basic level young employees are recruited from the external labour market, the traditional Japanese practice of filling more senior posts from within the company remains, notwithstanding the challenge of greater labour mobility. Some managerial vacancies may, however, be filled from outside (Zeng and Su, 2009; Zhang, 2007).

One incentive is increased renumeration and, to counter mobility, Honda's management has introduced performance related pay, the latter also being a condition for promotion. While traditionally in Japan wage increases have been based on length of service and seniority, Honda in China has enhanced the role of work performance assessment which also determines training opportunities (Zeng and Su, 2009; Zhang, 2007). Training may be vocational, involving training in-house or in educational institutions and may be a prerequisite for promotion to higher ranks (Zhang, 2007). Enshrining the principle of promotion through ability and work performance as a motivational device, with the agreement of the Chinese joint venture partner, Honda has departed from the erstwhile Japanese organizational model, and there are, as a result, implications for other domestic companies in China.

Previously, in Japan, age seniority tended to restrict promotion opportunities, given that the higher the stage of the managerial hierarchy, the fewer the positions to be filled, with potential consequential effects on motivation. Accordingly, Honda China has sought to broaden promotion opportunities for those at the basic levels of the managerial hierarchy and blue collar workers alike. Thus, selection for promotion is not only based, in the case of graduate entrants, on past scholarly attainment, but on performance in the production context. In addition, workers without formal academic qualifications may be promoted to Chinese managerial posts like departmental head but in practice no higher. To facilitate promotion for both managers and workers, personal technical development plans are designed. In effect, two kinds of advancement are available to those with proven ability: promotion to a higher rank or award of higher salary, mainly through bonuses, in their current position. In both kinds of promotion, quality of performance and experience are paramount. Another key to the promotion system is the practice of job rotation at Honda China by which managers and technical personnel are seconded to different departments to gain greater understanding of operations as a whole and forge personal links across the enterprise (Zhang, 2007).

Consequently, such human resource management practices are said to have enhanced motivation to an even greater extent than in other Japanese companies and, through competition, able young graduates from major Chinese universities have been promoted to, for instance, the rank of work team leader (Zhang, 2007). In turn, this flatter organizational structure is more suited to motivating those employees handling the information technologies integral to a knowledge economy.

In similar vein, moves towards the creation of a corporate culture have been facilitated by division of top managerial responsibilities between representatives of the two joint venture partners, the theory being that neither side will then be able to monopolize decision-making power. Thus, the head of the production manufacturing department is Japanese, while his deputy is Chinese. Conversely, the head of the finance department is Chinese and his deputy Japanese (Liu, 2007; Zhang, 2007).

Reference to division of managerial responsibility raises the issue of localization. The evidence cited above indicates the degree to which Honda China has modified Japanese human resource management practices and thus to that extent localized. In contrast, many Japanese companies in China have been slow to localize (Liu, 2007; Wang and Li, 2008).

In summary, the Honda case study demonstrates how Japanese human resource management may be modified in the Chinese context.

Questions

1 How suitable is Japanese human resource management to the Chinese context?

2 Select from the media examples of Japanese companies investing in China. How have they modified their human resource management in their Chinese operations?

3 Could it be said that employment in Japanese ventures in China will enhance Chinese managers' career prospects in the long term?

Sources

Liu, J.M. (2007) Discussing the question of cultural clashes in Japanese invested enterprises in Dalian [in Chinese]. *Guizhou Minzu Xueyuan Xuebao (Zhexue Kexueban)* [*Journal of Guizhou University for Ethnic Minorities (Philosophy and Social Science)*], 1: 54–56.

Wang, D.S. and Li, Y.N. (2008) Comparative Research into the Market Strategies of European and American as Opposed to Japanese and Korean Companies in China [in Chinese]. *Gongsheng Guanli*, 7: 79–83.

Zeng, X.Q. and Su, Z.X. (2009) The Challenges to and Changes in the Japanese Style Human Resource Management System in a Chinese Context [in Chinese]. *Jingji Lilun Yu Jingji Guanli*, 9: 69–75.

Zhang, C.H. (2007) The Management of Promotion in Sino-Japanese Joint Ventures and its Implications [in Chinese]. *Jinan University* (*Philosophy and Social Sciences*), 4, 46–51.

Web links

The Asian Development Bank: http://www.adb.org

China Daily: http://www.chinadaily.com.cn/

Xinhua:http://www.xinhua.org

References

Bolger, J. (2006) Woman Who Lost Her Heart to IBM Plans New Assault. *The Times*, 29 August.

Businessweek (2012) Don't Bet on the End of China's Growth Miracle, accessed 6 November 2013 at: http://www.businessweek.com/articles/2012-09-02/don-t-bet-on-the-end-of-china-s-growth-miracle

Censky, A. (2012) China's middle class boom. CNN money, 26 June 2012, accessed 6 November 2013 at: http://money.cnn.com/2012/06/26/news/economy/china-middle-class/

Chen, J. (2005) *Corporate Governance in China*. London: Routledge Curzon.

Child, J. (1994) *Management in China in the Age of Reform*. Cambridge: Cambridge University Press.

Child, J. and Pleister, H. (2004) Governance and Management, in R. Garnaut and L.G. Song (eds.) *China's Third Economic Transformation: The Rise of the Private Economy*. London: Routledge Curzon, pp. 192–208.

China Business Review (2012) Short Takes: Investment. Chinese Firms more than Tripled Investment in Europe in 2011, *China Business Review*, 3: 9.

China Daily (2012) China's foreign trade surges 22.5 per cent, accessed 6 November 2013 at: http://www.chinadaily.com.cn/business/2012-01/10/content_14415408.htm

Dean, J. (2006) China Turns to Western style Governance. *Sunday Times*, 8 October.

Dollar, D. (2007) China Faces its Environmental Challenges. *APEC Economies Newsletter*, 5.

Fu, J. (2004) Private Enterprises and the Law, in R. Garnaut and L.G. Song. (eds.) *China's Third Economic Transformation: The Rise of the Private Economy*. London: Routledge Curzon, pp. 166–177.

Garnaut, G. and Song, L.G. (2004) *China's Third Economic Transformation: The Rise of the Private Economy*. London: Routledge Curzon.

Hannan, K. (1998) *Industrial Change in China*. London: Routledge.

Hildebrandt, T. (2003) Making Green in Beijing, *China Business Review*, 6: 16–21.

Krug, B. and Polos, L. (2004) Emerging Markets, Entrepreneurship and Uncertainty: The Emergence of the Private Sector in China, in B. Krug (ed.) *China's Rational Entrepreneurs: The Rise of the New Private Business Sector*. London: Routledge Curzon, pp. 72–96.

Laaksonen, O. (1988) *Management in China During and After Mao*. Berlin: de Gruyter.

Melvin, S. (2001) Retaining Chinese employees. *China Business Review*, 6: 30–35, 43.

Meng, X. (2004) Private Sector Development and Labour Market Reform, in R. Garnaut and L.G. Song. (eds.) *China's Third Economic Transformation: The Rise of the Private Economy*. London: Routledge Curzon, pp. 146–165.

Naughton, B. (1997) Danwei: The Economic Foundations of a Unique Institution, in X.B. Lu, and E.J. Perry (eds.) *Danwei: The Changing Chinese Workplace in Historical and Comparative Perspective*. New York: M.E. Sharpe, pp. 169–194.

Newfarmer, R. and Liu, D.M. (1998) China's Race with Globalization. *China Business Review*, 4: 8–13.

O'Connell, D. (2006) Toyota to Sell China Cheapies. *Sunday Times*, 2 April.

Rawski, T.G. (2011) The Rise of China's Economy, *Foreign Policy Research Institute*, 16(6): 1–11.

Rosen, D.H. and Hanemann, T. (2012) The Rise in Chinese Investment and What it Means for American Businesses. *China Business Review*, 3: 18–22.

Sanders, R. and Chen, Y. (2005) On Privatization and Property Rights: Should China Go Down the

Road of Outright Privatization? *Journal of Chinese Economic and Business Studies*, 3: 231–245.

Shieh, S. (1999) Is Bigger Better? *China Business Review*, 3: 50–54.

Smith, D. and Rushe, D. (2004) Devoured by the Dragon. *Sunday Times*, 12 December, accessed 4 December 2013 at: http://www.thesundaytimes.co.uk/sto/business/article95259.ece

Solinger, D.J. (1997) The Impact of the Floating Population on the Danwei: Shifts in the Patterns of Labour Mobility Control and Entitlement Provision, in X.B. Lu, and E.J. Perry (eds.) *Danwei: The Changing Chinese Workplace in Historical and Comparative Perspective*. New York: M.E. Sharpe, pp. 195–222.

Steinfeld, E. (2000) *Forging Reform in China: The Fate of State Owned Industry*. Cambridge: Cambridge University Press.

Sutherland, D. (2003) *China's Large Enterprises and the Challenge of Late Industrialization*. London: Routledge.

Tang, J. and Ward, A. (2003) *The Changing Face of Chinese Management*. London: Routledge.

Taylor, R. (2005) China's Human Resource Management Strategies: The Role of Enterprise and Government. *Asian Business and Management*, 4: 5–21.

Taylor, R. (2007) Corporate Social Responsibility in China: The Enterprise and the Environment, in R. Sharpe and H. Hasegawa (eds.) *New Horizons in Asian Management*. Basingstoke: Palgrave Macmillan, pp. 81–99.

Taylor, R. (2011) China's Labour Legislation: Implications for Competitiveness. *Asia–Pacific Business Review*, 4: 493–510.

Turner, J.L. (2003) Cultivating Environmental–NGO Business Relationships. *China Business Review*, 6: 22–25.

Wang, X.M. and Liang, Y.G. (2000) Research Into Factors Governing the Success of EU Invested Companies in China. *Juece Jiejian* [*Policymaking Reference*], 6: 23–27.

Warner, M. (1986) The Long March of Chinese Management Education, 1979–1984. *China Quarterly* 106: 326–342.

Wu, L. (2009) Research into Human Resource Localisation in Multinational Companies. *Wuliu Gongchang yu Guanli* [*Logistics Engineering and Management*], 3: 114–115, 127.

Yabuki, S. and Harner, S.M. (1999) *China's New Political Economy*. Boulder, CO: Westview Press.

Vipin Gupta

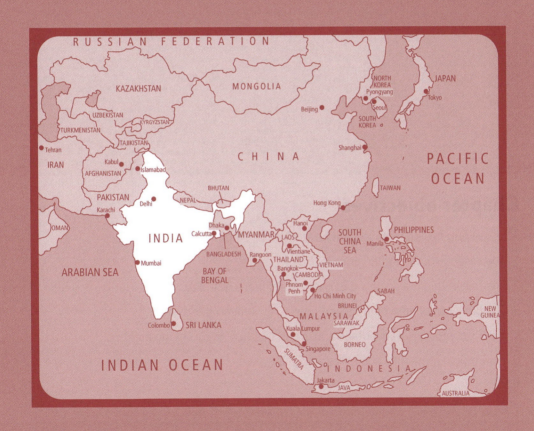

Chapter outline

- Culture of India
- The role of civil society and the institutions
- India's business system
- The changing trend in the Indian business system
- International activities of Indian firms
- Corporate social responsibility, governance and ethics in India

Chapter objectives

After reading this chapter you will have an understanding of:

1 The essence of the Indian culture.

2 The role of the civil society and of the institutions in India.

3 The business system of India and emerging shifts in this system.

4 India's comparative advantage and international activities of Indian firms.

5 How Indian firms fulfil social responsibility.

Introduction

Bounded by the Indian Ocean in the South, and the Himalayas mountain range in the North, India is the seventh largest nation in the world, with a total area of 1,222,559 square miles. The northern and eastern India is home to the Ganges-Brahmaputra river system, the western India to the Thar Desert, and the Southern India to the Deccan Plateau. With a population of over 1.2 billion, India is the largest democracy in the world today.

India has emerged as one of the most vibrant and fast growing economies since the mid-1990s, with a steady annual growth rate of 7–9 per cent, up from a historical rate of 3.5 per cent since independence. Even during the worldwide recession, the Indian economy has maintained more than 5 per cent growth. The growth has helped to reduce levels of poverty dramatically however, social inequities have also risen. There are growing challenges and demands for an inclusive approach. Indian culture is diverse and rich, and has formed the basis for itsr business system.

Culture

The GLOBE (Global Leadership and Organizational Behaviour Effectiveness) Research Project suggests using a nine dimension framework to study culture (House et al., 2004). We use House et al.'s dimensions as they relate to three business system perspectives: rationale, identity and authority.

Rationale

The cultural rationale for the business system can be understood through the GLOBE cultural dimensions of performance, future and humane orientation. Some business systems are designed to emphasize the norms of performance and futuristic goals, while others seek to protect people's identities and traditional authority structures. Further, performance and wealth creation in some cultures is intended for specific stakeholders, such as the shareholders or other types of power holders, while in others it is founded on the principles of humanism, fairness and universal justice.

Performance orientation

Indian society as a whole recognizes and celebrates accomplishments. Formal performance appraisal systems exist in most medium and large size organizations. At the same time, Indian society tries to not devalue failures; thus poor performance ratings are avoided. The leaders are accordingly expected to follow a nurturing style while maintaining a focus on performance (Chhokar, 2007). As such, weight is also sometimes given to an individual's identity and situational factors; for instance, seniority and suitability play a role in promotions, in addition to performance.

Future orientation

Indian society has historically prioritized acting now for improving the 'hereafter'. Saving money and resources is encouraged in families as well as organizations. Reusing and recycling resources and products is a common practice; even in services, firms strive to develop refined and mature processes to conserve human effort. A related doctrine of *mahurata* states that if time is not auspicious, then the actions may not be as fruitful. Given this complexity of balancing *act now* with *act at the right time*, outstanding leaders in India are expected to be visionary and inspirational.

Humane orientation

From very early times, India's culture has been characterized by a great sense of fairness in social and civic relations (Chhokar, 2007). Commenting on the culture of India in the 1st millennium BCE, Basham (1967: 8) noted: 'The most striking feature of ancient India's civilization is its humanity.' Managers in India tend to be highly sensitive to the rights of the workers, who are often seen as members of an extended family. The worker and consumer rights are also well protected by law. There is a strong tradition of benevolent rulers in India.

Identity

The cultural basis of identity in the business system can be understood through the GLOBE dimensions of institutional and in-group collectivism, and assertiveness. Some business systems are designed to promote collective institutional identities, while others emphasize interests of the individual participants based on assumed differences in capabilities, motivation and opportunities. Some business systems are designed along the lines of the belongingness of the members to various groups, while others dismiss group identities in terms of the irrational emotions and nepotism in business contexts. Finally, some business systems take a soft approach to the observed identity differences, while others take an assertive approach for negotiating the identity landscape.

Institutional collectivism

The community is a fundamental principle in Indian society. It is about nurturing each other's voice despite differences, and unity in diversity, communal harmony and democratic pluralism. Effective managers are those who are adept at finding a third solution as a way to reconcile the seemingly opposite interests. Simultaneously, defending one's self-esteem and uniqueness, in the face of oppressive, hegemonic and homogenizing forces is also a critical aspect of India's culture. Leaders are expected to be introspective, keep important secrets, protect followers and help save face.

In-group collectivism

The family is one of the basic units of Indian society. Support from the family, particularly parents-in-law, is an important factor for women working in non-family managerial and leadership positions. Key positions in family business management are often held by members of the extended family as well as close family friends and confidants. Professional managers in these businesses gain top leadership positions usually after having worked for several years (Gupta et al., 2008).

Assertiveness

In Indian society humility, gentility and charm go along with firmness. Indian media encourages and seeks multiple sides of an argument. Culturally speaking, meanings, reality and interpretations are seen as multidimensional in India, just like the multiple forms of God. Leaders in India are expected to be decisive, diplomatic and team integrators (Chhokar, 2007).

Authority

The cultural basis of authority in the business system can be understood through the GLOBE dimensions of gender egalitarianism, power distance and uncertainty avoidance. Some business systems associate authority more with men, and expect considerable differences in the power of those in authority and those who are not. Further, some business systems use expert, bureaucratic and technological mechanisms for reducing uncertainty and arbitrariness in the exercise of authority, while others consider such uncertainties to be sources of innovation and change.

Gender egalitarianism

Indian society has traditionally been male-dominated. Men primarily make the decisions in families, organizations and society, and there are very few women leaders at the top of such arenas. At the same time, several women role models are celebrated in Indian folklore. These role models have been invoked by the social reformers focused on the re-empowerment of women within a merit-based framework. As Gandhi (1947/2003) observed, 'Women, and for that matter any group, should disclaim patronage. They should seek justice, never favors.' To meet the challenges of skilled worker shortages, there is now an increasing emphasis on training, mentorship and enabling social attitudes, family systems and organizational structures for women in management.

Power distance

Indian society and businesses have traditionally been quite stratified. Historically, in the so-called caste system, Brahmins as educators were spiritual leaders, Kshatriyas as rulers were administrative leaders, Vaisyas as traders were business leaders, and Sudras as farmers and craftsmen were masters of their trade. During colonial times, the British introduced a hierarchical system of governance for society and organizations. Social reformers have sought to give voice to the underprivileged. In addition, deference to elders is an integral aspect of culture, and so employees tend to be respectful of the leaders. The power distance corresponds with the autocratic-paternalistic style of leadership and micro-management; but if the leaders are not nurturing, the employees may use their power of resistance or show dissent.

Uncertainty avoidance

Attempts to reduce and regulate uncertainty are common in Indian society. Life in India is guided by elaborate social customs and religious rituals, especially for major life events such as birth, marriage and death. Experiential knowledge and oral knowledge passed between generations are held high, though in recent years, professional academic qualification has become a passport to fast track careers. Leaders in India are expected to be administratively competent, that is, to enact policies fairly and proficiently.

In summary, the cultural image of Indian businesses is one of an action oriented force of development and change. In general, Indian society prefers proactive, morally principled and ideological system of business, rather than a reactive, pragmatic and instrumental system. A contemporary Indian business system is designed for the humane mobilization of group loyalties, while carefully negotiating the reduction of dysfunctional hierarchical and male-dominated power stratifications. It seeks to focus group energies using an egalitarian approach for constructive future and goal-oriented endeavours.

These cultural differences have important implications, particularly in relation to the roles of state and the civil society as discussed next.

The roles of the state and the civil society

The civil society is the space between the family and the state, and comprises non-government organizations and social movements. This concept is central to the Gandhian mode of peaceful political conduct, and popularly referred to *Gandhigiri*. In independent India, the civil society started to take shape in the 1970s, when activists began forming powerful broad-based social movements to advocate interests perceived to be neglected by the state. The farmer's movement organized hundreds of thousands of demonstrators to seek greater investment in rural areas. The Dalit movement sought to serve the interests of the underprivileged castes, the women's movement emerged to promote women's issues, and the environmental movement emerged to bring back respect for indigenous cultures and the environment in the development agenda.

In India, civil society organizations play four major roles as intermediaries between the State and the business system. First, they fill the institutional gaps by directly serving the interests of their constituents, for example, by innovating and experimenting with new approaches to social and economic problem solving. Second, they create consciousness among the constituents of their rights and connect them with the policy infrastructure and enforcement mechanisms that already exist. Third, they use their formal and/or informal membership base and mass appeal to use political pressure. That includes, seeking preferential allocation of resources for the advocated causes, as well as advocacy for specific legislation including participation in the legislation bill drafting committees. Fourth, as watchdogs of the activities of the State at various levels, civil society leaders and organizations have resorted to the use of public and social media, as well as of public interest litigation (PIL) entailing taking support of the judiciary to direct the State to act to protect the fundamental rights guaranteed by the Constitution of India.

The civil society movement and organizations have become increasingly sophisticated, with some also mobilizing the support of: the international community; Indian expatriates; social, religious and cultural celebrities; educated professionals; and corporate leaders. The growth of the civil society has been accelerated because of the funding offered by the State to non-government organizations through budgetary allocations, and recognition of their important role in inclusive and sustainable development, that is, representative of the voice of all, inclusive of all and serving all in the developmental process. As a result, there is heightened sensitivity for responsible institutions and business system. The reforms and the features of the institutions and the business systems are discussed next.

Institutions

Financial capital

The financial system in India is dominated by banks, with commercial banks accounting for 60 per cent of the financial assets, and cooperative banks accounting for another 5 per cent. Insurance firms dominate the non-banking sector, accounting for 20 per cent; followed by mutual funds who account for 6 per cent. Reserve Bank of India (RBI) is the Central Bank that acts as a multifaceted primary regulator, supervising the banking sector, the foreign exchange market, the credit and settlement market, and government securities. As of 2011, public sector banks account for about 74 per cent share in the commercial banks, foreign banks for about 7 per cent and private sector banks for about 19 per cent. Since the liberalization of the Indian economy in the 1990s, financial reforms have resulted in reduced concentrations and improved profitability in the banking industry.

Following a series of reforms since the 1990s, India now boasts a modern, transparent financial market of international comparison. There is a robust regulatory framework, led by Securities and Exchange Board of India (SEBI), and shared by the Ministry of Finance, the Ministry of Company Affairs and RBI. The number of listed domestic companies surged from about 200 in 1990 to about 1,400 in 2010; while the market capitalization rose from a few billion US dollars to about 5,000 billion dollars. Market liquidity increased tremendously because of the huge inflows from foreign institutional investors, but that also made India vulnerable in the global financial meltdown. Weak foreign equity flows and growing concerns about the commitment of the government of India to further economic reforms and to take a strong action against corruption, have contributed in nearly 50 per cent depreciation in the value of Indian currency over the past few years.

Retail participation in the equity market remains low, although growing because of the rise in the mutual funds. The penetration of banking services and resource mobilization by banks, measured as the ratio of bank credit and bank deposits respectively to gross domestic product, are also low and less than 50 per cent. As a result, firms have been forced to rely more on internally generated resources, on international capital markets, and on private placement to fund their capital requirements, especially as the disclosure requirements have been tightened. A downside is that the dominance of private placements further discourages retail participation, companies are forced to enter the market frequently to raise funds through small tranches, and the trading of these bonds in the secondary market is low because of limited transparency. Corporate debt as a percentage of gross domestic product is only 3 per cent in India. The government is taking steps to address the issues of credit assessment, transparency and regulatory framework that have limited the development of the public corporate bond market.

In the fiscal year, 2010–2011, public investment in infrastructure accounted for about 5 per cent of the gross domestic product and the private investment for about 3 per cent. The Planning Commission of India has projected a need to double the investment in infrastructure over the next five years, to sustain a 9 per cent rate of growth, creating urgency for further financial market reforms. Banks who account for about half of the financing debt are already overstretched, with excessive exposure to infrastructure and rising non-performing asset ratios and mismatches of asset-liability maturities. The government is seeking to simplify procedures, tap retail market through infrastructure debt funds, and more aggressively pursue public–private partnerships (Kohli, 2012).

Human capital

In the global surveys, Indian youth (16–29 year olds) have been found to be the happiest in the world. The AC Nielson Consumer Confidence Survey also finds that since 2001, Indian consumers are the most optimistic in the world, with faith in their personal finances (90 per cent) and job prospects (94 per cent). At the same time, Indian men and women also wish to balance family and social life, and are not solely focused on work.

India has strong educational and training institutions, including higher education, in various specialized fields, as well as many research and policy institutions. There is a considerable gap in the theoretically oriented and bookish education in the vast majority of educational institutions, and the practical realities of the globally relevant soft and technical skillset demanded by the employers. However, efforts towards academic accreditation, faculty development initiatives, industry–academic collaborations and global academic exchange are gradually helping to improve the quality of entry-level human capital. India now also boasts a qualified and effective mid-level executive cadre, capable of leading a very young workforce – given that those age under-25 constitute the majority of the workforce. Top-level executives in India are highly sought after by even the leading foreign multinational firms, because of their global mind set, technical knowledge, and innovative and creative leadership approaches.

Institutions in India put considerable emphasis on the diversity initiatives for broad-basing and augmenting talent at all levels, particularly at the mid and top levels. These have traditionally been dominated by urban men, mostly those belonging to more privileged castes. Three types of diversity initiatives are prominent: affirmative action involving underprivileged castes and tribes; engaging the base-of-the pyramid (the segment of population that lives on an income of less than $2 a day) particularly those living in the rural areas; and gender mainstreaming. Diversity in terms of alternative ability (e.g., physical handicap) is less recognized, though a 2012 television show *Satyamev Jayate* (Only Truth Wins) hosted by Bollywood Superstar Aamir Khan showcased a Pune-based company where the entire workforce is physically handicapped and able to perform all tasks proficiently, with an intended purpose to promote awareness and action.

The issue of affirmative action involving underprivileged classes and tribes carries strong political tone, and defines the agenda of several State political parties, and through them, of the multiparty coalition governments at the centre. Nearly half of the public sector positions in many States of India are reserved for these classes and tribes, despite controversies about whether quota based reservations damages the overall human capital strength of organizations. While there is strong public concern about the base-of-the-pyramid segment, non-government organizations have taken a lead in the programmes to develop and advance this segment and to promote entrepreneurial initiatives by connecting with the public sector and the private sector frameworks.

Private sector firms have been most prominent in taking leadership around the gender diversity, and these initiatives deserve some elaboration. The proportion of women employees in new economy businesses is twice the average urban rate of 15 per cent; and the percentage of women in managerial positions has doubled from 6 per cent in the late 1990s. However, many firms experience 50 per cent attrition in the women employees by the age of 30, as a result of marriage and/or childbirth. Firms such as IBM India, who have managed their gender-centring programmes well, report single-digit overall attrition rates, an even lower attrition rate for female employees, and an ability to rapidly and successfully scale up local operations.

Social capital

Institutions enhance social capital of the businesses by promoting trust-based transactions. Though there has been a gradual improvement over the recent years due to the vigilance of civil society, formal institutions in India are generally weak, characterized by a huge backlog of cases in the judiciary system, weak enforcement of laws, the high degree of corruption in public life, and generally low levels of transparency in management and governance. There is, therefore, a greater reliance on the informal institutions based on business and social relationships.

De and Singh (2009) examined the extent to which informal interfirm relationships are relational contracts that constitute social capital using a sample of 141 small and medium enterprises (SMEs) over a 10 year period 1996–2005. Findings show that informal relationships do enhance access to credit for the firms, but do not reduce the cost of credit for the borrowers; on the positive side, they do not increase the cost of credit either. Further when the parties are highly dependent on their relationship, that is, when a firm extends credit to a customer who has few or no other suppliers, then the firm extending credit tends to enjoy a profit premium, while the firm receiving credit in fact suffers from an excess cost of credit. In summary, the business system of India does offer its firms social capital based on their informal business and social relationships. These benefits are related more to improved access and offsetting any growth or profitability disadvantages for the underprivileged members of the community, and less to any significant profitability or growth advantage. Overall, thus, one can say that the institutions offer a moderate degree of social capital to the businesses.

The traditional nature of interfirm relationships offers additional insights into the reasons for the moderate level of institutionalized trust in India. Traditionally, Indian businesses have been differentiated along the different parts of the value chain system. Members of the same community occupy a given link of the value chain, and engage in trading relationships with the members of other communities who occupy other vertical and horizontal links in the value chain system. This reflects the principle of community-based specialization and division of labour, prominent in India from ancient times, and also the original basis for identifying the sub-castes within the business community. As noted earlier, identity in this culture is in-group and family based. Since different families within a community tend to operate and compete in the same market space, the level of identification with the firms who occupy supplier or customer relationships tends to be more limited.

Business system

Ownership

The major forms of ownership in India include the public sector, professional entrepreneurial firms, foreign owned firms, cooperatives, non-government organizations (NGOs) and closely held family businesses and/or interlinked family business groups. There has been a reduced emphasis on the public sector, especially since the 1990s when the government launched a major divestment program. Since then, there has been a growing emphasis on using public–private partnerships for major infrastructural projects. Since the 1990s, many entrepreneurial firms have also been set up by co-founding professional partners, using venture capital and other sources of funding. Many foreign firms have invested in India, using joint ventures, acquisitions, as well as new investments. Consistent with its grassroots democracy culture, India also has a large number of cooperatives, such as Amul, comprising a large number of individual and small dairy producers who collectively organize operations and share profits. Many NGOs also work with the underprivileged members of the community, and are engaged in business activities.

Family businesses are the dominant form of business organization in India. Most family businesses have closely held ownership structures, but many create interlinked ownership structures among the group firms to retain management control while enabling access to the open market capital. These structures allowed Indian family businesses to become well diversified conglomerates. In the 1990s, among the top 50 business houses, such as the Tata Group, there was an average of 18 businesses. To meet the competitive challenges of the new economy many diversified family businesses have gone through family splits. Managers often use family splits to recognize the synergies among different business operations and make each business group more focused and cohesive (Goswami, 2000).

Networks

The Indian business system is characterized by reliance on vertical networks and horizontal networks. Vertical networks represent interfirm relational contracts, that is, close and long-standing relationships between suppliers and customers. The automotive industry illustrates where a large network of component suppliers is linked to a few leading large automotive firms, and where a few leading component firms are also linked to a fairly large network of smaller automotive firms (Parhi, 2008). In the 1950s, several indigenous automotive firms were established within the context of a policy framework that through reservations and local content requirements encouraged vertical disintegration, and proliferation of small-scale automotive components firms. In 1982, Maruti was founded through a joint venture between Suzuki of Japan and the Government of India, under a phased program requiring increasing local content. The market for cars grew rapidly, with Maruti taking an 80 per cent share of the market by the end of the 1980s. Following the practices then prevalent in Japan, Maruti relied on close buyer–supplier collaboration including exclusive supplier relationships with some of the most technologically capable and reliable local component suppliers, and offered reduced uncertainty for the peripheral firms that enabled them to invest in technology upgrading to meet Maruti's exacting quality standards. In the 1990s, the passenger car industry was de-licensed, and foreign firms were permitted to form joint ventures with a majority equity stake. This offered opportunities for some of the leading automotive component firms to develop close relationships with several new players (Parhi, 2008).

The information-technology-enabled services sector is another notable example of vertical buyer–supplier networks, but here buyers are overseas customers who engage in business process outsourcing to the local vendors in India. Rathinam (2008) investigated the role of network relationships between the foreign clients and the Indian vendors. Results suggest that Indian software firms rely on their reputation, particularly in the form of formal quality certifications and repeated long-term relational contracting, to economize on the costs of writing costly contracts while dealing with complex high-end projects. Their reputation, based on their high quality and long-term relationships, gives foreign customers the confidence to forego legal protection.

Horizontal networks have been long prevalent in India, in the form of highly specialized regional clusters that are known for agglomerating a large number of firms within a particular industry. Several regions are known for being centres of excellence in particular niches, such as, farm products, handicraft products, manufacturing and services. Well known examples include: Mumbai's Bollywood and financial services sector; Pune's automotive component sector; Bangalore's software sector; Hyderabad's business process outsourcing sector; and Jaipur's handicrafts sector. Many regional clusters play an important global role, through exports and interfirm relationships. Network relationships within clusters are sustained through community links, third party support, and government and NGOs.

Management

Pre-British and British colonial roots have influenced management–labour relations and managerial discretion in India. This influence has resulted, after independence in 1947, in attempts to correct some of the past injustices and the adoption of some of the world's best practices after liberalization of the 1990s. The early model of human resource management in India was created in the British colonial factories (Ramaswamy, 1997). In busy times, the workers, including women and children, 'had to work 22 hours a day for seven consecutive days' (Indian Factory Labor Commission, 1908); 'Those working these excessive hours frequently died' (*British Parliamentary Papers*, 1888). The indigenous welfare movement gained pace with the establishment of the Dorabji Tata Graduate School of Social Work (later renamed as the Tata Institute of Social Sciences) by the Tata business family in 1936. The Tata School offered training in casework, group work and community organization techniques to deal with individuals, group and community problems in the workforce.

Under the 1947 Industrial Disputes Act, the Indian government established an elaborate management-labour dispute mechanism. In the public sector, industry-level bargaining on a nationwide scale is common in core industries such as coal, steel, banks, insurance and ports. In the private sector, industry-level bargaining on a regional scale flourishes in industries such as textiles, plantations and engineering, where professional managers from the industry association, the Confederation of Indian Industry (CII), negotiate region-cum-industry agreements for member firms. Basic wage rates, benefits and working conditions decided at the company level are adjusted for local conditions at the plant level. Guided by the concept of the Welfare State in the Constitution of India, the collective agreements cover every aspect of business that influences the workforce, including compensation, work norms, staffing arrangements, transfer and promotion procedures, job and income security, techniques and technologies (Venkata Ratnam, 1998). While about 90 per cent of the workforce in the public sector has been unionized, the private sector has sought to minimize the union effects by subcontracting to small and medium firms.

In the 1980s, private firms in India began pioneering approaches for flexible restructuring to cope with the restrictive labour legislation and the emerging global competition. There has been a shift from regional and national unions to enterprise-level unions, often not linked to the National Federations, to negotiate willingly on the basis of the business conditions of particular companies. The restructuring of the larger private sector firms has opened up subcontracting for small units in the informal sector.

Since the late 1990s, more dramatic changes have occurred in human resource management. To manage growth, firms have scouted for talent deep in the smaller cities. They have rapidly escalated the metrics to support HR's contribution to their organizations and help measure effectiveness. Many firms deal with attrition rates as high as 70 per cent. The firms with lower attrition rates are focused on increasingly complex, integrated and challenging projects to generate higher unit values and to prevent more valuable employees from leaving. Many local firms have formed collaborations with universities to start specialized programs. Similarly, some US firms have used their corporate universities, such as Motorola University and Cisco networking academies, to collaborate with vendors in India to provide training in soft and technical skills (Srivastava, 2007).

Comparative advantage

The developments in the institutional framework and the business system have correlated with the shifts in the national competitive advantage. Indian managers migrated from a mind set focused on opportunistic resource accumulation and trading that traditionally prevailed as the basis for the unrelated diversification strategy. In general, they started building a cost leadership, thereafter enhancing service leadership, and finally evolving into a recognized technology leader in the global marketplace (Das, 1999).

The traditional trading business families were not cost leaders – indeed they sought to keep their business within their communities, if not families, so they would not be undercut. Even today, an employee in a typical family-run *saree* (the dress traditionally worn by women in India) store unfolds a hundred sarees within minutes, trying to sell just one. Similarly, waiters in most family-run *dhabas* (the traditional Indian restaurants) deliver a customer's *thali* (a set meal) in two minutes. Many managers are now rediscovering the secrets of service leadership. Service leadership generates value by delivering superior service through trained knowledge workers.

Since the mid-1990s, Indian companies have shown the highest return on equity in Asia – about double that in China. India has followed a business-to-business model globally. However, domestically, the focus has been on a business-to-consumer model. Increasing salaries have resulted in increased consumer expenditure. It has allowed many entrepreneurs to make large investments and benefit from economies of scale. By 2012, India boasted the second highest number of billionaires in Asia – 45 people, valued at US$195 billion; it also had more than one million millionaires.

India's comparative advantage is led by value-added designs and services, which show a higher growth potential at the international level, as compared to the low wage manufacturing centre for exports model of comparative advantage traditionally pursued by China. Considering the world's top 50 companies in terms of market capitalization, India boasts the highest intangible component as a percentage of total enterprise value – 75 per cent – the same as that of the United States. In 2007, the global average among 32 nations was 65 per cent, with China at 58 per cent (Dhobal and Pande, 2007). While the growth in the 1990s was driven by information technology (IT), IT-enabled services and off-shoring, since the 2000s several other sectors are growing at double-digit rates including aviation, entertainment, real estate development, financial services and hospitality (Government of India, 2007).

The changing trend of the Indian business system

India's institutional policy and business system has evolved over a period spanning several decades, centuries and millennia. India was perhaps the wealthiest nation of the ancient world, and aptly nicknamed the 'Golden Sparrow.' India became a British colony by the eighteenth century after the 1765 Treaty of Allahabad. The British introduced a bureaucratic business system, characterized by a leisurely work ethic (*aaram*); things being left as they are (*chalta hai*); elaborate procedures and numerous approvals (*red tape*); expectation of private rewards for official work (*corruption*); public resources used for private indulgence and family favours (*nepotism*); an expectation of favours for bosses (*yesmanship*); and superficial employment (*employees who have little actual work*). To facilitate colonial administration, postal, telecom, and railroad technologies were introduced into India in the 1850s as 'engines of social improvement' (Bear, 1994). The interior of India was substantially altered. English machine-made goods, made from Indian raw materials, squeezed out skilled Indian village artisans, and transformed them into unskilled workers doing jobs in the colonial British factories.

At the time of independence in 1947, India's agricultural sector was growing at a mere 0.3 per cent, and its manufacturing sector was miniscule (Indian National Science Academy, 2001). India's first Prime Minister, Jawahar Lal Nehru, advocated adoption of the Soviet type Five Year Planning system, along with a Non-Alignment Policy (Nehru, 1936/1972). The 'Mixed Economy' policy entrusted heavy industry projects, such as steel and hydro-power, to the public sector, and introduced a 'License Raj' to regulate the investments of larger private sector companies. The public sector firms built 'extension service' networks with small-scale enterprises for sourcing various intermediate inputs. Similarly, the private sector subcontracted to the smaller enterprises in order to bypass licensing restrictions.

With foreign aid, in particular from the United States and the then Soviet bloc, institutions of higher education in management and technology (engineering), and medicine were created, and modern infrastructure was also created for agriculture and capital goods production. The policy allowed India to become considerably self-sufficient in capital goods, but substantial consumer goods supply constraints emerged, along with economic stagnation, inflation, unemployment of the educated and urban poverty.

In the 1980s, government policy called for an integrated development of software for the domestic and export markets. The imports of knocked-down computer kits were liberalized, allowing the rise of many software development firms. Indian software development firms created customer facing onshore sites particularly in the United States, which enabled them to develop capabilities to perform increasingly complex work for the foreign clients offshore in India (Mulhearn, 2000).

In the 1990s, a major liberalization of Indian markets was undertaken, and the markets were opened to foreign multinational firms. The charge for the economy was handed over to the private sector. Unviable public sector firms were closed, while the potentially viable ones were disinvested. A majority of the Fortune 500 companies outsourced their IT services to India (Raipuria, 2002). India rapidly evolved from the world's software programmer to the world's back office to the world's laboratory, where the knowledge workforce made the cost of risk-taking affordable for companies around the world. For many foreign companies, new India became a design house, a tooling centre, a components base and a manufacturing hub. For instance, Germany's Heubach group produces pigments in India, 90 per cent of which are exported to help paint the cars of Mercedes, General Motors, and other major auto firms in the United States, Europe and Japan (India Brand Equity Foundation, 2007). Concurrently, the strategy of large private sector firms relying on imported technologies, services and capital goods lost its early momentum. Many technology collaborations with foreign firms fell. Several large private sector firms, such as Reliance, started emphasizing internal R&D, rather than continuing to depend on imported know-how.

As the indigenous capabilities of the Indian firms evolved, the decade of the 2000s saw an unprecedented rise in the numbers of Indian multinational corporations. The worldwide expansion of Indian firms as discussed next.

International activities of Indian firms

Historically, constrained and shepherded by the policy environment, most Indian business groups competed on country-specific advantages built on the re-engineering of the Western know-how for the conditions of India, and were unable to internationalize through FDI. However, a few large business groups went beyond re-engineering of the Western know-how, and constructed indigenous-based manufacturing and marketing advantages that were appropriate to the conditions of the emerging markets. They excelled in entrepreneurial adaptation of foreign designs to local conditions of the developing nations such as non-availability or prohibitive costs of raw materials, peculiarities of local consumers, the climate and geography (Athukorala et al., 2009).

Since the 1990s, government policy has shifted towards global integration. Based on the deep internal and external reconfiguration of the core competencies, many Indian businesses realized that they already had a rich history of accumulating firm-specific advantages. In order to leverage and augment these, however, they needed to develop appropriate global linkages, encompassing financial channels, vendor networks, client networks, and various systems and processes. As the government liberalized capital controls, several business groups moved rapidly to acquire targets overseas to augment their firm-level technological bases. They also sought to construct vendor bases in other emerging markets to complement their capabilities to serve the global markets. Through exports and foreign direct investments, many Indian businesses have become important players in the global market, and taken market share leadership in a range of domains.

The global financial and economic meltdown of 2007–2009 and the subsequent recession, have brought forth several challenges for the international growth of the Indian firms. Many Indian firms have responded by striving to explore opportunities for growth in the domestic market. In this scenario, the inadequacies of the Indian institutional structures have become increasingly apparent, as corruption, corporate frauds and policy failures contributing to billions of dollars of public losses have become apparent. The civil society, led by the judiciary, the media, and NGOs, has played a key role in fighting for transparency.

Corporate social responsibility, governance and ethics in India

Historically, managers of Indian businesses sought to ensure multigenerational continuity of firms' values and resources by satisfying a variety of different interests of community and showed eco-centric values (Sundar, 1999). After independence, the government began enforcing social altruism values. Some public sector companies invested up to 5 per cent of their profits on corporate social responsibility (CSR) activities. The conventions of the International Labor Organization heavily influenced public policy. The high corporate and personal income taxes of up to 55 per cent and 98.75 per cent respectively, however, encouraged widespread tax evasion.

In the post 1980 era, the new professionally owned firms saw the government as a partner (Sidel, 2000). The Confederation of Indian Industry, India's largest industry and business association, developed a voluntary code of corporate governance conduct in 1996 for listed companies, ahead of the East Asian crisis. The initiative has propelled the capital market regulatory authority of India – SEBI – to introduce a statutory code to elevate the corporate governance to international standards. Financial institutions have adopted an aggressive market-oriented stand, lifting their unconditional support of management. They have begun converting their outstanding debt to equity, and selling their shares in under-performing companies to professional entrepreneurs and managerial groups.

The policy framework has sought to resolve the 'shareholder vs. stakeholder' debate by promoting the rights of shareholders, while ensuring that the interests of other stakeholders are not adversely impacted. Secured credits such as banks, financial institutions and insurance companies offering long-term debt have the right to appoint their representatives as 'nominee directors' on the board of the client companies. They have exercised this right with almost all major listed companies that have a sizeable debt. Well-defined laws protect the interests of employees, insofar as the labour market is very restrictive, where adjustments, retrenchments, and downsizing are difficult to implement. Increasing popularity of equity stock options, particularly for the managerial and leadership level, has aligned employee and shareholder interests.

As the firms have faced competition for capital, human resources, customers and public goods pressure groups have become vocal, asking for support in poverty alleviation, addressing unemployment, fighting inequity and carrying out affirmative action. Similarly, foreign clients have demanded new CSR activities, including advancing women to managerial and leadership teams, and grass-roots action for eliminating adverse impacts on the environment, human rights and child rights. The Indian CSR initiatives have evolved to cover employees, customers and stakeholders, as well as sustainable local and national development through corporate citizenship

In 2012, India ranked 94th out of 176 nations on the Transparency Index of the Transparency International. Public institutions continue to be compromised by corruption. In 2005, the Right to Information Act was passed to allow civic institutions to hold public institutions accountable and create an empowered citizenry. Indian judiciary has also supported Public Interest Litigation as a way to spur public bodies to positive social action. The economic growth has resulted in improved social indicators such as reduced poverty, morbidity and mortality rates, and higher literacy levels, with rapid improvements in the Human Development Index. However, with growing income inequalities, India's rank on Human Development Index in 2012 was 136 out of 186 nations.

Given the vast scale of the challenge, Indian managers recognize that for sustainable development, they need to take a greater responsibility for linking economic growth with social development. In addition to improving the overall quality of life and increasing social stability, it will also make India an international destination of choice for 'socially responsible investment' and differentiate Indian firms for long-term, high quality investors.

Chapter summary

- India is fast emerging as a major economic power. India has retransformed from a lower income to lower middle income nation. The role of government has shifted from that of tight control to partnership with the private sector for inclusive and sustainable development.

- The backbone of the growth of India's economy has been information technology, but new areas such as biotechnology are fast emerging as new growth drivers.

- Civil society has emerged as an important advocate for the rights of the underprivileged groups, and champion of inclusive initiatives.

- The informal institutions help build substantial social capital within communities, and help to remove the disadvantages of being less dominant. However, they do not necessarily offer a profit or growth advantage. The Indian business system relies on both vertical and horizontal networks.

- The Indian management style is built on craft traditions and community values. However, it is also influenced by British bureaucratic and human rights exploitation and welfare-oriented socialist policy.

- Women are playing an increasingly important role as entry-level workers and as managers in Indian companies, although the number of women in leadership remains quite limited.

Key concepts

Business-to-business model: direct relationship between two businesses or business partners.

Business-to-consumer model: a relationship where businesses interact with the end-consumers.

Cost leadership: developing an ability to compete on the basis of low cost structure.

Extension services: services offered by an academic or public institution to the larger public.

First generation family business: family businesses that are owned and run by the founders.

Green revolution: a significant increase in agriculture productivity arising from the introduction of scientific methods and systematic management models.

License Raj: the bureaucratic system of controlling the economy through license permits for investment capacity and production outputs.

Mixed economy: a system of economic governance where the public and private sector collaborate and play an equally important role.

Review questions

1 Describe the rationale, identity and authority in the Indian business system.
2 Explain the characteristics of financial capital, human capital and social capital in the Indian business system.
3 Describe the aspects of ownership, networking and management in the Indian business system.
4 How are Indian firms integrated in the international economy?
5 How would you describe the CSR in India? What role has the civil society played in the Indian business system?

Learning activities and discussions

1 Search for Indian businesses in your community, and evaluate them broadly (in terms of price, quality, ethnic uniqueness, product diversity, inclusiveness and service). What distinguishes them from similar businesses from other countries in your community? Think about whether and how the features of these Indian businesses can be related to the peculiarities of Indian management.

2 Imagine you are working for an Indian company. Discuss with your classmates how you would be able to deal with the Indian management style, and what would probably be the biggest cultural challenges for you to accommodate in such an environment.

Jaipur Rugs empowers the grassroots in India

N.K. Chaudhry founded Jaipur Rugs in the city of Jaipur as a small family business in the 1970s, and started exporting in 1986 By 2008, Jaipur Rugs was the largest manufacturer and exporter of Indian hand knotted rugs, and also produced tufted and flat woven styles.

The Chaudhry leadership was guided by a deep concern for the welfare of the weavers. The traditional, unorganized rug industry in India, as in many other low-income nations, was characterized by the use of similar traditional designs and materials. The firms faced significant competition, selling primarily in the local market, and commanding low prices. To remain viable, the use of low-cost child labour and women labour was rampant, while men were deployed to instruct, supervise and control this illiterate and impoverished workforce.

Mr Chaudhry began by removing the males from their middlemen and supervisory roles, and provided looms directly to the women weavers, organized into small groups, who worked together weaving a rug on their loom. More experienced women weavers were designated as leaders, who worked as weavers but also offered instructions to fellow less experienced weavers, who worked on the different part of the rug alongside them. This was possible because depending on the size and design complexity, a rug might require several women to work simultaneously for up to one year. Former experienced weaver supervisors, who had a deep appreciation of the weaving techniques associated with different designs, were retrained as designers. Since they were all illiterate, they were trained to work in a computer-based design centre using customized visually-based design software. Latest international design books were provided for inspiration, enabling creation of fusion contemporary designs, which commanded strong interest from wholesale rug buyers in the international markets – particularly the United States – the initial country of focus. Those who had some education were appointed to different managerial positions in the company.

The weavers were paid per piece (depending on the size, complexity of design, and quality of finished product in terms of defects and amount of rework required). Thus, rewards and punishments were built into the payment system. While most women weavers earned only the legal minimum wages when translated into daily wages, many chose to work for fewer than eight hours. The looms were situated in the villages at or near their homes, in order to provide a more humane working environment. That allowed women to take time off to take care of their household chores and children. Significantly, Jaipur Rugs was competitive and was able to scale up its model and its international demand, without the need to cut down on the wages or to hire child labour or to use exploitative methods. Further, women weavers were assured year-round consistent work because of the international demand, in an industry traditionally characterized by cycles of work and idling.

Mr Chaudhry sent all his five children for higher education in the United States. Two of his eldest daughters opened a marketing office in Atlanta. His eldest son and the youngest daughter returned to India to help with operations and marketing respectively. His youngest son was an undergraduate at a university in Boston. Mr Chaudhry was now looking to scale up the model of social responsibility that he had prototyped, and bring in the fresh ideas led by the next generation of his family and by the professional hires.

Questions

1 Which internal and external factors have helped Jaipur Rugs to succeed?
2 In which aspects has the management at Jaipur Rugs been typical for Indian management? In which aspects has it been atypical?
3 Do you think Jaipur Rugs has to transform itself fundamentally to remain successful in the future, as the second generation of family assumes leadership roles? Why or why not?

Web links

On the story of India: http://india.gov.in/
On the success story of Brand India: www.ibef.org
On news from India: http://www.samachar.com/

References

Athukorala, P.-C. Bandara, J.S. and Kelegama, S. (2009) *Trade Liberalization and Poverty in South Asia*. London: Routledge.

Basham, A.L. (1967) *The Wonder that was India*, 3rd edn. London: Sidgwick & Jackson.

Bear, L.G. (1994) Miscegenations of Modernity: Constructing European Respectability and Race in the Indian Railway Colony, 1857–1931. *Women's History Review*, 3(4): 531–548.

British Parliamentary Papers (1888) LXXVII, No. 321.

Chhokar, J.S. (2007) India: Diversity and Complexity in Action, in J.S. Chhokar, F.C. Brodbeck, and R.J. House (eds.) *Culture and Leadership Across the World: The GLOBE Book of In-Depth Studies of 25 Societies*. Mahwah, NJ: Lawrence Erlbaum, pp. 971–1020.

Das, G. (1999) The Problem. *Seminar* (Special Issue on Family Business: A Symposium on the Role of the Family in Indian Business): 482.

De, S. and Singh, M. (2010) Credit Rationing in Informal Markets: The Case of Small Firms in India, accessed 4 December 2013 at: http://www.isid.ac.in/~pu/conference/dec_10_conf/Papers/SankarDe.pdf

Dhobal, S. and Pande, B. (2007) India Emerges Top 3 Economy in the World, *The Economic Times*, 10 December.

Gandhi, M.K. (1947/2003) Gandhi on Women in Politics: A Voice from the Past. *The Hindu*, 28 September, accessed 6 November 2013 at: http://www.hindu.com/mag/2003/09/28/stories/2003092800280400.htm

Goswami, O. (2000) *The Tide Rises Gradually: Corporate Governance in India*. Paris: OECD Development Centre.

Government of India (2007) *The Economic Survey 2006–2007*. New Delhi: Government of India.

Gupta, V., Levenburg, N., Moore, L., Motwani, J. and Schwarz, T. (2008) *Culturally-Sensitive Models* of Family Business in Southern Asia: A Compendium Using the GLOBE Paradigm. Hyderabad: ICFAI University Press.

House, R.J., Hanges, P.J., Javidan, M., Dorfman, P.W. and Gupta, V. (2004) (eds.) *Culture, Leadership, and Organizations: The GLOBE Study of 62 Cultures*. Thousand Oaks, CA: Sage Publications.

India Brand Equity Foundation (2007)Home page, accessed 6 November 2013 at: www.ibef.org

Indian Factory Labor Commission (1908) *Report of the Indian Factory Labor Commission* Vol I. Simla: Government of India.

Indian National Science Academy (INSA) (2001) *Pursuit and Promotion of Science: The Indian Experience*. New Delhi: INSA.

Kohli, R. (2012) Indian Financial and Capital Markets: Implications for Infrastructure Funding, Paper presented at the Conference of the Policy Research Institute, Ministry of Finance, Tokyo, Japan.

Mulhearn, J. (2000) Birth, Evolution, and Globalization of the Indian Information Technology Industry: Protected Insular State Enterprises to Private Global Software Exporters, accessed 13 January 2005 at: http://www.contrib.andrew.cmu.edu/~mulhearn/india.html

Nehru, J.L. (1936/1972) Introduction to M.R. Masani: Soviet Sidelights. Reprinted in *Selected Works of Jawaharlal Nehru* (New Delhi, 1972) 7: 128–129.

Parhi M. (2008) Impact of Changing Facets of Inter-firm Interactions on Manufacturing

Excellence: A Social Network Perspective of Indian Automotive Industry. *Asian Journal of Technology Innovation*, 16(1): 117–141.

Raipuria, K. (2002) What Size the 'New' Economy? A Conduit Approach. *Economic and Political Weekly*, 37: 1062–1067.

Ramaswamy, E.A. (1997) *A Question of Balance: Labor, Management, and Society*. Delhi: Oxford University Press.

Rathinam, F.X. (2008) Determinants of Inter-firm Contractual Relations: A Case of Indian Software Industry. *The IUP Journal of Financial Economics*, 6(4): 73–85.

Sidel, M. (2000) New Economy Philanthropy in the High Technology Communities of Bangalore and Hyderabad, India: Partnership with the State and the Ambiguous Search for Social Innovation. Paper presented at the Rockefeller Foundation Conference 'Philanthropy and the City: A Historical Overview', 25–26 September.

Sundar, P. (1999) *Beyond Business: From Merchant Charity to Corporate Citizenship, Indian Business Philanthropy through the Ages*. New Delhi: Tata McGraw-Hill.

Srivastava, S. (2007) Indians to Get a Big Raise. *Asia Times*, February 9.

Venkata Ratnam, C.S. (1998) Industrial Relations in India, in A. Chandram, H. Mund, T. Sharan and C.P. Thakur (eds.) *Labor, Employment and Human Development in South Asia*. Delhi: BR Publishing Corporation.

11

The Business System of Korea

Martin Hemmert

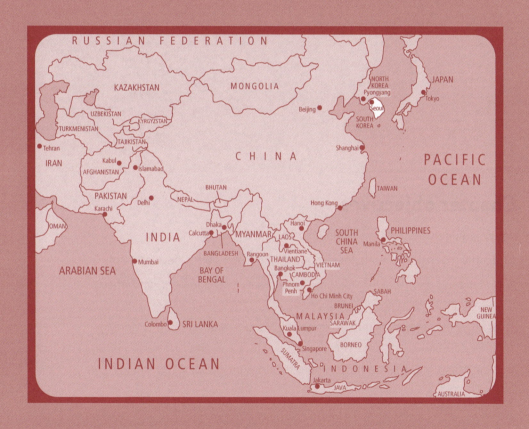

Chapter outline

- Economic development, corporate growth and business-government relations
- Korean culture, financial, human and social capital
- The Korean management system and the globalization of Korean firms
- Corporate social responsibility and working and living conditions in Korea

Chapter objectives

After reading this chapter, you should be able to:

1 Identify the major reasons for Korea's dynamic economic development.

2 Understand the specific features of Korean management and their cultural and institutional background.

3 Identify the major potential strengths and weaknesses of Korean management.

4 Understand how Korean firms globalize and exert social responsibility.

Overview of the Korean economy

South Korea (subsequently referred to as Korea) is a geographically small country with an area of approximately 100,000 km^2 which covers the southern half of the Korean peninsula. However, in contrast to its limited geographic size, it is a major economic power. The Korean GDP amounted to more than US$1,100 billion in 2011, which made it the fourth largest in Asia behind China, Japan and India. It has a population of approximately 50 million people, and the estimated per capita income in 2011 was approximately US$22,500 at current exchange rates and US$30,000 on a purchasing power parity adjusted base, illustrating the fact that Korea has reached the group of very high income countries, with the remaining income gap to the richest countries narrowing in recent years. Moreover, income level per capita has increased by approximately 250 times throughout the past 50 years, reflecting the country's stunning economic development (World Bank, 2012).

Despite being a small country the Korean economy shows a strong pattern of specialization. The weight of the manufacturing and construction sectors amounted to 39 per cent of the total economy in 2011 (with 3 per cent falling to agriculture and 58 per cent to services) and is thereby one of the highest in the world among developed countries (World Bank, 2012). Moreover, within manufacturing, Korean firms are strongly specialized in a few industries, such as automobiles, electronics, microelectronics, telecommunications, steel and shipbuilding, which account for most of the country's exports. Apart from this pronounced sectoral specialization Korea's economy is also very specialized in a vertical sense. Korean firms often focus on specific steps within the industrial value chain only. Whereas they concentrate largely on the final assembly of products such as cellular phones or digital displays, most of the parts and components are purchased from outside and often imported. Taken together, the Korean economy is characterized by a strong horizontal and vertical specialization in fields of activities where it possesses competitive advantages.

Korea's business sector also has some other distinctive characteristics. Most of the country's large companies are members of business groups (*chaebols*), which dominate the export oriented industries. However, most Koreans do not work in these large firms; small and medium-sized enterprises (SMEs) with less than 300 employees accounted for almost 87 per cent of the country's total business sector employment in 2010 (e-National Indicators, 2012). When compared to large firms, wages and salaries are much lower in these SMEs. In other words, a pronounced dualism between SMEs and large firms can be observed. Large firms possess a strong international competitiveness and are concentrated in the export oriented industries, whereas SMEs are mostly focused on domestic business activities.

Economic development, corporate growth and business-government relations

Although Korea, throughout its long history, has evolved as an independent kingdom, it was – much like other East Asian countries – technologically backward when Western colonization reached out to the region in the late nineteenth century. After a struggle to maintain independence, it eventually came under Japanese influence and was formally annexed by Japan in 1910. During the period of Japanese colonial rule, which lasted until 1945, the country's infrastructure was somewhat modernized, and an industrial manufacturing sector was created. However, all developmental priorities were set according to the preferences of the Japanese rulers, not those of the Korean people themselves.

After achieving independence from Japan, the country split into a southern half, which developed under US influence and a northern half under Soviet influence and, later on, Chinese influence. Following a military attack by the North, the country was devastated by the Korean War, which lasted from 1950 to 1953. This war cost not only the lives of three million people, but also destroyed large parts of the infrastructure and manufacturing facilities. In short, the Korean government after the war found itself in charge of a country that was extremely impoverished in technological, material and financial resources. Moreover, Korea had also been deprived of any autonomous development and leadership for the previous 50 years. As a result, apart from a gradual post-war reconstruction that was backed by development aid, no rapid improvement of the economic situation could be achieved in the first years after the war.

Rapid economic development and high growth since the 1960s

The situation changed, however, during the government of President Park Chung-hee, who seized power through a military coup in 1961. Under authoritarian rule, resources were concentrated on activities in specific sectors that were designed to achieve rapid industrialization. In the beginning, priority was given to the development of basic industries such as cement and petroleum and light, labour intensive industries, such as textiles and footwear (Chung et al., 1997). Since the late 1960s, however, the focus of Korea's industrial policy shifted to heavy industries such as steel and shipbuilding, and later on in the 1970s to advanced assembly industries such as automobiles and electronics. Korea's industrial policy during this period included not only concentration on specific sectors and industries, but also preferential treatment of specific companies and business groups in these industries, which were evaluated as most capable by the government to contribute to the country's economic and industrial development. These firms were provided with priority access to scarce resources through the granting of import licenses that secured availability to foreign exchange and almost unconditional bank loans.

The emergence of Korean business groups

Korea's industrial policy during this period was widely regarded as extremely successful. Double digit annual growth rates were continuously achieved, resulting in a rapid upgrade of the country's status from a developing to an emerging economy. The economic and technological development in the 1960s and 1970s clearly occurred under the leadership of the government, which steered and controlled private business activities through a wide range of direct and indirect measures (Chang, 2003). However, as a consequence, the corporate sector grew rapidly. In particular, numerous diversified business groups (*chaebols*) emerged in Korea. A common feature of these groups was that they expanded into a large number of products and industries, which were often technologically unrelated. This lateral corporate growth was partially the result of the preferential treatment of specific companies by the government, which allowed them to pursue aggressive expansion strategies. However, at least during the early stages of development, it was also a consequence of the lack of industrial development and weakness of markets for resources and intermediate products that induced companies to expand into other industries to become and stay competitive (Kim et al., 2004). To illustrate, LG chairman Koo Cha-kyung recalled the early development of his business group like this (Aguilar and Cho, 1985):

> My father and I started a cosmetic cream factory in the late 1940s. At the time, no company could supply us with plastic caps of adequate quality for cream jars, so we had to start a plastics business. Plastic caps alone were not sufficient to run the plastic molding plant, so we added combs, toothbrushes, and soap boxes. This plastics business also led us to manufacture electric fan blades and telephone cases, which in turn led us to manufacture electrical and electronic products and telecommunications equipment. The plastics business also took us into oil refining, which needed a tanker shipping company. The oil refining company alone was paying an insurance premium amounting to more than half of the revenue of the then largest insurance company in Korea. Thus, an insurance company was started. This natural step-by-step evolution through related businesses resulted in the Lucky-Goldstar group as we see it today.

In the 1980s, the government gradually retreated from the direct control of the corporate sector and its support of specific firms. By this time, some *chaebols* had grown into giant industrial groups that not only accounted for a large part of the Korean economy, but also competed globally in a wide range of industries. At the same time, many Korean firms also made rapid technological advances (Kim, 1997). Whereas they were strongly dependent on foreign technology in the early stages, starting in the1980s they increasingly acquired indigenous technological capabilities through research and development (R&D) activities. As a result, Korean firms moved into technologically advanced fields, such as semiconductors, cellular phones and digital displays. In certain fields, they emerged subsequently as global industry leaders, such as Samsung Electronics in the memory chip industry. Recently, supported by heavy investment in wireless communication networks, Korean companies are also rapidly advancing into internet related products and services.

The financial crisis of 1997 and structural reforms

In spite of the gradual reduction of government interference in the business sector and the country's democratization, which occurred in the late 1980s, Korea was still considered largely as a closed market by foreign investors in many industries until the 1990s. Many formal restrictions as well as informal practices, accompanied by a widespread hostility in the government and the business community towards foreign influences, made it difficult for multinational enterprises (MNEs) to penetrate the Korean market through imports or foreign direct investment.

However, the business climate drastically changed as a result of the Asian financial crisis of 1997 that had a huge impact on Korea and forced the government to seek the IMF's financial assistance in order stay solvent internationally. Subsequently, many restrictions for international investors were removed, and a large number of financially troubled Korean firms were acquired by foreign MNEs. At the same time, the *chaebols'* structure and business model, which have been praised before as a major reason for the country's economic success, came under strong attack. Nine of the 30 largest business groups became bankrupt or underwent bank-sponsored restructuring programs in the years immediately following the crisis (Hemmert, 2012), with Daewoo, which together with Samsung, Hyundai, LG and SK was one of the five leading *chaebols* in Korea but ceased to exist as a group after 1999, being the most prominent victim. Moreover, the *chaebols* were also criticized for their lack of transparency and poor corporate governance, which allowed the groups' owners to exert almost unlimited power regarding strategic business decisions through a network of majority ownership in group companies. The *chaebols'* management was urged to improve transparency through the setup of holding companies and to dispose of technologically unrelated activities.

Many *chaebols* made significant efforts to address these issues, with the Hyundai group, which split up into two groups – one being focused on the automobile business and some related activities and the other one accommodating most of the other group companies – being the most well-known case. Despite these developments most Korean business groups still have to be regarded as more strongly diversified when compared with conglomerate firms from other advanced economies, and the extremely strong influence of their owners prevails in most cases (Hemmert, 2007). In fact, some *chaebols* started to diversify again after the economic crisis had been overcome. Furthermore, whereas the government's influence on business has weakened in the course of the country's economic and political development, it still appears to be stronger than in most other OECD countries, as some politicians and administrators continue to interfere occasionally with the private sector through discretionary actions and rulings.

Taken together, notwithstanding the rapid transformation of Korea's economic and political system throughout the past 50 years, some previous important features of the Korean economy still partially prevail. In particular, large business groups continue to play an important role in Korea.

Korean culture

The country's cultural tradition is strongly linked to a specific interpretation of Confucianism, which traces back to the Yi dynasty that ruled Korea from 1392 to 1910 and made it the predominant ideology of the pre-modern Korean state. Korean Confucianism is very strict and particularly emphasizes the following values (Chang and Chang, 1994, Chung et al., 1997, Hemmert, 2012):

- loyalty to senior individuals within a hierarchy;
- filial piety and respect to parents;
- emphasis on education and diligence; and
- trust between friends and colleagues.

Consequently, Korean culture has several distinctive characteristics. First, power distance is very high, implying that individuals at the upper levels of organizational hierarchies are extremely influential and that their subordinates feel strongly obliged to follow their directions, even if they may have personally different views. Second, authority and power are strongly linked to the age of individuals. Consequently, top level positions in business and society are predominantly occupied by people of senior age. Third, all activities that are linked to learning and education are genuinely regarded as very valuable, even if their economic return is uncertain, resulting in a national education zeal, which is outstanding even by East Asian standards. Fourth, Korean people are generally group-oriented, although they tend to keep their individual ambitions when they join companies, other organizations or groups as members.

Financial, human and social capital

Financial capital

The Korean financial system has been primarily bank-based from the beginning the country's modern economic development. In the 1950s, some business groups expanded their operations into the financial sector. During the period of military government from the 1960s to the 1980s, however, banks were placed under tight government control, and *chaebols* were prohibited from holding significant stakes in them. The Korean government used the financial sector as a vehicle to allocate funds from domestic savings and development aid to selected and prioritized investment projects in the business sector.

Whereas the government's industrial policy was overall very successful, it prevented banks from developing genuine risk assessment and management skills. These shortcomings became apparent in the 1990s when the financial sector was gradually liberalized. Many Korean banks heavily borrowed overseas to increase their operating funds without controlling the exchange rate risk properly. Consequently, they fell into a serious crisis when the rate of the Korean Won against major global currencies fell by half in late 1997. The government was subsequently forced to restructure many ailing banks. At the same time, the financial sector was deregulated further. Foreigners are now allowed to invest in Korean securities and compete directly in the Korean financial industries, with much fewer restrictions. More recently, the government's banking supervision has also been modernized and reformed, resulting in increased transparency (Kwon, 2010).

The post-1997 restructuring of the Korean financial sector is widely regarded as a success. Korean financial institutions emerged from it in a much healthier state and have greatly improved their operating skills, though they are still primarily domestically oriented and lagging behind the competitiveness of their leading counterparts from Western countries. Securities markets have also significantly developed and globalized. Around one-third of the total capitalization of the Korean stock market is now under foreign ownership (KRX, 2012). Overall, however, the Korean financial system is still more strongly based on intermediaries than on financial markets. The financial sector is not as competitive as the manufacturing sector, but is no longer regarded as a liability of the Korean economy and business system.

Human capital

In contrast to financial capital, human capital has, throughout the past decades, been a relative strength of the Korean economy. Reflecting the traditionally strong inclination of Koreans to learn and study, their education level has been consistently very high when considering the country's level of economic development. In recent years, their educational achievements are among the highest in the world. Almost all young Koreans graduate from high school, and two-thirds of them take a university degree. At the same time, Korea sends more students abroad than any other OECD country (OECD, 2011). Through such global exposure and through educational reforms in Korea itself, many young Koreans now acquire critical thinking skills, which were less emphasized when the country's education system was more focused on rote learning.

Koreans are also well known for working very hard after entering the workforce. On average, they worked for 2,090 hours in 2011, which is more than 20 per cent less than two decades ago. However, even now Korea has the second longest working hours among all OECD countries, after Mexico (OECD, 2012b). It is considered normal to work until the late evening and weekends if there is important work to be done. Except from public holidays, vacations typically amount to only one or two weeks per year.

Despite the diligence and strong work ethic of Koreans, industrial relations have been troubled. During the period of authoritarian government from the 1960s to the 1980s, the labour movement was suppressed and labour unions were severely restricted regarding their permitted range of activities. In 1987, this repressive government regulation regarding industrial relations was largely removed (Chung et al., 1997). Since then, labour unions evolved as powerful negotiation partners for companies and have enforced high rates of wage increases and various other improvements in working conditions. While this development has certainly contributed to the improvement of living standards for many Koreans, it also drove up the labour cost for Korean companies and induced them to move significant parts of their operations to countries with lower wages, particularly China. Furthermore, many firms have increased the proportion of non-regular employees, as their compensation is much lower and they can be laid off easier. As a result, the share of non-regular employees has increased and now amounts to around 35 per cent of the total workforce (OECD, 2012a).

Furthermore, many labour unions developed a hostile attitude toward companies in the years after the country's democratization in the late 1980s, as they perceived business leaders to be part of the establishment that previously held them down. Due to the deep rooted mistrust between the firms' management and labour representatives, many labour unions have been readily calling for strikes if their demands were not fulfilled. These problems were so widespread that industrial relations were often raised as a major hurdle for investment in Korea by representatives of multinational firms. However, throughout more recent years, labour unions have become more modest in their demands, and industrial relations have gradually become more peaceful. The number of labour disputes and accompanying economic losses is now approaching the average of OECD countries (ILO, 2013).

Social capital

Korea has been classified as a 'low trust society', implying that Koreans tend not to trust people they do not know (Fukuyama, 1995). At the same time, however, Koreans engage extensively in social networking to compensate for this lack of general trust in society. Traditionally, the strongest bond that allows a high level of interpersonal trust is kinship in extended families. Furthermore, Koreans strongly cultivate regional ties (with individuals who originate from the same city or region), school and university ties (with individuals who have graduated from the same high school or university) and military ties (with people who have served in the same military units). More recently, friendships through study and hobby groups have evolved as a further strong bonding mechanism.

As a result, interpersonal trust is more strongly developed than institutional trust. Koreans have only limited trust in general institutions in society, such as the parliament, the police, the legal system or large companies (Lee, 2003). At the same time, they strongly trust those people they have personal bonds with. This precedence of personal trust over institutional trust often expresses itself through important decisions made by Koreans. For example, when a senior manager leaves a company and enters a different company, subordinates who have a close relationship with this manager often follow him or her to the new company.

The Korean management system

The roots of Korean management

The management system of Korean firms clearly differs from that of firms in other countries and has four different roots (Hemmert, 2012):

1. The country's strong Confucian tradition is reflected in a centralization of authority and a high power distance between managers and their subordinates in corporate organizations, a paternalistic leadership style, and a strong emphasis on education and training.

2. During the Japanese colonial period in the first half of the twentieth century, centrally controlled and highly diversified Japanese conglomerates (*zaibatsu*) became implicit role models for Korean firms. At the same time, Korean companies and managers acquired strong survival skills as they had to cope with a generally difficult economic environment as well as restrictive policies by the Japanese colonial administration.

3. The strong US presence in Korea in the decades after 1945 induced Korean firms to vigorously seek business opportunities emerging from government support and US economic aid. As the eligibility standards for these support measures greatly changed over time, Korean firms became very flexible and pragmatic in their business planning in order to seize opportunities. Moreover, many Korean managers acquired a global mind set by studying and working in the United States.

4. Through the military-led development policies of the Korean government in the 1960s and 1970s, companies became accustomed to working very quickly on highly ambitious and clear-cut targets and to meet these goals and their deadlines under any circumstances, as no excuses were accepted for failures.

The Korean management system is most distinct in the three fields of business strategy, leadership and human resource management, which are subsequently discussed.

Business strategy

The business strategies of Korean firms tend to be very bold and aggressive. As outlined before, Korean businesses typically lacked resources or competitive advantages when they started their operations in the first decades after liberation and the Korean War. Often, innovative and risk-taking approaches were the only way to overcome this situation and to make a business viable and sustainable. This risk-taking attitude has persisted in the managerial strategies of many Korean firms until today. It could be observed not only domestically, but also internationally. For example, Korean firms often entered emerging markets such as India or Central Asian countries in an early stage to grab business opportunities and achieve first mover advantages. Likewise, *chaebols* often advanced aggressively into new industries and product lines, leading to very high diversification levels, as discussed earlier in this chapter. Moreover, the Korean firms' aggressive expansion strategies were often extensively debt financed, resulting in highly leveraged balance sheets with debt/equity ratios of 5:1 or higher (Chung et al., 1997). Following the Asian financial crisis of 1997 and the subsequent restructuring, those companies and groups that survived have greatly reduced their financial debt in order to become less vulnerable to future economic shocks.

The entrepreneurial, risk-taking strategies of Korean firms bring certain opportunities and risks. On the one hand, their aggressive approach was often rewarded with high growth and profitability when new markets were successfully penetrated through product or geographical diversification. On the other hand, however, it also made them vulnerable to the consequences of managerial errors or unfavourable changes in the business environment. Therefore, it was not a coincidence that so many *chaebols*, notwithstanding their previous growth and profitability, became bankrupt during the Asian financial crisis.

Leadership and decision making

In a Korean business group or firm, the CEO is typically the owner. Thus, there is generally no separation between ownership and management. The CEO and company owner assumes the role of the father in a Confucian family. He makes all major decisions and expects his subordinates (the 'family members') to implement them swiftly without dissent. As a consequence, most of the power in Korean firms is centralized at the top level. Moreover, for top managers, there is no need for extensive consultation and consensus seeking within the organization before making major decisions.

In large *chaebols*, the owner typically relies on a staff organization, which is personally attached to him and named 'planning and coordination office', 'central planning office' or 'office of the chairman' to gather information needed to make important decisions (Chang and Chang, 1994). Following new regulations, after the Asian financial crisis, these staff organizations, which initially often were 'private' planning offices of the chairmen, had to formally integrate into group companies and have been somewhat downsized in recent years. However, they still play an important role in supporting the chairmen's leadership.

Korean business leaders motivate their subordinates by setting very ambitious and clearcut goals. For example, they may give them the target of becoming the domestic market leader or one of the three top global companies within the next three or five years or of reaching a specific market share within a specified time period. Setting such ambitious goals can be very motivating for employees, but at the same time can become very stressful for them when these goals are difficult to achieve. In this context, the behaviour of Korean executives can be referred to as 'leadership by crisis creation' (Hemmert, 2012). Even in the absence of an external crisis, corporate organizations are thrown internally into a crisis situation by being pushed to their limits in order to meet the very ambitious targets set by their leaders.

Another instrument of corporate leadership in Korea is the extensive use of company mottos (*sahoon*), which do not only cover important aspects of business performance such as customer satisfaction, but also often emphasize broader values such as 'trust', 'credibility', 'excellence' or 'responsibility' (Chung et al., 1997). Notably, the corporate values that are promoted through company mottos are strongly linked to the personal beliefs of the current corporate leaders and thereby aim to align the behaviour of the whole workforce with the directions given by top management.

The leadership of Korean companies is broadly supported by close relationships between managers and their direct subordinates and a generally strong coherence among their employees. Vertical human ties tend to be close in Korean firms and are often extended beyond narrowly defined working relationships. Managers expect their subordinates to be respectful and to do their best to follow their directions. At the same time, they assume personal responsibility for the well-being of their subordinates and give them advice on work-related and private matters. In sum, whereas harmonious human relationships are regarded as important in Korean firms, such harmony is particularly emphasized in vertical rather than horizontal relationships (Chen, 2004). However, all members of corporate organizations are also bound together by a collective sentiment, which is captured by the concept of 'jeong' (Yang, 2006). Jeong can be roughly translated as 'human affection' and expresses that members of collectives, such as colleagues in companies, are getting used to each other through their everyday exchanges and work effectively together, regardless of personal aversions or differences in character.

The Korean management and leadership style has a number of specific strengths and weaknesses. As there is little need for discussion and consensus seeking, managerial policies tend to be implemented with high speed in Korean firms. At the same time, the fate of Korean companies depends to a great extent on the quality of managerial decisions made by top managers. If a top manager is highly competent and his or her managerial directions are enlightened, Korean companies have the potential to emerge as extremely strong and dynamic competitors – domestically and internationally. However, if the prescribed managerial policies are bad, they can lead the respective companies into serious difficulties, as there is no effective organizational mechanism in place to control or correct them. Furthermore, a lack of professionalism has been identified as a major problem in some large chaebols and Korean companies. As ownership and management are not separate in most cases, it sometimes turns out that the competent management of large businesses is beyond the intellectual or professional capacity of their owners (Chang, 2003). In fact, many chaebols are now relying more and more on professional managers to overcome this problem (see for an example the mini case at the end of this chapter).

Human resource management

Korean firms devote a lot of attention to the field of human resource management. As Korea is not blessed with any significant natural resources they are compelled to rely on human skills and knowledge for developing competitive strength. Moreover, their human resource management strongly emphasizes education, which is a core value in the country's Confucian culture.

Recruiting

There are two groups of employees in Korean firms for which sharply different conditions and rules apply: regular and non-regular employees. For regular employees, a highly formalized recruiting process is applied, whereas non-regular employees are hired on a more casual base. Accordingly, job security is provided to regular employees, whereas non-regular employees are often laid off at the convenience of the company, such as during business downturns.

Regular employees are hired twice a year (in spring and autumn) by most companies, and traditionally the recruiting process has been centred on new university graduates.

In many large companies, only graduates from prestigious universities used to be hired as core employees to whom long-term career opportunities are provided. However, in recent years, a university degree has in many companies become a requirement to be considered as a normal regular employee, or sometimes even as a non-regular employee. The rising expectations of Korean firms regarding the qualifications of job applicants reflect the increasing competitive pressures they are exposed to, but are also a result of an education boom in Korea, which shows the strong emphasis on education in the country's society.

New employees are hired through an extensive review of application materials and multiple interviews. Moreover, large companies also conduct additional written tests and run assessment centres to screen the actual skills and capabilities of applicants (Chung et al., 1997). Apart from their formal education level and the reputation of the educational institutions from which they graduated, the applicants' personalities and their range of practical skills and foreign language capabilities are also strongly considered in the recruiting process. As an overall tendency, strictly performance-oriented criteria, as opposed to personal networks and social ties, have become more and more important in the selection process for Korean companies' new employees.

Training and skill formation

There are extensive internal training programs in Korean firms. Most large and meddle-sized firms have set up their own training facilities. Moreover, the companies' internal training centres are not exclusively targeted at providing basic training for new hires only, but also organize various skill enhancement programs for established employees. The great emphasis many Korean companies place on the training of their employees can be seen from the fact that they set aside around 5 per cent of their employees' regular working hours for participation in training programs (Chen, 2004). Except from skill development, the internal training is also aimed at enhancing the employees' group cohesiveness, esprit de corps and emotional attachment to their company.

Thus, Korean companies not only enhance the professional skills of their employees, but also promote collectivistic values, such as harmony and group cohesiveness. In this context, it is noteworthy, that Korean workers' and managers' work values and attitudes are strongly individualistic, though group oriented. Whereas they are willing to and are used to working in teams, they are also striving for individual achievement, such as receiving positive evaluations, within the group context. In other words, Koreans are group-oriented workers, but do not abandon their individual ambitions by becoming group members. In this sense, groups of Koreans can be qualified as 'salad bowls' in which each member keeps his or her individual profile, as compared with 'melting pot' groups in Japan which absorb each member's aspirations and create a coherent group consciousness (Chang and Chang, 1994).

Compensation, promotion and retirement

Koreans tend to be very diligent and ambitious, and the perspective for a promotion can motivate them strongly, as promotions come with recognition, prestige and status gains, which are highly valued rewards in a Confucian cultural context. However, wage increases and, in particular, job security are also strong motivators (Chen, 2004). To illustrate, as a result of the rising competitive pressures in the business sector that give many employees the feeling that their jobs may not be safe in the long run, many highly qualified individuals in Korea are applying for jobs in the public sector, which provides only moderate career opportunities and salary levels, but high job security.

Compensation and promotion systems traditionally used to be primarily seniority oriented. However, throughout the past few decades, performance orientation has become stronger and stronger. Some companies, such as Samsung Electronics, have become famous for strongly linking their managers' compensation to business results in their fields of responsibility (refer to the mini case at the end of this chapter), or even providing them with stock options. In general, whereas most Korean companies still retain a certain seniority component in their promotion policies, it appears that performance at individual and group level has become the predominant evaluation criteria for workers and managers. This change was further triggered by the impact of the Asian financial crisis, when many Korean firms were forced to lay off large numbers of their employees and had to abandon stable, long-term employment relations (Park and Yu, 2002). At the same time, the loyalty of many employees to their companies is not very high, although some Koreans still spend their whole working life within the same company. In recent years, partially as a reaction to the introduction of flexible employment practices by many companies and decreasing job security, many Koreans are open to consider a change of their employer when a better position or compensation is offered, and they actively search the external job market if they are unsatisfied with their current work or compensation level.

Companies have specific retirement ages which are commonly between 55 and 60. However, the retirement age often varies at different managerial ranks. Executives and senior managers are sometimes given the opportunity to stay for longer in their company if they are very successful. At the same time, however, they are also provided with less job security than lower level managers and workers who are protected by labour regulation. As a consequence, they face the risk of having to leave their company earlier.

The globalization of Korean firms

The growth and development of the Korean economy has been largely founded on the global expansion of its firms. Since the 1960s exports have grown dramatically and amounted to US$ 555 billion in 2011, which is equivalent to 50 per cent of the country's GDP. Outward foreign direct investment took off in the 1980s and exceeded US$20 billion annually in recent years (Bank of Korea, 2012). Leading *chaebol* firms such as Samsung Electronics, LG Electronics and Hyundai Motor have built comprehensive global business networks. They are selling their products almost everywhere in the world and have created major manufacturing hubs in all major regions. Apart from the established *chaebol* companies, more recently, smaller independent technology companies have aggressively entered international markets. Overall, Korean firms have been greatly successful in their international expansion and built strong or dominant global market positions in the semiconductor, mobile phone, household electronics, automobile and shipbuilding industries.

Korean firms largely relied on a home replication strategy when they first went international. Their international subsidiaries were built using the same organizational structures and processes as the home base company. However, over time they have gradually adjusted to the needs of their local workforces and the business cultures in each country or region. Likewise, Korean firms have also quite flexibly customized their products across regions according to the local preferences of customers. Whereas most of their international subsidiaries are still managed by Korean expatriate managers, many companies have recently begun to hire and nurture non-Korean talent for executive positions in its global networks as well as in Korea itself (Hemmert, 2012).

Corporate social responsibility in Korea

During the period of authoritarian rule, the Korean government gave preferential treatment to many firms and business groups in order to enhance the country's economic development. Part of this implicit contract between government and business was that the *chaebols* provided employment opportunities for many Korean people through their rapid growth. In this sense, Korean firms certainly exerted a high amount of corporate social responsibility to the public during that stage of economic development. Since the government retreated from the direct regulation of the business sector, however, firms have increasingly come under criticism for maximizing their profits only and not being responsible toward the general public, particularly after the Asian financial crisis that resulted in layoffs on an unprecedented scale. This public reaction shows that in Korea, large companies are expected to take some responsibility not only for the benefit of their shareholders and employees, but also for the Korean economy and the country as a whole. Many Koreans have ambiguous feelings about the *chaebols*. On the one hand, people are proud of the large firms and their achievements because they symbolize the country's economic achievements and success. On the other hand, *chaebols* are accused of selfish and irresponsible behaviour, particularly after corporate scandals, which are periodically surfacing.

Many *chaebol* owners have often shown a certain willingness to share their wealth with the Korean public. They have repeatedly given large donations for the development of educational infrastructure or other activities of high public interest. One particularly spectacular case was the endeavour of Chung Ju-yung, former chairman of the Hyundai group, to set up a tourist resort in North Korea's Kumgangsan region in the early 1990s, a time when there was still almost no communication between the two Koreas at the governmental level. Arguably, Chairman Chung, through this, made a major contribution to inter-Korean conciliation. The fact that Hyundai's tourist business in North Korea was never very profitable throughout its years of operation suggests that the whole initiative was indeed not primarily profit seeking, but rather intended to contribute to an improvement of the political situation on the Korean peninsula. (The resort was closed down as a result of a shooting incident in 2008 rather than its unprofitability.)

Working and living conditions in Korea

As mentioned earlier in this chapter, the Korean people undertook an intense national effort in the decades after the Korean War to reconstruct and develop their economy. During this period, annual working hours were among the longest in the world, and economic development was given clear priority over cultural or environmental concerns. As a result, the country has been perceived as exposing its population to harsh working and living conditions.

The situation has changed considerably since the 1980s, however. Working hours, while still being longer than in other OECD countries, have been much reduced, and the five-day working week has been gradually introduced since 2004. Moreover, infrastructure related to public transportation, culture and leisure activities has been rapidly built up, particularly in the metropolitan area around Seoul, which accommodates almost half of the country's population. Whereas environmental problems remain a concern, energy efficiency has been increased and air pollution has been significantly reduced in recent years, and efforts for a further improvement of the situation are on-going (OECD, 2012a). Taken together, working and living conditions in Korea have been greatly improved throughout the past few decades.

Notwithstanding these impressive achievements, however, many Koreans still perceive their everyday lives as stressful. Whereas the pressure to address material needs has subsided due to much higher income levels, strong competition is commonplace in the education system as well as in professional life, and those who do not succeed in this competition for educational and professional achievements often feel left behind and mentally depressed. Thus, it is no coincidence that Korea is globally one of the countries with the highest suicide rates.

From an international perspective, Korea has become a much easier place to live and work. English is more widely spoken now, particularly by the younger generations. The country's well-developed infrastructure combined with its natural beauty makes it a pleasant place to live in. Koreans also commonly show a friendly behaviour towards foreigners, particularly those from Western countries. In fact, surprise about the high level of development and the good overall living environment is a frequent experience made by foreigners who newly arrive in Korea, suggesting that its image in many other countries is outdated. The proportion of foreigners in the total population stands at about 3 per cent in 2011 and is therefore still lower than in many other countries, but has been rapidly increasing since the 1990s, reflecting Korea's greater openness to the world.

Chapter summary

- Korea is a geographically small country, but a major economic power. The country emerged within 50 years from extreme poverty to high affluence through an intense collaborative effort by business and government.

- The Korean economy has a large manufacturing sector and has strongly specialized in specific industries, such as automobiles, electronics, microelectronics, telecommunications, steel and shipbuilding. Highly diversified business groups (*chaebols*) play a leading role in it.

- The Korean management style is very distinct and built on Confucian traditions, but also received Japanese, US and military influences. It features bold and aggressive business strategies, a strong centralization of power, top-down management, authoritarian and paternalistic leadership, long-term oriented, but flexible, employment practices and a strong performance orientation.

- Korean workers and managers are very diligent and highly motivated. They work in groups, but their motivation is strongly individualistic. Korean companies select their regular employees carefully, train them extensively and expose them to strong performance pressures.

- Korean firms have built a strong overall presence on global markets. When internationalizing, they were initially relying on home country replication, but are now more strongly customizing their business in each country and region.

- Large firms are being criticized in the Korean public for displaying selfish profit-seeking behaviour, but occasionally make large donations to the society.

Key concepts

Confucianism and hierarchical Korean management: Korean cultural traditions support a paternalistic, top-down management style.

Economic dynamism: Korea has transformed itself from a low-income developing country to a major economic power in less than 50 years.

Entrepreneurial business strategies: Korean firms pursue aggressive growth strategies into new product lines and geographic regions.

Korean business groups (chaebols): large, diversified groups of companies that are tightly controlled by their owners.

Korean human resource management: employees of Korean firms are carefully selected, extensively trained, and exposed to strong performance pressure.

Review questions

1 What are the specific features of the Korean economy?
2 Why has the Korean economy developed so rapidly since the 1960s?
3 What are *chaebols*? Why are they important in Korea?
4 What is typical for Korean management? What are the implications of this management style for the competitive strategies of Korean firms?
5 How do Korean companies hire, train and evaluate their workers and managers?

Learning activities and discussions

1 Search the internet for information about the four largest *chaebols* (Samsung, Hyundai-Kia Automotive, LG, SK). Compare their structure with each other and with leading conglomerate firms from Japan.
2 Imagine you are working for a Korean company. Discuss with your classmates how you would be able to deal with the Korean management style, and what would probably be the biggest cultural challenges for you to accommodate to such an environment.

Samsung Electronics: the emergence of a Korean flagship company

Samsung Electronics was founded in 1969 as an affiliate of the Samsung group, which has become Korea's largest *chaebol*. Since the 1980s, it emerged as Samsung's leading group company and later on as the country's largest industrial enterprise in general.

The company's beginnings were humble, as it was established initially as Samsung-Sanyo Electric, a joint venture with Japan's Sanyo Electric intended to produce household and consumer electronics in Korea based on the Japanese partner's technology. In the 1970s, the company grew rapidly, and it produced relatively simple electronic products, such as TVs, refrigerators and microwave ovens. However, technological independence was gradually achieved during this period.

The next stage of the company's development in the 1980s was signified by a first wave of internationalization. Production and sales affiliates were established in different parts of the world, and a large part of the revenues now came from overseas markets. However, the company's business was still mainly focused on mature, low-tech products.

In 1987, Lee Byung-chul, Samsung's founder and chairman died and his son, Lee Kun-hee, became the new chairman of the Samsung Group. Later on, in 1998, he also assumed the chairmanship at Samsung Electronics. He led the company into a new direction by allocating more resources to hi-tech products, including semiconductors, digital panels and mobile devices. This strategy was apparently successful, as Samsung Electronics entered the highly competitive semiconductor industry from a latecomer position, but achieved global leadership in the memory chip market no later than 1992. It became the world's leading memory chip producer and has never given up this position. Its success has been largely attributed to its aggressive investment in R&D and production facilities and its ability to dominate rivals through shorter development and ramp-up cycles that are crucial in this industry where every few years one generation of products is replaced by a new one. In particular, Samsung's initial success was a result of its counter-cyclical investment behaviour during the global memory chip market recession of 1990–1991, when it aggressively built new capacity at a time when its main rivals cut or delayed their investments.

Whereas Chairman Lee's leadership definitely played an important role in the company's strategic direction throughout the past 20 years, his approach is clearly different from those of many other *chaebol* owners, as he transferred much of the responsibility for on-going business decisions to professional managers and focuses himself on the formulation of long-term, overarching strategies. A large part of Samsung's recent success is attributed to Yun Jong-yong, a manager not associated with the Lee family who was the company's CEO from 1996 to 2008, and his managerial team.

Since the late 1990s, the following managerial policies have been pursued at Samsung Electronics:

- *Technological leadership and innovativeness*: the company has continued to invest aggressively in R&D. It is now one of the leading R&D spenders in the world and accounts for more than a quarter of Korea's total business R&D. It has also become a globally leading patent producer. Moreover, employees of all ranks are encouraged to develop new ideas and problem-solving approaches.
- *Efficiency drive through internal competition*: internal business divisions, while still assisting each other when appropriate, have been induced resulting in intense company internal competition. At the same time, strong performance incentives have been introduced for individual managers as well as for divisional units as a whole.
- *Enhanced global marketing and brand management*: whereas the company's marketing and branding efforts had been formerly dispersed throughout the world, strong attention has been given to the creation of a strong, coherent Samsung brand. As a result, the company's brand value has been evaluated in 2012 as ninth in the world and as the highest among all Asian companies.
- *Further globalization*: Samsung Electronics' global sales, production and R&D networks have been considerably extended and deepened, giving it a strong presence in all parts of the world. In 2011, 30 per cent of its revenues came from the United States, 24 per cent from Europe, 16 per cent from Korea, 14 per cent from China and 17 per cent from other regions.

Recently, the company caught global attention through a series of spectacular achievements. It became the world's largest technology company in terms of revenues and took the largest global market share in the mobile phone industry. Notwithstanding all this success, Chairman Lee sent a strong sign that the company cannot rest on its laurels and warned all employees in 2011 that fundamentally the company is facing a crisis as most of its current products will have disappeared from the markets within 10 years.

As shown in Figure 11.1, the company has four large business divisions and as a whole is very profitable. However, the data hint at some on-going challenges Samsung is facing. Most of the company's profits are generated by the semiconductor and telecommunication divisions, whereas the other divisions are less successful.

At a more fundamental level, the company is likely to face two other key challenges. First, how to balance the innovativeness and creativity needed to be a global technology leader with traditional Korean top-down management. Second, how to become a truly global company not only as regards its business but also as regards its managerial leadership without giving up accumulated strengths which appear to be strongly embedded in the company's home base.

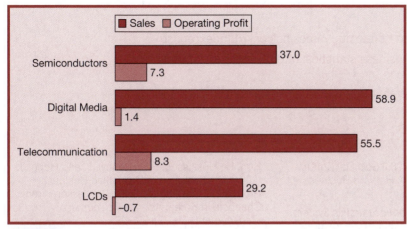

FIGURE 11.1 Samsung Electronics' Sales and Operating Profits by Division, 2011 (unit: trillion KRW)

Questions

1 Which internal and external factors have helped Samsung Electronics growing into its current position?

2 In which aspects has the management of Samsung Electronics throughout the past decades been typical for Korean management? In which aspects has it been atypical?

3 Do you think Samsung Electronics has to transform itself fundamentally to remain successful in the future? Why or why not?

Sources

CNN Money (2012) Fortune Global 500, accessed 7 November 2013 at: http://money.cnn.com/magazines/fortune/global500/2012/full_list/

Gartner Newsroom (2012) Worldwide Mobile Device Sales to End Users by Vendor in the Second Quarter of 2012, accessed 7 November 2013 at: http://www.gartner.com/it/page.jsp?id=2120015

Hankook Kyungja (2011) Short, Surprise, Shocking… Chairman Lee Kun-hee's '3S' has Worked, 17 June.

Interbrand (2012) Best Global Brands, accessed 7 November 2013 at: http://www.interbrand.com/ko/best-global-brands/2012/Best-Global-Brands-2012-Brand-View.aspx

Michell, A. (2008) *Samsung Electronics and the Struggle for Leadership in the Electronics Industry*. Singapore: Wiley.

Samsung Electronics (2011) Annual Report. Samsung Electronics, accessed 7 November 2013 at: http://www.samsung.com

Shin, J.-S. and Jang, S.-W. (2005) Creating First-Mover Advantages: The Case of Samsung Electronics, SCAPE Working Paper No. 2005/13, Department of Economics, National University of Singapore

Web links

Macro-economic data on Korea: http://ecos.bok.or.kr/EIndex_en.jsp

Korean economic and business statistics: http://kostat.go.kr/portal/english/index.action

On life and culture in Korea: http://www.lifeinkorea.com/

References

Aguilar, F.J. and Cho, D.S. (1985) *Gold Star Co. Ltd.*, Case No. 9-385-264. Boston: Harvard Business School.

Bank of Korea (2012) *Economic Statistics System*, accessed 7 November 2013 at: http://ecos.bok.or.kr/EIndex_en.jsp

Chang, C.S. and Chang, N.J. (1994) *The Korean Management System: Cultural, Political, Economic Foundations*. Westport, CN: Quorum.

Chang, S.J. (2003) *Financial Crisis and Transformation of Korean Business Groups: The Rise and Fall of Chaebols*. Cambridge: Cambridge University Press.

Chen, M. (2004) *Asian Management Systems: Chinese, Japanese and Korean Styles of Business*, 2nd edn. London: Thomson.

Chung, K.H., Lee, H.C. and Jung, K.H. (1997) *Korean Management: Global Strategy and Cultural Transformation.* Berlin: Walter de Gruyter.

e-National Indicators (2012) General Situation of Small- and Medium-sized Enterprises [in Korean[, accessed 7 November 2013 at: http://www.index.go.kr/egams/stts/jsp/potal/stts/PO_STTS_Idx-Main.jsp?idx_cd=1181andbbs=INDX_001 andclas_div=A

Fukuyama, F. (1995) *Trust: The Social Virtues and the Creation of Prosperity*. New York: Free Press.

Hemmert, M. (2007) The Competitive Potential of Asian Business Groups: A Comparative Analysis of Kigyo Shudan and Chaebo, in O.H.M. Yau and R.P.M. Chow (eds.) *Harmony Versus Conflict in Asia Business: Managing in a Turbulent Era*. Basingstoke: Palgrave Macmillan, pp. 182–208.

Hemmert, M. (2012) *Tiger Management: Korean Companies on World Markets*. London: Routledge.

ILO (International Labour Organization) (2013) ILOSTAT Database. Subjects: Strikes and Lockouts by Economic Activity, accessed 4 December 2014 at: http://www.ilo.org/ilostat/faces/home/statisticaldata/data_by_subject?_adf.ctrl-state=15ltqhhq56_4&_afrLoop=119156927867473

Kim, H., Hoskisson, R,E., Tihanyi, L. and Hong, J. (2004) The Evolution of Diversified Business Groups in Emerging Markets: The Lessons from Chaebols in Korea. *Asia Pacific Journal of Management*, 21(1/2): 25–48.

Kim, L. (1997) *Imitation to Innovation: The Dynamics of Korea's Technological Learning.* Boston, MA: Harvard Business School Press.

KRX – Korea Exchange (2012) *KRX 2011 Fact Book*. Seoul. Korea Exchange.

Kwon, O.Y. (2010) *The Korean Economy in Transition: An Institutional Perspective.* Cheltenham: Edward Elgar.

Lee, A.-R. (2003) Down and Down We Go: Trust and Compliance in South Korea. *Social Science Quarterly*, 84 (2): 329–343.

OECD (Organisation for Economic Co-operation and Development) (2011) *Education at a Glance 2011: OECD Indicators*. Paris: OECD Publishing.

OECD (Organisation for Economic Co-operation and Development) (2012a) *OECD Economic Surveys: Korea 2012*. Paris: OECD Publishing.

OECD (Organisation for Economic Co-operation and Development) (2012b) *OECD Statistical Extracts: Average Annual Hours Actually Worked per Worker*, accessed 7 November 2013 at: http://stats.oecd.org/Index.aspx?DatasetCode=ANHRS

Park, W.S. and Yu, G.C. (2002) HRM in Korea: Transformation and New Patterns. In Z. Rhee and E. Chang (eds.) *Korean Business and Management: The Reality and Vision*. Elizabeth, NJ: Hollym, pp. 367–391.

World Bank (2012) *World Development Indicators – Korea*, accessed 7 November 2013 at: http://data.worldbank.org/country/korea-republic

Yang, I. (2006) Jeong Exchange and Collective Leadership in Korean Organizations. *Asia Pacific Journal of Management*, 23(3): 283–298.

The Business System of Singapore

12

Tony Garrett

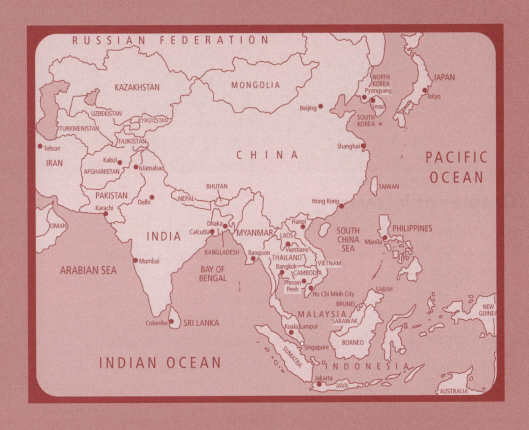

Chapter outline

- The Singapore business system
- Government role
- Ownership and management of the Singapore firm
- International activities of Singapore firms
- Corporate social responsibility (CSR) and Singapore business
- Working and living in Singapore

Chapter objectives

After reading this chapter, you should be able to:

1 Identify the major reasons for Singapore's dynamic economic development.

2 Understand the specific features of Singaporean management and their cultural background.

3 Understand the Singaporean approach to managing human resources.

4 Understand how Singaporean firms exert social responsibility.

Introduction

The Republic of Singapore (subsequently: Singapore) is a small island city state with an area of about 650 km² located at the tip of the Malay Peninsula. From the time of its inception as a city, Singapore's geographic location has helped it to become one of the major and successful hubs for the South-East Asian region.

One of Asia's four Tiger economies, Singapore has developed strong service and manufacturing sectors. It has a well-developed infrastructure, with its port, airport and roads among the best in the world. Singapore's GDP is US$300 billion with an average GDP growth rate of 5.4 per cent since 2009 (Statistics Singapore, 2013b), although there has been large fluctuations of this due to increasing international economic uncertainty (Ministry of Trade and Industry, 2013). It has, however, one of the region's highest GDP per capita of approximately US$50,000 (International Monetary Fund, 2012) and US$60,000 on purchasing power parity adjusted base, placing it as one of the wealthiest nations in the world, with some predicting that it will be the wealthiest in the not too distant future (Mahtani, 2012).

Singapore's relatively small resident population, 5.3 million, and dependence on external markets and suppliers pushed Singapore toward economic openness, free trade and free markets. Governmental policies that encourage and foster economic development underpin this and are key factors in Singapore's historically strong economic performance. The Singapore government, a key player in the economic life of Singapore, continues to pursue an outward-looking, export-oriented economic policy that encourages two-way flows of trade and investment. It has introduced policies to enhance Singapore's objective to become a global city that is a hub for financial, education, science based manufacturing, transport manufacturing and services. The 'knowledge-based innovation-driven economy' has been a key focus of the government's policies for Singaporeans (Ministry of Trade and Industry, 2011).

Singapore positions itself as the region's hub and proponent of economic development and reform. Singapore faces several challenges however. Globalization, the increasing competition from fast-growing lower-cost regional producers, its ageing population, and a need to upgrade and increase it manufacturing productivity highlight the need for Singapore to move from a labour intense manufacturing based economy to one which is focused on being a value-added services hub (Ministry of Trade and Industry, 2011). This chapter goes some way to explain how and why Singapore has emerged as a key economy to watch.

The Singapore business system

Culture and key historical influences

To understand the Singapore system, we start by examining the people of the country and its historic underpinnings.

Compared to many of the other nations in the region, the history of Singapore is relatively short. Although accounts exist of Singapore from the third century, it is commonly accepted that modern Singapore was founded in 1819, by Thomas Stamford Raffles, of the British East India Company, as a regional base for the British Empire to ward off the power of other colonial powers in the region, particularly the Dutch. Raffles found

Singapore to be an ideal location to establish a port, fulfilling basic requirements such as having a deep water harbour, water supplies and timber for the repair of ships. After negotiation with the Sultan of Johor, the nominal leader of the island, a treaty was signed to establish the colony of Singapore.

During its time as a British colony, Singapore developed as a key trading area, built upon the opening market of China and the raw products coming from Malaya. During this time, the colony attracted a number of immigrants, which reflects the multicultural makeup of Singapore today (Chinese 74 per cent, Malay 13 per cent, Indians 9 per cent and other 3 per cent, (Statistics Singapore, 2013a)). Prosperity existed until World War II when the Japanese occupied the colony from 1942 until 1945. The colony took some time to recover to pre-war levels of prosperity after the war, but notably the credibility of the British as its rulers took a blow since it was unable to defend the state from occupation. Subsequently, Singapore was granted self-government from the British in 1959 and after a brief period in the Federation of Malaysia, 1963–1965, became an independent republic.

Singapore was seen by many to be inadequate to survive as an independent national state, so the national policy initiatives made national survival its core basis for national policy (Koh and Wong, 2005). In a desire to prove its pundits wrong, its government and peoples are driven by the desire to succeed and to be the best.

With those of Chinese heritage making up the majority of the population and having governmental and economic power, many cluster Singapore with other Confucian Asian economies, such as, China, South Korea and Taiwan, in terms of its national cultural tendencies. These nations share similar values. They are known, for example, to be concerned with maintenance of harmony, face, collectivist, persistent, hierarchical and a respect for tradition. While Singapore conforms to most of these, there are distinctions. Using the GLOBE dimensions the culture of the nation is discussed (Hofstede, 1984; House et al., 2004).

Rationale

Performance orientation: Singapore is highly oriented towards performance at all levels of society. Singapore workers have been found to be oriented to individual success and career advancement (Garrett et al., 2006). This seems at odds with the society's Confucian principles however, Singapore has been geared towards economic and social success through its economic development. Individual performance, for example, is now becoming an HR practice norm. The National Wages Council (NWC) actively encourages pay scales to be based on competitive forces and individual performance than on seniority alone (Leggett, 2007).

Future orientation: Singapore is highly future oriented. The Singapore government is an exemplar of this through implementing future-oriented policy initiatives, which have been difficult but have led to economic success for the country. Organizational leaders and other members of the society are also expected to share the government's values. Students for example work diligently from an early age to secure a good future.

Identity

Institutional emphasis on collectivism versus individualism: Singapore's societal values lead to an institutional emphasis on collectivism, which are advocated strongly by the government. The focus on the overall community therefore is important. This is not shared, however, by some employees within the workplace. It is the workplace leaders and managers therefore who maintain in-group cohesion, rather than relying on the individual themselves. This is in keeping with the notion of the paternalistic state (Low, 2006b).

In-group collectivism: the family is one of the basic units of Singaporean society. Although the Singaporean family is getting smaller, the family and family occasions are very important. Seniority plays an important role within the family, and traditionally in the workplace.

Authority

Gender differentiation: Singapore has traditionally been male dominant although this is changing. Although their representation in government is low, similar to many other countries, women are now making large inroads into business and other key areas within society. Compared to other innovative countries, however, female participation in entrepreneurial activities is high (Gem, 2012).

Uncertainty avoidance: Singapore has been found to be very concerned about avoiding uncertainty. Singaporeans wish to avoid uncertainty generally. Singapore personnel for example would prefer to work for larger organizations, rather than risk face and finances on starting their own (Low, 2006a). High levels of codified procedures are found in Singapore organizations and upper management is expected to take responsibility for the workgroup (Garrett et al., 2006).

This dimension shares elements with Hofstede's dimension of uncertainty avoidance from his famous study conducted in the early 1970s (Hofstede, 1984). In this study Singapore was rated as one of the least uncertain avoidance countries in the world. The reversal in the interim time period has been hotly debated. In one study looking at the lack of entrepreneurial activity in Singapore, the following conclusions were made (Bhasin, 2007, Low, 2006a):

- Young people are cautious due to the People's Action Party (PAP) society being very compliant and lacking in diversity of ideas.
- The education system has a strong focus on learning facts and figures rather than being creative.
- Singaporeans in modern society are somewhat more pampered and less street smart, relying on text books and being left brain oriented.
- A strong reliance on government to do things for you.
- Failure is an embarrassment.

Power distance: Singapore has a high level of power distance. Although not necessarily born into a class-based society this is evolving with individuals seeing the way to break through this by education. Leadership tends to be autocratic and seniority based. Performance, however, is becoming an important criterion for success (Chia et al., 2007).

The government and the civil society

Singapore is a modern society epitomized by a combination of a modern capitalist system and high government intervention. It is the business system that has stemmed from this unique combination that has assisted its development into one of the leading economies in the region, to be envied by other societies (Ortmann, 2012).

Singapore government's role in the economy

Singapore is characterized by the (soft) authoritarianism of its government. Singapore has been ruled by a single political party, the PAP, since independence, despite there being some 23 other parties. The party holds 81 out of the 84 electable seats in parliament, gaining approximately 60 per cent of the popular vote in the 2011 elections, although this is one of the narrowest victory margins since Singapore's independence. In spite of the PAP's power, Singapore is regarded as one of the least corrupt, ranking fifth overall, and number one in Asia (Transparency International, 2012) and one of the easiest economies to do business in the world (International Finance Corporation, 2012). The PAP has been central to the state's political, social and economic development. Historically, the core ideology of the party was to ensure Singapore's survival using a social democrat model. The subsequent PAP ideologies have been pragmatism, meritocracy, multiculturalism and Asian values. Although it has rejected the idea of Western style of liberal democracy, many of the ideals of western liberalism do permeate government policies. The philosophy underlying governmental policy has been to 'maximize political cooperation and minimize contention' (Bhasin, 2007).

Core to PAP's success and ability to implement its policies has been the continuing vision, influence and charisma of the 'Father of Singapore' (Low, 2007), Lee Kuan Yew. Lee Kuan Yew cofounded PAP in 1954 and led it to victory; he stepped down in 1990. He was the leader and prime minister of the country until this time and subsequently he was appointed as 'Senior Minister' and then 'Minister Mentor' in 2004, until his retirement in 2011. A strong advocate of 'Confucian Democracy' he has been variously applauded and criticized in his approach to government. What is clear though is that he has been acknowledged in driving Singapore's transformation since independence. His legacy, might reside in his children, who are now in influential positions within Singapore's private and public sector, most notably Lee Hsien Loong, Prime Minister of Singapore since 2004, whose wife, Ho Ching is the CEO of Temasek Holdings.

The Confucian democracy that exists is central to understanding government policy. Opposition or disruption to the government role is regarded negatively. The government's view is that strong rule is necessary to promote political stability, which in turn leads to rapid economic development.

The Government has fostered economic development through the maintenance of peace and harmony among the multiethnic population, and to focus on needs for global market competitiveness (Bhasin, 2007; Haley and Low, 1998). They have done this through identification and careful management of the following core values for a good society (Bhasin, 2007; Haley and Low, 1998):

1. putting community before self;

2. upholding the family at the basic building block of society;

3. resolving major issues though consensus instead of contention;

4. stressing racial and religious tolerance and harmony;

5. honest government; and

6. compassion for the less fortunate.

The government maintains that these values are at the centre of the Confucian/Asian approach and would be the guide to structure a society that will serve and be successful in a changing global environment. The tenets of the stated values are for hierarchical structures and a compliant society, reminiscent of early Chinese society. The community, the centre of collectivism and Confucianism, rather than the individual is its important element.

These values manifest themselves in many elements of Singapore society through governmental campaigns to modify social behaviour such as, no littering, family planning (procreate more), be courteous. Legislation is implemented and strictly enforced, unfortunately causing the country to be labelled as a 'fines' country (Bhasin, 2007), referring to the number of monetary punishments that are imposed.

Governmental policy, however, has been instrumental in the development of the skills required for changes in the economic environment. Initially the focus was on meeting skills shortages for the MNCs who now dominate the society. Specialization is required at an early age, with a student's education path being stratified by their ability and aptitude, creating what is arguably a hierarchical society.

This is no more apparent by those who were drafted by the bureaucracy. The bureaucracy has historically recruited the best and brightest. This was through the education system and scholarships, to get the best people for the leadership in politics, military and business. Government traditionally therefore had a monopoly on the top talent (Bhasin, 2007; Chew and Sharma, 2005; Chew and Chew, 2003; Haley and Low, 1998).

The end result is that the government takes a somewhat technocratic approach to achieve the country's shorter term goals through the channelling of academic talent to meet their own aims. There has been some comment and criticism to this approach indicating that this is leaving a shortage of talent for entrepreneurial or innovative activity in the business sector (Agency for Science Technology and Research (a*Star), 2012; Chew and Chew, 2003)

Singapore Inc.

The term 'Singapore Inc.' is often referred to State's operation of Singapore. This has tended to be done through the use 'Government-Linked' Companies (GLCs).

GLCs were established in the 1960s and 1970s to help facilitate the building of infrastructure and to support economic development. GLC companies were also established in the 1980s and 1990s to further expand the privatization of government departments and statutory boards. There was a clear rationale stated by the government of the time to 'compensate for the lack of private sector funds or expertise' (Ramirez and Tan, 2003). Many of these GLCs have subsequently become monopolies and national icons. They are run purely on a commercial/profit basis and the government will have no hesitation in closing them down if they are failing.

GLCs have extended into many key sectors of Singapore's economy such as finance, trading, transportation, shipbuilding and services. Examples of GLCs include Singapore Airlines, Singapore Telecom and Natsteel. It is estimated that GLCs account for up to

60 per cent of the domestic economy (Bhasin, 2007; Low, 2006b; Ramirez and Tan, 2003) and approximately 22 per cent of its total GDP from them and government ownership of property (Bhasin, 2007).

There has been increasing argument about the progressive nature of these GLCs and their contribution to an entrepreneurial environment to meet the changes in the regional business environment (Bhasin, 2007). The link with government, particularly the ability to access funds, tenders and opportunities have been argued to close large areas of the economy to the private sector and have stifled the growth of entrepreneurship (Ramirez and Tan, 2003). Ramirez and Tan (2003) argued that GLCs were rewarded by this 'special' relationship with government through premiums of 20 per cent in financial markets.

GLCs tend to be funded through Temasek Holdings, the commercial mechanism of the Singapore government. Established in 1974, it has a portfolio of some US$160 billion (Temasek, 2012). With involvement in telecommunications and media, financial services, property, transportation and logistics, energy and resources, infrastructure, engineering and technology and pharmaceutical and biosciences, the company regularly announces shareholder returns of 18 per cent annually. It accounts for approximately 30 per cent of the economy.

The role of the government in Temasek Holdings is large. The company is 100 per cent owned by the Singapore Ministry of Finance, with the Chief Executive generally having strong political links. The government has strong connections to the management team of the organization.

The second important investment arm of the Singapore government is the Government Investment Corporation (GIC). This organization invests Singapore's foreign reserves. These reserves are some of the largest in the world, with estimates of its assets totalling some $US330 billion (*The Economist*, 2008). The fund managed by GIC is shrouded in secrecy. The government's stated rationale behind this is to ward off speculative hits on the Singapore dollar as foreign reserves are frequently used to stabilize the national currency (Bhasin, 2007).

Due to the turbulent environment there are increasing calls for the government to decrease its participation in private enterprise and show more transparency in its current involvement. These calls have come across the board. The response by government is to defend its involvement stating that foreign pressures should not be heeded if the Singapore public is happy in it, and government involvement fosters growth.

Government role in the phases of economic development

The government's efforts to transform the economy roughly transverse three key phases of development. The first phase in the 1960s–1970s focused on industrializing the nation by providing employment and diversifying away from a dependence on entrepôt trade. This was a factor driven growth strategy (Koh and Wong, 2005; Porter, 1990). The early focus of this phase was to attract foreign multinational investment into labour intensive export oriented manufacturing (Koh and Wong, 2005; Soon and Tan, 1993). By the mid-1970s a labour shortage developed that required the government to refocus its efforts in attracting foreign hi-tech business. By 1979 foreign firms were playing a significant role in the Singapore economy. The slowdown in industrialized economies around this time alerted the government the need to diversify the economy (Koh and Wong, 2005; Soon and Tan, 1993).

Phase two centred on developing a capital intensive economy (1980s–1990s). During the period 1979–1984 economic restructuring was implemented, whereby both the economic activities and markets were diversified and expanded. Wages were also adjusted upwards to discourage inflow of labour-intensive and low-tech investments that posed obstacles to upgrading and restructuring. Promotions were implemented to attract firms into 11 selected hi-tech industries. These included: automotive components, machine tools and machinery, medical and surgical apparatus and instruments, specialty chemicals and pharmaceuticals, computer, computer peripherals equipment and software development, electronic instrumentation, optical instruments and equipment, advanced electronic components, precision engineering products, and hydraulic and pneumatic control systems. Large inflows of foreign direct investments into these desired industries resulted, and they remain some of the cornerstone industries. MNCs became firmly established as a key element within the society.

The third phase saw the development of the knowledge intensive economy. In it the government focused on the development of the nation's science and technology capability. At the core of its efforts was to move from an economy that uses technology to one that creates it (National Science and Technology, 2000). Nine technology fields were targeted accompanied with large national investments: information technology; microelectronics; electronic systems; manufacturing technology; materials technology; energy, water, environment and resources; food and agro-technology; biotechnology; and medical sciences.

The key to this phase is the government's expansion of manpower capability through the development of expertise by identifying and providing scholarships to bright students and easing the entry requirements of foreign nationals with the right expertise (Ministry of Trade and Industry, 2011)

Alongside this support activities and incentives are in place to create an industrial environment that is conducive to R&D. Financial support, in the form of grants, is available for cofunding R&D activities. Physical infrastructure includes the development of a technology corridor; a 15km region containing a synergistic mix of higher education establishments, research institutes and private sector laboratories. The proximity of these institutions, like the 'Science Park', and 'One-North' provide an environment for researchers to network on a frequent basis.

Despite the major impetus and large funding given to R&D by the government, the private sector spending in R&D outstrips government spending. The private sector accounted for 62 per cent of the country's gross expenditure on R&D (GERD) in 2011 (Agency for Science Technology and Research (a*Star), 2012). This has been growing at a faster rate than publicly funded R&D.

The second core factor in driving a knowledge-based economy is the development of the local entrepreneur. As noted earlier, elements of Singapore society may in fact hinder entrepreneurial behaviour. The Global Entrepreneurship Monitor (GEM) 2012 rated the total early entrepreneurial activity in Singapore at 6.6 per cent, ranking 12th among the 24 innovation-driven nations surveyed (Gem, 2012). A number of agencies have been set up in Singapore to assist in the development of entrepreneurial activity including: Singapore Productive Innovation and Growth (SPRING), Enterprise One Singapore and

International Enterprise Singapore (Bhasin, 2007). Incentives for entrepreneurial activity were also given, such as tax exemptions for start-ups, tax incentives, government financing, and matching funds from the Economic Development Board Start-up Enterprise Scheme. Many of these are initiatives that have only occurred in the latest phase of economic development and although there is positive movement, comparison of the 2012 GEM survey with 2006, shows there is still some way to go to catch up with other innovation led economies.

Commentators have also commented on the lack of entrepreneurial activity concluding that 'although Singapore displays many of the characteristics typical of a knowledge based economy, Singapore's new economy seemingly lacks a stimulating climate conducive to imagination, innovation and adventure that will attract globally mobile talent' (Tan, 2003 cited in Wong et al., 2006). This concern is at the heart of the government's plan for the next decade (Ministry of Trade and Industry, 2011).

Singapore's business environment

In spite of the high government involvement in the economy, Singapore is symbolized by its ease of doing business and the state of its financial development, being ranked fourth behind Hong Kong SAR, the United States and the United Kingdom (World Economic Forum, 2012a).

Financial capital

Singapore has an open and free financial system, having transformed itself into a significant regional financial centre. Singapore's banking sector has a wide range of services from traditional lending and deposit to having high levels of corporate and investment banking activities. Commercial access to capital is ranked second in the world although retail access only is only 31st (World Economic Forum, 2012a). Financial institutions are monitored by the Monetary Authority of Singapore, which has garnered a stable banking system. Calls are still made though for more funding for start-up enterprises (Ministry of Trade and Industry, 2011).

Human capital

The management of Singapore's human capital has been a critical element for the country's success. As a country of limited natural resources, human capital has been a key cornerstone of Singapore's development both at the governmental and organizational levels, although human capital management is set to become even more important with the emphasis on a knowledge-based economy. This major strategic focus necessitates the development, recruitment, motivation and retention of highly skilled human capital, both local and foreign. This has large ramifications for local businesses in Singapore who, although having benefited from the government efforts to provide a well-educated workforce, have traditionally focused on technical and capital resources at the expense of their human capital (Horwitz et al., 2006, Low, 2006a). This is changing, with indicators showing that companies are becoming much better at retaining their workforce. Singapore still seeks knowledge workers and is consequently actively attracting skilled overseas employees (Ministry of Trade and Industry, 2013).

At the heart of the human capital plan is the educational development of the domestic workforce. Singapore has a highly centralized, developed and well-equipped education infrastructure, which has achieved worldwide acclaim. The Global Competitiveness report rated it second in the world on overall quality of the education system in 2011–2012 (World Economic Forum, 2012b) with many other international acclaimed rating agencies continually noting it has the ability to meet the demands of an increasingly competitive environment. Alongside its strengths in the sciences and mathematics education one of the system's key strengths is its focus on bilingualism. Bilingualism results from the student having to study an official Mother Tongue alongside English, the main teaching language. This develops assimilation and understanding within the society, but also increasing understanding of others and in particular the key emerging Asian markets.

Another cornerstone of the Singapore education system is its meritocracy. The identification and grooming of intellectual excellence for future leadership emphasizes academic performance when grading students in order for them to enter certain academic programs. The advantage is that the student has an equal chance whatever their background. However, the criticism is that it breeds elitism, fosters rote learning, thereby reducing creativity and critical thinking, and puts an enormous amount of pressure on students to succeed. This is inherent with other Confucian economies who emphasize education, and in spite of the Ministry of Education starting to stress creativity, critical thinking and other lifelong skills, it has been met with resistance by parents and teachers alike.

Singapore similarly has stable industrial relations. The government has played a key role in this. To encourage the economy's industrialization the Industrial Relations Ordinance was enacted, in 1960, with the purpose of regulating collective bargaining and dispute settlement. Unionists were brought together under the National Trades Union Congress (NTUC), which effectively saw the end of politicized labour and a decline in disruptive labour disputes in the period 1960–1967. During the 1970s the government enacted a number of laws that highly regulated industrial relations. The government wanted to work with the NTUC to assist in the economic development in a collective way, although by doing so the NTUC had to restrain its union activities. The end result is that industrial relations are highly regulated.

One further key advisory body, a tripartite forum with representatives from employees, trade unions and government, is the National Wages Council (NWC). Set up in 1972, this body: recommends annual wage increases for the entire economy; ensures that wage development promotes social and economic development; and assists in incentive schemes to help national productivity. Although its guidelines are not mandatory they are followed by the large public sector and it has a strong influence and is widely followed in the private sector. At times of national financial crisis its recommendations to cut or moderate labour costs, which were largely implemented, assisted Singapore in getting through successfully. Similar to the development of the knowledge-based society the NWC is influential in recommending a Competitive Base Wage System, which urges a move away from a seniority based wages with a 70 per cent basic wage, a 20 per cent annual variable component and a 10 per cent monthly variable component for task employees, and a 40 per cent and 50 per cent variable components for middle and top managements, respectively (Leggett, 2007). The aim is to make the compensation system more flexible. Alongside this the NWC is recommending a more inclusive approach to wages to slow down the growing disparity between rich and poor.

Social capital

Developing social capital in Singapore has been an increasingly important issue and is increasingly being raised at the highest levels in society (e.g., Asia One, 2012; Hoi, 2013). Singapore's low levels of social capital, in relation to its neighbours, and an understanding that high levels of social capital signify a mature modern society has highlighted the issue (Asia One, 2012), along with the fact that social capital should be one of the key tenets of a Confucian philosophy underpinning government policy. The levels of social capital, however, remain stubbornly low in spite of the efforts of the government and other community groups in promoting social capital values, such as increasing the levels of volunteering, philanthropy, mentoring, and societal awareness and understanding. In his 2012 new year message, for example, Prime Minister Lee Hsien Loong highlighted that social capital would determine Singapore's success as a nation and that Singaporeans must 'strengthen their values of tolerance, mutual respect and empathy as their country's success as a nation is increasingly defined not just in economic terms but also by the country's social capital' (Asia One, 2012).

Singapore's low levels of social capital have been attributed predominantly to the focus on meritocracy to guide the nation's development and the nation's cultural diversity (Chua, 2010). Meritocracy has been a key value that has made Singapore successful with society putting an emphasis on individuals being appointed on their own credentials, rather than on their personal networks (Chua, 2010; Meng, 2012): promoting individualism (Li, 2011). The upside of this is that during growth those with the 'best' skills to grow the country are given precedence (Chua, 2010). There are potential downsides. First, long-term success is not a function of education performance alone, however, with individual educational and professional performance being the principal focus, the space for social capital development is sacrificed (Asia One, 2012; Chua, 2010). Second, at the beginning of Singapore's development most of the citizenry started at a similar level, however, those who have been successful because of meritocracy are argued to be now using their resources to ensure that their offspring are also successful (Meng, 2012), resulting in greater inequality and lack of social mobility giving rise to elitism (Chua, 2010). Social capital distribution in society is therefore unequal with the elites, normally from the Chinese majority, now having greater social capital advantage (Chua, 2010). Data has shown that Malay Singaporeans are six times less likely to have university graduate contacts than their Chinese counterparts, and four times less likely to have someone they know who lives in a private dwelling (Chua, 2010). The multiethnic Singaporean society may also create low levels of social capital. Immigration and cultural diversity has been argued to reduce social capital (Putnam cited in Hoi, 2013) with different ethnic groups living in parallel societies with little opportunity to interact with one another (Li, 2011). With Singapore's objective to become a global city with the potential for even greater ethnic diversity, the problem may increase.

With the greater emphasis on social capital development, the government has implemented a number of measures to foster social cohesion and trust, particularly between ethnic groups and people from different economic backgrounds. These include ethnic quotas in Housing Board blocks, an education system that brings people from different backgrounds together and national military service, when young men are obliged to be together (Li, 2011). Similar measures are being investigated and are likely to be implemented.

The Singapore business system

Ownership

Business ownership is classified into three broad categories. As mentioned GLCs makes one category but these are broadly classified into two subcategories. First-tier GLCs are those in which the government owns at least 20 per cent of the voting shares and therefore the government is regarded as the owner of the company with the right to appoint the chairperson, some directors and senior management and direct board strategies. The Government also owns at least 20 per cent of the shares in second-tier GLCs, who are a subsidiary or associate entity of the first-tier GLC (Yin, 2003).

The second broad classification is local sector private companies. They are classified into small and medium enterprises (SMEs) and medium and large organizations (the big business organizations). The common definition of an SME is that they have at least 30 per cent local shareholding and employ less than 200 employees if they are non-manufacturers (Yin, 2003).

The third classification, are MNCs. There are no requirements for national or local participation in the equity or management of foreign-owned enterprises apart from restrictions in investing in essential service industries for example, port facilities or public utilities (Deloitte Touche Tohmatsu Limited, 2012). MNCs are the highest contributor to the country's GDP (Ministry of Trade and Industry, 2013)

Networking

Networks take on different levels in Singapore. Due to the large number of MNCs, western approaches to networking are widespread. At the other extreme, Chinese companies will follow Chinese business culture that stresses the importance of reputation, family ownership, and special personal relationships (*guanxi*) in their networks (Zang, 1999).

Government and other industry organizations have developed a number of initiatives to encourage greater networking, for example, the Science Park and SPRING to foster partnerships and interactions in order to meet the objectives of being global city and becoming competitive. These have achieved some success in bridging some of the gaps between MNCs and local employees.

Management

The fragmented nature of the Singapore company ownership has traditionally meant differing human resource management practices between Singapore owned and operated businesses and MNCs. MNCs have frequently been benchmarked by Singapore companies in order to understand the most effective strategies for competiveness and, in the case of larger local companies, progressing to Asian MNCs (Huang et al., 2002). Singapore companies are therefore in a state of transition (Stanton and Nankervis, 2011).

Orientations toward employees differ, for example, MNCs traditionally view human capital as being more crucial to their strategic performance than some of their local counterparts do (Chew and Horwitz, 2004; Huang et al., 2002). In addition Singapore companies have previously valued their employees on an historical cost or expenditure base rather than on a human capital asset base. The movement to a knowledge-based economy is changing this view among enterprises (Huang et al., 2002).

Job recruitment approaches are similar, Singapore places critical emphasis on good qualifications, whereas MNCs seek teamwork, honesty, creativity, intelligence and leadership in addition (Horwitz et al., 2006).

Extensive training programs in larger firms are the norm and expected among employees (Taorimina, 1998). MNCs and Singapore-based companies differ on the training and development focus. In line with the recruitment procedure for their employees, technical and IT skills are emphasized. MNCs will also focus on social-cultural training. In both cases training may lead to additional rewards from the company in terms of salary increments.

Singaporean knowledge-based employees tend to be individualistic in orientation. Key human resource strategies to motivate employees include having the freedom to plan and work independently, having challenging projects to work on, having access to leading edge technology and products, good top management support and fulfilling work (Horwitz et al., 2006). They are less motivated by flexible work practices, working with a large group of knowledge workers, generous funding for conference or studies, cash rewards for innovations and seeking recruits who fit the culture. Preferred retention strategies are similar. There is a high level of motivation for challenging work, financial rewards, such as competitive pay packets, performance incentives and bonuses, along with management support and opportunities to develop in a specialized field and access to leading edge technologies and products (Horwitz et al., 2006). These motivations appear to be at odds with the Confucian culture, although not at odds with the Singaporean desire to succeed.

International activities of Singapore firms

Singapore's economy has been strongly reliant on international trade and on the sale of services. Its merchandize trade to GDP ratio is the highest trade to GDP ratio in the world at 415.8 per cent (2009–2011) (World Trade Organization, 2012). Almost half of its merchandized exports involve entrepôt trade (re-exports) reinforcing Singapore's role as a trans-shipment hub. The majority of its exports go to the local region: Malaysia (12.2 per cent), Hong Kong SAR (11 per cent), Indonesia (10.4 per cent), China (10.4 per cent) and the European Union (9.6 per cent). Its major industries include petroleum refining, electronics, machinery, rubber products, processed food and beverages, ship repair, financial services and pharmaceutical manufacturing. However, Singapore is moving to reduce its reliance on manufacturing and exports by developing its services sector, as well as its chemical, petrochemical and biotechnology industries. Although manufacturing still accounts for 25 per cent of GDP, it has found new niches in marine engineering and biomedical firms, and it dominates the region in private banking.

Singapore is also a significant outward foreign direct investor with the total direct investment abroad accounting for 9.26 per cent of GDP in 2010 (World Bank, 2012), accounting for some S$407billion. Of this 55.8 per cent was destined for other Asian economies, and in particular China, followed by South and Central America (14.1 per cent) and Europe (12.9 per cent) (Statistics Singapore, 2012). Nearly half of the investment was centred on financial and insurance services (including investment holding companies) (48.3 per cent), with manufacturing (24 per cent) and real estate activities (8.1 per cent) (Statistics Singapore, 2012). The heavy investment in Asia is not surprising given the importance of the region to Singapore. Much of the investment in lower income Asian economies was encouraged as part of Singapore's regionalization strategy whereas investment in advanced economies was to facilitate the acquisition of new technology. GLCs were often used to do this (Ellingsen et al., 2006). The use of GLCs or Temasek in investment activities has often brought into question the links between Singapore's corporate or political motivations by some of its regional neighbours (Tripathi, 2006).

Singapore and corporate social responsibility

Social responsibility has been a key element underpinning the development of Singaporean society, although it is only recently that increasing attention has been paid to corporate social responsibility (CSR) (Lee et al., 2012; Tan, 2008). In 2005, a study indicated that Singapore had one of the lowest levels of CSR penetration compared to seven other (poorer) Asian countries (Chappel and Moon, 2005) and internationally its perceived western counterparts (Ioannou and Serafeim, 2012). These are not paradoxes that have been missed on government agenda. In 2004, a tripartite approach involving government, private sector and labour movement was set up to drive CSR. This culminated in the formation of Singapore Compact for Corporate Social Responsibility in 2005.

The government has been reliant on persuading organizations to work in accordance with Singapore's political and cultural values rather than strict legislative mechanisms (Tan, 2008). This is in line with the fundamental social responsible nature of these values. Recent research suggests that although larger Singapore organizations are taking their own more proactive CSR initiatives, small to medium sized enterprises in Singapore are somewhat behind (Lee et al., 2012). The explanations given for this low priority include a lack of resources, not a part of their business goals, stakeholder apathy and the current economic environment. Although the firms did not believe that they were engaging in CSR activities, this research found that they were in fact in compliance with government regulation.

Although the government's agenda has predominately been oriented towards organizations within the domestic environment, the rise of the Singapore MNC and Singaporean GLC's regional and international investments means that increasingly CSR and the Singaporean values that the organizations are being persuaded to use to apply outside the confines of Singapore. This is particularly apparent with some of the observed backlash against Singapore in the region (*The Economist*, 2007).

Ethical business considerations are becoming more and more important in Singapore. Consumer watchdog groups, such as the Consumer Association of Singapore (CASE) along with the government are increasingly making businesses accountable for their actions. The government's agenda and overall the public's desire to make Singapore a global hub for good business practice and the importance of CSR and business ethics will be more heavily promoted.

Living and working in Singapore

Singapore has built a country on the hard work and diligence of its residents and incomers. It has maintained its political and economic stability and is considered a safe country in which to live. The results of its economic success are evident. The streets are among the cleanest in the world and it has a cosmopolitan lifestyle.

Singapore is an easy place to live and provides a high standard of living. Although it is regarded as a city state, Singapore is not overly developed. With some 58 surrounding islands and the city covering one-third of the main island, there has been an attempt to give open leisure spaces for the population. Although clean, on occasions it can encounter air pollution problems often generated by the clearing of land by neighbouring Indonesia. The Government has also embarked on a number of infrastructure projects, such as the Marina Barrage project, which has the benefit of water storage, flood relief and recreational facilities. Importantly these projects offer citizens and visitors alike with iconic events, such as the Singapore Grand Prix and buildings such as the Marina Bay Sands Resort and the ArtScience Museum.

Singapore offers its residents a high quality of life. Results from the Asian barometer study have shown that Singaporeans are happy and enjoy life, although they do not feel that they have generally accomplished much in their life (Tambyah et al., 2009). The results from this survey have also indicated their overall priorities in life are to be healthy, having a comfortable home, having a job and spending time with the family. In the most part the government has responded to this by providing an excellent health system, affordable public housing, education and training opportunities and recreational facilities. Underlying this however is the Singaporean perception that they need to continue to work hard and to strive to be the best to counter the vulnerability they feel as a small nation in a region characterized by dynamic emerging larger economies.

The government therefore plays a large role in every aspect of people's lives. Singapore has often been referred to as a 'nanny' state with a large degree of social engineering, so for outsiders the country appears to be very restrictive and controlled. Although the 2011 election results suggest that there may be a change in people's views toward the 'soft-authoritarianism' of the PAP regime, in most cases the Singapore population accept and work within the status quo. The population, for the most part, place Singapore's success, economically, socially and for the quality of life in the city, on the highly regulated environment and they plan their lives in accordance with this regulation. However, some residents seek ways in which maximize the benefits and find loopholes in the system (Teo, 2010).

Although on the surface Singapore appears to be modern and western in its approach, the underlying Confucian principles in the population remain strong. There is a general pride among the people of the success of the country, which accords with the Confucian democratic principle the government has 'dictated.' For example, there is a strong degree of filial piety, which, many Singaporeans believe, distinguishes them from some of their western peers (Teo, 2010). This cultural adherence is strongly taught and advocated in the national education system.

Chapter summary

- Singapore has emerged as a major economic hub in South East Asia. It has moved from a manufacturing-based economy to a knowledge-based economy that creates its own technology. Governmental policies have encouraged foreign direct investment and supported GLCs to develop key infrastructure.

- Singapore's economy has grown through R&D with a focus on information technology, microelectronics, electronic systems, manufacturing technology, materials technology, energy, water, environment and resources, food and agro-technology, biotechnology and medical sciences.

- Singapore is a Confucian-based culture. Similar to other Confucian cultures it does have high power distance, uncertainty avoidance and performance orientation. Confucian principles also underlie government orientation for the society.

- Human resource management is key to the knowledge-based society. A large focus is being made on identifying best practice to make the knowledge-based economy a success.

- Principles that underlie Singaporean society are social responsible, although only being realized by corporations more recently.

Key concepts

Confucian approach: this is a cultural approach to government that reflects the view of the national culture. The government has formulated the nation in lines of these Confucian values.

Factor-driven growth strategy: a strategy followed by the Singapore government in the 1960s and 1970s that focused on building up economic fundamentals that allowed future growth. This included the policies that allowed foreign direct investment that built upon the manufacturing and skill base for the economy.

Knowledge-based economy: movement away from a reliance on manufacturing of technologies brought into the country, rather the development of unique technologies that will give the country a distinct competitive advantage.

Singapore Inc. and GLCs: Singapore Inc. is the colloquial name given for state intervention in the economy through the use of Government-Linked Companies (GLCs). These are large companies that often have a monopolistic position within the market, or have become national icons.

Value-added services hub: Singapore is set to become a central within the region to provide added value for services, whether this be education or R&D activities.

Review questions

1 How did the Singapore economy transform and grow so fast since the 1960s?
2 How has the Singapore government been instrumental in the success of Singapore?

3 What are GLCs? Why are they important in Singapore?

4 What are the distinguishing features of Singaporean society? What are the implications for the management and leadership of Singaporean firms?

5 What are key fundamentals of Confucian culture that should make the implementation of CSR easier?

Learning activities and discussions

1 Search the internet for information on two GLCs: Singapore airlines and SingTel. Compare their structure and management with other large multinational companies. Think about whether and how these GLCs can be related to the peculiarities of Singapore environment. Do they differ from other MNCs in the world?

2 Think about working in Singapore for a Singapore-based firm. Would you be able to work with the management style of the society, and what would you consider the biggest cultural challenges for you to adapt to in such an environment?

3 Singapore is a base for many multinational companies for the region. What cultural elements would you consider to be important for a MNC consider when doing business there? Do you think that Singapore companies could learn from the MNC?

MINI CASE

Marina Bay – Garden City by the bay

An iconic skyline is emerging in the central area of Singapore – the world-class development of Marina Bay. An extension of the central business district built on 360 hectares around a fresh water reservoir, Marina Bay supports Singapore's goal of becoming a major business and financial hub in Asia. The facilities, such as the world's most expensive standalone casino, Marina Bay Sands, with its three 55 story towers topped by a one hectare sky terrace, the Sky Sands Park, and its Eiffel Tower length infinity pool, indicate Marina Bay is a brand that epitomizes Singapore's push to be one of the most dynamic and forward thinking economies in the region (*The Business Times*, 2008).

The core of the Marina Bay brand is the 'three Es': Explore, where living meets the sky; Exchange, where the world connects with you; and Entertain, where the bay is your playground. 'Explore' refers to the development of residential areas that provide a seamless work-life environment such as The Sail @ Marina Bay; a 70-storey landmark development that provides six-star luxury housing (Marina Bay Singapore, 2013). To balance the high-rise residential developments, gardens and other recreational facilities have been carefully planned to provide residents with a good quality of life. 'Exchange' is for the development of a global business hub that is designed to attract leading financial institutions and businesses. Marina Bay, which the same size as Hong Kong's central financial district and larger than London's Canary Wharf, effectively doubles the size of the current financial centre. This reinforces the country's resolve to be a regional hub for financial commerce. The centre piece is the 3.55 hectare Marina Bay Financial Centre, three office towers situated on the waterfront. Finally Marina Bay is to be one of the key playgrounds of Singaporev – 'Entertain'. The building of nature destinations, such as the Gardens by the Bay, the hosting of major events, such as the 2008 Singapore Grand Prix, and the provision of major entertainment, cultural, and eating venues, such as the Marina Bay Sands integrated resort and the Esplanade – Theaters on the Bay, is certainly providing leisure and entertainment opportunities to Singapore's population and visitors. The range, uniqueness and vision of the facilities on offer in the bay meets the development's true vision to become a '24/7, thriving and energetic place where people live, work and play'(Marina Bay Singapore, 2013).

Marina Bay highlights the Singapore government's long-term initiatives to maximize the commercial potential and to satisfy the population's residential, transport and recreation requirements from its finite land resources (Henderson, 2012). With the mission 'to make Singapore a great city to live work and play in,' the Urban Redevelopment Authority (URA), a unit of the Ministry of National Development, administers these and other government urban planning initiatives (Urban Redevelopment Authority, 2013). Nothing is haphazard in the government's planning objectives. From as early as 1971, in the early years of Singapore's independence, the government had initiated a 40- to 50-year Concept Plan (Urban Redevelopment Authority, 2013). Revised every 10 years to take into account changing circumstances and needs, it sets a clear picture of the government's short- and long-term urban development directions. Marina Bay is a product of such long-term planning. Although the more tangible results of the Marina Bay project have only emerged from the late 2000s, initial planning for the project started in the 1970s with the reclamation the Telok Ayer Basin, with the view that extra land may be needed for the main business district in the longer-term (Marina Bay Singapore, 2013). In the process this meant that the Singapore River no longer flowed into the sea, which created, on the completion of the Marina Barrage, in 2008, a large and needed inner-city fresh water reserve, a lifestyle attraction, and effective flood control for the city. Marina Bay also fulfils many of the quality of life objectives of the latest 2011 Concept Plan that are the provision of a good living environment, an inclusive society, homes to which people feel that they belong, and economic growth (Henderson, 2012).

Marina Bay is one of the many planning transformations that are occurring in Singapore. Not only is it its own brand, it is also supporting Singapore's aim to be a global city that that also cares for its citizens. This does not happen on its own. It is a partnership.

Questions

1 What key challenges facing Singapore do you think that Marina Bay is addressing?

2 What do you think the 'place brand' of Singapore is? How is Marina Bay helping this brand?

3 Do you think that government should have a role in urban planning to the extent that it has in Singapore? Think of the positives and negatives of a development such as Marina Bay.

4 At the core of the URA (Urban Redevelopment Authority)'s mandate is to provide quality of life for the Singapore population. Do you think that Marina Bay can fulfil this objective alone?

Sources

Henderson, J. C. (2012) Planning for Success: Singapore, The Model City State, *Journal of International Affairs*, 65(2): 69–83.

Marina Bay Singapore (2013) Homepage, accessed 7 November 2013 at: http://www.marinabaysands.com

The Business Times (2008) Realising the Marina Bay Vision. *The Business Times*, 22 March, 7.

Urban Redevelopment Authority (2013) Homepage, accessed 7 November 2013 at: http://www.ura.gov.sg

References and further readings

Agency for Science Technology and Research (A*Star) (2012) National Survey of Research and Development in Singapore 2011. Singapore.

Asia One (2012) PM Lee's Delivers His New Year Message, accessed 7 November at: http://news.asiaone.com/News/Latest+News/Singapore/Story/A1Story20120122-323330.html

Bhasin, B.B. (2007) Fostering Entrepreneurship: Developing a Risk-Taking Culture in Singapore, *New England Journal of Entrepreneurship*, 10(2): 39–50.

Chappel, W. and Moon, J. (2005) Corporate Social Responsibility (CSR) in Asia: A Seven Country Study of CSR Web Site Reporting, *Business and Society*, 44(4): 415–441.

Chew, I.K.H. and Horwitz, F.M. (2004) Human Resource Management Strategies in Practice: Case-Study Findings in Multinational Firms, *Asia Pacific Journal of Human Resources*, 42(1): 32–56.

Chew, I.K.H. and Sharma, B. (2005) The Effects of Culture and HRM Practices on Firm Performance: Empirical Evidence from Singapore, *International Journal of Manpower*, 26(6): 560–581.

Chew, S.B. and Chew, R. (2003) Promoting Innovation in Singapore: Changing the Mindset, *International Journal of Entrepreneurship and Innovation Management*, 3(3): 249–266.

Chia, H., Egri, C.P., Ralston, D.A., Fu, P.P., Kuo, M.C., Lee, C., Yongyuan, L. and Moon, Y. (2007) Four Tigers and the Dragon: Values Differences, Similarities, and Consensus, *Asia Pacific Journal of Management*, 24: 305–320.

Chua, V.K.H. (2010) *Social Capital and Inequality in Singapore*. Toronto: University of Toronto.

Deloitte Touche Tohmatsu Limited (2012) *Taxation and Investment in Singapore 2012: Reach, Relevance and Reliability*. Singapore.

Economist, The (2007) Let's all bash Singapore, *The Economist*, February 8.

Economist, The (2008) Asset-Backed Insecurity, *The Economist*, January 12.

Ellingsen, G., Likumahuwa, W. and Nunnenkamp, P. (2006) Outward FDI by Singapore: A Different

Animal? *Transnational Corporations*, 15(2): 1–40.

Financial Times (2004) Temasek Strengthens Ties to Malaysia PM, *Financial Times*, November 12.

Garrett, T.C., Buisson, D.H. and Yap, C.M. (2006) National Culture and new Product Development Integration Mechanisms: A Cross-cultural Study between New Zealand and Singapore, *Industrial Marketing Management*, 35(3): 293–307.

Gem (2012) *Singapore Report 2011*. National University of Singapore Entrepreneurship Center.

Haley, U. and Low, L. (1998) Crafted-culture: Governmental Sculpting of Modern Singapore and Effects on Business Environments, *Journal of Organizational Change*, 11(6): 530–553.

Hofstede, G. (1984) *Culture's Consequences*. Newbury Park, CA: Sage.

Hoi, P.C.P. (2013) Why Social Capital is Missing in Singapore, *The Straits Times*, September 10.

Horwitz, F.M., Heng, C.T., Hesan, A.Q., Nonkwelo, C., Roditi, D. and Van Eck, P. (2006) Human Resource Strategies for Managing Knowledge Workers: An Afro-Asian Comparative Analysis, *International Journal of Human Resource Management*, 17(5): 775–811.

House, R.J., Hanges, P.J., Javidan, M., Dorfman, P.W. and Gupta, V. (2004) *Culture, Leadership, and Organizations*. Thousand Oaks, CA: Sage Publications.

Huang, G.Z.D., Roy, M.H., Ahmed, Z.U., Heng, J.S. and Lim, J.H.M. (2002) Benchmarking the Human Capital Strategies of MNCs in Singapore, *Benchmarking*, 9(4): 357–373.

International Finance Corporation (2012) *Doing Business: Measuring Business Regulations*. Singapore: Author.

International Monetary Fund (2012) World Economic Database, October 2012.

Ioannou, I. and Serafeim, G. (2012) What Drives Corporate Social Performance? The Role of Nation-Level Institutions, *Journal of International Business Studies*, 43(9): 834–864.

Koh, T.H. and Wong, P.K. (2005) Competing at the Frontier: The Changing Role of Technology Policy in Singapore's Economic Strategy, *Technological Forecasting and Social Change*, 72, 255–285.

Lee, M.H., Mak, A.K. and Pang, A. (2012) Bridging the Gap: An Exploratory Study of Corporate Social Responsibility among SMEs in Singapore, *Journal of Public Relations Research*, 24(4): 299–317.

Leggett, C. (2007) From Industrial Relations to Manpower Planning: The Transformations of Singapore's Industrial Relations, *International Journal of Human Resource Management*, 18(4): 642–664.

Li, X. (2011) S'pore Can't Afford to Stop Building Social Capital, *The Straits Times*, March 31.

Low, C.P.K. (2006a) Cultural Obstacles in Growing Entrepreneurship: A Study in Singapore, *Journal of Management Development*, 25(2): 169–182.

Low, C.P.K. (2006b) Father Leadership: The Singapore Case Study, *Management Decision*, 44(1): 89–104.

Low, C.P.K (2007) The Cultural Values of Resilience: The Singapore Case Study, *Cross Cultural Management*, 14(2): 136–149.

Mahtani, S. (2012) The World's Richest Country, *Wall Street Journal*, 15 August.

Ministry of Trade and Industry (2011) *Economic Vision*. Singapore: Author.

Ministry of Trade and Industry (2013) *Economic Survey of Singapore*. Singapore: Author.

Meng, S.S. (2012) Balancing the Benefits and Downside of Meritocracy. *The Strait Times*, 9 October.

National Science and Technology (2000) *National Science and Technology Plan 2005*. Singapore: Author.

Ortmann, S. (2012) The 'Beijing Consensus' and the 'Singapore Model': Unmasking the Myth of an Alternative Authoritarian State-Capitalist Model. *Journal of Chinese Economic and Business Studies*, 10(4): 337.

Porter, M. (1990) *The Competitive Advantage of Nations*. London: Macmillan.

Ramirez, C. and Tan, H.L. (2003) Singapore Inc vs. The Private Sector: Are Government-linked Companies Different? *IMF Staff Paper* 51(3)

Soon, T. and Tan, C.S. (1993) *The Lessons from East Asia: Singapore – Public Policy and Economic Development*. Washington DC: The World Bank.

Stanton, P. and Nankervis, A. (2011) Linking Strategic HRM, Performance Management and Organizational Effectiveness: Perceptions of Managers in Singapore, *Asia Pacific Business Review*, 17(1): 67.

Statistics Singapore (2012) *Singapore Investments Abroad*. Singapore: Author.

Statistics Singapore (2013a) *Monthly Digest of Statistics Singapore*, February 2013.

Statistics Singapore (2013b) *Per Capita GDP at Current Market Prices*. Singapore: Author.

Tambyah, S.K., Tan, S.J. and Kau, A.K. (2009) The Quality of Life in Singapore. *Social Indicators Research*, 92(2): 337–376.

Tan E. (2008) Moulding the Corporate Social Responsibility Agenda in Singapore, accessed 4 December 2013 at: http://www.smu.edu.sg/perspectives/2012/06/26/moulding-corporate-social-responsibility-agenda-singapore#.Uom37_CIrcs

Taorimina, R.J. (1998) Employee Attitudes Toward Organizational Socialization in the People's Republic of China, Hong Kong, and Singapore, *Journal of Applied Behavioral Science*, 34(4): 468–485.

Temasek (2012) *Temasek Review 2012*. Singapore.

Teo, Y. (2010) Shaping the Singapore Family, Producing the State and Society, *Economy and Society*, 39(3): 337.

Transparency International (2012) *Corruptions Perceptions Index 2012*. Berlin.

Tripathi, S. (2006) Temasek: The Perils of Being Singaporean, *Far Eastern Economic Review*, May 11.

Wong, C.Y.L., Millar, C.C.M. and Choi, C.J. (2006) Singapore in Transition: From Technology to Culture Hub, *Journal of Knowledge Management*, 10(5): 79–91.

World Bank (2012) *Foreign Direct Investment, Net Outflows (% of GDP)*. Washington, DC.

World Economic Forum (2012a) *The Financial Development Report 2012*. Geneva: World Economic Forum.

World Economic Forum (2012b) *The Global Competitiveness Report 2012–2013*. Geneva: World Economic Forum.

World Trade Organization (2012) *Singapore Country Profile*. Geneva: World Trade Organization.

Yin, S.C. (2003) MNSC and Other Business Organizations in Singapore, accessed 7 November 2013 at: http://choonyin.tripod.com/mncs/

Zang, X. (1999) Research Note: Personalism and Corporate Networks in Singapore. *Organizational Studies*, 20(5): 861–877.

The Business System of Malaysia

Axèle Giroud

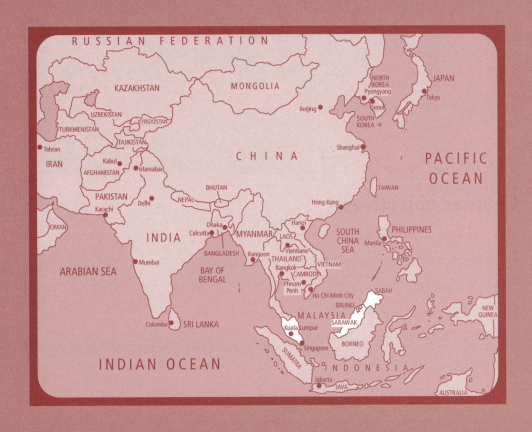

Chapter outline

- The Malaysian business system
- Comparative advantage
- Continuity and change in the Malaysian business system
- MNEs in Malaysia
- International activities of Malaysian firms
- CRS in Malaysia
- Implications for expatriates and foreign firms in Malaysia

Chapter objectives

After reading this chapter, you will gain an understanding of:

1 The essence of the Malaysian institutional environment.

2 The Malaysian business system.

3 The importance of multiculturalism in Malaysia.

4 The role played by MNEs in Malaysia.

5 The rise of Malaysian firms on the international business scene.

Introduction

Malaysia is a country of just over 28 million people located in Southeast Asia and is one of the fastest growing countries in the region. It is a multicultural society, rich in natural resources, with high inflows of Foreign Direct Investment (FDI) and is attractive to many for its beautiful and attractive tourist locations. The new government has published the Tenth Malaysia Plan, and launched an Economic Transformation Program to ensure the continued growth of the country, with the ambition of raising Malaysia from a middle income country to fully developed country status by 2020. The economic development strategy and economic goals of the Malaysian government reflect this ambition.

This chapter uses concepts developed by both the business systems and international business literature, and provides a historical and current factual analysis of the Malaysian business system. The key topics covered include multiculturalism, government intervention, natural resources, multinational enterprises (MNEs), the position of Malaysia within ASEAN, and how these considerations influence the current and future business system in Malaysia.

In Malaysia, the structure of business reflects the ethnic diversity and strong involvement of the country in globalization. The country has a rich socio-political history, and its government has applied an unusual mix of liberalization in the manufacturing sector with strong intervention in other parts of the economy. The chapter begins with an analysis of the institutional environment, spanning the political system, capital system, interfirm relationships system and labour system. The institutional environment is instrumental in explaining how firms combine resources and ultimately gain competitive advantages. Following this theoretical rationale will enable us to understand better the key role played by social contexts within Malaysia, and how various types of firms prevail in the country.

In the latter part of the chapter, the rise of Malaysian firms on the international business scene is explored, and the chapter ends with a mini case of one of Malaysia's best known firm, Petronas.

The Malaysian business system: culture and key historical influences

Rationale

Understanding firms and how they operate in Malaysia is intrinsically related to the social-cultural structure of society and key historical events.

Malaysia is a truly multicultural society. Malaysia's population of over 28.3 million inhabitants, is made up of 91.8 per cent Malaysian citizens and 8.2 per cent non-citizens. Of the Malaysian citizens, 67.4 per cent are Bumiputera, 24.6 per cent *Chinese*, 7.3 per cent *Indians*, and 0.7 per cent *Others* (mostly ethnic Thais, Khmers, Chams and the natives of Sabah and Sarawak) (Department of Statistics, 2011). Among the Bumiputera, the Malays are the dominant ethnic group, followed by the *Ibans* in Sarawak and *Kadazan/Dusun* in Sabah.

The presence of Chinese and Indians dates back to the British rule, when immigration was initiated as a means to increase the labour force. The Chinese are dominant in the business and commerce community. Though various ethnic groups live in relative harmony nowadays, racial tensions occurred during the 1960s, culminating on 13 May 1969, when Sino-Malay sectarian violence took place in Kuala Lumpur and 196 persons (official number) lost their lives. This prompted the government to launch the New Economic Policy, enforcing affirmative action to increase the participation of Bumiputera in economic activities.

Religious beliefs follow the multiracial nature of Malaysia; 61.3 per cent practice Islam, 19.8 per cent Buddhism, 9.2 per cent Christianity and 6.3 per cent Hinduism. The official language of Malaysia is Bahasa Malaysia, and English is widely used in business. Due to the ethnic diversity of the country, many other languages are spoken.

Malaysia has been influenced by different cultures over the centuries. Historically, the United Kingdom, Portugal, the Netherlands and Japan have had various influences over the country. Malaysia had Portuguese and Dutch influences dating back from colonial times, in the sixteenth and seventeenth centuries, when Malacca operated under Portuguese rule and later on under Dutch rule. The Malay kingdoms have operated under the British Empire since the eighteenth century, and obtained independence on 31 August 1957. Malaya united with Sabah, Sarawak and Singapore on 16 September 1963 to become Malaysia (until 1965 when Singapore opted out of the Federation).

Two main social-economic and historical aspects explain the business structure of Malaysia today, intervention by the government to ensure even participation across ethnic groups in economic activities and involvement of MNEs. Economically, Malaysia has thus transformed rapidly from a traditional, agricultural-based economy to a modern industrial-based economy since the 1970s. This transformation was based upon rapid expansion of trade, and is partly due to foreign multinational enterprises (MNEs) investment in the country.

Since the early 1970s and the Second Malaysia Plan of 1971–1975, the government has developed targets for Bumiputera participation in the private sector and initiated schemes to assist participation in commerce, such as the Bumiputera Commercial and Industrial Community (BCIC). This scheme has provided a platform to finance the Bumiputera Joint-Venture Scheme and the establishment of genuine joint ventures between Bumiputera and non-Bumiputera entrepreneurs, as well as various programs to facilitate the Bumiputera participation in strategic SMEs, notably with the support of government-owned companies, privatized and privately-owned firms.

In the Tenth Malaysia Plan, the BCIC focuses on the provision of direct assistance and capacity building to micro-enterprises, while support to large Bumiputera companies is to be merit based. More recently, Bumiputera entrepreneurs have received support from the government to engage in international trade. Overall, the policy has been successful, despite remaining disparities between ethnic groups in terms of income level and business participation. Chinese entrepreneurs still engage actively in trade, both domestically and internationally.

In the mid-1980s the Malaysian government became fully committed to a strategy of development based on MNE-led export-oriented manufacturing. Malaysia was particularly successful in attracting foreign direct investment (FDI) in higher technology manufactured exports (notably in electronics).

As a result of these changes, the composition of the GDP has changed with a rising share of the secondary sector. The primary sector share of GDP has declined from 28 per cent in 1990 to 12 per cent in 2011, while that of the secondary sector has increased from 30 per cent in 1990 to 40 per cent in 2011. That of the tertiary sector has increased more modestly from 42 per cent in 1990 to 48 per cent in 2011. The composition of the private sector has also changed. The ownership of share capital at par value of limited companies by Bumiputera has increased from 2.4 per cent in 1970 to 21.9 per cent in 2008 (EPU, 2010). As for MNEs, by 2011, foreign firms accounted for US$ 10,772.5 million of a total US$ 17,693.0 million approved total capital investment projects in the manufacturing sector (that is 60 per cent of all approved projects) (MIDA, n.d.).

In sum, government policy has encouraged the participation of Bumiputera in the business and commercial sector. Its economic development strategy has relied upon a large inflow of FDI and the diversification of GDP thanks to activities of MNEs in the manufacturing sector. Through high growth rates, Malaysia has succeeded in reducing poverty levels, and thereby ensured social harmony within the country. The Tenth Malaysian Plan (2010) mentions that poverty has declined from 49.3 per cent in 1970 to 3.8 per cent in 2009, with extreme poverty nearly eradicated at 0.7 per cent in 2009 (PMO, n.d.). The government has provided the general direction for economic development and the maintenance of social and economic order. Foreign investors have been welcome in the country since the liberalization program initiated in the late 1980s, and education has been widely developed to facilitate social mobility and provide a pool of educated workforce notably for foreign MNEs in the manufacturing sector.

Identity

Using data on cultural values and beliefs, Gupta et al. (2002) find that Malaysia belongs to the Southern Asia societal cluster, together with India, Indonesia, the Philippines, Thailand and Iran. The Malaysians have a relatively collectivist sense of identity and tend to put the interest of the group above that of the individual, irrespective of their ethnic origin. The collectivist attitude has been reinforced by the government's long-term development objectives, and notably the *2020 vision* of becoming a developed nation by the year 2020, launched as part of the Sixth Malaysia Plan in 1991. This continues to be a main national objective, and the Tenth Malaysia Plan 2011–2015 is still committed to the *1Malaysia* ideal to create a fair and socially just society with national unity as its ultimate objective.

The collectivist sense of Malaysians means that they favour a long-term, loyal commitment to the group (being family or extended relationships), and employer/employee relationships are led by collectivist considerations, strong sense of shame and loss of face. Malaysians tend to adopt a relaxed attitude towards rules, with flexible schedules and will work hard mostly when necessary. Malaysia is on the whole not a highly innovative society.

Authority

Malaysian society is strongly hierarchical, with authority relations structured along family, position and professional achievement lines. It is highly driven by success, and acceptance that all individuals are not equal within society. People accept a hierarchical order in society, managers are expected to be decisive, and employees expect to be told what to do. On the whole, challenges to leadership and authority in Malaysia are not well-received. Participation of women in work is widely accepted, though the participation rate of women in the labour force (at 45.7 per cent in 2008) is low compared to neighbouring Thailand (70.0 per cent) or Singapore (60.2 per cent) (MIDA, 2010), and female participation remains mostly in non-management positions. For this reason, the participation of women is a key objective of the Tenth Malaysia Plan.

The government: a tale of *laissez-faire*, intervention and liberalization

Malaysia operates under a federal constitutional elective monarchy. The system of government closely mirrors that of Westminster's parliamentary system, and the legal system is based upon the English Common Law. Executive power is vested in the Cabinet, led by the Prime Minister. Legislative power is divided between federal and state legislatures. The King is elected for a five-year term by and from one of the nine hereditary rulers of the Malay states (though there are 13 states, four are only titular governors). To understand fully politics and modern business ownership structures of what is now Malaysia today, it is essential to explore briefly the main stages in the Malaysian economic development pattern since its independence. Broadly, the political economy of what is now Malaysia can be divided into five phases (Searle, 1999: 27):

1. The pre-colonial phase (before 1874).

2. The phase of the colonial economy (1874–1957).

3. The post-colonial economy (1957–1969) when the government adopted a largely *laissez-faire* approach.

4. The period of state intervention (1970–1985).

5. The period of economic liberalization (since 1985).

Key legacies from the colonial rules are worth noting. It has been argued that the prestige of the sultans as symbols of the Malay community was strengthened under British rule. Foreign assets dominated under colonial rule and a dual economy prevailed, with large corporations based on venture capital engaging in plantations, mining, banking, manufacturing, shipping and public utilities, in parallel to peasant small holdings. Foreign activities were linked with large inflow of low-cost immigrant labour from China and India. This resulted in a demographic shift and the rise of a plural society. The agricultural/commercial divide widened between Malays and Chinese during this time, especially because Chinese were excluded from holding senior administrative positions in the Malay States.

On 31 August 1957, the Federation of Malaya gained its independence. The government was formed by the Alliance between the United Malays National Organization (UMNO), the Malayan Chinese Association (MCA) and the Malayan Indian Congress (MIC), UMNO being the dominant party, Islam being the state religion and the Malay Sultans being preserved within the framework of a constitutional democracy. In the pre-1969 period, the state did not actively promote Malay advances into the capitalist sector, which resulted in a marginalization of the Malays and a lack of development of Malay capitalism. Economic disparities between Malays and non-Malays were later on identified as the main cause for the social riots that took place in 1969.

The New Economic Policy (NEP) was launched in 1971 with the aims of eradicating poverty and restructuring the Malaysian society to eliminate the identification of race with economic function. The Industrial Co-ordination Act (ICA) of 1975 was intended to control the growth of the manufacturing sector and ensure advancement of Malay capitalism. Under the NEP, the Ministry of Trade and Industry and Bank Negara, the central bank, became important regulatory bodies. It is also at that time that the political hegemony of UMNO was consolidated. The *laissez-faire* alliance was replaced by a more interventionist orientation.

In 1981, Dr Mahathir's assumption of power as Prime Minister was the catalyst for a shift in the political system towards a patrimonialist cast. An influential core of Bumiputera businessmen developed and power was concentrated in a few key regulatory state agencies. Malaysia engaged in a heavy industrialization program, with the setting up of the Heavy Industries Corporation of Malaysia (HICOM), a series of heavy and chemical firms in sectors such as steel, cement, automobiles, chemicals, and paper and pulp. HICOM was to promote growth through backward and forward linkages and the expansion of the capital goods sector. The *Look East Policy*, *Malaysia Incorporated*, and *Vision 20/20* were key policies launched in the early 1980s to support Malaysia's industrialization. The Malay elite changed, from politicians and administocrats to a combination of politicians and businessmen. In this context, it was those who were loyal to the leadership rather than those who were technically competent who were rewarded with influential positions.

A number of factors, including the economic recession of 1984–1985, the stagnation of foreign capital flows, growing reliance on foreign MNEs and HICOM's growing financial problems prompted the government to move away from policies of state intervention and emphasis on ownership restructuring towards liberalization policies, with a focus on deregulation, profit, growth and public sector restraint. New investment incentives were launched with the Promotion of Investments Act in 1986, interest rates were kept low and bureaucratic restructuring took place. It is argued (Searle, 1999) that rent-seekers (often Malays whose survival in business was dependent upon access to state patronage) have been gradually losing out to a growing class of entrepreneurs who were moving beyond state support. Further liberalization and efforts towards greater transparency in the economy has been prompted following the Asia crisis in 1997, although Malaysia was not as strongly affected as Thailand or Indonesia.

To summarize, over the past four decades, key Master Plans have broadly built upon the core economic development objectives of reducing poverty, widening Bumiputera participation in business and commerce, welcoming foreign investment, and diversifying economic activities, notably through the promotion of key clusters. The government has generally been friendly to foreign MNEs and encouraged FDI inflows, while promoting 12 National Key Economic Areas. These 12 NKEAs are composed of oil and gas, palm oil and related products, financial services, wholesale and retail, tourism, information and communications technology, education, electrical and electronics, business services, private healthcare, agriculture and greater Kuala Lumpur.

Business environment

Financial capital

Financial capital in Malaysia is embedded in the hands of the state or well-connected businesspeople.

Major reforms and market liberalization of the financial capital market occurred in Malaysia following the Asian crisis in 1997, and in the early 2000s. In 2009, the government launched the Central Bank of Malaysia Act, which recognized both the conventional and Islamic financial systems as equally important. In practice, the Bank Negara Malaysia's (BNM) monetary policy leans towards an inflation-targeting regime, using the interest rate as its monetary instrument to target inflation. Over the past decade, BNM has made progress to be more transparent regarding its monetary strategy, notably through the publication of regular monetary policy statements.

Malaysia adopts a managed (rather than free floating) exchange rate for the ringgit. For instance, during the Asia crisis, the government decided to peg the ringgit against the US dollar, as well as apply selective capital controls.

BNM is generally considered to be closely linked to the government, as opposed to operating independently. This is reflected in the fact that some bank lending takes the form of state-directed lending. The Central Bank of Malaysia Act of 2009 does contain provisions to increase the independence of BNM in its monetary policy decisions. The act provides for a dispute settlement procedure in case of disagreement between the finance minister and the central bank. The Act specifies that the central bank governor is to be appointed by the king for a five-year term, while deputy governors are to be appointed by the minister of finance for a three-year term.

The Malaysian financial system is regulated by the BNM (which regulates the financial sector), and Securities Commission Malaysia (which regulates the capital market), with the number of banking institutions and ownership determined by the government. As of 2009, there were 141 financial institutions in Malaysia (Yap and Tend, 2012: 121), 63 banking institutions (of which 21 were foreign banks, which do not conduct normal banking business but rather services to allow businesses in Malaysia to liaise with their counterparts overseas) and 78 non-banking financial institutions (of which 23 were foreign).

Since 1983, Malaysia provides the legal basis for the establishment of Islamic banks, and the first Islamic bank was Bank Islam Malaysia. Today, Malaysia has 11 domestically controlled, six foreign-controlled and two international Islamic banks operating through a network of 2,651 branches and offering over 40 different Islamic financial products (Yap and Tend, 2012: 124). The Malaysia Islamic Financial Centre was launched in 2006 within the BNM, and August 2009 saw the launch of the Bursa Suq Al-Sila', a shariah-compliant commodity trading platform for Islamic banks.

Human capital

In its goal to achieve a high-income economy status, the Tenth Malaysia Plan puts special emphasis on up-skilling the current workforce.

Malaysia has invested in education and gross enrolment ratios have increased from 88.2 per cent in primary in 1970 to 96.7 per cent in 2005, 52.2 per cent in 1970 in lower secondary to 84.4 per cent in 2005, from 20.1 per cent in 1970 to 71.7 per cent in upper secondary and from 0.6 per cent in 1970 to 9.1 per cent in 2005 in tertiary (Lee and Nagaraj, 2012: 215). Such improvements in education are reflected in the composition of the labour force. As of 2005, 19.3 per cent of the labour force worked as professional and technical (against 4.8 per cent in 1970), 25.1 per cent in production (19.4 per cent in 1970) and 14.3 per cent in services (8.2 per cent). By contrast employment in agriculture has decreased from 53.6 per cent in 1970 to 12.6 per cent in 2005.

Despite these improvements, one of the three main obstacles mentioned in the World Bank's Enterprise Survey of Malaysia remains an inadequately educated workforce. This is partly because of changes in skills requirements as the country develops, and partly as a result of improvements still required in the quality of education being received. With the ambition in the Economic Transformation Program to boost the development of higher value-added activities in manufacturing and encourage the expansion of the service sector, the education system in Malaysia must be improved further.

Malaysian universities are not among the world's top performers, the number of R&D researchers per million remains low as do academic publications. There is ethnic stratification in education (with favoured access for Bumiputera especially in the tertiary sector) as well as in public sector (where 80 per cent of public service jobs are held by Bumiputera). Many non-Bumiputera choose either to enrol in private universities, or to study abroad as a result, and often do not return home, which creates a loss of talent. Brain drain is a concern, which the government wishes to address in the Tenth Malaysia Plan. It is estimated that two out of ten graduates from Malaysia work abroad.

Private sector education has grown significantly over the past decade, especially in the tertiary sector. Private colleges and universities tend to use English as the main language of instruction, rather than Bahasa Malaysia, which means their graduates are often favoured by foreign multinational enterprises as good English language skills ease communication at work.

The government encourages a variety of training through various schemes, such as the Human Resource Development Fund (HRDF), which encourages companies to train employees for the number of skills through a variety of levies and training grants (http://www.hrdf.com.my/wps/portal/PSMB), or SME targeted training centres such as the Penang Skills Development Centre, which partners with MNEs to identify and provide relevant skills training for local SMEs. Altogether there are 12 similar skills development centres across Malaysia.

Unemployment rate is low in Malaysia, standing at 3.7 per cent in 2009 (Trading Economics, n.d.). For this reason, employees tend to change job several times during their career, especially those who have skills that are attractive to employers. Labour turnover can, in some cases, represent a difficulty for employers as hiring new employees can involve training costs.

As of 2011, women represented 49.1 per cent of the population, but only 36.6 per cent of the workforce. Women remain under-represented in senior positions and in the public sector, and they only have 16.5 per cent of the members of parliament (Economic Planning Unit, 2012).

Labour migration is important for the Malaysian economy, as migrants make up about a quarter of the workforce. Net migration inflows ranges between 80,000 and 90,000 per year. The majority is planned and authorized, but there is also illegal immigration, which is composed predominantly of young workers from poor neighbouring countries who engage in activities where wages are low such as agriculture or construction. The number of illegal immigrants in Malaysia is estimated to be between 1 and 2 million.

Malaysia has recently seen its expatriate population decline, partly as a result of slow movement towards higher-end economic activities. These considerations have been acknowledged in the New Economic Model for Malaysia issued in 2010.

Social capital

Social capital tends to be high in Malaysia, particularly when considering people's close family and friends' relationships. Involvement and participation of individuals in groups is high, with close social ties and relation with others in society.

However, Malaysia is a plural society (with, as mentioned earlier in this chapter, four main ethnic groups that are Malays, Chinese, Indians and indigenous people of Sabah and Sarawak), and considering the country's diverse socio-cultural fabric, social capital is a highly debated topic in Malaysia. Through various policies (the NEP, the NDP (National Development Policy) and more recently the National Vision Policy), the government has made attempts to promote national unity, especially with the Vision 2020 of attaining developed nation status. Overall, quality of life has increased, poverty has been substantially reduced and education strengthened. Reasonably high growth rates have also ensured that standards of living have risen for the majority of the population.

There remain two main concerns. The first is regional disparity, as all regions do not perform similarly well economically, and in fact, a large share of economic activity remains concentrated around the Kuala Lumpur area. The second one relates to levels of social capital, which can still be strengthened on an ethnic-based level. Generally, social ties tend to be stronger within rather than across ethnic communities, with high trust and solidarity and generally strong collective action and cooperation within ethnic groups.

Given its objective of moving the country's position from middle-high to high income status, the government needs to pay particular attention to the transition to a knowledge-based economy, given the potential strains that can be created a labour force so diverse in terms of ethnicity, socio-economic, religious, educational and linguistic background. Unity is a key component of continued economic growth for Malaysia, and much of this success relies upon the ability of the government to ensure that particular economic sectors are not dominated by one particular ethnic group.

Business system

Ownership

Since the early 1970s, the Malaysian government has endeavoured to increase the participation of Bumiputera in business. Throughout the 1980s and 1990s, the government has continued to pay attention to corporate ownership patterns. A number of well-connected businesspeople have emerged as owners of large publicly quoted conglomerates, such as Halim Saad, Tajudin Ramli or Rashid Hussain. It is to be noted that well-connected non-Malays have also been able to build large firms with state support and patronage at that time, such as Vincent Tan Chee Yioun, Ting Pek Khing and T Ananda Krishnan.

Bumiputera ownership of corporate equity has, as a result, increased from 1.5 per cent in 1969 to 21.9 per cent in 2008 (Gomez, 2012: 65). Chinese ownership remains high at

34.9 per cent in 2008. Overall, the most noticeable change resides in the reduction of foreign ownership from a high of 62.1 per cent in 1969 down to 37.9 per cent in 2008. Of course, the number of foreign firms has continued to increase, but their share in overall corporate ownership has declined.

The government currently wishes to boost private investment, because its levels have not been considered high enough to ensure sustained economic growth. Key measures introduced for this purpose include a 10-year exemption on venture capital, investment incentives in some regions, and scaling back government involvement in the economy by divesting stakes in 33 companies.

Since the mid-2000s, as outlined in the Ninth Malaysia Plan 2006–2010, more emphasis is placed on supporting small and medium-sized Bumiputera enterprises. One strategy is to foster niche markets for *halal* food and other Islamic products, notably by supporting networks between SMEs and large enterprises (including MNEs such as Tesco and Carrefour) to promote national and export competitiveness.

The electronics and electrical industry accounts for a large share of economic activity (including exports) for Malaysia. The industry continues to be largely led by foreign multinational firms. Although too few domestic players have developed, some have established themselves as competitive firms, such as MEC, Khind, and Pensonic, and a few are making small inroads into export markets. In the components sub-sector, domestic companies can mostly be found in semiconductor packaging and assembly (with names such as Malaysian Pacific Industries, Unisem, Globetronics Technology and AIC Corporation), unfortunately, there are still too few of these suppliers of key parts and components, and foreign firms primarily purchase many parts from other foreign firms or from abroad.

Networking

Malaysia may not generally be considered a network economy. Despite major improvements in information gathering and sharing, more transparency can be achieved, for instance, to understand fully monetary policy decisions adopted by the government.

Business networks can be found among major manufacturers within, notably, the electronics and electrical sector with major MNEs having developed strong relationships with a number of local vendors. In part, some of those relationships arose following government initiatives to strengthen existing clusters, through tax incentives, specific institutional arrangements, vendor development schemes, local content requirements, subcontracting exchange schemes and information provision and exchange. Specific initiatives included the Industrial Linkages Program, encouraging large companies to link with small vendors, or the Global Supplier Program (Giroud, 2003).

Management

As a hierarchically oriented country, decision making in Malaysian firms is often concentrated at the top of organization, employees expect managers to provide clear guidance and make decisions, and they would not normally question decisions taken by senior management. As such, it is important for Malaysians to have a clear idea of hierarchy within their organization and know who to report to. Promotion is not necessarily merit based, and in some cases, routes to promotion can lack transparency.

There is generally respect for seniority in Malaysian organizations. It is also expected that managers will ensure their employees do not lose 'face'. Given that all ethnic groups in Malaysia are group-oriented, Malaysians tend to be good team players, rather than focused on own individual targets. Communication in Malaysia involves politeness and diplomacy, and open confrontation is generally avoided. While people will happily engage in discussion related to family, sports, or Malaysia itself, other topics such as politics, religion and ethnicity are less common in business conversations.

Comparative advantage

Malaysia draws its comparative advantages from natural resources (for instance, Malaysia is among the world's top exporter of natural gas), its geographical location and tourism potential, regional economic relations and its trade and the manufacturing sector. Its biggest comparative disadvantages lie in slow private investment (though private investment has increased recently, partly as a result of changes implemented in the Economic Transition Plan), dependence on trade and lack of innovation capacity.

Malaysia's main export oriented industries include electronic and electrical products (about half of exports), oil and gas (nearly a fifth of exports), palm oil (about one-tenth of exports), and chemicals and chemical products (about one-tenth of exports). This means that Malaysia is sensitive to the volatility of global commodity prices, and exports of electronics and electrical products have been sensitive to the economic crisis in Western countries. The role of the services sector in the economy is rising (together with its share of GDP). Key services include wholesale and retail trade, finance and insurance, transportation and communication, and government services. Government revenues rely heavily on the oil and gas sector, and in an effort to reduce this dependence, the government plans to broaden the tax base by introducing new taxes on goods and services.

Given its ambition to reach developed country status by 2020 and in a drive towards diversification of the economy, the government encourages a shift to higher value-added sectors (these include notably new sectors such as biotechnology, Islamic finance, communications technology and tourism – including health tourism), but this is not an easy process and some adjustments are still needed in the country, such as, stricter enforcement of intellectual property rights.

Continuity and change in the Malaysian business system

Over the past few decades, Malaysia has achieved great economic success, and has reached middle income status. There is much debate as to whether it is now trapped in the middle income, and whether it will succeed in its ambition to reach developed country status. It has proved resilient to various crises however, both internally and externally. The government has combined export-orientation policies with strong protectionism of specific sectors, and a strong hold over some economic activities notably through state ownership. A strength lies in its multicultural society and the adaptability of people. These explain why Malaysia resumed growth quickly after the 1997 Asia crisis.

Malaysia is a country of contrasts, and it embraces diversity in its efforts to support growth. For this reason, foreign MNEs have been welcome in the manufacturing sector, and it is those firms that drive a large share of export, especially in the electronics and electrical sector. In parallel, the primary sector and many services remain subject to foreign ownership restrictions. Malaysia ranked at 18 (out of 183 countries) in the 'Doing Business 2012' ranking, but only at 53 in terms of economic freedom.

Changes within the Malaysian business system may occur, especially if changes are needed for the country to continue to grow. Some of the positive changes that may continue to occur include more transparency and continued effort to provide strong and reliable information regarding monetary policy and the structure of the economy. Access to information is essential for businesses to thrive. Government intervention in business and socio-economic affairs may also decline alongside a strengthening of the legal system in relation to intellectual property protection, and continued support for innovation within the country.

MNEs in Malaysia

Malaysia has been, over the past three decades, a key host for global FDI to developing countries. In fact, in the late 1980s and early 1990s, Malaysia was among the top 10 developing country FDI recipients. The main explanations behind the attractiveness of Malaysia lie in its sound macro-economic success (notably fast growth rates), good physical infrastructure (in terms of sea, rail, air and train transports as well as in terms of electricity supplies), knowledge infrastructure (in terms of primary, secondary and increasingly tertiary education too) and business infrastructure (with numerous industrial and technology parks, the Malaysian Super-Corridor), a favourable living environment (in terms of good quality of life), attractive government policies towards businesses and foreign investors, and its regional geographical location (within ASEAN). As shown in Table 13.1, inward FDI flows into Malaysia have increased steadily since 1970 (when they totalled US$94 million) to a peak of US$11.9 billion in 2011. Amid a slowdown in global FDI flows, this demonstrates that Malaysia remains very attractive to foreign investors.

Malaysia has, in the past, experienced setbacks in terms of inward FDI flows, first after the Asian crisis (FDI inflows reached an annual average of US$5.8 billion over the 1992–1997 period, before decreasing to US$2.7 billion in 1998), and again in 2001 (down to US$554 million) and 2009 (down to US$1.4 billion) following crises in the United States and Europe. These declines demonstrate that the Malaysian economy is sensitive to regional and global crises.

The importance of inward FDI to the Malaysia economic is best represented by the share of inward flows in GFCF, which is almost double the average world share in 2010 (18.8 per cent for Malaysia against 9.5 per cent for the world average). Such figures demonstrate the importance of foreign firms to the Malaysian economy.

If foreign MNEs are important to the local economy, it is likely that the country is, in turn, influenced by foreign institutional contexts. In the case of Malaysia, the main sources of foreign investment have changed over the past decades. Japan and the NIEs (Taiwan, South Korea, Hong Kong and Singapore) emerged as major investors in Malaysia in the 1980s and 1990s. In the late 1990s, Singapore was the most important investing country, while in the early 2000s, the United States and some European countries also started to invest significantly.

About half of all FDI is directed to the manufacturing sector, and the services sector attracts just over a third of inward FDI flows. The manufacturing sector is key to the

TABLE 13.1 Key facts about FDI in Malaysia

	1970 (million US$)	1980 (million US$)	1990 (million US$)	2000 (million US$)	2005 (million US$)	2010 (million US$)	2011 (million US$)
FDI Inflows	94	934	2,611	3,788	4,065	9,103	11,966
FDI Outflows	...	201	129	2,026	3,076	13,329	15,258
FDI Inward Stocks			10,318	52,747		101,510	114,555
FDI Outward Stocks			753	15,878		96,896	106,217
Share of Inward FDI							
% in GFCF (Malaysia)	16.5	11.9	17.5	16.0	14.4	18.8	N/A
% in GFCF (Average World)	1.8	1.9	4.1	20.1	9.9	9.5	N/A
% in GDP	2.6	3.7	5.7	4.0	2.9	3.8	4.3

NOTE: GFCF Gross Fixed Capital Formation.
SOURCE: Data extracted from UNCTAD Database, http://www.unctad.org.

success of the Malaysian economy. It makes up 25 per cent of GDP, employs 16.7 per cent of the workforce and is dominated by export-oriented producers of electronic products.

In this section, I have demonstrated that foreign MNEs, through large annual inward FDI flows, have a significant role in the success of the Malaysian economy, and they represent key business partners in the country. They operate predominantly in the manufacturing sector, which is a driving force behind Malaysia's economic growth. The Malaysian government has been instrumental in facilitating the activities of foreign firms, notably by introducing FDI-friendly policies, and by treating foreign and local investors equally.

International activities of Malaysian firms

Malaysian firms' international activities abroad were very low in the 1980s, but have increased significantly since 1993 and remained high throughout the 2000s (see FDI outflows and outward stocks in Table 13.1). Over the period 2008–2011, Malaysian investment abroad was directed primarily towards ASEAN neighbouring countries (35 per cent), Africa (19 per cent), Central and South America (13 per cent), Europe (12 per cent), Oceania (7 per cent) and South Asia (7 per cent) (Bank Negara Malaysia, 2013). The main recipients of Malaysian outward FDI were Singapore (15 per cent), Indonesia (13 per cent), Mauritius and Australia (6 per cent respectively), the United Kingdom and Thailand (3 per cent respectively). Over the same period, 52 per cent of Malaysian investment abroad occurred in services (with more than half in financial and insurance activities), 29 per cent in mining and quarrying (29 per cent), 9 per cent in agriculture, forestry and fishing, and 7 per cent in manufacturing.

Three types of Malaysian companies engage in overseas activities, namely GLCs (Government Linked Companies), resident private companies (those in which residents have equity stake of more than 50 per cent), and non-resident private companies (those in which total non-resident shareholding is more than 50 per cent). Malaysian GLCs and resident private companies account for just under two-thirds of outward FDI from Malaysia. They invest mostly in developing countries, especially ASEAN and in Africa.

Petronas is the only Malaysian company to be ranked among the world's top 100 non-financial MNEs. According to UNCTAD, six Malaysian companies rank among the world's largest MNEs from developing countries, namely Petronas, YTL Corp. Berhad, MISC Berhad, Sime Darby Berhad, MUI Berhad and Kumpulan Guthrie Berhad. Four of these are GLCs and three are diversified groups.

Malaysian firms have core ownership advantages that are best exploited in other developing countries, especially in neighbouring Asia. Petronas and other plantation companies invest overseas in search of resources (such as oil fields and plantation land). In oil and gas and plantation, Malaysian firms have relevant knowledge and expertise in exploration/extraction and technical competencies in plantation management and production. Other firms have also invested abroad in search of new markets, or to improve their export competitiveness.

Corporate social responsibility in Malaysia

Since the 1980s, Malaysian firms have been under pressure to engage in CSR activities. This followed the privatization program implemented in the early 1980s, with the understanding that privatized firms should achieve social objectives and should not focus solely on profit maximization. Although it has gained in importance over the past two decades, CSR in Malaysia is not as widely spread and applied as in neighbouring Asian countries such as Singapore or South Korea. Corporate CSR reporting in the country remains low and companies are yet to fully integrate concepts within their overall strategies.

The Bursa Malaysia CSR framework defines CSR as 'open and transparent business practices that are based on ethical values and respect for the community, employees, the environment, shareholders and other stakeholders' (Said et al., 2009: 213). The government actively encourages companies to adopt CSR practices, for instance, through the Prime Minister's CSR awards. However, CSR disclosure is voluntary.

The levels of CSR disclosure in Malaysian companies is low overall, even though many companies now include some information in their annual reports. Ownership structure is an important factor influencing disclosure, in particular director ownership and the government as a substantial shareholder (two common business attributes) (Ghazali, 2007: 261). This means that, in Malaysia, companies with higher levels of government shareholding, or those with a higher proportion of non-executives sitting on the audit committee board, show higher levels of CSR disclosure (Said et al., 2009).

Implications for expatriates and foreign firms in Malaysia

Over the past few decades, Malaysia has been attractive to foreign firms, and many expatriates live there. These firms are well established and have found Malaysia to be a profitable place to operate, mostly as an export platform to regional and world markets.

There are some considerations that foreign expatriates might want to take into account when doing business there.

- *Respect the unique blend of cultures in Malaysia*: one of Malaysia's strength is its multiculturalism, but this can also create tension if not handled carefully. For instance, many employees may follow different faiths, and respect for religious practices should be carefully integrated into the work environment.

- *Make clear decisions*: a manager is expected to guide employees and take clear decisions. There is respect for hierarchical relationships in Malaysia, which should not prevent a manager from caring for his/her employees and it is generally good to show interest in employees' private lives.

- *Take part in government initiatives*: the government is keen to ensure long-term economic growth of the country. This is why there exist many schemes to encourage relationships between foreign and local firms. Taking part in these schemes can be advantageous financially through tax reduction, and is also positively perceived by authorities. This may provide good business opportunities and enable your firm to discover good local longer-term business partners.

- *Contemplate regional potential*: Malaysia is located in ASEAN, and much of its trade and investment is directed at or comes from neighbouring economies. Thus, being located in Malaysia opens up further business opportunities across the region. Some companies have created regional production networks, while others benefit from the recently implemented Free Trade Agreement in the region.

Conclusion

In this chapter, the past and current trends in the Malaysian Business System have been discussed. Malaysia presents distinct features in terms of key government policies, economic development objectives and a multicultural society. Numerous MNEs have chosen to operate there, and they have done so for a long time. Malaysia is has competitive home MNEs that invest abroad in a variety of sectors.

Despite its economic success over the past few decades, it may not be easy for Malaysia to reach the full developed country status by 2020. Yet, this is a country that has adapted over the years, and as such, it will be worth observing future successes and whether and how it achieves its long-term objective.

Readers will find various questions below that will further enhance understanding of key issues of interest in the case of Malaysia. In particular, the case study of Petronas will provide useful insights into the uniqueness of some globally competitive government-owned Malaysian firms.

Chapter summary

- Malaysia has a multicultural society with some common management features across ethnic groups that mean it is a highly hierarchical group-orientated society, with a strong respect for rules.

- The government has a strong role within the economy, and is interventionist. It engages in positive discrimination in favour of Malays, with emphasis on wider participation in business and access to education.

- Personal relationship building in business can be very important, and social capital is generally strong in Malaysia.

- MNEs have played an important role in the economy over the past few decades, and the government has actively encouraged foreign firms to come and set up businesses within Malaysia.

- Malaysia is a middle-income country with aspiration to be a developed nation by 2020.

- ASEAN countries are important partners commercially for Malaysia, both in terms of trade and FDI.

- Malaysia relies on export for its international competitiveness, and foreign investment accounts for a large share of investment domestically.

- The Chinese ethnic minority is an important actor in business, this has been consolidated by the regional integration and increased commercial links with Mainland China.

- Islam is the primary religion in Malaysia, and the government actively promotes economic activities related to Islam, such as Islamic Finance.

Key concepts

ASEAN: The Association of Southeast Asian Nations is a regional political and economic organization which was established on 8 August 1967 in Bangkok, Thailand, by Indonesia, Malaysia, the Philippines, Singapore and Thailand, with the signing of the ASEAN Declaration. Today, there are 10 ASEAN members, the five founding states, Brunei, Burma (Myanmar), Cambodia, Laos and Vietnam.

Bumiputera: this is a Malaysian term that refers to the *son of the soil*, and is used in the country to describe Malay people. Since the 1970s, affirmative action in public policy favours the participation of Bumiputera in a number of ways, from education to participation in economic activities. As part of the NEP, the Malays were provided a special position in the constitution, especially in Article 153.

Malaysia Master Plan: Malaysia is currently in its tenth plan covering the period 2011–2015. The Malaysia Master Plan provides the broad policy guidelines established by the government to achieve continued economic growth and specify the economic development program, with the aim of achieving high-income status by 2020.

MIDA: the Malaysian Industrial Development Authority is the government's principal agency for the promotion of the manufacturing and services sectors in Malaysia. It was established in 1967 and assists foreign and local companies in their investment project application and implementation.

MNEs: foreign multinational enterprises account for a substantial share of economic activities in Malaysia. They operate in a number of economic sectors, and have a dominant position in the electronics and electrical industry.

Multiculturalism: this refers to ethnic diversity in a country. It is important in Malaysia because its population is composed of multiple cultures, and multiculturalism affects all socio-political and economic issues of the country.

NEP: the Malaysian New Economic Policy was launched in 1971 and ended in 1990, when it was replaced by the National Development Policy. The NEP was a socio-economic restructuring affirmative action program launched to eradicate poverty and inequalities between Malays and non-Malays and grants Malays special preferential treatment to increase their participation in the economy.

NKEA: there are 12 National Key Economic Areas identified in the Malaysian Economic Transformation Program, which cover 11 industries and one geographical territory, namely oil, gas and energy, palm oil, financial services, tourism, business services, electronics and electrical, wholesale and retail, education, healthcare, communications content and infrastructure, agriculture, and the Greater Kuala Lumpur/Klang Valley.

Overseas Chinese Business: a share of corporate ownership is in the hands of people of Chinese origin in Malaysia. Across Asia, Overseas Chinese Business (OCB) refers to companies owned and run by Chinese immigrants. It is often associated with *guanxi* and family lineage, and the concept 'bamboo network' that represents business relationships among OCBs across Asia.

Vision 20:20: this Malaysian ideal was launched by former Prime Minister Mahathir bin Mohamad in 1991, and depicts the vision to achieve full industrialized nation status by the year 2020.

Review questions

1 Describe the role of multiculturalism in Malaysian business, human capital and policy.
2 Explain the characteristics of financial capital, human capital and social capital in the Malaysian business system.
3 What main industries have led to economic growth over the past two decades in Malaysia? Why?
4 What roles have MNEs played in the Malaysian economy over the past three decades and how important are they likely to be in future growth?
5 To what extent have Malaysian firms expanded overseas, in which key sectors and why?

1   FDI is important to the Malaysian economy for a number of reasons. Discuss the advantages and disadvantages of an economy relying on inward FDI, and the importance of also engaging in outward FDI.

2   The Malaysian government has been interventionist in selected areas of the Malaysian economy. Split into two groups. One group will prepare an argument in favour of less intervention by the government in the economy. The other group will prepare an argument in favour of continued strong intervention. The two groups should then enter into a debate and jointly decide as an outcome whether they would suggest more or less intervention.

MINI CASE

Petronas: a multinational of choice

May 2013, Petronas Brazil E&P Limitada prepares to reach an agreement with OGX Petróleo e Gás S.A.. The objective is to acquire 40 per cent of OGX's interest in two offshore blocks, some 95 km off the coast of Rio de Janeiro. This is an important step in consolidating the firm's presence in Brazil, one of the world's top holders of hydrocarbon reserves.

The Petronas – Petroliam Nasional Berhad Group was incorporated in 1974 and is an integrated international oil and gas company. Wholly-owned by the Malaysian Government, it is one of the 13 largest state-owned energy companies in the world; others include Saudi Aramco, Gazprom (Russia), China National Petroleum Corps., National Iranian Oils Co., Petróleos de Venezuela, Petrobas (Brazil). Collectively, state-owned companies control the lion's share of crude oil production. State-owned firms benefit from considerable financial and political support from their home government. Similarly, even when state-owned firms compete for drilling rights at home with multinationals, they have the advantage of also acting as industry regulators.

However, state-owned firms also face the pressure of global competition, variations in global demand and prices, or other challenges such as the production shutdown in South Sudan that caused Petronas' revenues to slip 3 per cent early 2012. Petronas' contractors were asked to cut costs when the company's profits declined in recent years.

The company is very important for Malaysia. The government relies on Petronas' payments to fulfil some of its socio-economic and political objectives. It subsidizes fuel and gas consumption – which contributes to a rising deficit. Malaysians enjoy some of the lowest electricity rates and petrol-pump prices in Asia. Petronas is the country's largest taxpayer and largest source of revenue, and the dividends paid go towards reducing the fiscal deficit. Petronas funds have also, over the years, been channelled towards large construction projects. But large pay-outs slow new investment projects by the company. With declining domestic supplies, Petronas needs to invest in global oil and gas exploration. In fact, Malaysia may become a net oil importer within the coming years.

At home, Petronas manages all of Malaysia's energy reserves, yet, accessing such reserves requires substantial resources. In order to reverse a decline in production, Petronas needs to spend on discovering new energy reserves, and consider international partnerships, such as the joint investment plan with Royal Dutch Shell Plc to recover oil off the coasts of Sarawak and Sabah. The government helps by offering incentives to companies ready to explore deeper and less-profitable fields.

The company is a successful state-owned multinational firm. It ranks among the top 100 of the Fortune Global 500 list. Only one-fifth of its rev-enues is domestic, while nearly half comes from international operations and a little more than a third from exports. Petronas has a presence in most regions of the world, mainly in Asia and Africa. It started exporting to Japan in the mid-1970s and conducted its first direct investment in Vietnam in 1989. The company pursued its internationalization strategy in the 1990s and 2000s to access natural resources (including petroleum reserves), expand its market and access technology and strategic assets. International activities have further helped the company in enhancing competences, staff quality and corporate governance. To succeed, Petronas has a portfolio of cooperative arrangements with other large oil and gas corporations around the world. With strong support at home and increasing international presence, it is no wonder the company's vision is to become a 'Leading Oil and Gas Multinational of Choice'.

Questions

1 What advantages and disadvantages does state ownership have for Petronas?

2 How important is Petronas for the Malaysian economy?

3 Petronas is investing abroad. What are the core advantages it can exploit in foreign markets, where should it operate and what impact does state ownership have on its potential for overseas activities?

Students may also wish to visit the company website and annual reports published online at: http://www.petronas.com.my

Web links

Economic statistics, information on doing business in Malaysia and government support: http://www.mida.gov.my and http://www.miti.gov.my

Social and economic statistics www.statistics.gov.my/

ASEAN statistics: http://www.aseansec.org

References and further reading

ASEAN Secretariat (2013) *ASEAN Investment Report 2012: The Changing FDI Landscape*. Jakarta.

Athukorala, P.C. and Waglé, S. (2011) Foreign Direct Investment in Southeast Asia: Is Malaysia Falling Behind? *ASEAN Economic Bulletin*, 28(2): 115–133.

Athukorala, P.C. (2001) *Crisis and Recovery in Malaysia: The Role of Capital Controls*. Cheltenham: Edward Elgar.

Bank Negara Malaysia (2013) Monthly Statistical Bulletin, accessed 4 December 2013 at: http://www.bnm.gov.my/

Department of Statistics (2011) Population Distribution and Basic Demographic Characteristics, Population and Housing Census of Malaysia, homepage accessed 7 November at: www.statistics.gov.my/

Economic Planning Unit (2012) *The Malaysian Economy in Figure*, Prime Minister's Department, homepage accessed 7 November at: www.epu.gov.my/

EPU (Unit Perancang Ekonomi) (2010): Tenth Malaysia plan, accessed 7 November 2013 at: http://www.epu.gov.my/en/tenth-malaysia-plan-10th-mp-;jsessionid=8BDD6DCC91EEED9EAFF1381C53DC69E8

Ghazali, N.A.M. (2007) Ownership Structure and Corporate Social Responsibility Disclosure: Some Malaysian Evidence. *Corporate Governance*, 7(3): 251–266.

Giroud A. (2003) *Transnational Corporations, Technology and Economic Development: Backward Linkages and Knowledge Transfer in South East Asia*. Cheltenham: Edward Elgar.

Gomez, E.T. (2012) The Politics and Policies of Corporate Development: Race, Rents and Redistribution in Malaysia, in H. Hill, T.S. Yean and R.H.M. Zin, (eds.) *Malaysia's Development Challenges: Graduating from the Middle*. New York: Routledge, pp. 63–82.

Gomez, E. and Jomo, K.S. (2002) *Malaysia's Political Economy: Politics, Patronage and Profits*. Cambridge: Cambridge University Press.

Gupta, V., Hanges, P.J. and Dorfman, P. (2002) Cultural Clusters: Methodology and Findings, *Journal of World Business*, 37: 11–15.

Hill, H., Yean, T.S. and Zin, R.H.M. (2012) (eds.) *Malaysia's Development Challenges: Graduating from the Middle*. New York: Routledge.

Jomo, K.S. and Wee, C.H. (2003) The Political Economy of Malaysian Federalism: Economic Development, Public Policy and Conflict Containment. *Journal of International Development*, 15(4): 441–456.

Lee K. H. and S. Nagaraj (2012) The Crisis of Education, H. Hill, T.S. Yean and R.H.M. Zin, (eds.) *Malaysia's Development Challenges: Graduating from the Middle*. New York: Routledge, pp. 213–232.

MIDA (Malaysian Investment Development Authority (n.d.) Homepage accessed 7 November 2013 at: www.mida.gov.my

PMO (Prime Minister's Office of Malaysia) (n.d.) Homepage accessed 7 November 2013 at: www.pmo.gov.my

Rasiah, R. (1995) *Foreign Capital and Industrialization in Malaysia*. Basingstoke: Macmillan.

Rasiah, R. (2008) Drivers of Growth and Poverty Reduction in Malaysia: Government Policy, Export Manufacturing and Foreign Direct Investment. *Malaysian Journal of Economic Studies*, 45(1): 21–44.

Reinhardt, N. (2000) Back to Basics in Malaysia and Thailand: The Role of Resource-Based Exports in their Export-Led Growth, *World Development*, 28(1): 57–77.

Said, R., Zainuddin, Y.H. and Haron, H. (2009) The Relationship between Corporate Social Responsibility Disclosure and Corporate Governance Characteristics in Malaysian Public Listed Companies, *Social Responsibility Journal*, 5(2): 212–226.

Searle, P. (1999) *The Riddle of Malaysian Capitalism: Rent-Seekers or Real Capitalists?* Singapore: Allen and Unwin.

Trading Economics (2009) Accessed 7 November 2013 at: http://www.tradingeconomics.com/malaysia/unemployment-rate

Wei, Y.A. and Balasubramanyan, V.N. (eds.) (2004) *Foreign Direct Investment: Six Country Case Studies*. Cheltenham: Edward Elgar.

Yap, M.M.C. and Tend, K.K. (2012) Monetary Policy and Financial Sector Development, in H. Hill, T.S. Yean and R.H.M. Zin, (eds.) *Malaysia's Development Challenges: Graduating from the Middle*. New York: Routledge, pp. 106–130.

Yeung, H.W.C. (1998) Transnational Economic Synergy and Business Networks: The Case of Two-Way Investment between Malaysia and Singapore, *Regional Studies*, 32(8): 687.

Yusof, Z.A. (2003) Malaysia's Response to the China Challenge. *Asian Economic Papers*, 2(2): 46–73.

The Business System of the Philippines

14

Mari Kondo

Chapter outline

- The Philippine business system
- Comparative advantage
- Changing trends in the Philippine business system
- International activities of Philippine firms
- Corporate social responsibility (CSR) and Philippine business
- Implications for expatriates and foreign firms in the Philippines

Chapter objectives

After reading this chapter, you should be able to:

1 Understand the business system of the Philippines, especially, how the prolonged high level of inequality has created institutions that harm the competitiveness of Philippine industries (inequality trap).

2 Understand how globalization has reshaped the Philippine comparative advantages, especially in the business process outsourcing sector.

3 Understand the continuity and changes in the Philippine business system, especially in the system of exporting people (migration trap).

4 Understand CSR practices in the Philippines, especially, their important strategic roles in firms and for the public as well as their possible downsides.

Introduction

The Republic of the Philippines lies close to the world's most dynamic and best perform-ing economies, such as China, Korea and Singapore. To many, the performance of the Philippine economy has been a great puzzle. After it gained independence from the United States in 1946 on through the 1950s the Philippines was Asia's second richest country. Half a century later, it is one of the poorest. In 2012 the estimated GDP in real exchange was US$250.3 billion or US$423.7 billion in PPP[1] base, which makes per capita GDP US$4,300 in PPP base (CIA, 2013). The Philippines' self-rated poverty was around 50 per cent in 2011 (SWS, 2013). In 2006, more than 10 per cent of the population fell under the $1-a-day absolute poverty line (ADB, 2007a; PIDS, 2012). Why?

Internationally, the Filipinos are known to be a pleasant, capable and well-educated English-speaking people. The Philippines' population of 97.7 million (December 2013 estimated), mainly of Malay origin, registered as the top 12th most populous in the world and has Asia's highest rate of increase (CIA, 2013). Its literacy rate is 92.6 per cent. The people's official languages are 'Filipino' and English, but 78 languages and 500 other dialects have been identified in the country. Eighty three per cent of Filipinos are Catholic (CIA, 2013).

In 2012, the Philippine economy consisted of a large and growing service sector (57 per cent of GDP), which absorbed 53 per cent of employment. The service sector includes business process outsourcing (BPO) entities such as call centres and back offices, as well as semi-informal sector jobs for the urban poor. The relatively smaller and stagnating industry sector (31 per cent) accounted for only 15 per cent of the jobs; and an even smaller, low-productivity agriculture sector (12 per cent) absorbed 32 per cent most prob-ably the rural poor (CIA, 2013).

The poor performance of the Philippine economy is ascribed primarily to the industry (manufacturing) sector, which is supposedly the engine of growth but remains small and internationally uncompetitive. Except in electronics assembly, usually conducted by foreign MNCs at the export processing zones, low productivity and low technological capabilities characterize domestic manufacturing, which has a high share of low value-added industries such as food, beverage, tobacco and textiles. Since the 1960s this sector has only been able to employ 10 per cent to 15 per cent of the workforce. Consequently, the Philippines has high unemployment (7.1 per cent) and high underemployment (20.9 per cent) rates (NSO, 2013). But why has the Philippine industry not become competitive? Many factors explain why the Philippine economy has not achieved its full potential. For example, the Philippines has a particularly inefficient public administra-tion, endemic corruption and very low levels of trust beyond the specific clan circles. Yet, if asked to name a single root cause for its poor performance, one might advance inequality of wealth and power as a possible answer.

The Philippines is often called the 'Latin America of Asia' because of its unique past experience of both Spanish colonization and US rule. Like those of many Latin American economies, the Philippine economy has been built and run by big elite busi-ness families, some of them descendants of landowners during the Spanish rule. With the Gini coefficient hovering at 40–47, inequality in the Philippines stands out for its persistence and level among Asian countries (ADB, 2007a; Usui, 2012). In 2006, its Gini coefficient was 45.8, ranking it 36th of 136 countries in the world (CIA, 2013). In 2009, the poorest 50 per cent of total households accounted for 20 per cent of total income, while the richest 20 per cent accounted for 52 per cent of total income (IBON Foundation, 2011).

There is growing evidence that this long enduring, very high level of inequality adversely impacts various aspects of competitiveness and the long-term prosperity of society. Society can be caught in a so-called 'inequality trap'.[2] Inequalities reproduce themselves through the interaction of political, economic and socio-cultural inequalities, because the initial existence of unequal power tends to shape institutions that regenerate initial conditions, or exacerbate the status quo. If a high level of inequality persists, it makes reduction of poverty difficult even as the economy grows. It can also hurt economic growth bringing with it political instability and undesirable social consequences (Cornia and Cort, 2001; World Bank, 2005).

Centuries of inequality have influenced the development of the Philippine business system and as a result of these processes it is difficult to make Philippine industry competitive. As a result industry is unable to provide sufficient numbers of jobs so most of the population remains poor. Business institutions and the inequality trap are discussed later.

While the Philippines' industry sector stagnated, globalization and the advancement of IT technologies brought new opportunities to the Philippines. The economy is now exporting its people's skills. With many young English speaking workers business process outsourcing (BPO) is flourishing. This phenomenon is explained in the section on comparative advantage, together with the BPO's limitations for employment and the economy.

To survive, many migrate and work abroad, most of them sent through the country's state coordinated system. In 2009, the estimate of overseas Filipinos was 8.6 million (POEA, 2013), while the country's domestic labor force was estimated at 40.4 million in 2012 (CIA, 2013). Their remittances constituted US$21.4 billion in 2012 (Bangko Sentral ng Pilipinas, 2013), while the balance of Philippine trade was US$9.7 billion (NSO, 2013). It is their remittances and their families' spending that keeps the Philippine economy afloat.

Although the state led migration was started in the 1970s as a temporary measure, now the entire Philippine society leans towards migration. People in the Philippines acknowledge the serious negative effects of migration including brain drain and Dutch disease,[3] which weakens Philippine industries, and therefore makes the Philippine society more dependent on migration. In the changing trends section, I discuss the emerging business system of exporting workers, together with the pitfalls of the 'migration trap'.

In the remaining sections, the international activities of Philippine firms, though limited, and the importance of strategic CSR for firms to operate in the Philippines are described. The final section considers implications for foreign firms and precious lessons that the case of Philippine business systems can provide.

The Philippine business system

In describing the Philippine business system, the following section uses the framework Redding (2005) developed. The major characteristics are presented in Figure 14.1. Large firms are the key players of the economy though they constitute only 3 per cent of enterprises but account for more than 80 per cent of revenues and assets in 2005 (ADB, 2007b). Thus, the characteristics described relate to larger rather than smaller enterprises.

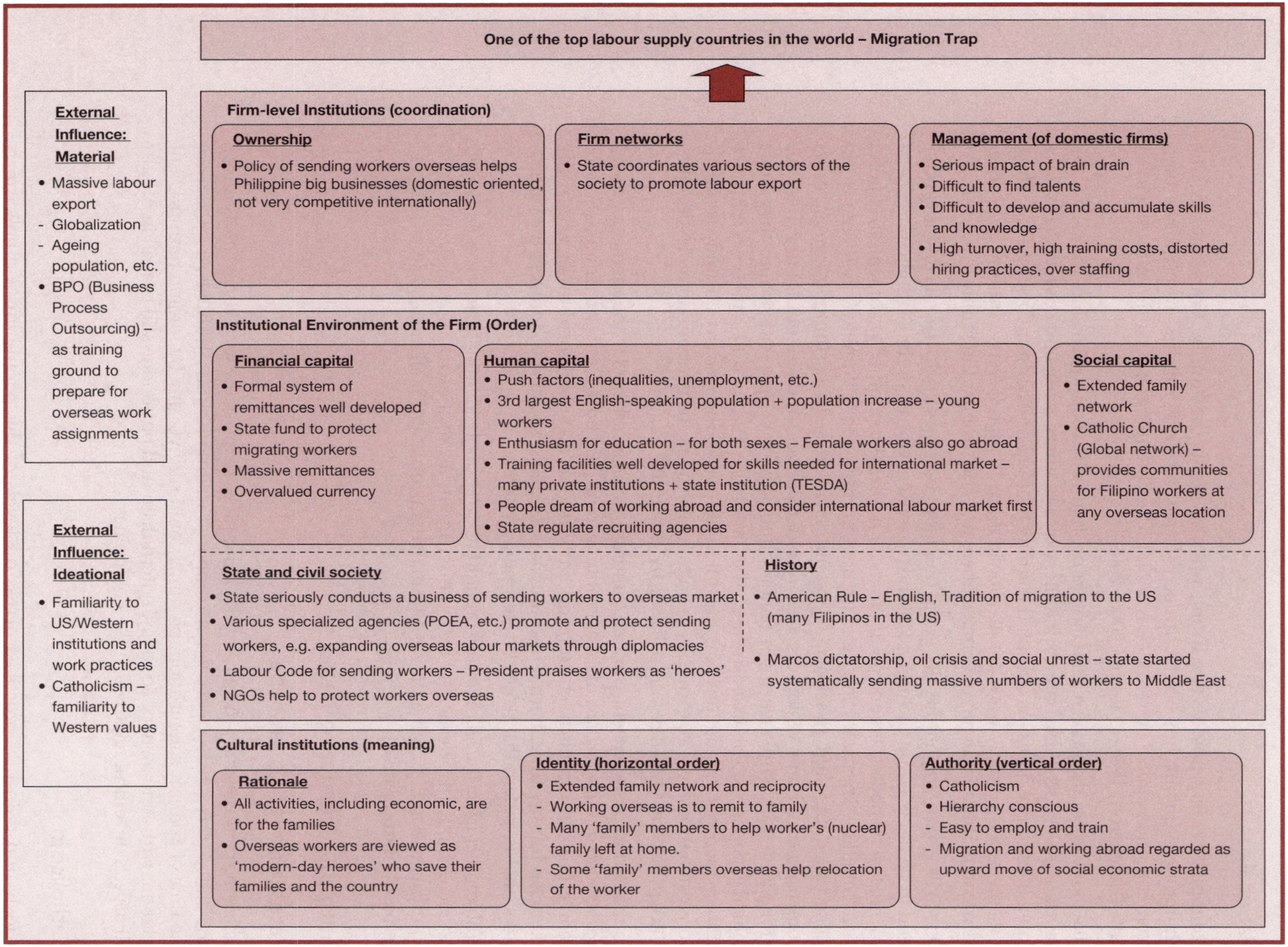

One of the top labour supply countries in the world – Migration Trap

External Influence: Material
- Massive labour export
- Globalization
- Ageing population, etc.
- BPO (Business Process Outsourcing) – as training ground to prepare for overseas work assignments

External Influence: Ideational
- Familiarity to US/Western institutions and work practices
- Catholicism – familiarity to Western values

Firm-level Institutions (coordination)

Ownership
- Policy of sending workers overseas helps Philippine big businesses (domestic oriented, not very competitive internationally)

Firm networks
- State coordinates various sectors of the society to promote labour export

Management (of domestic firms)
- Serious impact of brain drain
- Difficult to find talents
- Difficult to develop and accumulate skills and knowledge
- High turnover, high training costs, distorted hiring practices, over staffing

Institutional Environment of the Firm (Order)

Financial capital
- Formal system of remittances well developed
- State fund to protect migrating workers
- Massive remittances
- Overvalued currency

Human capital
- Push factors (inequalities, unemployment, etc.)
- 3rd largest English-speaking population + population increase – young workers
- Enthusiasm for education – for both sexes – Female workers also go abroad
- Training facilities well developed for skills needed for international market – many private institutions + state institution (TESDA)
- People dream of working abroad and consider international labour market first
- State regulate recruiting agencies

Social capital
- Extended family network
- Catholic Church (Global network) – provides communities for Filipino workers at any overseas location

State and civil society
- State seriously conducts a business of sending workers to overseas market
- Various specialized agencies (POEA, etc.) promote and protect sending workers, e.g. expanding overseas labour markets through diplomacies
- Labour Code for sending workers – President praises workers as 'heroes'
- NGOs help to protect workers overseas

History
- American Rule – English, Tradition of migration to the US (many Filipinos in the US)
- Marcos dictatorship, oil crisis and social unrest – state started systematically sending massive numbers of workers to Middle East

Cultural institutions (meaning)

Rationale
- All activities, including economic, are for the families
- Overseas workers are viewed as 'modern-day heroes' who save their families and the country

Identity (horizontal order)
- Extended family network and reciprocity
- Working overseas is to remit to family
- Many 'family' members to help worker's (nuclear) family left at home.
- Some 'family' members overseas help relocation of the worker

Authority (vertical order)
- Catholicism
- Hierarchy conscious
- Easy to employ and train
- Migration and working abroad regarded as upward move of social economic strata

FIGURE 14.1 Philippine business system based on the Redding model (2005): massive labour export and migration trap

Culture

Rationale

Philippine society has a very strong orientation to the family. Consequently, the Philippine economy has been arranged largely for elite families, who possess both economic and political power (McCoy, 1993). The Philippines is a patrimonial oligarchy state (Hutchcroft, 1988: Quimpo, 2005, 2009).

Like many in Southeast Asia, the Filipinos are bound by cognatic kinship, whereby families trace their roots along both their fathers' and mothers' lines, and boys and girls have equal inheritance rights. As a result the family is broad and constantly spreading. Thus, a member of the family works for an individual as though it were a mutual insurance/help system; hence, the more members there are, the stronger the family.

Due to its expanding nature, the group boundary becomes unclear, and Filipino groups tend to be flexible and inclusive. Filipinos extensively observe the Catholic practice of having several godfathers and godmothers for baptisms and other sacraments to expand their 'families'. They sometimes end up having hundreds of 'families', including workplace colleagues and superiors, to extend social ties. In a similar manner, one's hometown and home region are seen as extensions an individual's family; Filipinos strongly identify with their town/region, language or people with whom they have shared experiences. This extensiveness, the families and clans, and sometimes alliances of them, become foundations of competition for power and resources. Family competitions can be observed, for example, in national elections, local labour union leaderships, office politics and business competitions by elite families.

To make the family system work as a mutual insurance/help for the members, social norms such as *utang na loob* (debt of gratitude to be paid back) and *awa* (compassion for people in need) are instilled from an early age to give reciprocal order within the extended family; these norms also function to create social mechanisms for vertical order, that is, paternalism and the patronage system.

With those norms, the Filipinos are brought up to strongly identify themselves with their extended family. However, the extreme sensitivity to reciprocity in relations tends to obfuscate rationality and professionalism, which can cause inefficiencies in public and corporate management.

Authority (vertical order)

Paternalism and patronage

Reflecting centuries-long inequality, the Philippines is one of the largest power-distanced and status-conscious societies when compared internationally (Hofstede, 1980). Since the time of Spanish colonization, peasants could survive only by forging patron–client relations with land owners. So today, paternalism and patronage still prevail in almost all aspects of vertical relations in the Philippines.

Catholicism

Widely and diligently practiced across all levels of the population, Catholicism is often understood as reflecting their 'worldview', which includes animism and family-centeredness. Catholicism provides symbols and analogies for familial and authoritarian norms that are often used to cement society or organizations.

History and state

History

Before the Spanish (around 1565–1899) and US (1899–1941, 1945–1946) rule, the Philippines consisted of fragmented chiefdoms. While nearly 400 years of colonization brought Catholicism, basic education in English and other numerous influences, it also effected a concentration of wealth among the landed, business and/or highly educated elite families, with political, economic and socio-cultural institutions to support it. Having inherited those initial conditions and institutions, the post-independence Philippine economy has suffered inequality and stagnant growth, while its Asian neighbours, particularly those that gained equality through land reform have been enjoying rapid economic growth.

Post-independence Philippine history can be divided into three. During the first period, Philippine democracy was strongly influenced by the elite families. Reflective of the elite families vested interests Philippine industries were protected by an import-substitution policy, overvalued local currencies and high import tariffs (1950s and 1960s). These created oligopolies with an orientation toward domestic markets (Saldaña, 2001).

During the second period, under the 20-year rule of President Marcos, a dictator, tariff protections for government-preferred industries remained. His rule ended in 1986 following the first 'people power' movement, a peaceful popular mobilization organized by NGO coalitions and alliances of the business elite, the middle classes, the military, labour and the Catholic Church.

During the third period, electoral democracy was restored, again under strong elite influence, but this time, with some NGO voice. Gradual liberalization started in the late 1980s, and later accelerated in the 1990s (Abinales and Amoroso, 2005).

State and civil society

The Philippine state is predatory, but the power of elite business overwhelms state and civil society (Quimpo, 2009).

Weak bureaucracy

The basic structure of the Philippine government is similar to that of the United States. Unlike many other Asian countries the Philippines inherited a poorly-developed bureaucratic structure with 'public service' creating opportunities for corruption. The Philippines has twice as many politically appointed positions as the US, to accommodate families and friends of those in power (World Bank, 2000).

In 2012 the Philippines Corruption Perception Index score was 34[4] giving it a position of 105th worldwide one of the most corrupt in Southeast Asia (Transparency International, 2012).

Regulatory captures

Regulatory capture is the situation whereby an agency that regulates an industry for public interest acts in the industry's interest. It usually happens as a result of political influence or an understanding of the technical knowledge of the industry concerned. Philippine regulators are often 'captured' by the business they are supposed to regulate, and therefore allow high entry barriers and lucrative rent-seeking practices, which lead to the high cost, low quantity and quality supply of goods and services, including key services, for example, electricity (Hutchcroft, 1998; World Bank, 2008).

Resource constraints

The Philippine state suffers from resource constraints because it cannot collect adequate taxes from the wealthy. The Philippine government cannot therefore provide basic services to the population or the infrastructure for business competitiveness.

Unreliable judicial system (rule of law)

A well-functioning, independent judicial system is essential for rule of law, and thus the protection of property rights, to ensure sound investments and exchange decisions. The Philippine judicial system has been perceived to be notably weak, with judges seen to be serving mostly the interest of the wealthy (World Bank, 2000).

Imperfect democracy

Unequal power allows the wealthy to influence the decisions of the masses through vote buying, violence and patronage. As a result, historically, the landed and/or business elite have controlled Philippine legislature. The narrow representation makes it hard to adopt policies to promote the efficient distribution of resources (ADB, 2007b).

'Civil society' of ambiguous natures

The Philippines has a vibrant NGO and PO (People's Organization, such as membership associations of farmers) sector, the third largest in the developing world. These are the key players in the 'people power' democracy (Quimpo, 2005). Yet, some function as extensions of the state (Abinales and Amoroso, 2005) or business (Hedman, 2006; Silliman and Noble, 1998).

Institution

Social capital

Societies with a very high level of inequality possess certain commonalities – erosion of social cohesion, social conflicts and uncertain property rights (Cornia and Court, 2001). The Philippine society is no exception. The general level of trust among Filipinos is much lower than international standards (European Values Study Group and World Values Survey Association, 2006), as is their level of trust towards social institutions.

As described in the above section, a weak public sphere and strong wealth and familial influences means that credentials, such as licenses, are sometimes forged and accounting audits may be weak (World Bank, 2006a). The crime rate is high and there is easy access to guns. Both communist and Muslim insurgencies occur frequently. Property rights are not well protected.

So which institutions are trusted? Discounting family loyalties, the Church enjoyed the highest trust among the institutions studied in 2001(Abad, 2006), showing that family and religion are the backbones of Philippine society.

Financial capital

Banks dominate the small Philippine financial sector. All large domestic Philippine commercial banks are controlled by a few powerful elite families. A long history of regulatory capture and high spread cartel practices have been reported (Hutchcroft, 1998). Most of the people are too poor to save, and the interest rates for savings are low. On the lending side, the World Bank (2008, p. 40) reported that 'Most banks, given their corporate ownership, lend within their conglomerate, limiting access to outsiders or unconnected companies, which face a declining availability of credit.'

Likewise, the stock market of the Philippines is thin, volatile and highly concentrated. As public stock offerings dilute family control, families have been hesitant to go public or if they do, the owning family effectively controls the business through a multilayered pyramid structure. This structure can easily create minor shareholder rights issues, making the market unattractive to investors (Saldaña, 2001).

Philippine corporations use retained earnings for their operations and project investments, with only a few relying on equity (5 per cent) and bank financing (15 per cent) (World Bank, 2006). Meanwhile, small and medium-sized enterprises (SMEs) suffer from difficulties in obtaining finance and its high cost (ADB, 2007b). The small and highly concentrated financial sector has made limited contribution to reducing migration and financing business.

Human capital

Unemployment, inequality, deteriorating education, the brain drain and highly protected formal labour characterize human capital.

Deteriorating public education

In a society with a high level of inequalities, the education of the wider public tends to be neglected because this requires the transfer of resources from the wealthy, who can afford high-quality private education (Birdsall, 2007). In the case of the Philippines, the aforementioned, coupled with the increasing population, has caused the quality of public education to seriously deteriorate. In 2009, the Philippines' expenditure (per GDP) to education was 151th out of 173 countries in the world (CIA, 2013).

Protected formal labour

In order to avoid social and/or labour unrests, the government and business try to buy 'peace' from formal labour. Doing so is easy because the proportion of formal labour is relatively small and tends to be in the traditionally protected sectors, which enjoy high rents. Thus, it is a matter of rent transfers.

The Labour Code issued in the 1970s, when the militant unions linked with the insurgents ensures workers, particularly the rank and file, both job and income security regardless of their performance. Labour unions remain well protected, though they are not as active as before. Institutions that buy 'national labour peace' make formal labour more expensive, generate more informal sector workers and casual workers, and push an increasing number of people to find work overseas.

Business system

Ownership

Family-owned

Almost all the domestic firms in the Philippines are family businesses. By and large, the Philippine economy serves powerful elite families, who constitute a very loosely organized, wealth-based social group, comprising around 60 families (Krinks, 2002). Ethnically, the elite families are mostly composed of the Chinese-Filipinos, descendants of Spanish colonial elites, and the wealthy indigenous groups.

Networking

Highly diversified

The major elite families tend to own highly diversified conglomerates, which reflect their responses to rent-seeking opportunities (Hutchcroft, 1998). Lack of specialization hinders international competitiveness.

Chinese-Filipino business network

For a long period, the Philippine state adopted an exclusion policy towards the ethnic Chinese. However, with their collective power to fund elections through what they called their 'war chest', ethnic Chinese businesses gradually emerged as political allies, and especially in the 1990s, were fully recognized in society (Abinales and Amoroso, 2005).

Overseas networks

Overseas networks are important to create access to resources, including technologies, and for political reasons (see the mini case at the end of the chapter).

Management

Philippine (domestic manufacturing) organizations experience difficulties in coordination, innovation and skill formation. Much of the management effort is concerned with monitoring workers.

Vertical communication: a high level of inequality creates broad differences among workers in terms of their education, proficiency in English, lifestyles and cognitive orientations. In addition, people feel a large power-distance, which inhibits upward communication. The vertical flow of information within the organization is constrained.

Horizontal communication: society is mistrustful. Individuals tend to keep information to themselves – critical knowledge being the source of power.

Engagement: business and firms are run with the owner's family as the focus. As employees are not family members, they tend to feel exploited and are thus less engaged.

Human talents: the deteriorating quality of education and the brain drain restricts the availability of talented workers especially knowledge workers.

Rigid and protected regularized workers: although rank and file workers cannot be promoted, their wages and jobs are secure regardless of their performance. It is hard to motivate them to acquire skills.

Casual labour: because employment of regularized workers is expensive and rigid, management extensively resorts to casual workers. The law only permits them to work for a six-month period. Skill development possibility is minimal.

Moral hazards and monitoring: many Filipino firms suffer from moral hazard behaviours (AIM Hills Governance Centre, 2005) as a result of weak property rights protection, excessive family centeredness, mistrust and a feeling of being exploited, a protective labour law and difficulties in communication and information sharing. Much of the management effort is used to monitor workers. Family business owners directly involve themselves in management to protect their business and properties.

Patronage and paternalism: confronted by the challenges described above, many managements resort to patronage and paternalism to bring 'family' into the organization. Hierarchies of patron–client networks are observed from the top (the owner), to the bottom (casuals) of the organization, and quietly but strongly affect every aspect of people management (Selmer and de Leon, 2001). Many Philippine corporations try to blend a patronage into meritocracy, in order to minimize its negativity (Kondo, 2008). Business organizations try to convey a godfather image to their employees. However, both patronage and paternalism may harm organizational efficiencies. For example, to bring in 'family', Philippine managers tend to show considerable tolerance for workers' moral hazard behaviours.

The following section explains why institutions under the Philippine business system, described above, can be seen as exemplifying 'inequality-trapped capitalism' and how these institutions complement each other.

Culture and state

The power of big businesses owned by elite families overwhelms the state. The weak state favours big business through various methods: corruption, inappropriate tax collection, regulatory capture, inefficient resource allocation and state-related business opportunities such as privatization. Uncollected funds are directed to the rich and as a result the state cannot invest enough on infrastructure such as roads and basic services like education. People in the rural areas are poorly educated and stay poor. The result of regulatory capture is that input prices tend to be high and people and entrepreneurs suffer as a result (Kondo, forthcoming).

Institutions

- *Financial capital*: big business families enjoy wealth created in their banks, while infusing funds to their conglomerates. As deposit rates are low, the peoples' savings are not mobilized. The growth of SMEs is hindered by high finance cost. The small size of the stock market does not help entrepreneurs. The financial sector, which cannot promote efficient resource allocation, manages to widen the gaps further (Kondo, forthcoming).

- *Human capital*: deteriorating public education has been widening socio-economic gaps. The part of rents channelled to regularized workers expands the gaps between them and the non-regularized workers (Kondo, forthcoming).

- *Social capital*: a prolonged high level of inequality might have induced the low trust that people hold of the system and society, including property rights and the law. The fragile social capital hinders transactions and investments, and directly hampers many functions of society that could have helped narrow gaps: the financial system (e.g., from trust to mutual funds), corporate governance (e.g., from trust to auditing), management (e.g., from trust, to people, to delegation and coordination), employment relations (e.g., firing), skills formation (e.g., meritocratic HR practices so workers will be motivated to invest in skills acquisition), and networks (e.g., inter-elite collaboration) (Kondo, forthcoming).

Business system

- *Ownership*: corporations, including public ones, are de facto owned and controlled by families. They can take advantage of minority shareholders because corporate governance is weak. This is because big conglomerates own banks, the stock market is small and the number of circulated shares is limited. Further the directors on the independent board of directors tend to be friends of the family (Kondo, forthcoming).

- *Network*: Filipino elite families lack inter-elite collaborations that could help promote the country's broad developmental objectives (De Dios, 2011).

- *Management*: Reflecting socio-economic divisions, business organizations tend to take on hierarchically divided structures, which further widen gaps. The patron–client system generally discourages workers from engaging and investing in upgrading their skills, thereby widening gaps further (Kondo, forthcoming).

Comparative advantage

While the Philippine industries stagnated, growth in the service industry was the main driver of the economy, accounting for 66 per cent of GDP growth in the past 30 years (Usui, 2012). In the 2000s especially, business process outsourcing (BPO) inclusive of call centres, back office services, software development, and so forth, became the fastest growing sector in the country, growing at an average annual rate of over 30 per cent, and accounting for 5 per cent GDP in 2011 (Usui, 2012). The Philippines has become a top BPO destination, surpassing India. In 2010, Tata Consultancy even established a call centre in Manila. The advantages that the Philippines have that may explain BPO's stunning growth are as follows: (a) it is the third largest English-speaking country in the world (CIA, 2013); (b) it is a young country, registering the third highest increase in its working population; and (c) it maintains cultural ties with the United States.

Yet, some are cautious about exaggerations pertaining to the contribution that BPO and the service sector can provide to Philippine society overall. First, in terms employment: although employment in the BPO sector grew by 35 per cent between 2004 and 2009, its overall impact is limited. In 2009 the BPO sector employed around 1.2 per cent of the total labour force and is forecast to employ only 3 per cent in 2016 (Usui, 2012). The second issue has to do with the fact that low-end call centre jobs dominate Philippine BPO. To sustain its current growth, moving up the knowledge ladder is necessary, which requires highly specific skills in various specialized fields such as banking or accounting (Usui, 2012). The third issue is labour productivity, especially when Philippine industries stagnate. Usui (2012) pointed out that the Philippines is the only country in the region where the industry sector reduced its output and employment shares from 1980 to 2009. The development of the service sector alone is not sufficient for competitiveness.

Continuity and change in the Philippine business system

In the 1970s, the Philippine state started to coordinate the sending of migrant workers as a way of averting social unrest that was occurring as a result of high unemployment, poverty and the foreign economic crisis. Eventually, this evolved into a well-organized national system. Domestic businesses began to enjoy higher consumption and expanded partly due to the remittances received by the families of overseas Filipino workers. Over time, motivating and exporting workers became a very serious state business, with the President of the republic referring to these workers for being 'modern-day heroes' during a national ceremony in the presidential palace. President Arroyo reiterated this accolade annually.

A massive number of people have migrated through the years such that the Philippines has emerged as one of the top suppliers of migrant labour. Having heard the praise conferred by the president on returning workers and witnessing how the workers' families have become apparently well-off in their communities, many Filipino children dream of migrating rather than working in the Philippines. Through the years, the Philippines has developed various migration institutions, which are recognized as among the most sophisticated in the world (Ruiz, 2008). Some of the features of the emerging business system in the Philippines that promote migration follow.

Culture

Extended family systems with the culture of supporting each other make it easy for a worker to decide to migrate abroad. Many family members provide support at home, such as taking care of children, and the worker can also depend on his/her relatives abroad.

The Catholic Church maintains its anti-birth control stance. As a result, the country enjoys a young and growing population. The admiration for migrant workers as heroes has prevailed.

History and state

The historical relationship of the Philippines with the United States has provided the Filipino people a facility for English and familiarity with western culture. It has also influenced Filipinos to think of migration as a way of moving upward in the socio-economic stratum.

The Philippine state actively develops foreign labour markets always including it in the agenda of trade negotiations. The state orchestrates the systematic exportation of a massive number of workers, 1.6 million in case of 2011, through the Philippine Overseas Employment Administration (POEA) and other agencies (POEA, 2013). The state mounts campaigns extolling migrant workers as 'heroes' of the Philippines. Civil-society NGOs try to protect migrant workers, sometimes in coordination with the state.

Institutions

Financial systems for remittances are well developed and regulated. On the negative side, the Philippine peso tends to appreciate with the volume of foreign currency remittances, thereby hurting the export industry in the country. For many Filipinos today, the labour market is not merely domestic but international. Many private education institutions provide training for international hiring, quickly responding to the skills needed by international labour markets. The POEA and other agencies, in consonance with the provisions of the Labour Code, regulate private recruitment agencies and provide some protection to migrant workers. In terms of social capital, alongside extended family networks, the global network of the Catholic Church provides the social capital needed in overseas communities.

Business system

The interests of the elite and large business conglomerates in the Philippines are well protected by the sending of Filipino workers abroad. This is because domestic oriented businesses, which they operate, flourish even in the absence of international competition.

The state coordinates various related sectors, including finance, education, media and NGOs. The BPO industry serves as a training ground that prepares workers for migration. Migrations affect the management of Philippine firms. The brain drain is a serious problem. Firms need to keep training their skilled workers, professionals and managers. Many firms just give up on skills and knowledge accumulation, thus giving up gaining international competitiveness.

Although the sending of workers abroad may serve as a quick fix, in the long run, it further burdens Philippine society by making it difficult for industries to become competitive. In the absence of international competitiveness, industries cannot provide much needed employment to Filipino workers. This makes it necessary for workers to seek employment abroad. This is a vicious circle and the economy and society of the

Philippines seem to be trapped in the sweetness of sending workers abroad. This situation can be described as the 'migration-trap'.

As discussed, because Philippine capitalism is 'inequality-trapped', it is not possible to develop a competitive industry sector to provide sufficient employment and therefore it is necessary massive numbers of workers to work abroad to earn foreign exchange and ease the pressure of the unemployed population. For the workers, the only way out from capitalism where comprehensive systems of regenerating inequality exist is to move out of the Philippines and work outside the inequality-trapped system. We may say that a trajectory from 'inequality-trapped' to 'migration-trapped' capitalism in the Philippines seems to exist.

International activities of Philippine firms

Philippine firms are not very active internationally. The obvious reason behind this phenomenon is that Philippine firms, especially in manufacturing, are not competitive: most of them are not interested in international expansion. Yet, some firms are operating internationally.

- SM Investment Corporation (SMIC) stated in 1948 as a shoe manufacturer and a shoe store. Then it became a department store and eventually a mall developer, with two banks under its name. SM has opened six malls in China (Gutierez and Rodrigues, 2013; SMIC, 2013).

- Bench started by selling men's T-shirts in 1987. As of January 2013, Bench has 595 domestic stores, and 83 stores internationally, particularly in the United States, the Middle East and China (Bench, 2013).

- VMV Hypoallergenics is a skincare and cosmetic brand established in 1979. It now has stores in Italy, Mexico, Singapore, Thailand, the United Arab Emirates and the United States (VMV Hypoallergenics, 2013).

- Jollibee Foods Corporation, which started in 1978, enjoys the largest share in the fast food market in the Philippines. There are 750 Jollibee restaurants in the country and more than 80 stores internationally (in the United States, the Middle East, Southeast Asia and China) (Jollibee Foods Corporation, 2013; Gutierez and Rodrigues, 2013). In March 2012, it was reported that as a group, it had 2,004 outlets throughout the Philippines and 509 stores abroad (Gutierez and Rodrigues, 2013).

- The San Miguel Corporation, founded in 1890, is the food, beverage and packaging giant in Southeast Asia. SMC enjoys a large market share, with its beer accounting for 95 per cent of market sales. As its performance was affected by domestic economic rises and downturns, SMC internationalized aggressively in the late 1980s to the 1990s for risk diversification, and further in the 2000s. It has operations in China, Australia, Vietnam and various other Southeast Asian countries. Its flagship, San Miguel Beer, is one of the world's top 10 beer brands (Gutierez and Rodrigues, 2013; San Miguel Corporation, 2013).

The international activities of Filipino firms have four characteristics:

1. Most of the internationally active Filipino firms are in light industries including food, beverage and clothing or are in services.

2. Consumer-oriented businesses tend to select locations where many Filipinos migrate temporarily or permanently. These locations include the United States, the Middle East, Hong Kong and some Southeast Asian countries.

3. Firms of Filipino Chinese owners tend to expand to mainland China and/or Taiwan.

4. Some giants which experienced saturation levels in the Philippine domestic markets have chosen to expand internationally, in search of higher growth and risk diversification.

Corporate social responsibility (CSR)

Philippine CSR, largely conducted by elite business including well-established multinationals and traditionally understood as philanthropy, has been very active and even highly praised internationally. Philippine CSR has a long history, having originated in the donations made to churches and hospitals. After government allowed donations for social development to be tax deductible in 1958, many big firms created their own corporate foundations (Magno, 2004).

In 1970, hoping to counter the rise of social unrest and insurgency, elite businesses jointly formed an umbrella CSR NGO, which eventually promoted community relations (comrel) techniques among member companies (Philippine Business for Social Progress, 2000). In essence, comrel is a firm's way of depicting itself as the socially just paternalistic 'godfather' of the community. Widely practiced, it has helped contain insurgency at the community level.

With the emergence of 'people power' in mid 1980s, a popular mobilization mechanism, as a new concept of 'democracy', the capability to organize the masses through a coalition of NGOs became critical for business elites to maintain their influence over state power – including ousting two presidents in the process. Philippine CSR further evolved as the 'people power' movement in the late 1980s to the 1990s, with the formation of nationwide CSR NGO networks for issues beyond comrel's purview (Roman, 2007). Meanwhile CSR NGO executives, who became political appointees to cabinet positions, started to address the concerns of the poor.

In the 2000s, global enthusiasm represented by the UN Global Compact to achieve its Millennium Development Goals enhanced the legitimization of Philippine CSR institutions. A social consensus appeared to be developing whereby big business should consolidate CSR efforts to shoulder national development agendas such as education (Roman, 2007).

At the same time, the big conglomerates of the Philippines started to realize the importance of the bottom of the pyramid market and the value of their accumulated knowledge on dealing with the poor, for example, Ayala's Manila Water Corporation realized profits from providing piped water to poor (see the mini case at the end of the chapter for details).

Reflecting a weak state vis-à-vis strong business, Philippine CSR is becoming a national institution. At the annual 'CSR Expo', rich corporations posited that they have been shouldering responsibilities along the lines of what, traditionally, the state should be assuming. Given the constrained resources of the state, the Philippines has been left with no choice but to promote philanthropic CSR.

Vogel (2005, p. 170) argues that, 'Not only is CSR not a substitute for effective government, but the effectiveness of much civil regulation depends on a strong and well-functioning public sphere.' A survey found that donations to communities and other charities may discourage the elite from paying higher taxes (Clarke and Sison, 2003). The state that cannot collect enough tax from the wealthy cannot provide much needed basic services to the wider public. Although unintended, the Philippine CSR may, in fact, result in weakening the state's power further. This can, in turn, lead to further dependence of the state on the CSR of big business.

Implications for expatriates and foreign firms in the Philippines

The Philippines is a pleasant country to work in because of its being largely English-speaking and the existence of US business systems. Thanks to their cognatic kinship, which values both genders equally, the Filipinos accept either gender with amazing ease. Yet, expatriates and foreign firms in the Philippines face challenges, as well as opportunities, from the business systems described so far.

Concerning the high level of inequalities, initially, an expatriate may feel the Philippines as a paradise because most of the country's systems are made for the wealthy. Many expatriates can thus afford to live in huge houses resembling resort villas in gated residential communities, complete with swimming pools, beautiful tropical gardens, and special quarters for domestic helpers and a driver.

Nonetheless, living in the Philippines means living in a dichotomy. The high incidence of crime necessitates that gated residential areas be protected by armed security guards, just like one's office. Expatriates should not forget about the large power distance. Filipino subordinates tend not to tell bad news directly. They may expect a certain level of paternalism toward them, their family members and even their communities.

The massive levels of migration create serious challenges for human resource management. Finding managers and professionals with the right experience and skills is difficult. Therefore, most large Philippine corporations, besides giving on-the-job training, provide good western style training to managers and professionals at their training centres (Ofreneo, 2003). Still they face difficulties in retention, as reflected in high turnover rates (Di Gropello, 2010).

The more talented they are, the more likely the employees are to take international assignments and leave – effectively draining the supply of knowledge workers in the Philippines (Alburo and Abella, 2002). To cope, some multinational corporations take various measures, such as: encouraging global assignments of talented workers within the multinational company; avoiding the hiring of top notched talent because they will leave soon; training and promoting relatively low qualified employees so that they will stay; making the workplace more staffed than necessary to prepare for the eventuality that some employees will leave.

Conclusion

1. As the Philippine economy has not been a successful one compared to many other Asian countries, it can be easily ignored. However, the country can provide precious insights to other societies in the midst of the current globalization.

2. The Philippine case provides a good example of inequality-trapped capitalism. The Philippines is a democratic country, with an educated population. Nobody in the country believes it is good to have a society where a high level of inequalities persists. Yet, in reality, it is hard to change the system. Under the on-going globalization, inequalities are growing in many countries. The Philippine experience alerts us to exert considerable efforts to make societies inclusive, before inequalities widen and persist further.

3. The Philippine case also provides a good example of migration-trapped capitalism. In the Philippines, nobody believes it is good to keep sending workers abroad permanently. Yet, again, in reality, it is hard to change the country's dependence on migrant workers. Under the on-going globalization, domestic and international labour markets are converging and massive numbers of people are migrating to work in many parts of the world. The Philippine experience alerts us to seriously look at the costs and benefits of migration in societies and the world at large, especially in the long-term.

Chapter summary

- The Philippine economy has not achieved its full potential, though it had and still has many elements for success. Its industry sector has remained small and uncompetitive, and cannot provide enough jobs to the growing population.

- The Philippines is a patrimonial oligarchy state. Its economy has been basically run by and made for big elite business families. The Philippines is a highly unequal society with only a few rich and very many poor people. Even when the economy grows, poverty eradication is slow.

- The prolonged high level of inequalities has hurt its economy and hindered its becoming more competitive. Prolonged high level of inequalities also shape political, economic and social institutions to regenerate inequalities, so that the powers can be maintained, making it difficult to address inequalities. The Philippines may in fact be experiencing an 'inequality-trapped' capitalism.

- Amid globalization, the Philippines exports its peoples' skills through business process outsourcing, a business which is currently flourishing. Yet, the contribution of BPO to the country's employment and economy can only be limited, and cannot serve as a replacement for a competitive industry sector.

- The Philippines has become one of the top suppliers of migrant labour worldwide. Various business system institutions that enable the sending of massive numbers of workers abroad have been developed. Migration causes brain drain and Dutch disease, which has hurt Philippine industries to the extent of limiting its international competitiveness, thereby further deepening the country's dependence on overseas workers to keep the economy afloat. The Philippines may be experiencing 'migration-trapped' capitalism.

- The international activities of Filipino firms are limited in light industries and services. They tend to expand to where many Filipino workers migrate, or in China and/or Taiwan in the case of Filipino Chinese owners. Some giant corporations, including San Miguel, which dominate the local Philippine markets, have chosen to expand internationally in the quest for higher growth and to diversify risks associated with the ups and downs of the Philippine economy.

- Philippine firms conduct strategic CSR in order to secure a right to operate and tackle the BPO market. The Philippines may need to strengthen its public sphere. Otherwise, the active philanthropic CSR of Philippine big business may indirectly harm the state's role and power over business and its citizens.

- Although the Philippines can be easily ignored because its has not been as successful as neighbouring countries it may provide valuable insights when considering future business systems amid globalization.

Key concepts

Cognatic kinship: Filipinos subscribe to cognatic kinship, which reckons equal descent through males and females. As a result of the extensiveness created by the system families and clans become the foundation of competitions for power and resources.

Inequality traps: inequalities reproduce themselves through the interaction of political, economic, and socio-cultural inequalities (Prolonged severe inequality can hurt economic growth, and bring political instability and undesirable social consequences).

Migration trap: the Philippine state coordinates 'people exports' to earn foreign exchange and ease social unrest. Because of the brain drain it creates migration restrains the economy's competitiveness, which further deepens the dependence of the economy on the remittances of workers overseas.

Philippine CSR: Philippine CSR, which started as a business response to social unrest, has evolved to an important subsystem in the country.

Review questions

1 What are the characteristics of the Philippine economy?
2 Why can the Philippine economy not achieve its full potential? How does this phenomenon relate to its business system?
3 How has globalization affected the Philippine economy?
4 How has sending workers overseas affected Philippine society? What are the benefits and downsides of migration?
5 What roles has Philippine CSR played in society, and for business competitiveness?

1 Search the internet for the countries that have had high levels of inequalities over a long period. Discuss with your classmates the impacts of inequalities on their business and management systems.

2 With your classmates, discuss the migrant policy of your country. Considering the costs and benefits of migration to sending and receiving countries, what are the possible measures for making migration beneficial to both sides?

MINI CASE

The Ayala Group: BPO as its competitive edge

The Ayala Group of Companies is one of the most reputable conglomerates in the Philippines. Pyramidically arranged, the Ayala family's Mermac, a private corporation, holds the majority of the shares of the public Ayala Corporation (AC). AC effectively controls several public operational companies and their subsidiaries, through direct or cross shareholdings.

Founded in 1834, Ayala has grown with the history of the Philippines. For example, its Bank of the Philippine Islands issued the country's first currency notes. After World War II, Ayalas successfully converted their Hacienda Makati into the country's biggest business centre. Then, during the Marcos era, Ayala avoided sequestration by incorporating AC to allow wider shareholdings, inviting Mitsubishi of Japan from where Marcos obtained large funds as aid; and strictly upholding the family policy of not being 'clearly' involved in politics.

In the 1990s, Ayala entered the liberalized sectors through alliances with multinationals, thereby creating the nation's second largest telecommunications company and the world's most successful water utility to service urban poor. Ayala also developed an export-oriented industrial park that has helped attract many hi-tech FDIs. In the 2000s, Ayala started to invest in IT and the BPO industries. Currently, their diversification targets are BPO and infrastructure, including international property development.

Many consider the Ayala management as having various advantages vis-à-vis other Filipino family conglomerates. Ayala's organizational characteristics are: (i) one side of the Ayala family holds majority of Mermac, while another manages AC; (ii) Ayala purposely restricts the number of family members involved in top management to three, with 60 as the mandatory retirement age for all; and (iii) it has paternalistic policies, through which Ayala has instilled 'stewardship' even among its non-family management teams. Ayala is also known for the Ayala Foundation, which has had a long history of community relations and other CSR activities that seek to contribute 'to the eradication of poverty in all its forms'.

The excellence of the Ayala management vis-à-vis other Filipino family conglomerates is demonstrated by its water concession business, the Manila Water Company (MWC). In 1997, the Metro Manila Water System was privatized. Metro Manila was partitioned into two service areas, and the concessions were awarded to two competing firms – Manila Water Company, which was to provide water service for Manila's lowest-income area (60 per cent of the population), and Maynilad, which was to service the remaining population. In the following years, Maynilad went bankrupt, MWC, on the other hand, has been thriving.

From the start, MWC regarded the bottom of the pyramid market as a business opportunity rather than as a charity case, and integrated this value into its corporate strategies. The challenges for the MWC were many. It needed to expand the reach of water services to unserved communities, where the average monthly income in low-income areas was US $133. In some areas, banking institutions for payment collection did not exist, and even if these existed, the poor did not have access to them. Eighty per cent of the low-income households are informal settlers, that is, they do not have legal property rights and live in shanties that lack taps, toilets or even access roads. Illegal water connections are rampant in these communities, making them a major source of 'non-revenue water' that also causes damage to pipes.

Initially, people in these communities were hesitant to pay a one-time installation fee for 'piped-in' water despite the fact that vended water would be nearly ten times more expensive in the long run. MWC worked with community leaders to implement programs that educated the people about the benefits of legal, 'piped-in' water. It offered flexible payment and delivery schemes, allowing customers to pool resources for installation payments. By facilitating group payments, MWC managed to make the poor pay. Ayala Foundation and its people's BPO knowledge accumulated through years of community relations activities greatly helped in the conceptualization of these schemes.

After partnering with local communities in developing a profitable yet mutually beneficial relationship, the company reported record high profits in 2012. MWC has also expanded its interests in Vietnam, acquiring nearly 49 per cent of a Ho Chi Minh City water utility. Ayala's ability to manage the bottom of the pyramid has become its competitive edge, valuable even in international markets.

Questions

1 What internal and external factors have helped Ayala grow?

2 In which aspects has the management of Ayala been typical or atypical of Philippine business?

3 What roles can conglomerates, such as Ayala, play to advance the Philippine society?

Sources

Ayala Corporation homepage, accessed 8 November 2013 at: www.ayala.com.ph

Ayala Foundation homepage, accessed 8 November 2013 at: www.ayalafoundation.org

Batalla, E. (1999) Zaibatsu Development in the Philippines, *Southeast Asian Studies*, 37(1): 18–49.

Gibson, K. (2002) A Case for the Family-Owned Conglomerate, *McKinsey Quarterly*, 4: 126–137

Manila Water homepage, accessed 8 November 2013 at: http://www.manilawater.com/Pages/Index.aspx

Wright, C. (2006) All about Ayala, *Asia Money*, 26–28 May.

Wu, X. and Malaluan, N. (2008) A Tale of Two Concessionaires, *Urban Studies*, 45(1): 207–229.

Web links

Socioeconomic data and research papers: http://www.pids.gov.ph/

On culture: http://www.filipinolinks.com/

On society: http://www.sws.org.ph/

Notes

1   PPP, or Purchasing Power Parity, is the exchange rate between two currencies that gives equal purchasing powers in the two economies involved.

2   The mechanism of the trap was explained as follows: 'The interaction of political, economic, and sociocultural inequalities shapes the institutions and rules in all societies. The way these institutions function affects people's opportunities and their ability to invest and prosper. Unequal economic opportunities lead to unequal outcomes and reinforce unequal political power. Unequal power shapes institutions and policies that tend to foster the persistence of the initial conditions' (World Bank, 2005).

3   Dutch disease is the negative impact on an economy of a sharp inflow of foreign currency usually caused by an increase in the exploitation of natural resources. The currency appreciation, as a result, makes the other products of the country, often from the manufacturing or agricultural sector, less competitive in both export and domestic markets, and can lead to deindustrialization or the weakening of the sector concerned.

4   A score of 100 indicates a country is considered very clean and free of corruption whereas a score of 0 indicates a highly corrupt society.

References and further reading

Abad, R.G. (2006) *Aspects of Social Capital in the Philippines: Findings from a National Survey*. Manila: Social Weather Stations.

Abinales, P. and Amoroso, D. (2005) *State and Society in the Philippines*. Lanhan, ML: Rowman & Littlefield.

ADB (2007a) *Key Indicators 2007: Inequality in Asia*. Manila: Asian Development Bank.

ADB (2007b) *Philippines: Critical Development Constraints*. Manila: Asian Development Bank.

AIM Hills Governance Centre (2005) *Towards Improved Corporate Governance: A Handbook on Developing Anti-Corruption Programs*. Manila: Asian Institute of Management.

Alburo, F.A. and Abella, D.I. (2002) Skilled Labor Migration from Developing Countries: Study on the Philippines. International Migration Papers, 51. Geneva: ILO.

Bangko Sentral ng Pilipinas (2013) Overseas Filipinos Remittances, accessed 8 November 2013 at: http://www.bsp.gov.ph/statistics/keystat/ofw.htm

Bench (2013) Homepage, accessed 8 November 2013 at: http://www.bench.com.ph/

Birdsall, N. (2007) Inequality Matters: Why Globalization Doesn't Lift All Boats. *Boston Review*, March/April 2007.

CIA (Central Intelligence Agency) (2013) The World Factbook, accessed 4 December 2013 at: https://www.cia.gov/library/publications/the-world-factbook/geos/rp.html

Clarke, G. and Sison, M. (2003) Voices From the Top of the Pile: Elite Perceptions of Poverty and the Poor in the Philippines, *Development and Change*, 34(2): 215–242.

Cornia, G.A. and Court, J. (2001) Inequality, Growth and Poverty in the Era of Liberalization and Globalization, *Policy Brief*, 4.

De Dios, E.J. (2011) Governance, Institutions, and Political Economy, in D. Canlas, M.E. Khan and J. Zhuang (eds.) *Diagnosing the Philippine Economy*. London: Anthem Press, pp. 295–336.

Di Gropello, E. (2010) *Skills for the Labor Market in the Philippines*. Washington DC: World Bank.

European Values Study Group and World Values Survey Association (2006) European and World Values Surveys Four-wave Integrated Data File, 1981-2004, V. 20060423, 2006. Inter-University Consortium for Political and Social Research, accessed 4 December 2013 at: http://www.icpsr.umich.edu/icpsrweb/ICPSR/studies/4531

Gutierrez, B.P.B. and Rodriguez, R.A. (2013) Diversification Strategies of Large Business Groups in the Philippines. *Philippine Management Review*, 20: 65–82.

Hedman, E.E. (2006) *In the Name of Civil Society: Contesting Free Elections in the Post–colonial Philippines*. Honolulu: University of Hawaii Press.

Hofstede, G. (1980) Motivation, Leadership and Organization: Do American Theories Apply Abroad? *Organizational Dynamics*, 9(1): 42–63.

Hutchcroft, P.D. (1998) *Booty Capitalism: The Politics of Banking in the Philippines*. Quezon City: Ateneo de Manila University Press.

IBON Foundation (2011) Submission by IBON Foundation, a Philippine NGO, to UN Human Rights Council (UNHRC) for Universal Periodic Review (UPR) of the Philippines during the 13th UPR Session (21 May–1 June 2012), accessed 8 November 2013 at: http://lib.ohchr.org/HRBodies/UPR/Documents/session13/PH/IF_UPR_PHL_S13_2012_IBONFoundation_E.pdf

Jollibee Foods Corporation (2013) About Us, accessed 8 November 2013 at: http://www.jollibee.com.ph/about–us

Kondo, M. (2008) Twilling *bata-bata* into Meritocracy: Merito-Patronage Management System in a Modern Filipino Corporation. *Philippine Studies*, 56: 251–284.

Kondo, M. (forthcoming) The Philippines: Inequality Trapped Capitalism, in M. Witt and G. Redding (eds.) *The Oxford Handbook of Asian Business Systems*. Oxford: Oxford University Press.

Krinks, P. (2002) *The Economy of the Philippines: Elites, Inequalites and Economic Restructuring*. London: Routledge.

Magno, F.A. (2004) Investing in Corporate Social Responsibility: Corporate-Community Engagement in Cebu City, Philippines, in M.E. Contreras (ed.) *Corporate Social Responsibility in the Promotion of Social Development*. Washington DC: Inter-American Development Bank.

McCoy, A.W. (1993) An Anarchy of Families: A Historiography of the State and the Family in the Philippines, in A.W. McCoy (ed.) *An Anarchy of Families: State and Family in the Philippines*. Madison, WI: University of Wisconsin Press, pp. 1–32.

NSO (National Statistics Office) (2013) Statistics, accessed 4 December 2013 at: http://www.census.gov.ph/index.html

Ofreneo, R.E. (2003) Philippines, in M. Zanko and M. Ngui (eds.) *Handbook of Human Resource Management Policies and Practices in Asia-Pacific Economics*. Cheltenham: Edward Elgar.

Philippine Business for Social Progress (2000) *Our Legacy*. Manila.

Philippine Institute for Development Studies (2013) Economic and Social Database, accessed 8 November 2013 at: http://econdb.pids.gov.ph/tablelists/table/484

PIDS (Philippine Institute for Development Studies) (2012) Economic and Social Database, accessed 8 November 2013 at: http://econdb.pids.gov.ph/tablelists/table/303

POEA (Philippine Overseas Employment Administration) (2013) Stock Estimate of Overseas Filipinos, accessed 8 November 2013 at: http://www.poea.gov.ph/stats/Stock per cent20Estmate per cent202009.pdf

Quimpo, N.G. (2005) Oligarchic Patrimonialism, Bossism, Electoral Clientelism, and Contested

Democracy in the Philippines, *Comparative Politics*, 37(2): 229–250.

Quimpo, N.G. (2009) The Philippines: Predatory Regime, Growing Authoritarian Features. *Pacific Review*, 22(3): 335–353.

Redding, G. (2005) The Thick Description and Comparison of Societal Systems Of Capitalism, *Journal of International Business Studies*, 36(2): 123–155.

Roman, F.L. (2007) Philippine CSR over Five Decades: Networks, Drivers, and Emerging Views, in V. Santos (ed.) *Doing Good in Business Matters: CSR in the Philippines*. Manila: Asian Institute of Management and De La Salle Professional Schools, pp. 44–91.

Ruiz, N.G. (2008) Managing Migration: Lessons from the Philippines. *Migration and Remittance Brief 6*. Washington DC: World Bank.

Saldaña, C.G. (2001) Philippines, in M. Capulong, D. Edwards, D. Webb and J. Zhuang, (eds.) *Corporate Governance and Finance in East Asia*. Manila: Asian Development Bank, pp. 155–228.

San Miguel Corporation (2013) Homepage, accessed 8 November 2013 at: http://www.sanmiguel.com.ph/

Selmer, J.C. and de Leon, C. (2001) Pinoy-style HRM: Human Resource Management in the Philippines, *Asia Pacific Business Review*, 8(1): 127–144.

Silliman, G.S. and Noble, L.G. (1998) Citizen movements and Philippine Democracy, in G.S. Silliman and L.G. Noble (eds.) *Organizing For Democracy: NGOs, Civil Society, and the Philippine State*. Honolulu: University of Hawaii Press.

SMIC (SM Investment Corporation) (2013) Homepage, accessed 8 November 2013 at: http://sminvestments.com/smic/?p=248

SWS (Social Weather Stations) (2013) Self-rated Poverty: Families Who are 'Mahirap': Philippines April 1983 to Sep 2011, accessed 4 December 2013 at: http://www.sws.org.ph/

Transparency International (2012) Corruption Perception Index 2012. , accessed 8 November 2013 at: http://cpi.transparency.org/cpi2012/

Usui, N. (2012) *Taking the Right Road to Inclusive Growth: Industrial Upgrading and Diversification in the Philippines*. Manila: Asian Development Bank.

VMV Hypoallergenics (2013) Homepage, accessed 8 November 2013 at: http://www.vmvhypoallergenics.com/

Vogel, D. (2005) *The Market for Virtue*. Washington DC: Brookings Institution Press.

World Bank (2000) *Combating Corruption in the Philippines*. Washington DC.

World Bank (2005) *World Development Report 2006: Equity and Development*. Washington DC.

World Bank (2006a) *Philippines – Report on the Observance of Standards and Codes (ROSC): Accounting and Auditing Update*. Washington DC.

World Bank (2006b) *Philippines – Report on the Observance of Standards and Codes (ROSC): Corporate Governance Country Assessment*. Washington DC.

World Bank (2008) *Rising Growth, Declining Investment: The Puzzle of the Philippines Breaking the 'Low–Capital–Stock' Equilibrium*. Washington DC.

15

The Business System of Thailand

Pornkasem Kantamara

Chapter outline

Chapter objectives

After reading this chapter, you should know about:

Introduction

The Kingdom of Thailand (previously known as Siam) is a developing country situated in Southeast Asia covering an area of nearly 513,115 square kilometers. It is roughly the size of France. Thailand shares land borders with Myanmar (Burma) in the north and west, the Andaman Sea in the west, Laos in the north and north-east, Cambodia and the Gulf of Thailand in the east, and Malaysia in the south. With the shape of the country resembling that of an ancient axe, with the peninsula being the handle, combined with the richness of its natural resources, Thailand is also called 'A Golden Axe'.

Thailand's capital and largest city is Bangkok or 'Krung thep' in Thai language, which means 'City of Angels'. The national and official language is Thai, while English is widely spoken by: the younger generation, particularly school or university students; business people in Bangkok; and in business circles. The population of Thailand was estimated at 67 million in 2013, more than 10 million of whom live in Bangkok. Furthermore, according to the National Economic and Social Development Board (NESDB), the biggest ethnic group of Thailand is Thai (75 per cent), with Chinese 14 per cent and others 11 per cent. Almost 95 per cent of Thai people are Buddhist, 4.6 per cent Muslim, 0.7 per cent Christian and others 0.1 per cent (NESDB, 2007).

An overview of the Thai economy

Thailand is an agricultural country that enjoys an abundance of natural resources: mountains, forests, rivers, minerals, sea and natural gas. The saying, 'Nainammeepla, nainameekhao', which means 'there are fish in the water, there is rice in the paddies', depicts Thailand and the fertility of its land well. Approximately 68 per cent of the Thai population lives in rural areas and the majority are farmers with incomes reliant upon subsistence agriculture. Key agricultural products include rice, tapioca and rubber. Rice is the country's most important crop. Thailand has been the world's largest exporter of rice since 1981.

Thailand has been open to trade, commerce and diplomacy with foreign countries ever since the Ayutthaya period, the great era of international trade, particularly, during the reign of King Narai the Great (1656–1688). The first European countries that traded with Thailand included the Netherlands, England and Portugal. Apart from Europeans, Chinese, both from the mainland and later those who became ethnic Thais, are another significant influential group contributing to the development of trade and commerce in Thailand. In fact, most current successful conglomerates in Thailand today are of Chinese descent. The United States and Japan did not start business relations with Thailand until the nineteenth century (1832 and 1887 respectively). However, these two countries have become important business partners of Thailand as well with the United States being its number one exporter and Japan its number one supplier.

While agriculture is still the major part of the Thai economy with 49 per cent of its work-force, Thailand has become more commercialized and industrialized with an increasing number of multinational companies and industrial plants in different parts of the country. Its main industries include textiles, agricultural processing, electric appliances and components, computers and part and integrated circuits. Having numerous and diverse beautiful natural attractions, tourism has also become one of the key income-generating industries.

In 2011, the World Bank announced that Thailand's income categorization had been upgraded from a lower-middle income to an upper-middle income economy (a country with per capita GNI between US$3,706 and US$11,455) in 2009. This is due to Thailand's progress in social and economic development, despite facing a number of political challenges. As such, Thailand has been one of the great development success stories, with sustained strong growth and impressive poverty reduction.

The Thai business system

Cultural and key historical influences

Previous studies suggested that culture influences management practices (Dao and Sorensen, 2007; Ralston et al., 1999). Thus, learning about Thai culture increases understanding of Thai people and their behaviours. In this section, Hofstede's cross-cultural framework will be applied to provide perspectives on Thai culture. This framework comprises five dimensions: long-term vs. short-term orientation; individualism vs. collectivism; masculinity vs. femininity; power distance and uncertainty avoidance.

Rationale

Long-term orientation: historically, Thai people owned plenty of land upon which they grew their own foods. There was no such thing as 'business' as it means nowadays. Bartering systems might occur when people had too much for themselves and wanted to trade for something different. Thai people bartered with Chinese, Indians and Europeans. Formal business started after the domestic conflicts and the big war with Burma ended and Thailand welcomed many Chinese migrants who greatly helped boost trade and the economy in Thailand. Most businesses in Thailand were started and owned by Chinese migrants.

Due to the strong belief in Buddhism and the influence of Confucius in this region, Thai (mostly ethnic Chinese) people in the business sector have a long-term orientation. This has a strong influence on the rationale for business in Thailand. Even though Thai firms are established to generate profit for the owner, other key stakeholders are not neglected either. The attempt to maximize resources for the highest profit and effectiveness is less in Thai firms when compared to Western firms. Relationship between business partners and stakeholders are to be prolonged and cherished. Any investment of the firm is made slowly and with great care. Thai people are persistent and have a sense of shame. Saving, thriftiness and perseverance are considered important.

Identity

Collectivism: Thailand is a highly collective country. Thai people grow up within an extended family. Children are used to being surrounded by not just the parents and other children, but also grandparents, uncles, aunts and cousins. They learn to think of themselves as part of a 'we' group. During the harvest season, Thai farmers in the past had a tradition called '*long kaeg*' or 'collective labour', which was the time when the farmers in the same village gathered together to assist with the rice harvesting on the plot of one household. Then, the *long kaeg* rotated to cover the other households. An organization is like a family with employees as its members.

Femininity: according to Hofstede, 'A society is called feminine when emotional gender roles overlap: both men and women are supposed to be modest, tender and concerned with the quality of life. A society is called masculine when emotional gender roles are clearly distinct: men are supposed to be assertive, tough and focused on material success, whereas women are supposed to be more modest, tender and concerned with the quality of life' (Hofstede and Hofstede, 2005: 120). Thai people are generally neither assertive nor ambitious. The culture places more value on relationships and quality of life rather than wealth and material possessions. Thai people look for cooperation, modesty, caring for the weak and quality of life. Society at large is more consensus-oriented. Communication in Thailand involves politeness and diplomacy, and open confrontation is generally avoided.

Authority

Large power distance: Hofstede defined power distance as 'the extent to which the less powerful member of institutions and organizations (i.e., juniors) within a country expect and accept that power is distributed unequally' (Hofstede and Hofstede, 2005: 46). Thailand was rated high in the dimension of power distance. Inequality within Thai society is visible and accepted in the existence of different social classes divided by economic status (rich vs. poor); education (low vs. high); profession (blue vs. while-collar); position (subordinate vs. supervisor); family relation or seniority (parents vs. children), for example. This does not come as a surprise, given that Thailand had been ruled with absolute monarchy for hundreds of years. 'Each Thai person who is trained to be a functioning member of society learns, early in life, what rank he or she holds and how he is supposed to treat others according to that rank. The 'others' in his life are reckoned as his juniors, his seniors or his peers' (Holmes and Tangtongtavy, 1997: 26).

From early childhood: Thai children are taught to respect, obey and not to argue with adults; therefore, in a hierarchical society like Thailand, seniority is very important. Inevitably, this large power distance, resulting from seniority or authority, carries over into business and affects management.

Strong uncertainty avoidance: this dimension refers to the way people handle uncertainty, whether they tolerate or avoid it. Thailand is also found to rank high on uncertainty avoidance dimension. This makes most Thais to possess the mentality of 'What is different is dangerous'. They generally are not risk takers and fear change, which brings uncertainty and anxiety, and is perceived as a threat. Job hopping is unpopular among Thai people. Most of them prefer working for the government, which offers lifetime employment, security and better benefits, despite a low salary. However, the younger generation seems to share this value less and less.

The King's philosophy of sufficiency economy

Similar to numerous other Asia-Pacific countries, Thailand's economic policies have for decades been directed towards fostering economic growth. The desirability of the growth that has resulted is therefore of great interest. Obviously, the value of economic growth is open to question on many grounds, including its environmental impacts, its effects on traditional cultures, rates of urbanization, and so forth (Warr, 1993). After the 1997 financial crisis, most Thai firms were forced to seek a new management approach to survive, as an alternative to the prevailing Anglo/US business model. The Philosophy of Sufficiency Economy was one of the options.

His Majesty King Bhumibol Adulyadej, who is the soul of Thailand, has graciously reminded the Thai people through his royal remarks on many occasions of a step-by-step and balanced approach to development, which is now known as the Philosophy of Sufficiency Economy. Particularly, after he saw how globalization affected Thai people's way of life. The Philosophy provides guidance on appropriate conduct covering numerous aspects of life. The following is one example of an excerpt from His royal speech in 1974:

> Development of the nation must be carried out in stages, starting with the laying of the foundation by ensuring the majority of the people have their basic necessities through the use of economical means and equipment in accordance with theoretical principles. Once a reasonably firm foundation has been laid and in effect, higher levels of economic growth and development should be promoted. (His Majesty the King's royal speech given to the graduates of Kasetsart University on 18 July 1974, quoted in Sufficiency Economy, n.d., p. 1)

After the economic crisis in 1997, His Majesty reiterated and expanded the concept to point out the way for recovery that would lead to a more resilient, balanced and sustainable development, better able to meet the challenges arising from globalization and changes that may bring future economic insecurity. The philosophy can be summed up as follows:

> Sufficiency Economy is a philosophy that guides the livelihood and behavior of people at all levels, from the family to the community to the country, on matters concerning national development and administration. It calls for a 'middle way' to be observed, especially in pursuing economic development in keeping with the world of globalization. Sufficiency means moderation and reasonableness, including the need to build a reasonable immune system against shocks from the outside or from the inside. Intelligence, attentiveness, and extreme care should be used to ensure that all plans and every step of their implementation are based on knowledge.
>
> At the same time we must build up the spiritual foundation of all people in the nation, especially state officials, scholars, and business people at all levels, so they are conscious of moral integrity and honesty and they strive for the appropriate wisdom to live life with forbearance, diligence, self-awareness, intelligence, and attentiveness. In this way we can hope to maintain balance and be ready to cope with rapid physical, social, environmental and cultural changes from the outside world. (Medhi, 2003)

At first glance, this Philosophy may sound unrealistic, idealistic and impractical for today's world. However, it has been proved time and again by numerous Thai business owners and scholars that the Philosophy was effective and necessary for the survival and sustainability of the businesses (Kantabutra, 2005; Kusumavalee, 2005; Nuttavuthisit, 2005; The Thai Chamber of Commerce, 2008).

The Philosophy of Sufficiency Economy, based on adherence to the middle path, is advocated to (a) overcome the economic crisis that was brought about by unexpected change under conditions of rapid globalization, and (b) achieve sustainable development. The Philosophy of Sufficiency Economy framework (see Figure 15.1) comprises three main characteristics and two underlying conditions (Piboolsravut, 2004).

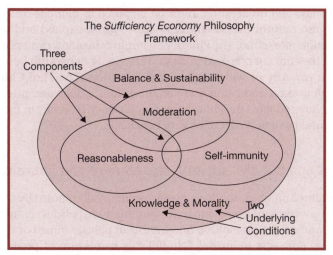

FIGURE 15.1 Philosophy of Sufficiency Economy framework (Kantabutra, 2008)

The three characteristics are:

1. *Moderation* has two components; sufficiency and appropriateness. The word enough means not lacking in anything but have everything in appropriation, that is, not too much nor too little. A balance in all our actions leads to sustainable development.

2. *Reasonableness* means evaluating the reasons for any action and understanding its full consequences with the conditions of having knowledge and ethics as the basis for decision-making.

3. *Self-immunity* is the readiness and the ability to cope with shocks from internal and external changes by carefully assessing the situation and considering both short-term and long-term consequences.

The two underlying conditions necessary to achieve *sufficiency* are:

1. *Knowledge* consists of accumulating knowledge from various subjects from the past, present and future.

2. *Morality*, which embracing the four virtues namely kindness, unity, honesty and justice that if practiced will bring peacefulness and prosperity to the individual and also the public (Thai Chamber of Commerce, 2008).

> There has been some confusion about the term Sufficiency Economy. Most people usually associate this with the poor or with farmers whereas trade and industry were on another level, and therefore not applicable. This is a misunderstanding. Sufficiency Economy is a philosophy that can be applied at all levels ranging from people's daily lives and society, to business and the nation. (Dr AjvaTaulananda, Member of Sufficiency Economy Movement Sub-Committee and Chairman of Private Sector Working Group, Thai Chamber of Commerce, 2008: 17)

To integrate the Philosophy of Sufficiency Economy and the ability to increase trade capacity, business people need to apply cautiousness in decision-making. They need to approach with rationale and moderation, must be prepared to manage and take any risks incurred. It is also natural that businesses need to grow, expand and achieve a productive goal through marketing. The Philosophy reminds business owners to be wise and not to act when they are not prepared to do so. They need not perform business that is beyond their own capacity or with no proper preparation (The Thai Chamber of Commerce, 2008). Nowadays, more and more organizations, public and private alike, no matter what size, have adopted the Philosophy of Sufficiency Economy in their organizational operation and have proved it to be very beneficial.

The government and the civil society: *laissez-faire* and liberalization

Thailand has maintained an open, market-oriented economy dominated by the private sector, together with government leadership in facilitating trade policies centred around import substitution and export promotion, and industrial policies aimed at the protection and fostering of domestic industries. Thailand is a mixture of predatory and developmental states. The state has significant predatory or corrupt aspects, to the extent that there are elites using the system for personal enrichment; but there has also been give-and-take, with bribes being paid in exchange for policy measures required for business to prosper. The outcome of economic development in the past four decades suggests that the Thai state has been controlled by a ruling elite, comprising the military, vested-interest groups (mostly ethnic Chinese) and bureaucrats, who seem to plunder without providing adequate welfare to their citizens (Suehiro and Wailersak, forthcoming; Witt, 2013).

Thailand's economy has always been very much based on decentralized free enterprise, and the laws are very similar to those in the free economies of the West. Sectors like telecommunications, energy and other infrastructure have been more like European quasi-monopolies than US deregulation. Thailand enjoys one of the best ratios of quality infrastructure to GNP per capita. Thailand's economy was one of the fastest growing in the world in the 1980s and early 1990s (in terms of percentage of GNP annually), but the 1997 Asia economic crash was the end of that. It is currently growing at approximately 4–5 per cent per year. There are some key restrictions to foreigners, such as owning companies and property.

The Thai government is able and willing to protect its people from the negative consequences of foreign corporate exploitation, even during the 1980s and 1990s with the domestic policies to attract the large flows of FDI in Thailand. Thai bureaucrats insisted on regulations such as demanding a certain percentage of domestic content in goods manufactured by MNCs in Thailand, and the 51 per cent share-holding rule, under which an MNC starting operations in Thailand must form a joint venture with a Thai company, the idea being that a company with 51 per cent Thai control is better able to keep jobs and profits in the country.

Regarding civil society, most civil society organizations (CSO) in Thailand that were established at the early stage worked in the field of rural development and welfare. However, through the 1990s, the dynamics of CSO changed, in parallel with economic growth leading to inequality between urban and rural areas. The core activities of most CSOs in Thailand are directed towards poverty alleviation, natural resource restoration, humanitarian relief, self-organization and professional development, non-violence, help for people living with HIV/AIDS, for example. However, there are still some areas in which CSO's role are still modest and limited including advocacy and transparency. The role of watchdogs to expose corruption by party cadres and government officials requires increased effort from CSOs.

Business environment

Financial capital

The financial system in Thailand is regulated by the Bank of Thailand (BOT). The BOT's monetary policy leans towards an inflation-targeting regime, using the interest rate as its monetary instrument to target inflation. The BOT is generally considered to be operating independently but cooperatively with other core agencies in economic policy-making: the National Economic and Social Development Board (NESDB), the Fiscal Policy Office (FPO) of the Ministry of Finance and the Bureau of Budget (BOB) of the Prime Minister's Office. The governor of the BOT is to be recruited by the Minister of Finance, endorsed by the Cabinet and then appointed by the King for a five-year term.

Similar to many Asian countries, the main source of financing for Thai firms is commercial banks. After the 1997 Asian Financial Crisis, which put an end to Thailand's economic boom during the 1980s and the 1990s, the Thai government initiated many reforms in financial sectors. For instance:

- The Deposit Insurance Act was launched in 2004.

- Supervision of financial institutions by providing consolidated supervision and risk-based supervision employing the following three pillars: (1) minimum capital requirement, (2) supervisory review process and (3) market discipline.

- Stringent corporate governance of financial institutions.

- Establish a Credit Bureau and declare Credit Bureau Act in 2003.

The above measures provide the bank with clear and specific guidelines to help the bank reduce financial risks caused by unpredictable external factors. Banks' lending allocation for loans before the crisis is based on the strength of existing business relationship; however, after the crisis it is a mixture of relationship and government input. With the financial institution reform there have been also many joint-ventures between Thai and foreign banks.

Human capital

The current Eleventh National and Economic Development Plan (2012–2016) continues to adopt the model of holistic 'people-centred development' starting from the Eighth Plan (1997–2001) focusing on applying the Philosophy of Sufficiency Economy to enhance Thailand's self-resilience by strengthening its economic and social capital and improving risk management in order to effectively handle internal and external uncertainties. This will lead the country to sustainable development and a 'Happy Society' (NESDB, 2012). Despite this ambitious plan, one key obstacle for Thailand is the regional disparity of quality education, especially at the primary and secondary level.

Overall the quality of education in Thailand has improved greatly over the past 10 years. However, the true problem is the regional disparity. Quality schools, teachers and education only concentrate around Bangkok and big cities in each region. Therefore, children in remote areas have to travel a long distance for quality education. Moreover, there are not sufficient well-trained teachers for the whole country. Nowadays, there are more public or private universities that provide higher education. There is a lack of technical and vocational training in the labour market, because young people prefer to work as a white-collar in an office where they earn higher salary and work in a better physical environment. Skill acquisition in Thailand is provided by employers and the employment tenure tends to be short and unpredictable, especially in the private sector. However, employees are well protected by Thai labour law and receive their lawful rights.

As a feminine society, organized unions are not common in Thailand, because it indicates a lack of trust and antagonism. There are only a few organized unions in state enterprises where their employees want to protect their rights and attractive benefits and to increase their bargaining power. Most Thai people still prefer to obtain a long-term, stable job either with the government or state enterprise and work there until their retirement. However, them generation seems to share this idea less and less and seem to prefer entrepreneurship.

Despite the most recent increase in the daily wage to 300 THB (or US$10.28), Thailand is currently facing a serious problem of the lack of low-level labour, for example, factory workers, fishery, construction workers, housekeepers and agricultural workers. These Thai workers prefer to work for higher wages in another country. As a result, the country has to loosen the policy and open the labour market to workers from the neighbouring countries, such as Laos PDR, Myanmar and Cambodia.

Moreover, there are two characteristics that are unique for Thailand. First, it is the only country in the region that was not colonized by a Western power during the European colonial period (1500s–mid-1900s). Thus, people generally have a strong sense of pride in the country. Second, despite having many different ethnic groups living in the country, such as Chinese Indian, Malay, hill tribes and other minority groups practising different religions, speaking different languages, life is relatively peaceful and harmonious. Thailand does not suffer from serious internal ethnic conflict. The Thai government never usually forces people to assimilate into the mainstream. The government also takes good care of them, especially those in the remote areas, by providing schooling, infrastructure, healthcare, and so forth. At school children speak, read and write central Thai (official) language, but at home they can speak own ethnic language. People are, in fact, encouraged to preserve their own ethnic authenticity. Moreover, His Majesty King Bhumibol Adulyadej made a great effort to travel all over the country to visit his people to witness their living conditions for himself. This made them feel a part of the big family visited by their 'porluang' or 'royal father' no matter where they live.

Social capital

As a collective culture, social capital tends to be high in Thailand, particularly when considering people's close family and friends' relationships. This interpersonal trust also comes from strong influence from the Sufficiency Economy philosophy and people's religions and philosophy, be it Buddhism, Islam or Confucianism (NESDB, 2005). There have been many examples of community members from all walks of life, for example, monks, farmers, teachers, doctors, students and parents coming together to share ideas, knowledge, skill and labour to solve the problem that they are facing together, such as the problems with the sustainable use of community forest, contaminated public water sources, orphans, quality of education and drop-out students. From the old days doing business in Thailand is often based on this interpersonal trust and relationship. Legal contract started when business with westerners occurred.

The picture is different with regards to institutionalized trust. Thai people have low level of trust in institutions. According to the World Economic Forum's Global Competitiveness Report 2010/2011, Thailand ranked 38th out of the 139 surveyed countries in overall score. However, it indicated a disgraceful status in both 'public trust in politicians' (83rd) and 'irregular payments and bribes' (70th). There is still a significant concern about weak law enforcement, corruption in public life and low level of transparency in management and governance. People generally do not think rule of law can protect them that its application to the Thai economy is minimal.

Business system

Ownership and corporate governance

There are three levels of business communities in Thailand: basic activities, such as agriculture and small trades; medium to large businesses which are the major group; and big businesses including joint ventures with foreign capital, those with state concessions, and those listed in the SET. Prior to the 1997 Asian Financial Crisis and even after, family owned firms are the dominant form of ownership in Thai businesses, at least in terms of the number of listed companies (not in terms of capitalization) (Suehiro and Wailerdsak, 2013). Thus, management control of firms also rests with families. In general, families usually retain a controlling stake in firms even if they decide to list them on stock exchanges. However, the 1979 crisis weakened Thailand's business families, leaving many firms vulnerable to foreign investment. There are two channels that families use to maintain both ownership and control in Thai businesses – holding shares directly in their names and through a pyramidal structure, in which the family hold a majority of shares in a holding/investment (parent) company that, in turn, held a majority of shares in an operating company or subsidiaries (Suehiro, 2006; Suehiro and Wailerdsak, 2013).

The corporate governance reforms initiated by the SET and Office of the Securities and Exchange Commission (SEC) resulted from strong pressure from international financial institutions (IMF and World Bank) in the wake of the 1997 financial crisis (Suehiro, 2001). Since 1998, many measures have been taken to improve corporate governance in Thai firms, for example, the SET issued requirements for all listed companies to have an audit committee and guideline: the Code of Best Practices Directors of Listed Companies. Despite these clear measures and guidelines, corporate governance in Thai firms is still considered at the moderate level. The problem lies in enforcement, business ethics and practices (Suehiro and Wailerdsak, 2013).

Networking

Thailand is becoming more of a network economy in response to the ever changing environment. This networking is formed in all levels of the country from the grassroots to the national level. In agricultural sector at the grassroots level, as mentioned before, farmers help each other on the fields during the planting and harvesting season for the well-being of everyone in the community. If there were any problems, for example, pests in the rice field, they would come together to solve the problem by consulting the local wisdom experts and governmental officials in the area, because if the problem cannot be solved, the damage will spread to their fields as well. The forms of networking at the local level include cooperatives, community enterprises, housewife groups, associations and clubs and the products or businesses normally focus on agricultural products, ecological tourism, and so forth. With the use of the internet and the concept of the knowledge-based economy, this level of networking has improved greatly. Additionally, with much stronger emphasis on CSR, Thai firms are more connected to the community they serve.

Likewise, at the national level and wider scope, larger firms also routinely exchange information, coordinate and cooperate with a number of actors, such as other firms and government agencies. The prevalence of business groups in Thailand is *glum thurakit*, or group of businesses, where firms within the same industry collaborate to increase bargaining power, solve industry-related problems, deal with crises and exchange R&D, for example. Many associations are formed to accommodate this kind of networking. In addition, many Thai companies maintain dense networks with suppliers and distributors, while collaboration with competitors exists but is still kept at arm's length.

Management

As described in 'Identity' above, Thailand is a hierarchical country and decision making in Thai firms is normally made at the top of the organization. Autocratic leadership style prevails in Thailand; top-down and centralized management is common in an organization. Employees would not normally question decisions made by senior management. Accordingly, the degree of delegation in Thai firms is generally low. Management below the top level is usually a conduit of orders from the top, supervising whether instructions are properly executed. As such, it is important for Thais to have a clear idea of hierarchy within their organization and know to whom they are to report. In return for good work, employers are expected to take good care of their employees at least to meet or exceed the basic needs to create job satisfaction. A charismatic manager with paternal characteristics seems to be more popular among Thai employees because they expect to receive protection from him. This is the influence of the traditional family-owned business, where the owner would use the father-figure style of management with their employees and treat them as family members. Thai people are also good team players.

However, nowadays there are more multinational companies doing business in Thailand. They introduced new management styles to become more responsive to needs of the rapidly changing world. For example, they use a more systematic and participative management style. The traditional criteria for promoting people have been merit-based or personal relationship and seniority, that is, the number of years one has worked in the company. This sometimes leads to favouritism and unfairness. Currently, many companies employ a performance-based system as the basis for promotion decision in order to increase transparency. However, most governmental agencies still use merit-based or relationship and seniority promotion policies.

Comparative advantage

Thailand's comparative advantage is generally based on natural resources and skilful labour, among other factors. Thai labourers are known as fast-learners, highly-skilled and intelligent. According to UNDP's Human Development Index 2013 Report, between 1980 and 2012 Thailand's HDI rose by 1.5 per cent annually from 0.49 to 0.69, which gives the country a rank of 103 out of 187 countries with comparable data. The HDI of East Asia and the Pacific as a region increased from 0.432 in 1980 to 0.683 placing Thailand above the regional average.

Thailand is the hub of ASEAN. It is ideally located at the crossroads of Asia, with easy access to the region's dynamic markets, including its own booming domestic consumer market of 67 million people. Thailand has long been a proponent of free and fair trade and its attractiveness as a production base for leading international companies is enhanced by a number of free trade agreements, and Thailand is certain to be a beneficiary of the ASEAN Economic Community (AEC), which will be in force in 2015.

Thailand has well-defined investment policies focusing on liberalization and encouraging free trade. Foreign investments, especially those that contribute to the development of skills, technology and innovation are actively promoted by the government. Thailand consistently ranks among the most attractive investment locations in international surveys, and the World Bank's 2012 Ease of Doing Business report places Thailand as the 17th easiest country in the world (and second-ranked country in Southeast Asia) in which to do business. Likewise, the United Nations Conference on Trade and development (UNCTAD) ranks Thailand as the 10th most attractive host economy in the world.

Continuity and change in the Thai business system

Various factors have an influence on the changing trends of the business system in Thailand. First, the global economy and global environmental concerns, for example, economic slowdown, accumulative debts in Europe and terrorism continue to affect the Thai business system and how firms make business-related decisions, especially for export/import businesses. The pain and the lessons from the 1997 Asian financial crisis caused Thai businesses to become more cautious and risk-aware, which led to structural reforms and contingency planning.

Despite the fast recovery from the crisis and the impressive economic growth in Thailand afterward, the country is now facing many challenges to move forward. The most significant one comes with the arrival of the AEC in 2015, which will open the door to the free flow of labour among member countries. This new working context requires a new set of skills and competencies of Thai workforce at all levels. Already globalization brings about a borderless business stage; with the AEC the impact is more evident and significant. The effective strategies are needed to collaborate with the AEC members to maximize the mutual benefits of over 200 million people in the region.

While the external change is unstoppable, businesses need to put one foot on the brake to prioritize the change and to help people manage the many expected changes. In fact, one of the factors leading to the 1997 Asian economic crisis was businesses trying to make too many changes at the same time hoping they would lead to more wealth. The Sufficiency Economy philosophy is, as mentioned, one of the ways to caution Thai people not to be lured by the global trend and try to do business for the country's sustainable development.

International activities of Thai firms

Thailand has been open to trade with westerners for a very long time. Today, with the modern format of business, Thai firms' international activities abroad are high. The United States is Thailand's number one export market. With its abundant natural resources, Thailand's main exporting products are agricultural products (raw and processed, for example, rice, tapioca, corn, fish. In addition to agricultural products, Thailand also exports clothes, furniture, handicraft, electrical goods, electronics and automotive parts. The Office of Foreign Trades of the Thai government promotes international activities of Thai firms by providing data about countries interested in doing business with Thai firms, and information on specific steps they have to take in doing so. However, the major drawback of the international activities of Thai products seems to be that their quality might not meet the conditions of those potential buying countries. Thus, Thai firms have to be more stringent in improving the production process in order to increase exports.

Corporate social responsibility in Thailand

Corporate social responsibility (CSR) is the current social mantra in the business world. Although many Thai firms might have been conducting some type of social responsible activities for many years, the concept of CSR as it stands today has emerged only recently. There is no legislative framework on CSR in Thailand. As in many other countries, 'the development of CSR in Thailand has been somewhat slow, piecemeal, reflective of a number of disparate positions, as well as lacking a clear theoretical framework' (Ratanajongkol et al., 2006: 67). In the past, only a few firms gave it much attention and saw the link between CSR and their business operation and its competitive advantage. Most companies only focused on increasing revenue and short-term profits and maximizing shareholder value. Some firms are simply too busy trying to survive during the economic downturn to think about CSR.

In Thailand, only 11 per cent of Thai companies donate to charities, well under the global average of 65 per cent, according to a survey by the consultancy Grant Thornton (Board of Investment, 2008). Most companies do not, and are not required to, have social responsibility policies. However, recently the trend on ethics and CSR practices companies shows an impressive increase, particularly, among large, leading, well-established Thai companies or joint ventures and multinational companies (MNCs).

After the 1997 economic crisis, public oversight and pressure became more common for Thai companies. The press was asking tough and sophisticated questions of business leaders in areas beyond financial reporting. Human rights, human dignity, social responsibility and equitable treatment within stakeholder groups were issues raised by activists, reporters, analysts and the public at large. As a result, all listed companies were asked by the Stock Exchange of Thailand to appoint an audit committee before the end of 1999. Starting from 2013, all listed firms are mandated to disclose their CSR practices and include them in their annual report. This effort was aimed at building awareness and promoting implementation of corporate governance and CSR practices in Thailand in a more sustainable way.

In Thailand, the manufacturing sector has the highest record of CSR disclosure of the industry sectors with the dominant theme of the environment, whereas the service sector has the lowest disclosure on the same theme (Ratanajongkol et al., 2006). Triple bottom line reporting is becoming more important and more common in Thai companies due to the pressure from consumers, government, NGOs and the wider society.

Chapter summary

- Thailand has a broad-based economy with strong agricultural, service and industrial sectors. It is a middle income newly-industrialized developing country with free-enterprise. The government encourages foreign direct investment. Before the Asian financial crisis, the Thai economy was the fastest growing in the world. The country has now fully recovered from the crisis mainly through the acceleration in exports and private investment.

- The King's Philosophy on Sufficiency Economy comprises three main characteristics: moderation, reasonableness, and self-immunity with two underlying conditions necessary to achieve sufficiency: knowledge and morality. This Philosophy can be applied to every unit of society, including business.

- Autocratic leadership style is prevailing in Thailand, thus top-down and centralized management and change implementation are common in an organization.

- There is no legislative framework for CSR in Thailand; however, the trend for it is increasing particularly among leading, well-established Thai and multinational companies. However, SET has mandated all listed companies to report their CSR practices in their annual report with the intention that these companies will become role models for other companies.

- Thailand is a Buddhist country and Buddhism plays a major role in every part of Thai's life. Thai culture has high power distance, collectivism, femininity and high uncertainty avoidance.

Key concepts

ASEAN Economic Community (AEC): the economic integration transforming ASEAN into a single market and production base by 2015. The economic integration goals will include the elimination of tariffs, free professional movement, capital and a faster customs clearance procedure. Free Trade Area (FTAs) will be a key strategy for ASEAN to gain greater market access into trading partners and to attract foreign direct investments. In short, the AEC will transform ASEAN into a region with free movement of goods, services, investment, skilled labour and freer flow of capital. ASEAN Member States include Negara Brunei Darussalam, Cambodia, Indonesia, Lao PDR, Malaysia, Philippines, Singapore, Myanmar, Vietnam and Thailand.

Civil Society Organizations (CSOs): a large number of groups, organizations and associations including mass organizations, professional associations, local NGOs and community-based organizations.

Philosophy of Sufficiency Economy: his Majesty King Bhumibol Adulyadej of Thailand initiated the Philosophy of Sufficiency Economy to guide Thai people to cope with the drastic changes brought by globalization with consciousness. The Philosophy emphasizes taking the middle path and comprises three main characteristics: moderation, reasonableness, and self-immunity system; and two underlying conditions: knowledge and morality.

Small and Medium Enterprise (SME): normally, a family or community-owned business with 1 to 20 employees. The business can be either domestic or international. The structure and management of the organization is generally not as complex as a large, multinational enterprise.

Triple bottom line: this is when an organization expands its traditional values and criteria for measuring its success by considering social and environmental performance in addition to financial performance.

Review questions

1 Despite its impressive growth, Thailand is notable for the near-absence of companies that could truly be called world-class, such as Korea's Samsung and LG, China's Huawei and Lenovo, India's Tata, or Singapore's Singapore Airlines. A recent study by the Boston Consulting Group (BCG) showed that only two companies from Thailand meet the standards required to belong of the 100 largest multinationals from emerging economies. In your opinion, what are the causes of this? How can Thailand improve and develop to be able to meet those standards?

2 Do you think the Philosophy of Sufficiency Economy is practical as a business management approach in your country, given its social, economic and cultural context?

3 Discuss some of the things you should be aware of, should you become a manager in Thailand. How do you think you can be successful in your job?

4 Despite having many ethnic groups and many religions in Thailand, why do you think Thailand remains peaceful and united generally? How do you think this characteristic of Thailand helps Thailand grow?

Learning activities and discussions

1 Assume that you work for multinational company. Your head office sends you to replace the previous country manager in Thailand, who had some

problems working with local staff leading to a drop in performance and productivity. What would be your strategy to solve the overall problem?

2 Search for more information on the Philosophy of Sufficiency Economy on the internet. Conduct a debate on its advantages and disadvantages for doing business in today's world.

3 With the information you have on Thailand, discuss the strengths and weaknesses for doing business in this country when compared with other Asian countries.

MINI CASE

Bangchak and its corporate social responsibility commitment

Bangchak Petroleum Public Company Limited is the only Thai petroleum company in Thailand was established by the Cabinet of Prime Minister Major-General PremTinsulanonda. Its aim was to operate the old Bangchak oil refinery, which had accumulated huge losses, to maintain energy security for the benefit of the Thai public. The company was established with the following goals:

1. To be a secure Thai company operating a petroleum business consistent with the common good.
2. To be a company that helps to develop a better quality of life for all Thais.

This brought efficient management and activities that stressed the overall benefit of fostering a secure and progressive business, guidelines of self-reliance and a corporate culture of creativity, ingraining in all staff that they should be 'good people, knowledgeable, to benefit others'. Within five years, the company achieved profits of 500 to 800 million baht per year. It became one of the top 10 Thai businesses in terms of sales and was praised by influential members of the community as having set a good example, in terms of both organization and people. The company's success at that time was credited as a major success of the government.

The company's longer term vision is Greenergy Excellence – creating an energy business that is environmentally friendly and sustainable. Its value statement includes B – beyond expectation, C – continuing development and P – pursuing sustainability. The vision statement also includes:

Business culture – develop a sustainable business, while safeguarding environment and society.

Employee culture – to be respectable, knowledgeable and helpful to others.

It expects its executives and employees to adhere to the following six principles to support its corporate governance:

• Accountability
• Responsibility

- Transparency
- Equitable treatment
- Vision to create long-term value
- Ethical

Towards a process for community relations

In 1990, Bangchak partnered with the Si Prachan Agriculture Cooperative in Suphanburi Province to establish the first cooperative gas station to provide agriculturists with low-priced gas to help them decrease production costs, while also providing them with technical and management consultation. The cooperative/community gas station was so successful the number grew to over 500 stations and provided useful benefits to over 1 million agricultural families around the country. With the economic downturn in 1997, there were many non-performing loans and many big businesses went bankrupt. But, the community gas stations coped with the crisis and continued to serve their customers because the businesses are simple and did not require much investment, big bank loans or foreign funding.

The start of a community gas station was simple. In 1987, Bangchak started the lunch program at schools in Suphanburi province. One day the committee of the Si Prachan Agriculture Cooperative visited Bangchak oil refinery and the school lunch program. They came up with the idea to exchange oil with rice, since they were all farmers. This was the first step of the collaboration between community and the company.

Realizing a sufficiency economy

With its continuous work developing a good quality of life for Thai society, Bangchak embraced the Philosophy of Sufficiency Economy in accordance with the suggestions of His Majesty the King. This philosophy directs Bangchak's operations and is in its employees' DNA. The community gas station is one example of creating self-immunity. Another activity following the Sufficiency Economy is Bangchak's establishment of Lemon Farm shops, which sell natural agricultural products from rural community organizations, providing health benefits to consumers, as well. This has grown into Lemon Farm Pattana Cooperatives, Ltd., providing a mechanism for Thais to help each other establish enterprises and provide benefits to society. Furthermore, Bangchak has assisted in the promotion of guidelines for a sufficiency economy to help communities become self-sufficient and encourage the use of Thai products, in order to save foreign currency. Community members are encouraged to sell their products at shops in the service stations. Bangchak was the first gas station in Thailand that gave away bottles of drinking water to customers after a minimum sale price was reached – a practice followed later by other brands. Bangchak does not see this as a marketing strategy but as the way to give back to their customers even though it means a reduction in profit. Sometimes, when there is an overflow of agricultural products, such as lemons, eggs or fruits, Bangchak would buy them for a reasonable price to ease problems in the agricultural sector, and then give these products or sell them to their gas customers. This would never happen with a foreign gas company.

To the future with pride

Bangchak will continue to follow the principle of 'developing a sustainable business, environment, and society' by coordinating community networks, in order to provide a 'community platform network for community businesses'. This will lead to the development of organizational or business networks at all levels from local to provincial and encourage business organizations at the national level to belong to the people. Bangchak service stations are also providing opportunities for community business, in order to benefit both urban communities/consumers and rural communities, at the same time strengthening Bangchak itself.

Questions

1 Do you think what Bangchak has achieved (from the case) are examples of corporate social responsibility? Why? Why not?

2 Given the concept of the Philosophy of Sufficiency Economy explain how Bangchak applied this philosophy to the activities it implemented.

3 It is obvious from the establishment of Bangchak that the company does not operate to maximize short-term profit. As the only Thai petroleum company, it has to take care of its different stakeholders as well, including customers, community members, the country, environment. Doing this certainly reduces profit. If you were the president of Bangchak, would you continue this way of doing business? Or, would you alter it? Why and how?

Note

This case was written based on publicly available information. It is intended solely to stimulate class discussion.

Web links

General statistics on Thailand: http://portal.nso.go.th

Thailand economy and business: http://www.boi.go.th

The Philosophy of Sufficiency Economy site: http://www.sufficiency economy.org

ASEAN Economic Community (AEC) site: http://www.asean.org/communities/asean-economic-community

References

Board of Investment (BOI) (2008) Accessed 4 December 2013 at: http://www.boi.go.th

Dao, T.L. and Sorensen, O.J. (2007) The Interplay between Expatriates and Local Managers from a Learning Perspective. The 3rd VDIB-Workshop in Hanoi, November.

Hofstede, G. and Hofstede, G. J. (2005) *Cultures and Organizations: Software of the Mind*, 2nd edn. New York: McGraw-Hill.

Holmes, H. and Tangtongtavy, S. (1997) *Working with the Thais*, 4th edn. Bangkok: White Lotus.

Kantabutra, S. (2005) Applying Sufficiency Economy Philosophy in business organizations: A case of Sa Paper Preservation House. Unpublished manuscript, Sufficiency Economy Unit, Office of National Economic and Social Development Board, Thailand.

Kusumavalee, S. (2005) Applying Sufficiency Economy Philosophy in business organizations: A case of Siam Cement Group. Unpublished manuscript, Sufficiency Economy Unit, Office of National Economic and Social Development Board, Thailand.

Medhi, K. (ed.) (1994) The Making of the Fifth Tiger, in *Thailand's Industrialization and its Consequences*. Basingstoke: Macmillan.

NESDB (National Economic and Social Development Board) (2005) *Construction of Social Capital for Resilient Communities*, [in Thai]. Bangkok: NESDB.

NESDB (National Economic and Social Development Board) (2007) *The Seventh National Economic Development Plan*. Bangkok: NESDB.

NESDB (National Economic and Social Development Board) (2012) *The Summary the Eleventh National Economic and Social Development Plan (2012–2016)*, accessed 4 December 2013 at: http://www.nesdb.go.th/Portals/0/news/academic/Executive%20Summary%20of%2011th%20Plan.pdf

Nuttavuthisit, K. (2005) Applying Sufficiency Economy Philosophy in business organizations: A Case of Pranda Jewelry. Unpublished manuscript, Sufficiency Economy Unit, Office of National Economic and Social Development Board, Thailand.

Piboolsravut, P. (2004) Sufficiency Economy. *ASEAN Economic Bulletin,* 21(1): 127–134.

Ralston, D.A., Nguyen, V.T. and Napier, N.K. (1999) A Comparative Study of the Work Values of North and South Vietnamese Managers. *Journal of International Business Studies*, 30(4): 655–672.

Ratanajongkol, S., Davey, H. and Low, M. (2006) Corporate Social Reporting in Thailand: The News is All Good and Increasing. *Qualitative Research in Accounting and* Management, 3(1): 67–83.

Suehiro, A. (2001) Asian Corporate Governance: Disclosure-based Screening System and Family-Business Restructuring in Thailand [in Japanese]. *Shakai Kagaku Kenkyu*, 52(5): 55–98.

Suehiro, A. (2006) *A Study of Family Business: Agents of Late Industrialization* [in Japanese]. Nagoya: Nagoya University Press.

Suehiro, A. and Wailerdsak, N. (forthcoming) Thailand: Post-Developmentalist Capitalism, in M.A. Witt and G. Redding (eds.) *The Oxford Handbook of Asian Business Systems*. Oxford: Oxford University Press.

Sufficieny Economy (n.d.) The Royal Development Study Centres and the Philosophy of Sufficiency Economy for the Ministerial Conference on Alternative Development: Sufficiency Economy, 8–10 November 2004 by Office of the Royal Development Projects Board, accessed 4 December 2013 at: http://www.sufficiency economy.org/old/en/files/14.pdf

The Thai Chamber of Commerce (2008) *Sufficiency Economy: A New Philosophy in the Global World – 100 Interviews with Business Professionals*. Bangkok: The Thai Chamber of Commerce.

Warr, P.G. (1993) The Thai Economy in P.G. Warr (ed.) *The Thai Economy in Transition*. Cambridge: Cambridge University Press.

Witt, Michael A. and Gordon Redding (2013) Asian Business Systems: Institutional Comparison, Clusters, and Implications for Varieties of Capitalism and Business Systems Theory. Socio-Economic Review, 11(2), accessed 4 December 2013 at: http://ser.oxfordjournals.org/content/11/2/265.full.pdf+html

World Bank (2008) Thailand Country Brief, accessed 8 November 2013 at: http://www.worldbank.or.th

World Bank (1993) *East Asia's Economic Miracle*. New York: Oxford University Press.

Chapter outline

- The Vietnamese business system
- Comparative advantage
- The changing trend of the Vietnamese business system
- International activities of Vietnamese firms
- Corporate social responsibility in Vietnam
- Working and living conditions in Vietnam

Chapter objectives

After reading this chapter, you should be able to understand

1 The essence of the Vietnamese culture, institutions, and the business system.

2 Areas of Vietnam's comparative advantage.

3 Changes in the Vietnamese business system.

4 International activities of Vietnamese firms.

5 Corporate Social Responsibility in Vietnam.

6 Working and living conditions in Vietnam.

Introduction

Located in South East Asia, Vietnam is a developing country bordered by China in the north, and Laos and Cambodia in the west. It has approximately 3,400 km of coastline. The total land area is about the size of California. With a population of nearly 90 million (2012) Vietnam has the third largest population in the Southeast Asia (after Indonesia and the Philippines) and the thirteenth largest in the world.

The Vietnamese government launched *doi moi* policy (economic renovation) in 1986, shifting the command economy to a market-oriented system. As a result of *doi moi*, Vietnam has obtained remarkable achievements in economic development and well-being indicators. The country has enjoyed impressive GDP annual growth rates of around 7 to 8 per cent since 1991. Although the economic growth of the past few years has declined due to the impact of the economic crisis and the worldwide recession, it still remains over 5 per cent in the period 2011 to 2012.

Vietnam joined the WTO in 2007 and continues to move towards the objective to become an industrialized country by 2020. Vietnam has become a lower-middle income country with a modest per capita income of over $1,000 since the end of 2010. The conclusions of the October 2011 Vietnamese Communist Party Plenum recognized the strong need for economic restructuring and identified restructuring of public investment, SOEs and the financial sector as priorities for the coming years. This restructuring of the economy shows the changing trend of moving towards more effectiveness and suggests big changes in the Vietnamese business system. This chapter examines components of the Vietnamese business system following the framework suggested by Redding (2005).

The Vietnamese business system: culture

The first level of the business system refers to culture, which consists of rationale, identity and authority (Redding, 2005). These three dimensions are used to present the culture of Vietnam.

Rationale

Previous studies often refer to Vietnam as a country associated with Confucian heritage and collective cultural values. Confucian values place strong emphasis on the importance of society and group. These values have influenced Vietnamese society and promoted those people and organizations devoting their efforts for the benefit of the community and of the country as a whole.

Vietnam is a socialist country. The political system in Vietnam stresses the primacy of collective goals (collectivism) in which the society's goals are more important than those of the individuals. For a long period of time before *doi moi*, the centrally planned economy was dominated with the state-owned enterprises (SOEs), while the private sector was hampered. Since the Vietnamese government is considered representative of the people at large, all the government's decisions were expected to be made for the sake of the entire country's benefits. The economic development's goals were to bring wealth for all the people in the country. Therefore, the SOEs operating under the government direction were certainly expected to generate benefits for the people and society.

After the collapse of the Former Soviet Union in 1991, Vietnam began to rigorously transform into a market-oriented economy with features of both a state-directed economy and a mixed economy. Privatization, which is often referred to as equitization in Vietnam, has increased since 2006. Therefore, in addition to SOEs, there have been an increasing number of firms that belong to the non-state sector. SOEs, as the government's important macro-regulation tool, have long been considered to hold a directive role in the economy. They have been given priority and many resources by the government. However, the flagship role of SOEs has been controversial as a result of the SOEs' low effective performance. There have also been big concerns, in society, about the 'interest groups' that could sway the decision-making process.

For non-state firms, with large groups of small and medium family types, although profit and owner/shareholder value may be very important goals of doing business, in general, the firms are expected to exist for the sake of society's benefits. Growth of these firms should be perceived as a driver of the improvement of economic well-being of citizens through generating wealth and employment at the grassroots level and having a significant impact on societal systems (Paswan and Tran, 2012). In fact, private sector enterprises have: substantially contributed to job creation, poverty reduction, social-economic stability; promoted of Vietnam's image internationally; and made a considerable contribution to GDP. In Vietnam, there has been also a recent trend of social enterprises caring for community development and social issues. The term 'corporate social responsibility' (CSR) has received much attention over the past few years, including private firms, which are considered to be heavily profit-oriented.

Identity

The influence of Confucian cultural values in Southeast Asian countries, including Vietnam, has been well documented. The characteristics of Confucianism are often identified as diligence, hierarchical relationships (filial piety), thriftiness, respect for authority, value of collective effort, harmony and humility. Vietnam has been typically regarded as a traditional and collectivist country. Vietnamese people are highly patriotic and have a high level of national pride.

Doi moi in Vietnam has changed the traditional value systems that were premised on a centrally planned and subsidized economy. The modern influences brought about by *doi moi* tend to coexist with many of the values, attitudes and behaviours that are associated with the traditional Vietnamese culture (Shultz et al., 1994). Nguyen (1994: 97) noted that 'today, Vietnam is witnessing a great synthesis and integration of the various cultures present in Vietnamese society: tradition with modernity, Oriental values with Western values, preservation of national culture with international integration'.

Along with economic renovation, Vietnamese people, especially among the young middle class seem to demonstrate increasing levels of materialism and individualism, while holding relatively low levels of consumer ethnocentrism. In the past, people could have a happy life without placing importance on material values. At present, however, material objects, especially imported products have become strongly desired by many people. It appears that an increasing number of Vietnamese use material symbolism to signal their success and achievements, which reflect their own competencies. This can help them display prestige and gain trust from business partners, which is especially important for first impressions (cf. Nguyen and Tambyah, 2011).

Similar to those in many other Asian countries, Vietnamese people stress the importance of relationships and the group. Vietnamese business relationships often develop into social relationships. Developing good personal relationships with business partners and relevant authorities is often seen as a tip for success. In Vietnamese enterprises, especially in SOEs, policies and procedures tend to be more 'high-context'. Organizational processes rely more on social relationships than on written descriptions. Informal networking and relationships create favourable conditions. However, they also create unpleasant obstacles to business and management, such as the difficulties in overcoming the bureaucratic administration system or accessing reliable information.

Vietnamese culture often tries to avoid personal conflict. Harmony is preserved and keeping face is desirable. Support, trust and respect are important factors in building relationship between partners. Westerners may see the humility and modesty of the Vietnamese people as indirect and deceitful, while the Vietnamese may see the individual assertiveness of Westerners as arrogant and tactless (Aswhill, 2007). Therefore, working and getting along well with business partners may be a challenge for both sides. The Vietnamese also wish to be respected. This can show itself in daily decision making and communication.

With regard to decision making in doing business, in Vietnamese SOEs, the collective approach is more often taken. In local small and medium-sized family businesses, the practices, however, would be different. The organization, in this case, is often highly centralized in terms of power, and the decisions are often made centrally.

Authority

Influenced by Confucianism, Vietnam tends to lean towards the high hierarchy and indeed, there is the existence of relatively strong hierarchical values in Vietnam. Respect for authority and social rites are very important. The organizational structure of many Vietnamese companies, especially SOEs, tends to be multilayered. Management style is more authoritative than participative. Decision making in firms is prevalently characterized as top-down and the extent of delegation is low (Witt and Redding, 2012).

In Vietnam, one is expected to show respect to people who are senior in age, status or position. Respect is part of the concept of filial piety at home. Outside the family, respect should be paid to elderly people, teachers, employers and people in high positions.

In Vietnam, education always receives very much attention – from families and to the wider society. Vietnamese people often give priority to education and the pursuit of high levels of education is an important goal in their life (Nguyen and Tambyah, 2011). Receiving a higher level of education is often seen as the avenue of advancement. Vietnamese families often sacrifice much for their children's education. The findings of a recent study by TNS (2011) show that education tops Vietnamese consumers' spending. Costly overseas education has become increasingly popular in Vietnam in recent years due to people's low trust in the current local education system and also because overseas education is expected to offer better future employment. There is currently a big concern in society about the slow pace of international integration of the local education system at all levels. Since individual's achievement of higher level of education can bring honour and pride to family members, relatives and ancestors, a degree-oriented society is also an issue that many people worry about.

Similar to many other Asian nations, Vietnam is a strong male-biased society. Although it is stated that Vietnamese men and women are equal under the law, gender prejudices, gender stereotypes and patriarchal thinking are still predominant in many areas of the society. These habitualized attitudes effectively weaken respectful attitudes and practices towards women. However, there has been an increasing active participation of Vietnamese women in business and social activities recently. Women are recognized to contribute significantly to the economic and social development of Vietnam.

The role of the government and the civil society

Vietnamese government is expected to play a guiding role in all affairs, including maintaining the development of the national economy. Before economic reform, Vietnamese government controlled almost all economic sectors and allocated resources through its planning system. SOEs were used as a vital economic tool and the government held responsibilities for the SOEs' performance. Under the centrally-planned management mechanism Vietnamese SOEs, which were dominant in the economy, did not perform effectively and efficiently. This led to the urge radically to reform the economy, particularly noticeable since the early 1990s.

A key element in the economic reform is the reduction of state intervention in business. The government has been trying to reduce its direct role in supervising the economy and to provide support to the private sector to enhance its crucial role in the economy. In addition, significant state efforts have been spent to build a more effective and responsible state apparatus, to develop a more responsive and clean development administration, and to create a more equitable business environment for all participants in the economy. However, the government still needs much more effort and stronger commitment to deal with the remaining concerns such as corruption, which is still considered pervasive with rank of 104 out of 142 countries in 2011 (Truong, 2013).

The Vietnamese government has set the ambitious goal of moving towards an industrialized and modern country by 2020. In order to achieve this goal, it needs to strengthen its role in ensuring the macroeconomic stabilization and place greater emphasis on a more balanced and 'quality-focused' economic growth pattern (Truong et al., 2010).

To support the country's renovation, Vietnam's politics and society have gradually evolved towards greater openness and opportunity for citizens to participate in governance. The Eleventh Congress of the Communist Party of Vietnam, in 2011, promoted greater citizen participation and unity. In Vietnam, however, the concept of civil society is still a relatively new and it has been only been employed more frequently in very recent years. Although there have been debatable views of civil society, in the context of Vietnam, it is considered to be broad based and comprises of a large number of groups, organizations and associations including mass organizations (MOs), professional associations, Vietnamese NGOs (VNGOs) and community-based organizations (CBOs) (Norlund, 2006).

The core activities of most civil society organizations (CSOs) in Vietnam are directed towards poverty reduction, humanitarian relief, self-organization and professional development. CSOs' efforts have contributed significantly to promoting some specific values such as poverty reduction, non-violence, gender equality and equal rights for people living with HIV/AIDS. However, there are still some areas in which the CSOs' role are still modest and limited. These include advocacy and transparency. CSOs have mainly taken on the role of service delivery organizations and have not strongly pursued advocacy. The role of watchdogs to expose corruption by party cadres and government officials still requires further effort from CSOs.

The United Nations Development Program (UNDP), the World Bank (WB) and International Non-governmental Organizations (INGOs) have provided significant efforts to support and promote civil society in Vietnam. The understanding of the concept and the role of CSOs therefore has been increasingly improved. CSOs' contribution to Vietnamese society has also been increasingly recognized.

Institutions

Financial capital

Similar to many Asian countries, the main source of external financing for Vietnamese firms is banks. Vietnamese firms, especially SOEs rely heavily on bank loans. Firms often have high demand for mid-term and long-term loans, but some difficulties for Vietnamese banks to meet this demand exist.

As a result of the economic renovation, the banking system in Vietnam has changed considerably. It have move towards a market-oriented financial sector and is more complex with multiple participants. Currently, the banking system is quite large which includes the State Bank of Vietnam (SBV) and a system of credit institutions. Currently, there are five big state-owned commercial banks (SOCBs) that are 100 per cent owned by the state or in which the state's share is dominant. In addition, there are 37 joint stock banks, 54 foreign banks' branches, five completely foreign-owned banks, five joint venture banks, 17 financial companies, 12 finance leasing companies, a Vietnam Central People's Credit Fund and others. In the credit market, the local credit institutions, especially SOCBs currently have a crucial role with a market share of more than 90 per cent (Nguyen, 2012).

Capital allocation in Vietnam is based heavily on the state and relationships. The State has a major influence on the banks and their lending (Witt and Redding, 2012). Currently, SOCBs are dominant in the banking system and engage in policy-driven lending, with preference given to SOEs despite their loss-making and their large non-performing loans. However, the role of joint stock commercial banks has been significantly increasing despite the difficulties they face in the restructuring process.

In the transitional economy of Vietnam, banks face greater uncertainties, partly due to: the absence of developed market institutions, the lack of transparency, and the limited availability of reliable data within the financial sector. In this circumstance, when providing loans to SMEs, the banks often make decisions relying on collateral, relationships with borrowers, credit scoring and pricing when determining risk. Loan decisions are often based on heuristic judgment that may be subject to serious consequences.

Over the past few years, the Vietnamese banking system has expanded quickly; the banks' management of risks remained weak. SBV's monitoring and surveillance system has not kept pace with the bank's development. Recently, the high level of bad debt has become a serious problem of the SOCBs, of which SOEs, especially the big groups and corporations account for a major part. Being stuck in this problem limits the banks' capacity and willingness to extend loans to the private sector, which is often associated with high risk. Many private firms have experienced severe difficulties in terms of capital shortage due to inability to access bank loans. During 2010 the interest rates were quite high, around 16–20 per cent per annum. The conditions for loan applications are so complex that private firms often fail to meet them. Therefore, private firms commonly resort to alternative sources of capital such as the informal market (loan sharks), which accounted for about US$20.8 billion in 2010 GDP value, making up as much as 20 per cent of GDP (Truong, 2013). The shortage of finance has resulted in thousands of firms going out of business. Further restructuring of the financial and banking system with focus on Vietnamese commercial banks is still considered a vital task for the near future.

Human capital

Vietnam has attained a high adult literacy rate (94 per cent in 2010). However, the education system, including higher education in Vietnam is considered to have many shortcomings. Education quality is criticized to be far behind from the international and regional standards, and the system does not provide enough qualified human resources for the development of the economy. Recruiters are still concerned much about the new graduates' poor qualifications and lack of critical and creative thinking at work. This practice calls for a comprehensive reform of the Vietnamese education system at all levels.

The Vietnamese workforce is often recognized to be young, bright, hardworking and eager to learn. It is also characterized by the shortage of skilled employees with a professional working style, as well as a dearth of managers equipped with strategic thinking and competence in business management. Despite a relatively high growth rate in overall labour productivity, the absolute level remains much lower in comparison to most countries in the region. Managers, especially those who work for SOEs, are found to hold modest levels of entrepreneurial orientation, especially when considering the innovativeness and proactiveness components, which mainly result from lack of necessary business and management knowledge and skills (Nguyen, 2011). However, Vietnamese managers are generally eager to learn modern management practices. For instance, in many international joint ventures, local managers have learnt, from their foreign partners, modern management styles and practices such as flexibility, systematic thinking, directness, taking responsibilities, keeping promises and being punctual. The learning process, however, may not be the same for different groups of local managers. MNCs tend to look for young Vietnamese executives who have experienced international standards rather than those with experiences associated with the former central planning system.

There are two types of labour markets in Vietnam: the primary or the formal labour market and the secondary or the informal labour market (Zhu, 2011). In the primary labour market people get permanent jobs with relatively high pay, upward mobility and social security. In the secondary labour market, people often get part-time, non-taxable and low-paying jobs, temporary positions and no social security. Women account for a considerable portion of the secondary labour market.

In Vietnam, the Vietnam General Confederation of Labour (VGCL) is the sole national trade union centre. It was founded in 1929 as the *Red Workers' General Union* in Northern Vietnam, and extended into the entire country after the national unity in 1976. All trade unions in Vietnam are required to affiliate to the VGCL. Legally, according to Trade Union Law (1990), the roles and activities of trade unions include educating the workforce about the Labour Code, promoting work discipline and productivity, organizing social activities, managing the labour force and checking on management, resolving labour disputes and signing Collective Labour Contracts. However, in practice, the roles of Vietnamese trade unions have been mainly limited to administrative functions and the provision of welfare-type services for employees (Vo and Rowley, 2010). Recently, trade unions have been granted more autonomy and there have been some positive changes in their roles such as adopting a more representative role on behalf of workers, engaging more in collective bargaining, signing collective agreements as the representative of employees, and participating more in the decision-making process on wages and working conditions (Zhu, 2011).

Social capital

The third element of institutions is social capital, which refers to interpersonal trust and institutionalized trust. In transition economies such as Vietnam with common characteristics of underdeveloped market institutions, social capital may have a particularly salient role. It is evaluated that the level of interpersonal trust in Vietnam is high while the level of institutional trust is low (Witt and Redding, 2012).

In Vietnam, laws are going to have an increasingly important role in regulating businesses, and in fact a number of laws have been promulgated, including the Enterprise Law, the Labour Code and laws to protect intellectual property. After joining the WTO in early 2007, Vietnam began working on improving its legal framework to bring it into closer alignment with international standards. Many policies have been issued to enhance transparency and financial accountability, and to ensure effective corporate governance. All this effort helps improve the business environment in Vietnam, and thus contributes to greater FDI attraction and promotion of all domestic economic sectors' potential for development.

However, in general, the formal institutions in Vietnam still remain weak, manifested through weakly enforced laws, significant concerns about corruption in public life and a low level of transparency in management and governance. The market institutions and protection of private interest have not been adequately developed. Due to the lack of trust in institutions, firms may need to rely extensively on trust in their business partners. Westerner managers who wish to work with Vietnamese firms need to learn about their Vietnamese partners and it may be critical for the partners to gain a fair amount of trust before any contract can be signed (Nguyen, 2005). In a study by Baughn et al. (2011) trust and cooperation between the partners is found to be an important factor leading to successful performance of international joint ventures (IJVs) in Vietnam.

Briefly, personal relationships and social networks play an important role. Under the absence of effective market institutions, actively building trust through interfirm networks as a substitute for formal markets is essential, especially for private firms. Developing social capital in the setting of poorly defined legal systems, as in Vietnam may be particularly crucial, given the high context and relationship-based orientation of the Vietnamese people.

Business system

Ownership

Prior to 1986, the Vietnamese economy was a command economy in which the state owned all businesses and allocated resources to SOEs, while restricting the development of private enterprises. There were only two legally recognized forms of ownership in Vietnam: state entities and collectives.

Vietnam's economic reform, initiated in 1986, has transformed the centrally planned system from SOE dominance to a market-oriented economy that has a multisector structure and a multiownership system. The reforms have resulted in a phenomenal growth of private enterprises, while, since the end of 1990s, the SOE sector has been significantly downsized mainly through equitization programs. The fast growing non-state sector has developed a dominant portion in the total of enterprises in Vietnam, while FDI enterprises have remained consistent at around 3 per cent, and SOEs have declined from 13.62 per cent in 2000 to only 1.15 per cent in 2010. However, SOEs are still considered to be 'pillars" of the economy, and the scope of SOEs' operation has been considerably increased, especially through establishing big economic groups. Many resources are still allocated to SOEs including land use and preferred access to ODA capital and credit despite this, many SOEs, including the big economic groups and corporations, generally report poor performance, low return on the resources and decreased contribution to the economy. A recent survey by the World Bank and VCCI of many organizations and businesses clearly shows the preference for private ownership, while very small percentage gave favour to state ownership (cf., Nguyen, 2012).

Under the market-oriented economy and in the context of international integration, Vietnamese SOEs have faced increasing competition from other firms in the form of private, limited liability companies, joint-stock companies, partnerships, joint ventures and 100 per cent foreign-owned enterprises. Therefore, to enhance SOEs' productivity and efficiency, the government has sought to continue to reform SOEs in the direction of cutting most subsidies and other privileges while giving greater autonomy to private firms. The Eleventh Congress of the Communist Party of Vietnam in January 2011 re-affirmed Vietnam's approach to state-led development, but also revised key policy documents to place greater emphasis on market processes and non-state ownership of economic assets. Restructuring SOEs with the focus on big economic groups and corporations is considered one of three vital components of economic restructuring in the coming time.

Networking

Globalization brings about several types of production like Japanese integral produc-tion with *monozukuri* spirit and US/Chinese modular production as well as changes in consuming styles.[1] There are different types of production network subject to different economic sectors and types of ownership. FDI companies like Japanese companies, Korean companies and Taiwanese companies dominate production chains of automo-tive, motorbike and electronic industries. Domestic companies dominate textile and garment industries, real estate, banking and finance, mining and electricity production.

Developing industrial parks and processing zones is an important Vietnamese govern-ment policy. It has promoted industrial parks and clusters in which companies are given favourable conditions such as, good infrastructure, labour training and help with administrative procedures. Over the past twenty years, to September 2012, there have been 283 industrial parks established in 58 provinces and cities. These have attracted many investors, especially FDI firms.

Since 2005, the Vietnamese government has established and promoted economic groups. They are expected to operate like big business groups in Japan (*keiretsu*) and Korea (*chaebol*). Up to December 2012, there were 12 economic groups the areas of: telecommunications; rubber; shipping; coal and mineral; petroleum; textile and garment; electricity; insurance; chemical; construction and housing industries. Vertical and horizontal coordination of production chains are also promoted. Management, development of internationally competitive capabilities and performance are currently big issues of these economic groups that raise urgent need for further comprehensive restructuring.

Management

Deeply-rooted in the long-standing centrally planned system, Vietnamese firms are often associated with characteristics such as, centralized decision making, complex structures with multilayers and departments, task duplication, and cumbersome procedures (Truong, 2013). These characteristics are manifested strongly especially in SOEs. The culture of SOEs is often characterized by collective responsibility, ambiguity of decision responsibility, and an absence of feedback on performance. In other words, it is a 'no-owner company' culture. As a result, SOEs' performance has often been poor.

Through the equitization process, the Vietnamese government strongly believed that the equitized SOEs (ESOEs) would perform better than their former SOEs. Changes in ownership and market conditions have made ESOEs increasingly market and people oriented (Vo and Nguyen, 2011). To face fierce competition successfully, ESOEs need to raise managerial competencies, including human resource management (HRM). In practice, the ESOEs have begun to apply HRM practices that are generally common in FDI firms.

FDI firms, such as those from Japan, Korea and the United States often bring their own management styles and show strong commitment to manage existing businesses in this style. They have clear business and management processes and policies on quality, cost, delivery, motivation and environment (QCDME). Vietnamese firms, especially private businesses, are learning by doing and observing. Some Vietnamese managers who work closely with foreign business partners understand and exercise international standards in running their businesses. Others are struggling with learning QCDME.

In Vietnam, seniority is very important at work, especially in SOEs and in the public sector. It is necessary to show appropriate respect according to position, age and education level. In promotion, seniority is heavily considered although merit and capability is receiving more attention in some firms.

Comparative advantage

Vietnam's comparative advantage is still largely based on the country's endowments of labour and natural resources. Vietnam's major exports have been primary products: agricultural and fishery commodities such as rice, coffee, tea, seafood, vegetable, rubber; and mining products such as crude oil, coal and various metal ores. However, these products are, in the main, raw and unprocessed commodities, and therefore do not bring much added-value (Le, 2010). Vietnam's exports are moving from 'agricultural' to 'industrial' with emerging export value in garments, footwear and electronic products.

Vietnam is rich in terms of its people, having a large and young population. Vietnamese workers are known to be hardworking, talented, with a high willingness to learn.

Vietnam ranked 127th out of 186 in terms of the Human Development Index (HDI) according to UNDP's report 2012. The HDI of Vietnam has increased over the past 10 years, which reflects factors such as, increased life expectancy, real income and especially education attainment.

The salary of Vietnamese workers is less than those in neighbouring countries such as Thailand, Malaysia, Indonesia or the Philippines. Managers working in Vietnam must be aware of the job-hopping issue. Theoretically, in rapidly growing economies like China and Vietnam, not only managers, but also engineers and workers have opportunities to move to other companies with higher compensation. However, it is not always the case since there are also other factors to retain employees.

Vietnam is facing a shortage of skilled labourers, while an abundance of unskilled labourers exists. Only 20 per cent of the total labour force is considered to be trained labour. In addition, work discipline is one weakness of Vietnamese workers (MOLISA, 2004). At the same time, Vietnamese highly skilled labourers are mostly in Hanoi and Ho Chi Minh City. These two cities are the motivators and power-houses for the economic development of Vietnam.

The cost of doing business in Vietnam is lower than it is in other countries in the region. Vietnam is improving its infrastructure system to facilitate businesses including the rehabilitation of roads, railways, seaports, airport networks and enhancement of the IT platform. Broadband internet is available in Vietnam with more than 31 million users as of October 2012 (VNNIC, 2012).

The changing trend of the Vietnamese business system

In January 2007, Vietnam became the 150th member of the WTO and as a result, laws were to be modified to meet international standards. Nowadays, the legal system in Vietnam has rules and laws on enterprises, property rights, anti-corruption and contracts. Contract law is regulated in the Civil Code as in other countries that apply civil law.[2]

Before 2005, different laws governed the operations of different types of enterprises, which were categorized into SOEs, FDIs and non-state enterprises. The unified enterprise law, or the Law on Enterprises, came into effect on 1 July 2006 and ensures that all enterprises in Vietnam are governed under the same regulations. Under this law, SOEs must be transformed into limited liability companies or shareholding companies by 2010.[3] FDIs may choose to change their legal status, it is not compulsory.

The common Investment Law in Vietnam also came into effect on 1 July 2006 and legislates that all investors, regardless of nationality, are promoted in the same manner. There is no separation of Law on Promotion of Foreign Investment and Law on Promotion of Domestic Investment. Under the Investment Law, the Vietnamese government commits to open its market, eliminate trade related investment measures (TRIMs), and protect the rights of investors including exemption of nationalization.

In the period of 2008–2012, Vietnam's economy witnessed the shortcomings of the management of 12 big state owned economic groups, the price bubbles of real estate and stock market, and the bad debt of the banking system. These require sectors require clear, strong restructuring.

Several business clubs and associations are in operation. The active ones include the American Chamber of Commerce in Vietnam (Amcham), the European Chamber of Commerce in Vietnam (Eurocham), the Japanese Business Association (JBA), the Vietnamese Business Forum (VBF), and the Vietnamese Chamber of Commerce and Industry (VCCI). These clubs and associations are facilitating fruitful discussions between businesses and governments.

International activities of Vietnamese firms

Since implementing *doi moi* policy, Vietnam has become more open to the global market. The country has maintained a high growth rate in non-oil export and increased share of manufacturing export albeit not yet becoming a significant player in international production networks. Vietnamese products have been exported to many countries over the world, with the major destinations including the United States, China, Japan and Korea. FDI firms have increasing role in exports. In 2012, FDI firms contributed more than 60 per cent of the total export values with the main export items including technology, and garment and footwear products. Domestic firms' achievement was recognized mainly in exporting agricultural products. Vietnam became the largest exporter of rice and coffee in 2012.

Outward FDI from Vietnam increased from 12 projects with registered capital at US$9,061 million to 718 projects in September 2012 with registered capital at US$9,061 13,052.36. Laos and Cambodia are most popular destinations followed by the United States, Singapore, Korea, Russia and Japan in terms of number of projects. Most popular sectors are mineral, electricity production, agriculture and aquaculture, art and leisure activities, post and telecommunications (MPI, 2012). Some big business groups such as Viettel have been very proactive in international investment activities. A number of non-state companies such as Trung Nguyen coffee and Pho24 have also been active in expanding their business in international markets with ambition to build global brands.

Corporate social responsibility in Vietnam

Corporate social responsibility (CSR) is well regulated in the Labour Code of Vietnam, Law on Environmental Protection, Anti-Corruption Law and Intellectual Property Law. The concepts and issues of child labour, forced labour, gender inequality, social insurance, environmental protection, intellectual property, bribery and corruption are not new to Vietnamese society. A number of forums, workshops and discussions have been organized for various topics related to CSR. In addition, a number of international cooperation projects have been carried out in an attempt to promote CSR practices in Vietnam, including 'Occupational Safety and Health', 'Cleaner production in industry sector', 'comprehensive plan for pollution prevention'. However, there are still many challenges for Vietnamese firms, especially private ones, to integrate CSR initiatives into their long-term corporate strategy including limited knowledge on CSR and lack of financial and human resources to set up CSR standards.

CSR practices initially were manifested in the FDI sector and among export-oriented firms under the pressure of various stakeholders of the business community to become more ethical suppliers to compete in the international market. For instance, SA8000 first was launched in Vietnam in 1997 for exporting manufacturers in footwear and garment and textile industries in response to the requirements of their foreign customers from the United States and Europe. However, there are still many related concerns in society, such as fake products, low product quality and safety, and environmental pollution caused by many businesses. Working conditions and workers' welfare are still a common problem that has led to strikes in several big factories. Although child labour may still be controversial subject, several recent studies have suggested a dramatic decline in child labour in Vietnam (e.g., Edmonds and Pavcnik, 2002).

In Vietnam, numerous natural disasters such as storms and floods occur every year. In addition, post-war consequences are still evident in many Vietnamese families. The Vietnamese Fatherland Front is an organization known as a pioneer and leader to deploy society's resources to help overcome the consequences caused by natural disasters as well as to support the poor and the handicapped in the country. An increasing number of companies in Vietnam actively participate in the programs initiated by this organization. This is a way that companies demonstrate their social responsibility. At the same time, the public image of the companies is promoted.

Working and living conditions in Vietnam

In Vietnam, common working hours are from 8am to 5pm, Monday to Saturday. Businesses often work until 6pm. The Labour Code of Vietnam governs labour related issues such as labour relations and management of labour. It was first introduced in 1994 and amended in 2002, 2006 and 2007. The law regulates an eight hour-working day and 48 hour-working week. The total over time working for employee is limited to 200 hours per year. Vietnam also has a Law on Gender Equality, which came into effect on 1 July 2007. These two laws provide a sound framework for labour management in Vietnam, and help move the population toward a more civilized society as well as sustainable development.

Officially recognized by the constitution and laws of Vietnam, the VGCL represents the working class in Vietnam. It has offices in all 63 provinces in Vietnam. As of 20 November 2011, VGCL had 7,535,584 members in its 111,319 trade unions (VGCL, 2012). With such figures the power of trade unions would appear to be great; however, at industry and company levels trade unions are not eager to bargain for rewards and wages for their members. They have little control over recruitment and selection of employees, or over employee development. Collective bargaining relates more to support from management in cultural, sportive and holiday activities for employees. There are few demonstrations by workers in Vietnam. Some have happened though in FDI firms where official trade unions are not set up or promoted.

Vietnam is considered to be safe country in which to live with beautiful landscape and great destinations for tourism. It is also known for its good weather, lively culture, relatively low cost of living and the steady improvement in infrastructure. Vietnamese people are friendly and the English language is becoming more popular, especially in urban areas. However, traffic congestion is a big issue in large cities like Hanoi and Ho Chi Minh City. People face difficulties in commuting to and from work. Local authorities concentrate substantial effort on improving the infrastructure and traffic systems. Both cities want to enhance their public transport services, including introducing buses and urban mass rapid transit (UMRT). In addition, pollution, red tape and bureaucracy are still concerns in life.

- Vietnam is a developing country in Southeast Asia. It has shifted from a command economy with the dominance of SOEs to a market-oriented economy with a multi-sector economic structure and multi-ownership system, following a process known as *doi moi*. Vietnam joined WTO in early 2007 and became a lower-middle income nation in 2011.

- Vietnamese culture is deeply affected by Confucianism. Personal networking and relationships are important to business and management practices.

- Vietnamese government has been trying to reduce its direct role in supervising the economy and providing support to the private sector. Restructuring the financial and banking system, SOEs, and public investment are considered three vital components of economic restructuring in the coming time.

- The concept of civil society is still relatively new in Vietnam, and the core activities of most civil society organizations are currently directed towards poverty reduction, humanitarian relief, self-organization and professional development.

- The Vietnamese workforce is often recognized to be young, bright, hardworking and eager to learn. It is also characterized by shortage of skilled employees with a professional working style, and a dearth of competent managers. Young Vietnamese executives who have experienced international standards are much sought after by MNCs.

- In Vietnam, market institutions are still underdeveloped. The level of interpersonal trust in Vietnam is high while the level of institutional trust is low.

- Vietnam has become more open towards the global market with the increase in export and import activities.

- In Vietnam, CSR is well regulated by the legal system but still remains an issue in practice.

Key concepts

Civil Society Organizations (CSOs): a large number of groups, organizations and associations including mass organizations, professional associations, local NGOs and community-based organizations.

Doi moi: economic renovation or 'change for the new', which guided the Vietnamese economy toward an open market economic system.

Equitization: a process to transform a part of state ownership to private ownership. The state first sells shares to employees in the SOEs. It then sells shares to the public through the stock market. The state remains the dominating owner in selected enterprises.

Industrialization: a process to transform an economy from agricultural base to industrial base.

International integration: a process in which an economy becomes an active part of the global market.

Transitional economy: economy going through a period of transition from a planned economy to a market economy.

Review questions

1 Describe the rationale, identity and authority in the Vietnamese business system.
2 Explain the characteristics of financial capital, human capital and social capital in the Vietnamese business system.
3 Describe the aspects of ownership, networking, and management in the Vietnamese business system.
4 How are Vietnamese firms integrated in the international economy?
5 How would you describe the CSR in Vietnam? What role has the civil society played in the Vietnamese business system?

Activities and discussions

1 Search for Vietnamese businesses or products in your community/country, and evaluate their competitive advantages compared to similar businesses/products from other countries in your community/country. If they are not yet available, in which industry should Vietnamese firms invest in order to gain a comparative advantage in your country?

2 Joint ventures (JVs) are a very common form of FDI in Vietnam. In many cases, the local partners are SOEs, which may have very different management styles and lack the knowledge and experience associated with a market economy. Discuss with your classmates potential conflicts in management styles of JVs in Vietnam and how to solve the problems.

Trung Nguyen Coffee: an ambition to become a global brand
Nguyen, T.T. Mai and Nguyen, T.H. Ha

Vietnam is the world's largest coffee exporter. The country, and particularly the Dak Lak province, is well known for advantages to develop coffee industry pertaining to the land of the Central highland favourable for the best quality coffee production, weather conditions suitable for the growth of coffee trees, and huge labour forces.

In Vietnam, Trung Nguyen is the largest domestic coffee brand. The Trung Nguyen Coffee Company currently operates a nationwide chain of over 1,000 coffee shops and 50,000 retail outlets. The first coffee shop was opened in October 1998 in Ho Chi Minh City, two years after the company's establishment in Buon Ma Thuot, Dak Lak – the country's main coffee growing province. In Hanoi, the capital city, the first coffeehouse was opened in 2000.

Trung Nguyen Company is aiming for $1 billion in sales by 2015 and its CEO shows great ambitions to become a global brand like Nescafé and Starbucks. Currently, Trung Nguyen coffee has been exported to over 60 countries and territories. Over the past few years, franchises have been opened in Japan, Singapore, Thailand, Cambodia, Malaysia and China. The first outlets outside Asia were opened in Germany and New York City in 2006.

Trung Nguyen's chairman and CEO is Dang Le Nguyen Vu, who is regarded as the Vietnam's Coffee King. According to Vu, there are three main important areas that an entrepreneur needs to focus on if he wants to be successful: passion, planning and an aptitude for networking. It also the strategic vision, creativity and ambition of this CEO is also notable. The intention to expand his own business leads Vu not to limit his brand to a small group of clients, but claims the ambition to 'serve the world'. Trung Nguyen wishes to connect with and develop the range of coffee-lovers all around the world through not only an authentic flavour but also the symbol of creativity and sustainable development that the brand pursues. What makes Trung Nguyen products spectacular is the combination of the following factors: good quality, high technology, secrets which create amazing Eastern coffee and the very new perspectives on the way people enjoy coffee. The most valuable asset of Trung Nguyen is considered as the creativity, innovation and a sustainable development strategy. Trung Nguyen leader always pursues his greatest ambition. He threw himself into a competitive market. His national pride drives his ambition to promote a worldwide positive image of Vietnam.

The philosophy of Trung Nguyen's leader pertains to designing business not only to generate personal wealth but also to enrich the lives of employees and the prosperity of the Vietnamese society as a whole. Vu says: 'We make the most specialist coffee in the world, and through coffee we want to create a sustainable development model, using coffee to come up with value for society and for the environment.' Trung Nguyen is proud to follow the key aspiration, which is to support the community to overcome poverty and reach for a sustainable development. The Vietnam's Coffee King states: 'If I can say only a few words to entrepreneurs who have been seeking for growth in the next decade, it would be the wholehearted focus on sustainable and green development – not just for themselves, but for the good of all society.'

In Vietnam, Trung Nguyen is a pioneer in launching many for-community programs, such as 'Creation for Vietnam's brand 2003', and 'Vietnamese agricultural products brand development 2003'. Trung Nguyen has also established the 'Fund for creation 2005', which greatly support new entrepreneurs, and together with the Youth Union it has co-organized a number of events including the interesting forum 'Vietnam is small or not?' Recently, Trung Nguyen and the Youth Union have reached an agreement to develop a program that supports the young generation and it titled 'Creativity for Vietnamese aspiration', offering free 100 million starting-business books for 23 million Vietnamese young people. Trung Nguyen hopes that his effort will boost Vietnamese youths' entrepreneurship ambition, help them overcome all difficulties and obstacles to achieve their goals in life.

Development always accompanies challenges. The misunderstanding in copyright of the Australia Coffee Association (http://baohothuonghieu.com/banquyen/tin-chi-tiet/ca-phe-trun g-nguyen-bi-nang-ten-mien-tai-australi a/404.html) is a clear indication for Trung Nguyen to be much more careful in protecting their brand. Besides, there are more and more competitive brands wishing to claim the No.1 Brand in Vietnam such as, Nestlé and Starbucks. Is Trung Nguyen's core values of 'great ambition and unceasing creativity and breakthrough' capable of sustainably ranking in the top in the domestic market, and of being successful in becoming a global brand?

Questions

1 Which factors have helped Trung Nguyen to succeed?

2 What is the role of leadership in Trung Nguyen's success?

3 Do you think Trung Nguyen will be able to successfully achieve its ambition to become a global brand in the increasingly competitive business environment?

Sources

http://thegioicf.com/no-passion-no-success/

http://vietnamnews.vn/economy/business-insight/236854/coffee-company-builds-global-brand.html

http://khatvongtuoitre.com/index.php?option=com_content&task=view&id=20&Itemid=11

http://dddn.com.vn/20120831035044614cat44/vua-ca-phe-dang-le-nguyen-vu-chinh-tri-nhat-thoi-ca-phe-la-vinh-cuu.htm

Notes

1   Integral manufacturing is implemented by Japanese manufacturers. It requires unique parts for each product and continuous technical improvement. Modular manufacturing is implemented by Chinese and US firms where parts are easily assembled to products. *Monozukuri* spirit is a Japanese term that is difficult to be translated into English. Its meaning resembles 'dedication and commitment of leaders/managers to drive a company toward success'.

2   Civil law is exercised in Germany, France, and other European countries. Common law is exercised in some countries such as the United Kingdom, the United States, Australia, and New Zealand.

3   We must not equate the transformation of company types, which is mainly related to legal management of companies with the transformation of ownership.

References

Ashwill, M. (2007) Interview with Christopher Runkel on the book *Vietnam Today: A Guide to a Nation at Crossroad*, published in 2005 by Intercultural Press, accessed 11 November 2013 at: http://www.business-in-asia.com/books/vietnam_today.html

Baughn, C., Neupert, K.E., Phan, T.A. and Ngo, M.H (2011) Social Capital and Human Resource Management in International Joint Ventures in Vietnam: A Developing Country Perspective, *International Journal of Human Resource Management*, 22(5): 165–185.

Edmonds, E. and Pavcnik, N. (2002) Does Globalization Increase Child Labor? Evidence from Vietnam. NBER Working Paper No. 8760, accessed 11 November 2013 at: http://www.nber.org/papers/w8760

Le, Q.P. (2010) Evaluating Vietnam's Changing Comparative Advantage Patterns. *ASEAN Economic Bulletin*, 27(2): 221–230.

Ministry of Labor, War Invalid and Social Affairs (MOLISA) (2004), *Labor-Employment in Vietnam 1996-2003*. Center for Informatics, MOLISA. Labor and Social Publishing House.

MPI (2012) Outward FDI of Vietnam: Success and limitations, accessed 11 November at: http://fia.mpi.gov.vn/News.aspx?ctl=newsdetailandp=3.22andaID=1164

Nguyen, D.T. (2012) *Facing Challenges of Economic Restructuring* (*The Vietnamese Economy Annual Report 2012*) Hanoi: Vietnam National University's Publishing House.

Nguyen, T.H. (1994) Vietnamese Traditional Culture: A Historical Approach. *Journal of Vietnamese Studies*, 95–97.

Nguyen, T.T.M. and Tambyah, S.K. (2011) Antecedents and Consequences of Status Consumption among Urban Vietnamese Consumers, *Organizations and Markets in Emerging Economies,* 2(1): 75–98.

Nguyen, T.T.M. (2011) An Exploratory Investigation into Entrepreneurial Orientation in Vietnam: A Study across Types of Ownership, Firm Sizes, Operation Fields, Entrepreneur's Age and Gender. *International Vision*, 15: 7–18.

Nguyen, T.V. (2005) Learning to Trust: A study of Interfirm Trust Dynamics in Vietnam. *Journal of World Business*, 40: 203–221.

Norlund, I. (2006) The Emerging Civil Society: An Initial Assessment of Civil Society in Vietnam. *Report of Vietnam Institute of Development Studies (VIDS):* UNDP Vietnam, SNV Vietnam, CIVICUS Civil Society Index.

Paswan, A.K. and Tran, P.T. (2012) Vietnam and Entrepreneurial Private Enterprises: A Macromarketing Perspective, *Journal of Macromarketing*, 32(1): 18–30.

Redding, G. (2005) The Thick Description and Comparison of Societal Systems of Capitalism, *Journal of International Business Studies*, 36(2): 123–155.

Shultz, C.J., Pecotich, A. and Le, K. (1994) Changes in Marketing Activities and Consumption in the Socialist Republic of Vietnam, in C. Shultz,

R. Belk and G. Ger (eds.) *Research in Consumer Behavior*, 7. Greenwich, CT: JAI Press, pp. 225–257.

TNS (2011) Education Tops Consumers' Spending, accessed 11 November 2013 at: http://insightviet-nam.wordpress.com/2011/07/02/education-tops-consumerss-spending-source-tns/

Truong, Q. (2013) Vietnam: An Emerging Economy at a Crossroads. Working Paper No. 2013/09. Maastricht School of Management.

Truong, Q., van der Heijden, B.I.J.M. and Rowley, C. (2010) Globalization, Competitiveness and Human Resource Management in a Transitional Economy: The Case of Vietnam. *International Journal of Business Studies*, 18(1): 75–100.

VGCL (2012) Development of members under the 10th National Congress of VGCL, accessed 16 September 2013 at: http://www.congdoanvn.org.vn/details.asp?l=1andc=58andm=5565

VNNIC (2012) Statistics of Internet in Vietnam, accessed 11 November 2013 at: http://www.vnnic.vn/en/stat/report-internet-statistics

Vo, A.N. and Rowley, C. (2010) The Internationalization of Industrial Relations? Japanese and US Multinational Companies in Vietnam. *Asia Pacific Business Review*, 16(1–2): 221–238.

Vo, T.Q. and Nguyen, D.K. (2011) Corporate Ownership Structure and Organizational Culture in a Transition Economy: The Case of Vietnam. *International Journal of Economics and Finance*, 3(4): 36–47.

Wischermann, J. (2010) Civil Society Action and Governance in Vietnam: Selected Findings from an Empirical Survey. *Journal of Current Southeast Asian Affairs*, 29(2): 3–40.

Witt, M.A. and Redding, G. (2012) Asian Business Systems: Institutional Comparison, Clusters, and Implications for Varieties of Capitalism and Business Systems Theory. Working paper. INSEAD.

Zhu, Y. (2011) Labor Market in Vietnam: Development under the Economic Reform and Globalization, in J. Benson and Y. Zhu (eds.) *The Dynamics of Asian Labor Markets: Balancing Control and Flexibility*. London: Routledge, pp. 148–164.

Conclusion

Harukiyo Hasegawa and Carlos Noronha

It is now time to reflect on and conclude the discussions in the book. It is also time to consider remaining issues of the theoretical framework and its linkage to other disciplines.

The chapters in Part I assessed the realities of Asian business and management within a theoretical framework of business systems. They focussed on six key functional topics. We presented business systems theory as a logic applicable to any country, that is, the framework has the capacity to compare and identify strengths and weaknesses in any system. The importance of meaning, order and coordination as key components of Asian business systems was emphasized as efficacious in spite of different political inclinations alongside the common trajectories of economic development. In-depth attention was given to the importance of a cultural understanding of Asian business and to relevant theories and views.

In our layered schema, meaning is considered a foundation for order and coordination, although in the long term coordination will conversely also influence meaning. It is an accepted fact that mutual influences among factors will persist due to the continual evolution of a system. This means that while in the narrow sense of the word the business system is to be found at the top layer of coordination, this layer is itself likely to be influenced by factors in the meaning layer, for example, we commonly apply characterizations such as Japanese-style, Korean-style or Chinese-style management. Accounting, finance and corporate governance are influenced by globalization, particularly by multinational companies, while small and medium-sized companies will have less influence and will not converge in the same way as multinationals, but will remain divergent, reflecting local cultural and institutional arrangements. Human capital is an important factor in the order layer, not only because it provides employees, professionals and executives for the system, but also because the level of education and values these people hold will determine the quality of human capital. Science and technology represent a key material logic for systems – without them, any system will find it difficult to increase productivity and innovation.

The discussion of regionalism and production networks in Asia showed how the theoretical framework can expand beyond national business systems, and demonstrates the scope of flexibility within that framework. The final chapter in Part I, on sustainable development and corporate social responsibility, provided an opportunity to discuss how the global-scale problem of sustainability can be accommodated by business systems logic, in particular by the meaning layer, and also by local issues of democracy, as in inequality of wealth distribution.

Part II featured nine countries, and hence nine national business systems. The first group – Japan, Korea and Singapore – are the most mature in terms of economic development, in both quantity and quality. This group, compared to other systems, shows relatively low economic growth and higher GDP per capita, although their systems present various differences. The second group comprises two emerging giants, China and India, which differ sharply in character in areas such as religion, culture and political perspective. They are, however, both commonly understood as systems transiting from a socialist-oriented state to market economy. Their economic trajectory has been similar, towards higher economic development, and they have similar growth rates and GDP, although China is growing faster and has much larger GDP than India. In the final group are Malaysia, the Philippines, Thailand and Vietnam. Each of these countries has its own unique contextual conditions and their systems differ in terms of factor content and system operation, due to their differing histories, political inclinations and cultures. Malaysia is unique in its pragmatic approach to development, while the Philippines face challenges in consolidating the foundations of its development. Thailand is testing a unique philosophy of 'Sufficiency Economy', while Vietnam has the task of blending three sets of values simultaneously: Confucianism, Socialism and Liberal Ideology.

Our framework posits a model within which the existence of Asian business systems – and the similarities and differences between them – can be understood. For example, across East Asia we find similarities in cultures and values deriving from a shared historical background of Confucianism – but it operates with considerable variation, as we can see in the case of China, Japan and Korea. The difference in function of factors in each business system, together with political preferences and historical events, technology transfer, and so on, have influenced the way these business systems have evolved, demonstrating diversity.

Models by definition have limitations of which we must be mindful. Recent events that do not easily lend themselves to explanation include the Asian economic crisis, China's transformation in political economy, Japan's socio-economic stagnation and environmental problems, Thailand's 'redshirts' civil unrest in 2009 and various other social movements across Asia. A systems approach can suggest that these events are attributable to imbalances between the factors within the system and the remedy may be to restore balance in an appropriate manner. However, such issues may be more receptive to explanation from other perspectives, such as political economy, sociology or Marxism. The strength of a systems approach is to explain the function of a system containing a certain number of factors; the more constant the factors are, for instance, like chemical materials or mechanical components, the more scientific and predictive it may become.

Acknowledging such strengths and limitations of the system approach, we posit two real challenges in the contemporary world that need to be directly addressed by business systems, though they may, at first sight, seem to lie beyond the logic of the business systems model. The first is the material challenge of the environment and sustainable development, and the second is the ideational challenge of democracy, particularly as represented by inequalities in wealth distribution and freedom of expression. Is it possible to articulate these challenges within the business system approach? The answer is 'yes', but only within a system and where the issues are originally generated within the business system. This implies that a business system that is operated and managed by factors at the top layer, namely ownership and management factors, will have limits in addressing the consequential issues of sustainability and social inequality at national or global level. Therefore, our system can explain only those issues for which corporations are responsible, such as CSR and sustainability relevant to corporations. Critical political changes such as those in China and other countries can be better explained by the logic of political economy; issues of sustainable development and inequality across a whole society can be better explained by interdisciplinary theory from fields such as economics, natural science, sociology, political economy, Marxism or philosophy. Business systems theory, therefore, should be seen not as a catch-all social theory, but as a theory that can be of considerable help in understanding and anticipating issues of business within a social context.

We hope that this book has contributed towards meaningful discussion of business and management issues in Asia and has been useful in formulating a grasp of the complex realities of business in Asia and beyond.

Notes: **bold type** = extended discussion or term emphasized in text; f= figure; n = endnote or footnote; t = table.

A

C

F

G

INDEX

J

K

L

M

N

O

S

U

V

W

Y

Z